DEAD BEATS

A MUSICAL HORROR ANTHOLOGY

EDITED BY JOE CORALLO AND ERIC PALICKI

Cover Illustration: LISA STERLE
Book and Production Design: NICOLA BLACK DESIGN, LLC
Dead Beats Logo: TIM DANIEL

Dead Beats
A Musical Horror Anthology
ISBN: 978-1-949518-03-0
First Printing: October 2019

Printed in Canada.

TYLER CHIN-TANNER President/Co-Publisher
WENDY CHIN-TANNER Executive Director/Co-Publisher
LISA Y. WU VP of Sales & Marketing
JOSEPH ILLIDGE Editorial Director
NICOLA BLACK DESIGN, LLC Brand Strategist/Art Director
JUSTIN ZIMMERMAN Media Director

WWW.AWBW.COM

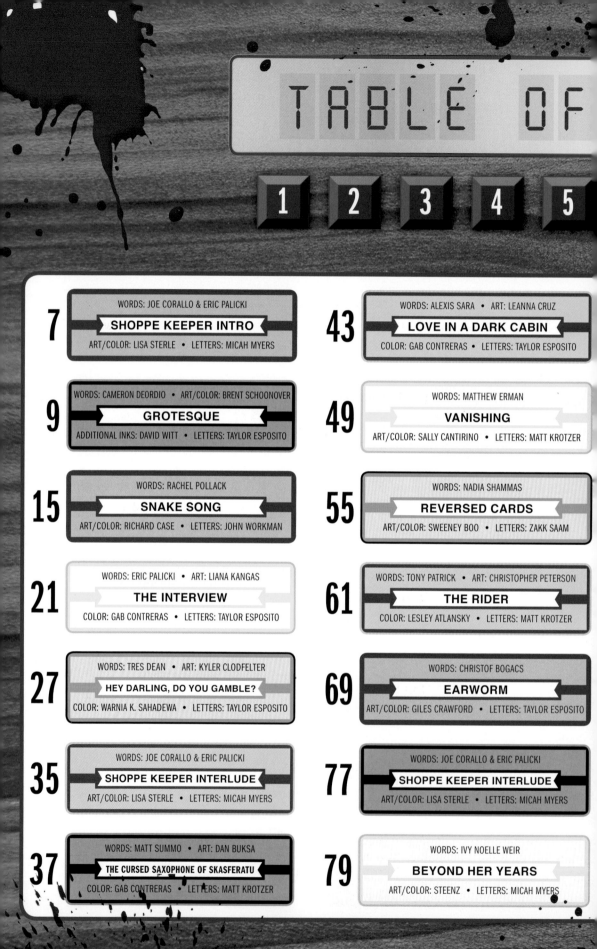

TABLE OF

1 2 3 4 5

CONTENTS

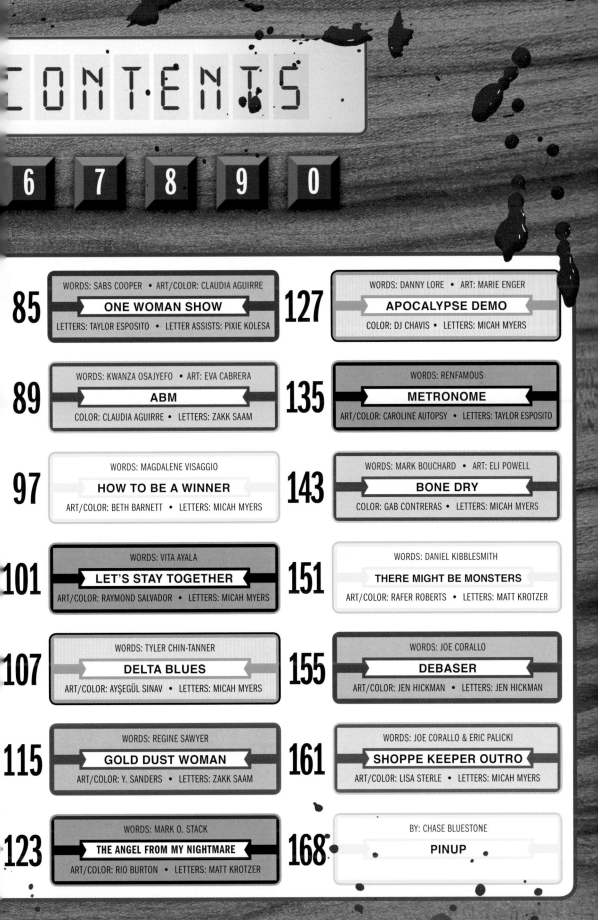

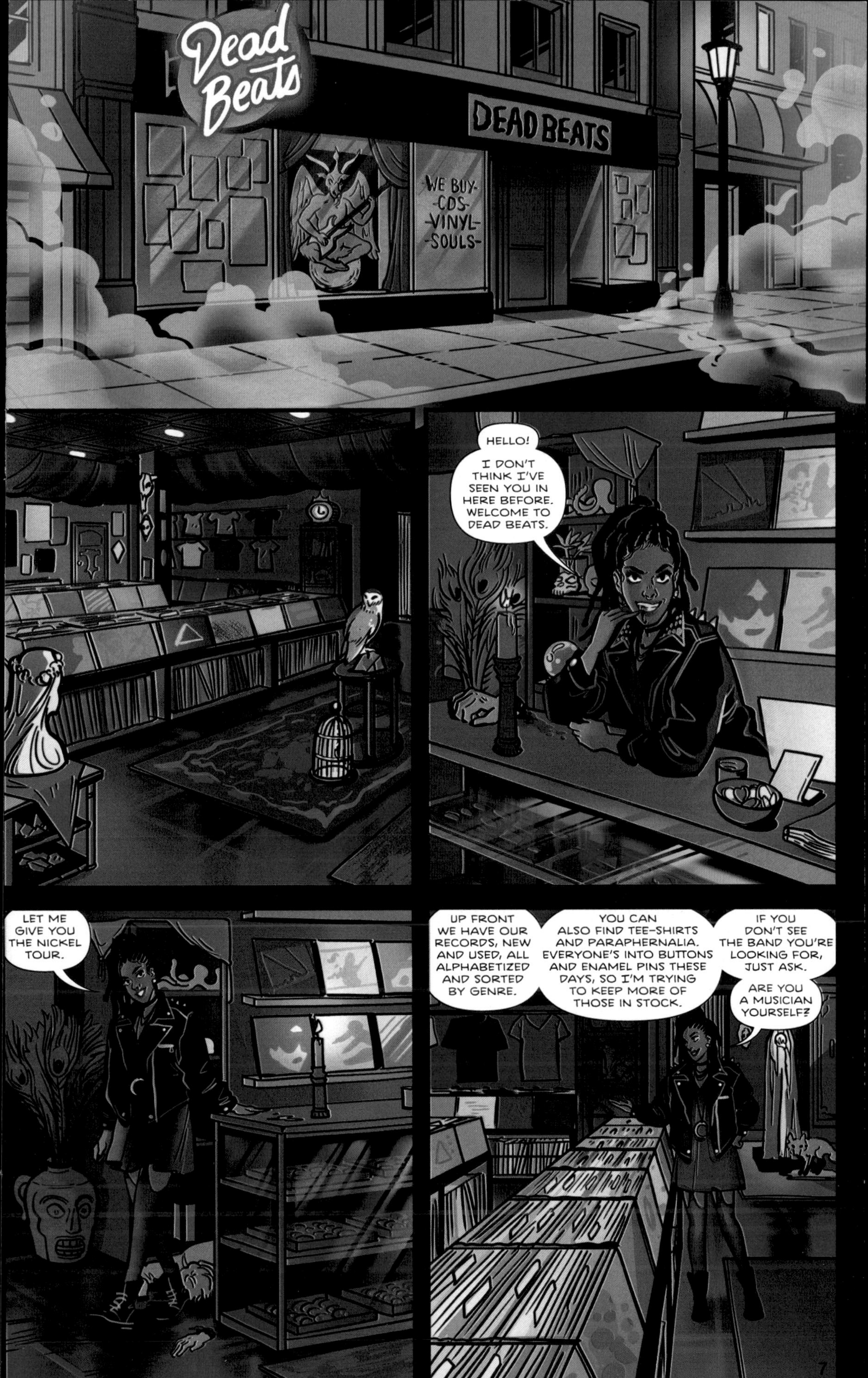
Dead Beats
DEAD BEATS
-WE BUY-
-CDS-
-VINYL-
-SOULS-
HELLO!
I DON'T THINK I'VE SEEN YOU IN HERE BEFORE. WELCOME TO DEAD BEATS.
LET ME GIVE YOU THE NICKEL TOUR.
UP FRONT WE HAVE OUR RECORDS, NEW AND USED, ALL ALPHABETIZED AND SORTED BY GENRE.
YOU CAN ALSO FIND TEE-SHIRTS AND PARAPHERNALIA. EVERYONE'S INTO BUTTONS AND ENAMEL PINS THESE DAYS, SO I'M TRYING TO KEEP MORE OF THOSE IN STOCK.
IF YOU DON'T SEE THE BAND YOU'RE LOOKING FOR, JUST ASK.
ARE YOU A MUSICIAN YOURSELF?

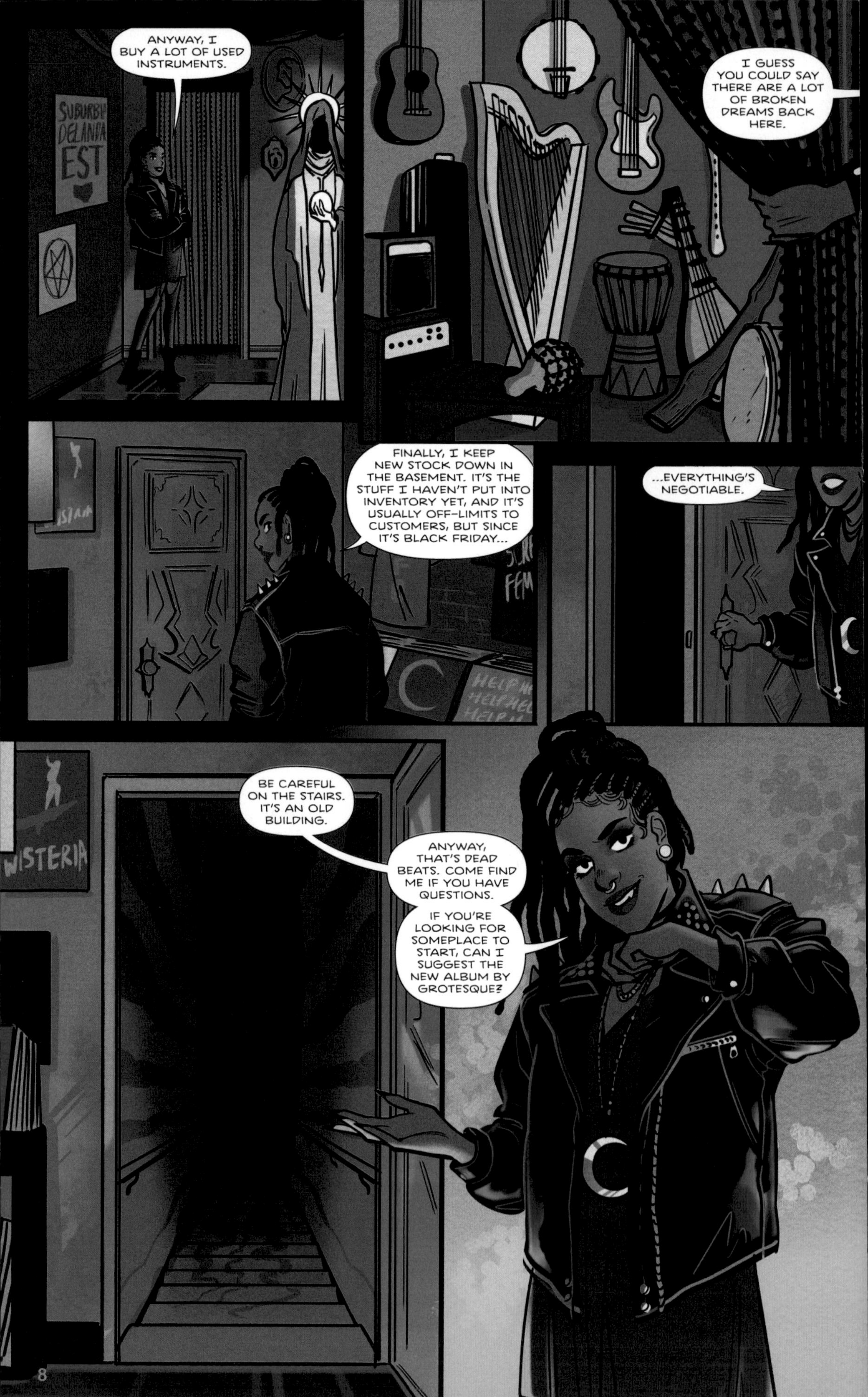
ANYWAY, I BUY A LOT OF USED INSTRUMENTS.
SUBURBIA DELANDA EST
I GUESS YOU COULD SAY THERE ARE A LOT OF BROKEN DREAMS BACK HERE.
FINALLY, I KEEP NEW STOCK DOWN IN THE BASEMENT. IT'S THE STUFF I HAVEN'T PUT INTO INVENTORY YET, AND IT'S USUALLY OFF-LIMITS TO CUSTOMERS, BUT SINCE IT'S BLACK FRIDAY...
...EVERYTHING'S NEGOTIABLE.
BE CAREFUL ON THE STAIRS. IT'S AN OLD BUILDING.
WISTERIA
ANYWAY, THAT'S DEAD BEATS. COME FIND ME IF YOU HAVE QUESTIONS.
IF YOU'RE LOOKING FOR SOMEPLACE TO START, CAN I SUGGEST THE NEW ALBUM BY GROTESQUE?

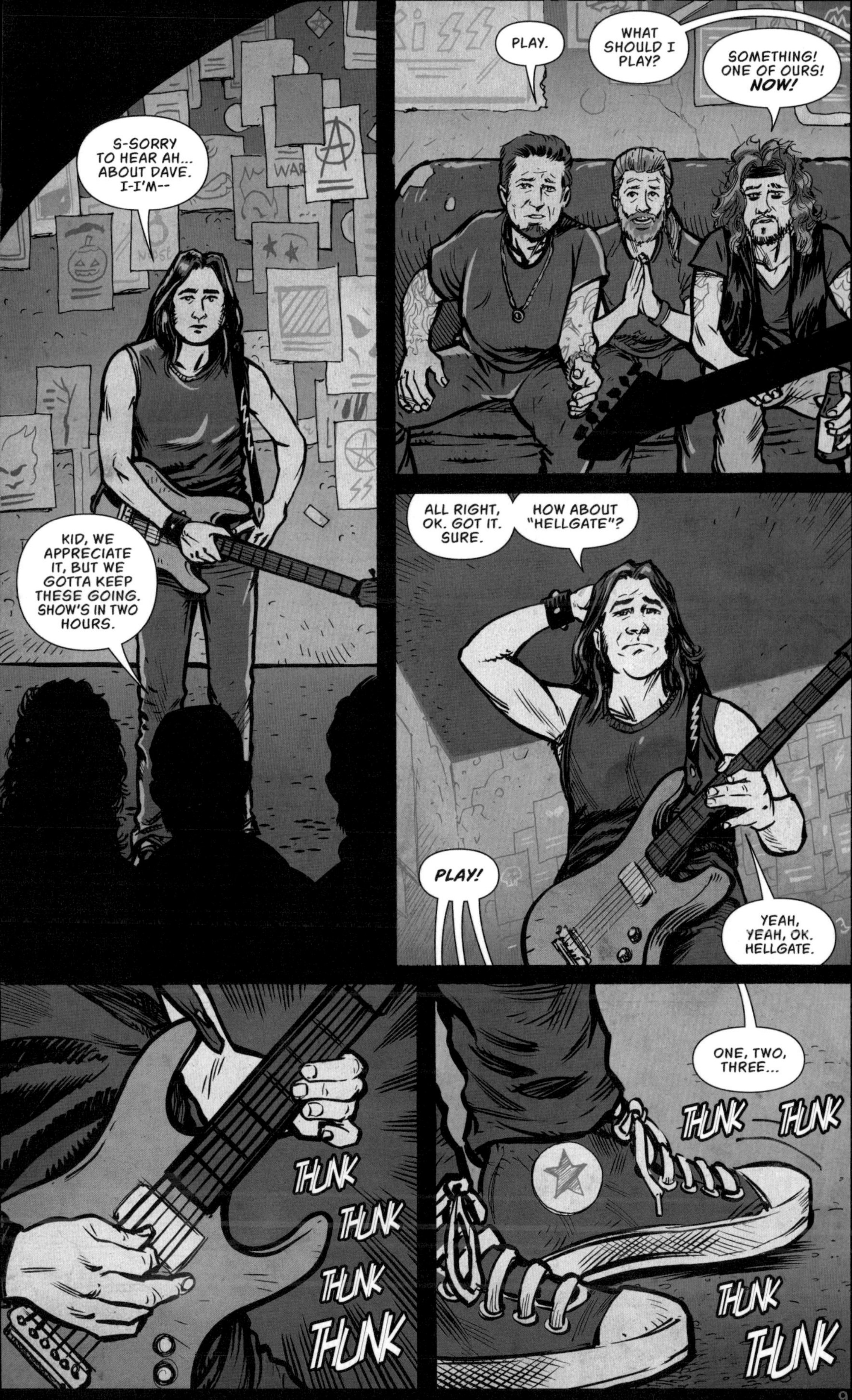

S-SORRY TO HEAR AH... ABOUT DAVE. I-I'M--
KID, WE APPRECIATE IT, BUT WE GOTTA KEEP THESE GOING. SHOW'S IN TWO HOURS.
PLAY.
WHAT SHOULD I PLAY?
SOMETHING! ONE OF OURS! NOW!
ALL RIGHT, OK. GOT IT. SURE.
HOW ABOUT "HELLGATE"?
PLAY!
YEAH, YEAH, OK. HELLGATE.
THUNK
THUNK
THUNK
THUNK
ONE, TWO, THREE...
THUNK THUNK
THUNK
THUNK

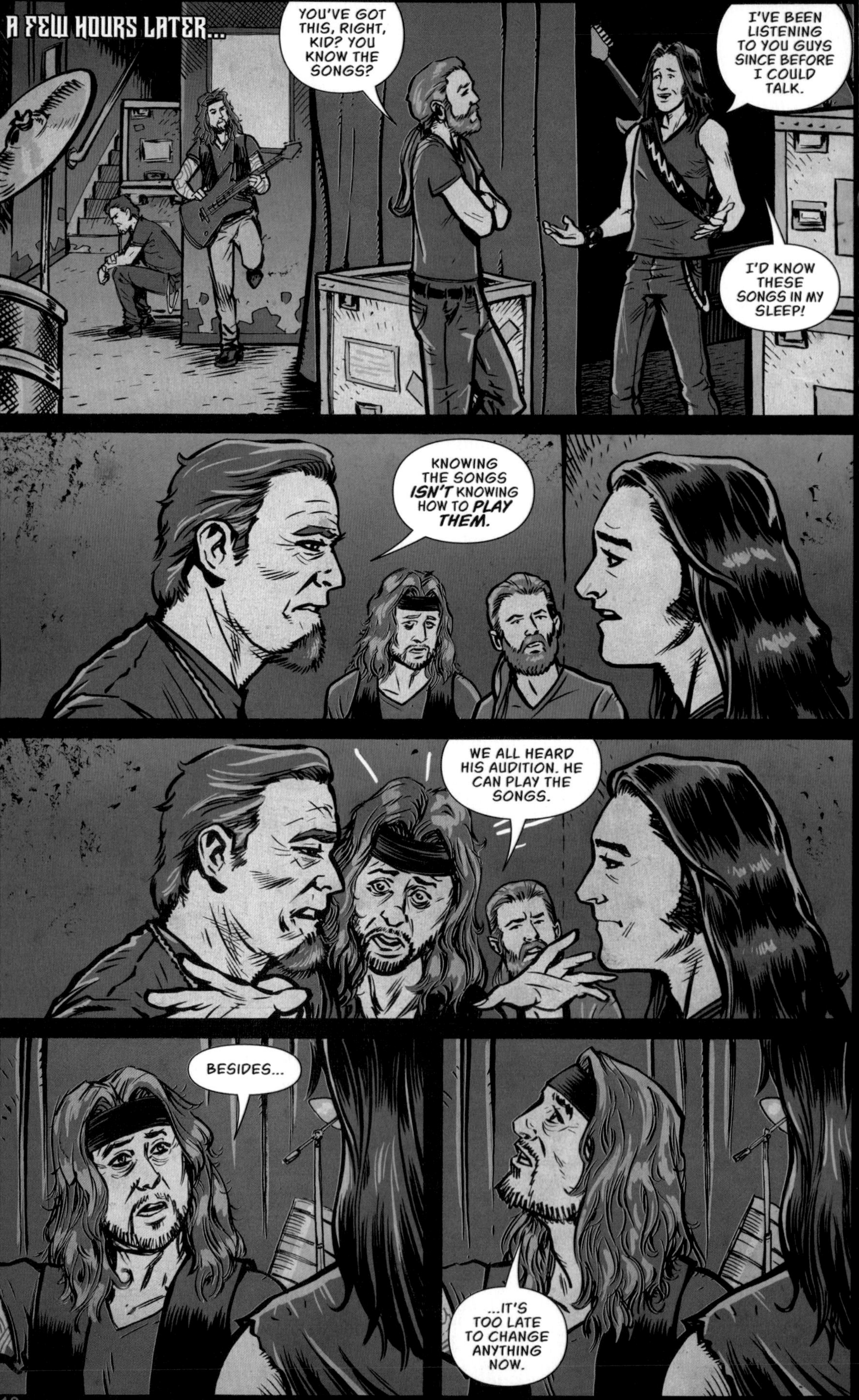
A FEW HOURS LATER...
YOU'VE GOT THIS, RIGHT, KID? YOU KNOW THE SONGS?
I'VE BEEN LISTENING TO YOU GUYS SINCE BEFORE I COULD TALK.
I'D KNOW THESE SONGS IN MY SLEEP!
KNOWING THE SONGS ISN'T KNOWING HOW TO PLAY THEM.
WE ALL HEARD HIS AUDITION. HE CAN PLAY THE SONGS.
BESIDES...
...IT'S TOO LATE TO CHANGE ANYTHING NOW.

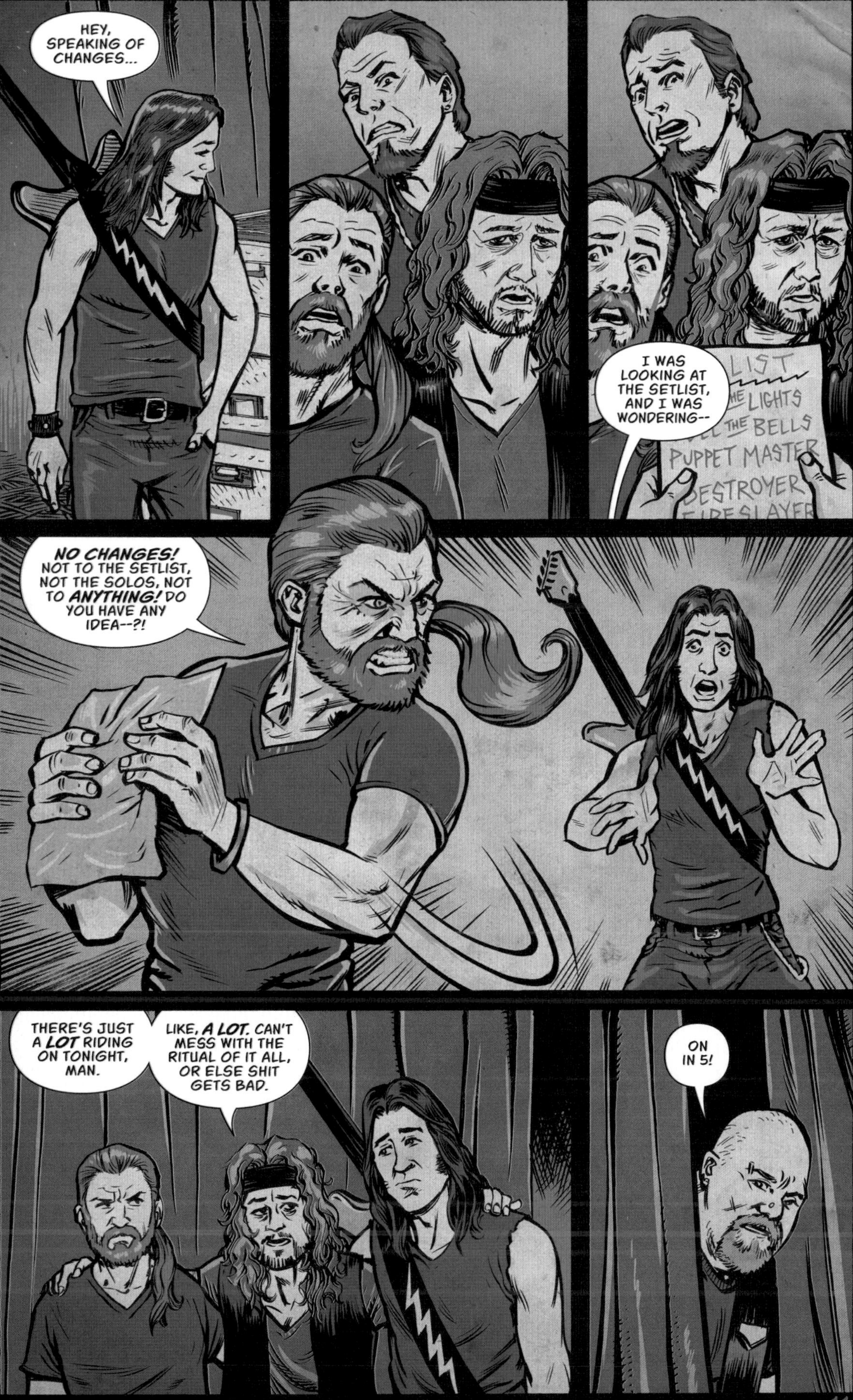
HEY, SPEAKING OF CHANGES...
I WAS LOOKING AT THE SETLIST, AND I WAS WONDERING--
PUPPET MASTER
DESTROYER
NO CHANGES! NOT TO THE SETLIST, NOT THE SOLOS, NOT TO ANYTHING! DO YOU HAVE ANY IDEA--?!
THERE'S JUST A LOT RIDING ON TONIGHT, MAN.
LIKE, A LOT. CAN'T MESS WITH THE RITUAL OF IT ALL, OR ELSE SHIT GETS BAD.
ON IN 5!

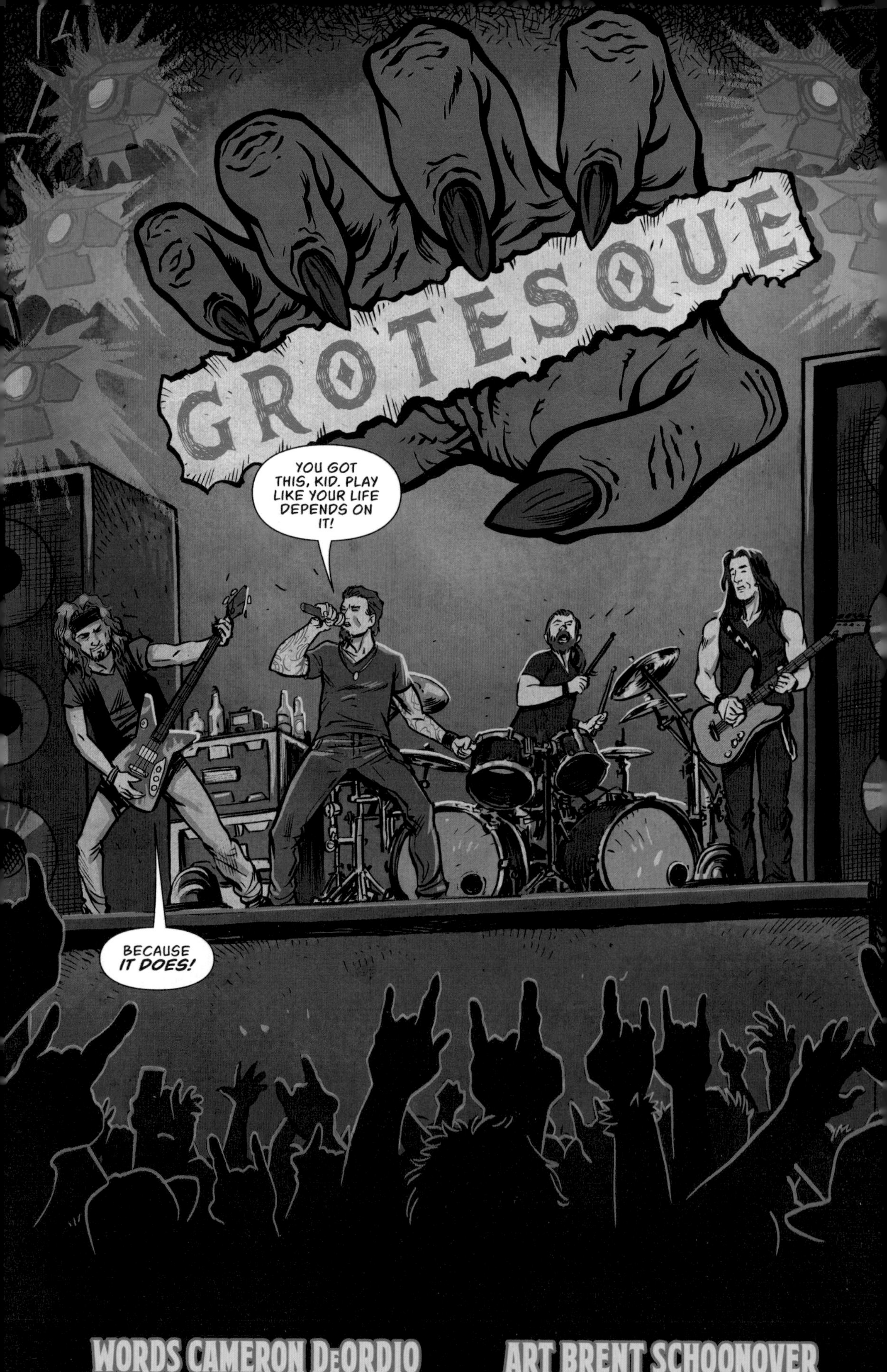
GROTESQUE
YOU GOT THIS, KID. PLAY LIKE YOUR LIFE DEPENDS ON IT!
BECAUSE *IT DOES!*

WORDS CAMERON DeORDIO ART BRENT SCHOONOVER
ADDITIONAL INKS DAVID WITT LETTERS TAYLOR ESPOSITO

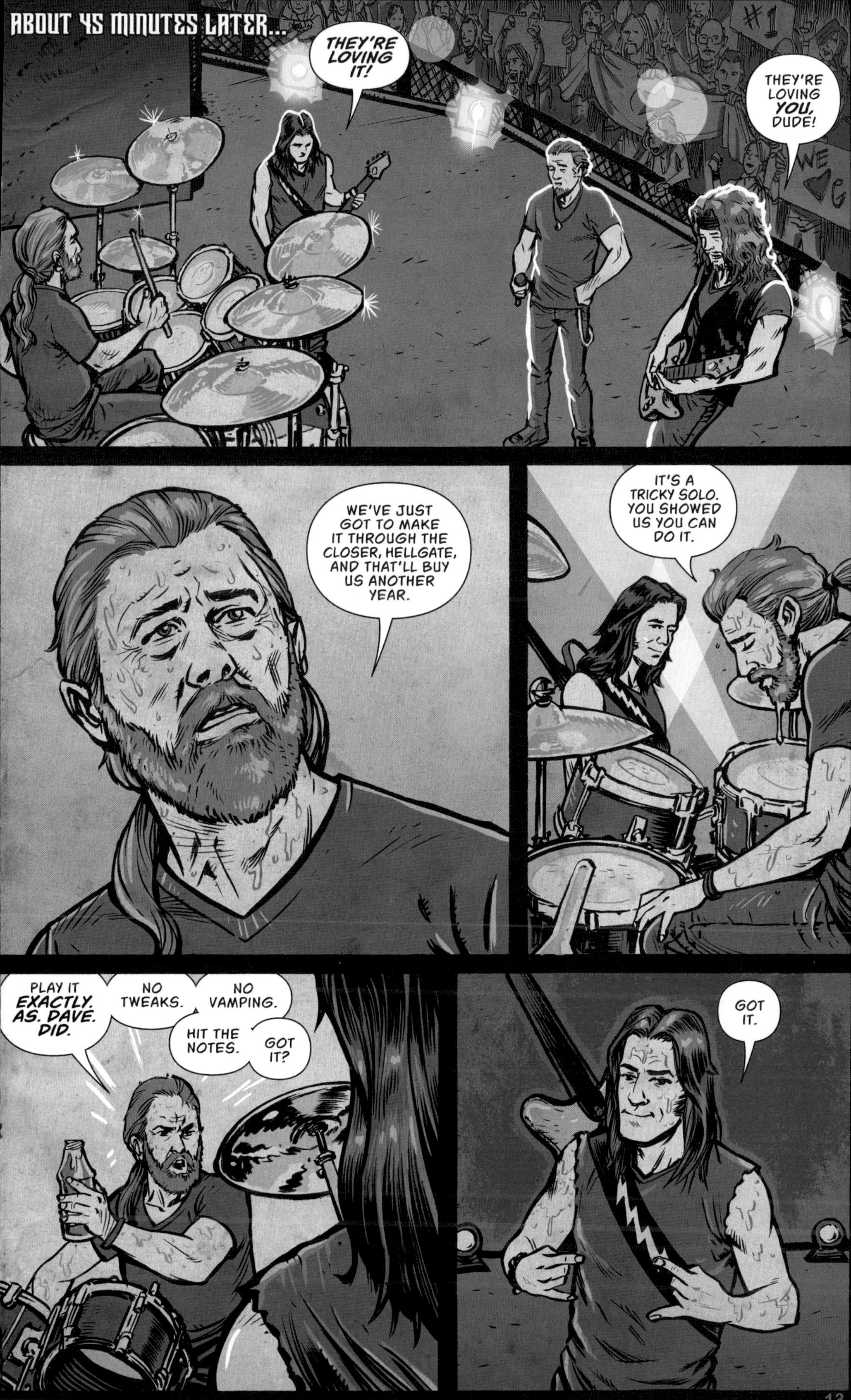
ABOUT 45 MINUTES LATER...
THEY'RE LOVING IT!
THEY'RE LOVING YOU, DUDE!
WE'VE JUST GOT TO MAKE IT THROUGH THE CLOSER, HELLGATE, AND THAT'LL BUY US ANOTHER YEAR.
IT'S A TRICKY SOLO. YOU SHOWED US YOU CAN DO IT.
PLAY IT EXACTLY. AS. DAVE. DID.
NO TWEAKS.
NO VAMPING.
HIT THE NOTES.
GOT IT?
GOT IT.

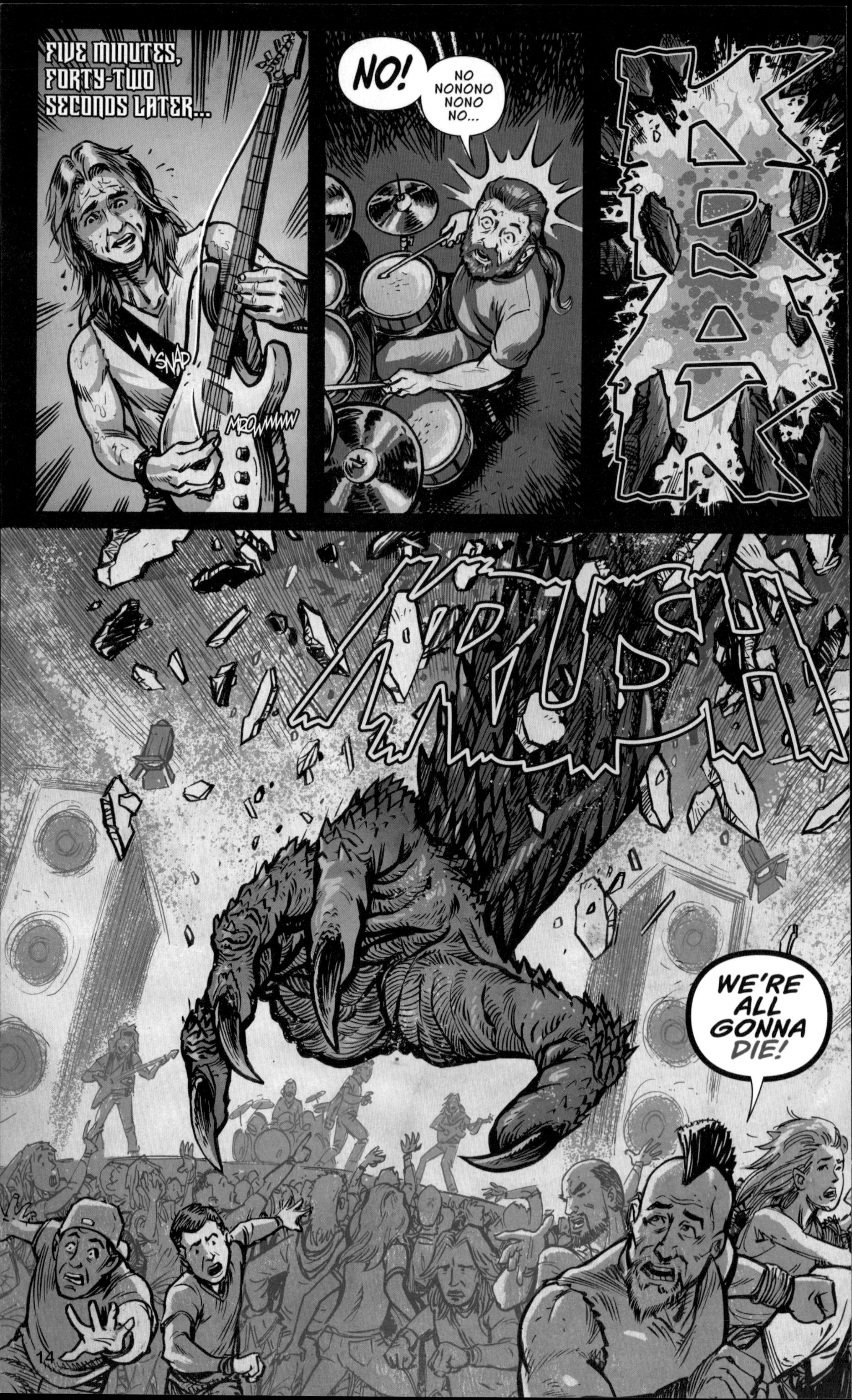
FIVE MINUTES, FORTY-TWO SECONDS LATER...
SNAP
NO!
NO NONONO NONO NO...
WE'RE ALL GONNA DIE!

SNAKE SONG

POLLACK•CASE•WORKMAN

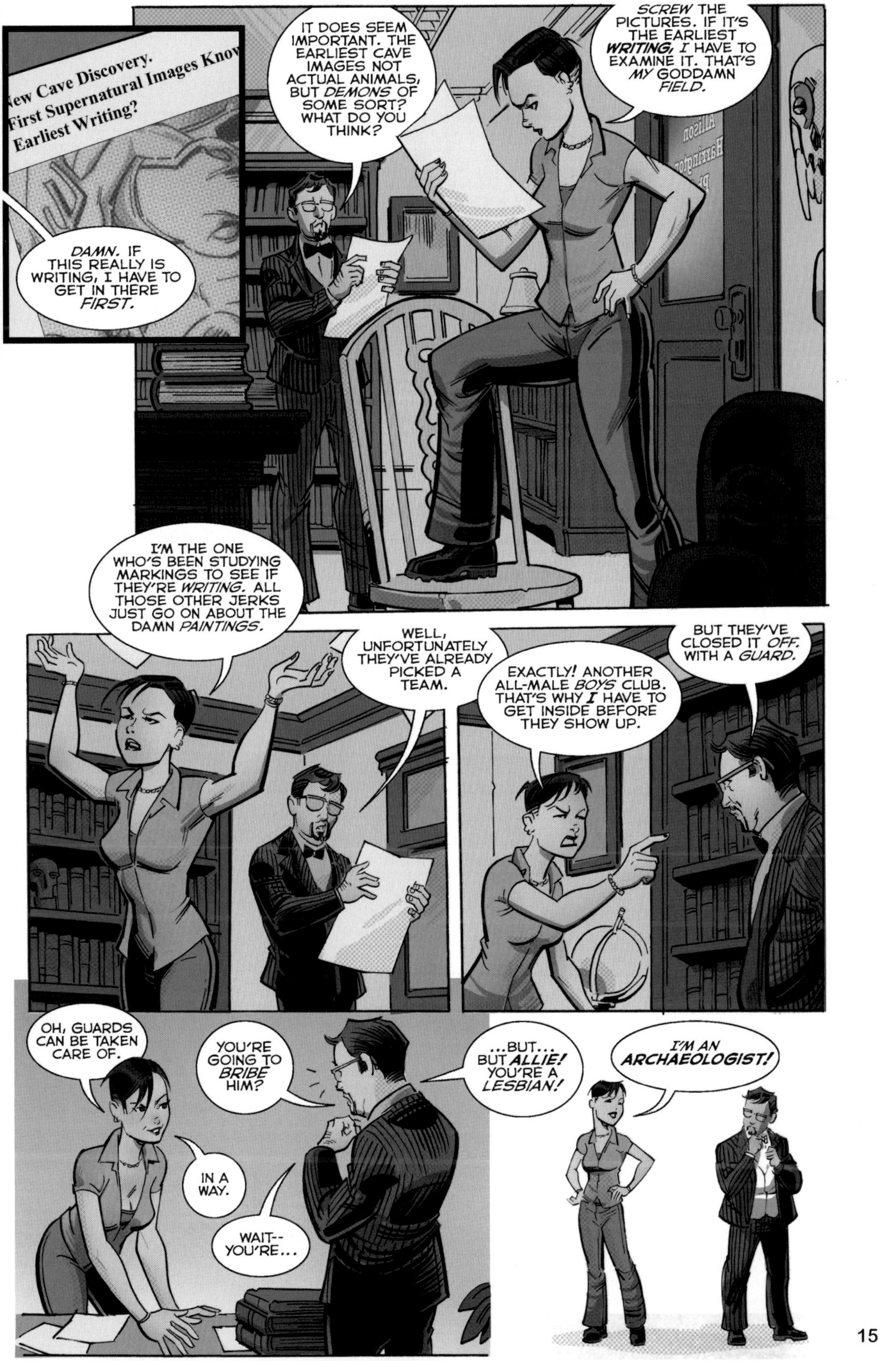

New Cave Discovery.
First Supernatural Images Know
Earliest Writing?
DAMN. IF THIS REALLY IS WRITING, I HAVE TO GET IN THERE FIRST.
IT DOES SEEM IMPORTANT. THE EARLIEST CAVE IMAGES NOT ACTUAL ANIMALS, BUT DEMONS OF SOME SORT? WHAT DO YOU THINK?
SCREW THE PICTURES. IF IT'S THE EARLIEST WRITING, I HAVE TO EXAMINE IT. THAT'S MY GODDAMN FIELD.
I'M THE ONE WHO'S BEEN STUDYING MARKINGS TO SEE IF THEY'RE WRITING. ALL THOSE OTHER JERKS JUST GO ON ABOUT THE DAMN PAINTINGS.
WELL, UNFORTUNATELY THEY'VE ALREADY PICKED A TEAM.
EXACTLY! ANOTHER ALL-MALE BOYS CLUB. THAT'S WHY I HAVE TO GET INSIDE BEFORE THEY SHOW UP.
BUT THEY'VE CLOSED IT OFF. WITH A GUARD.
OH, GUARDS CAN BE TAKEN CARE OF.
YOU'RE GOING TO BRIBE HIM?
IN A WAY.
WAIT-- YOU'RE...
...BUT... BUT ALLIE! YOU'RE A LESBIAN!
I'M AN ARCHAEOLOGIST!

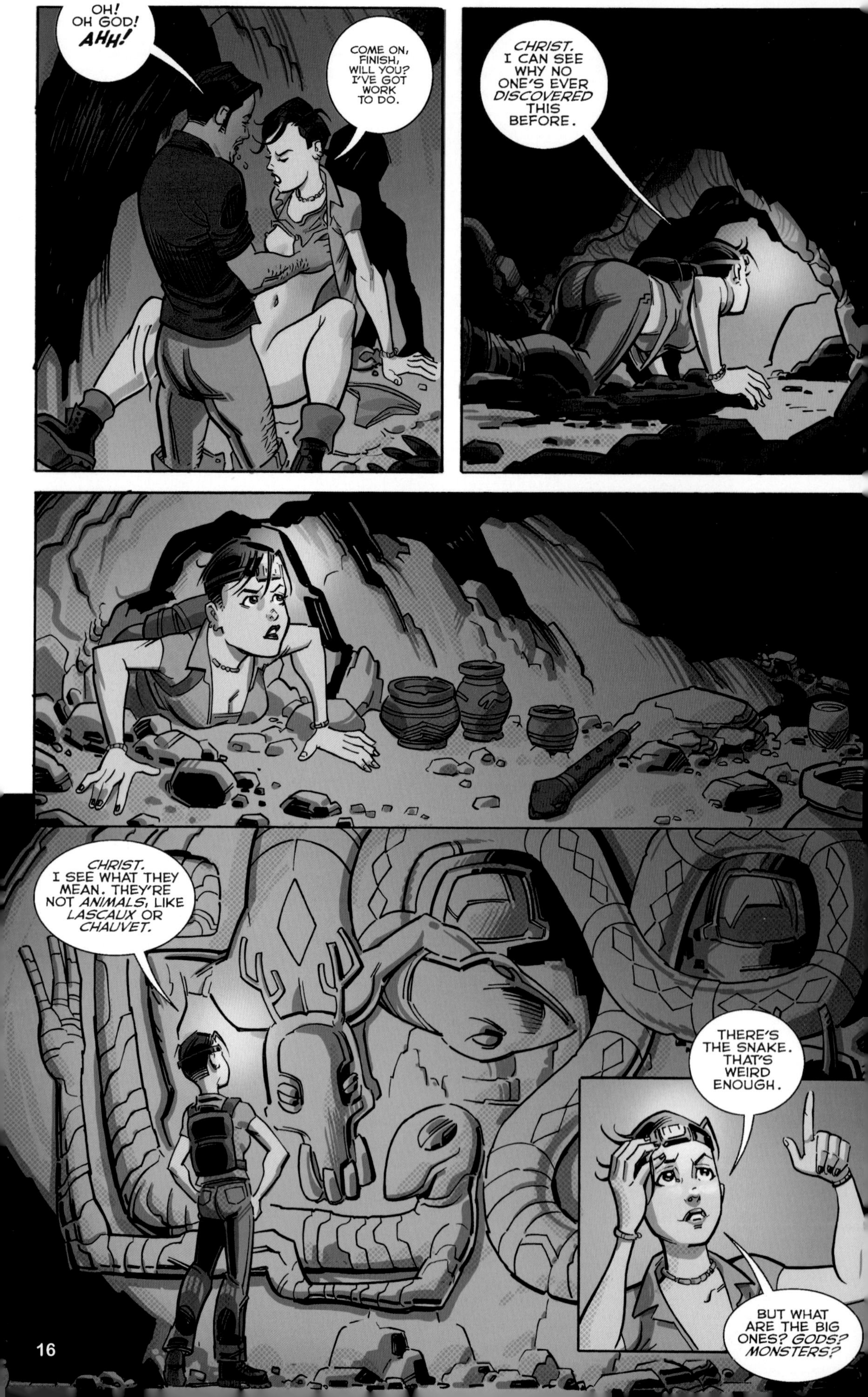
OH!
OH GOD!
AHH!
COME ON, FINISH, WILL YOU? I'VE GOT WORK TO DO.
CHRIST. I CAN SEE WHY NO ONE'S EVER DISCOVERED THIS BEFORE.
CHRIST. I SEE WHAT THEY MEAN. THEY'RE NOT ANIMALS, LIKE LASCAUX OR CHAUVET.
THERE'S THE SNAKE. THAT'S WEIRD ENOUGH.
BUT WHAT ARE THE BIG ONES? GODS? MONSTERS?

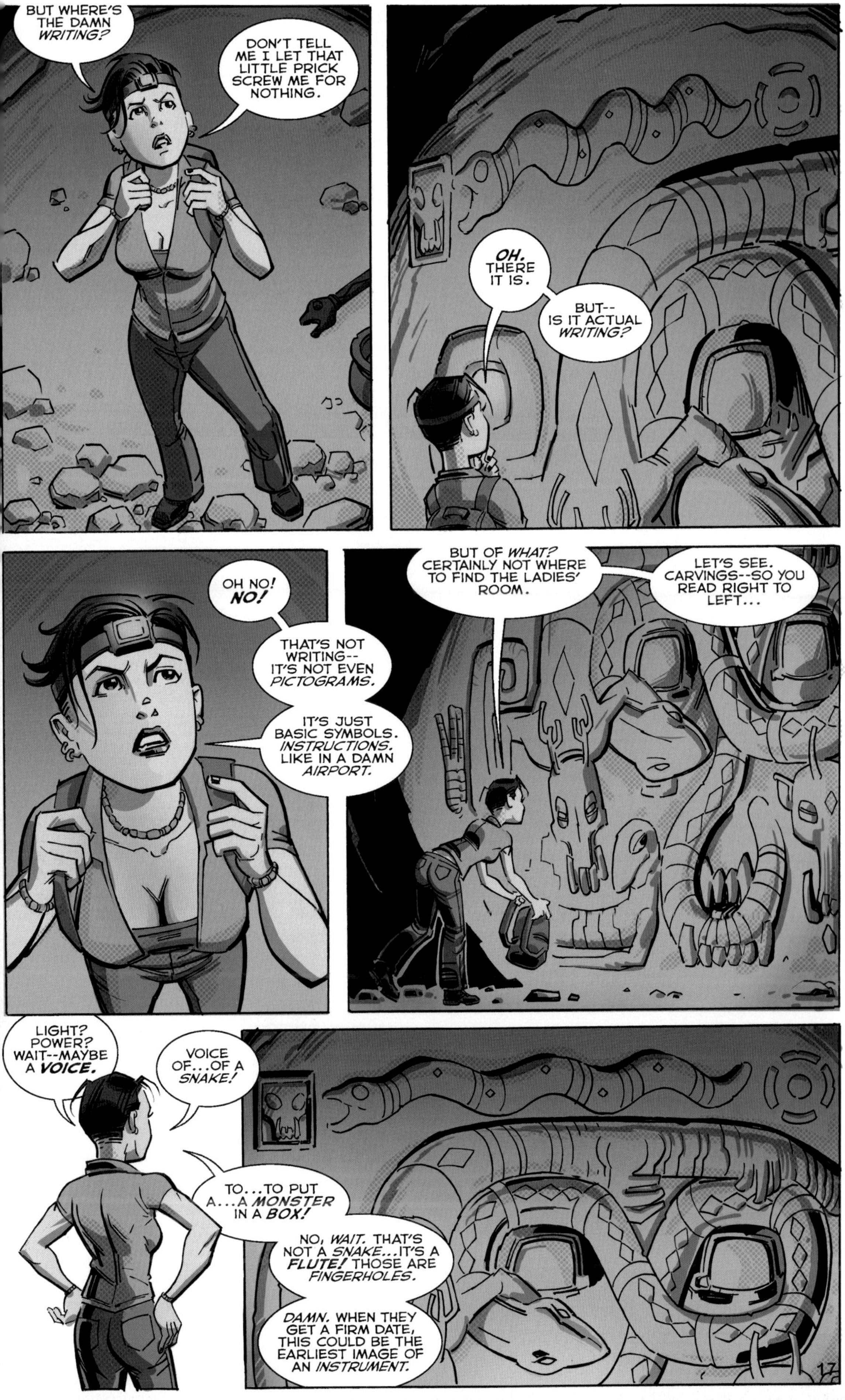

BUT WHERE'S THE DAMN *WRITING?*
DON'T TELL ME I LET THAT LITTLE PRICK SCREW ME FOR NOTHING.
OH. THERE IT IS.
BUT-- IS IT ACTUAL *WRITING?*
OH NO! ***NO!***
THAT'S NOT WRITING-- IT'S NOT EVEN *PICTOGRAMS.*
IT'S JUST BASIC SYMBOLS. *INSTRUCTIONS.* LIKE IN A DAMN *AIRPORT.*
LET'S SEE. CARVINGS--SO YOU READ RIGHT TO LEFT...
BUT OF *WHAT?* CERTAINLY NOT WHERE TO FIND THE LADIES' ROOM.
LIGHT? POWER? WAIT--MAYBE A ***VOICE.***
VOICE OF...OF A *SNAKE!*
TO...TO PUT A...A ***MONSTER*** IN A ***BOX!***
NO, *WAIT.* THAT'S NOT A *SNAKE*...IT'S A ***FLUTE!*** THOSE ARE *FINGERHOLES.*
DAMN. WHEN THEY GET A FIRM DATE, THIS COULD BE THE EARLIEST IMAGE OF AN *INSTRUMENT.*

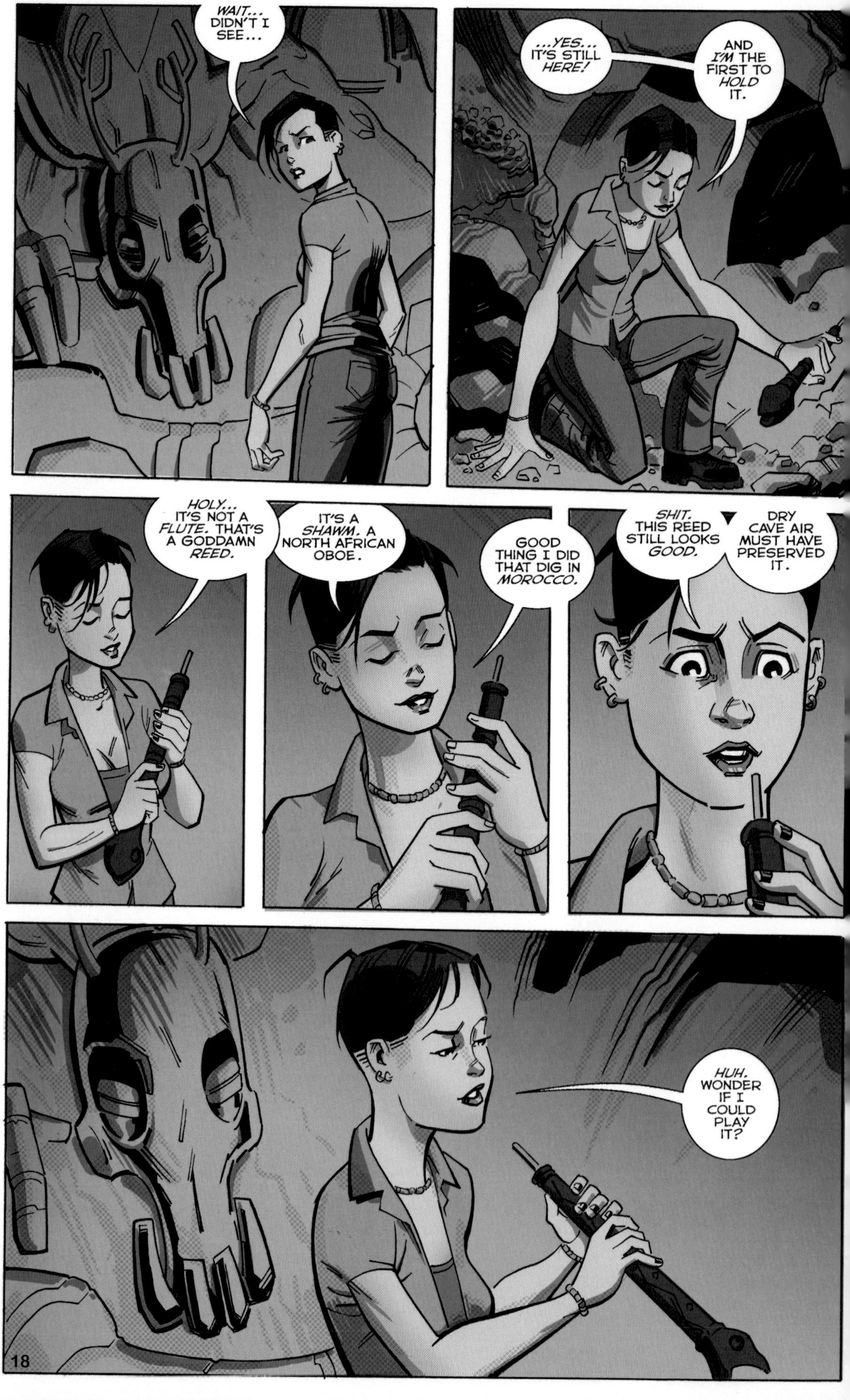
WAIT... DIDN'T I SEE...
...YES... IT'S STILL HERE!
AND I'M THE FIRST TO HOLD IT.
HOLY... IT'S NOT A FLUTE. THAT'S A GODDAMN REED.
IT'S A SHAWM. A NORTH AFRICAN OBOE.
GOOD THING I DID THAT DIG IN MOROCCO.
SHIT. THIS REED STILL LOOKS GOOD.
DRY CAVE AIR MUST HAVE PRESERVED IT.
HUH. WONDER IF I COULD PLAY IT?

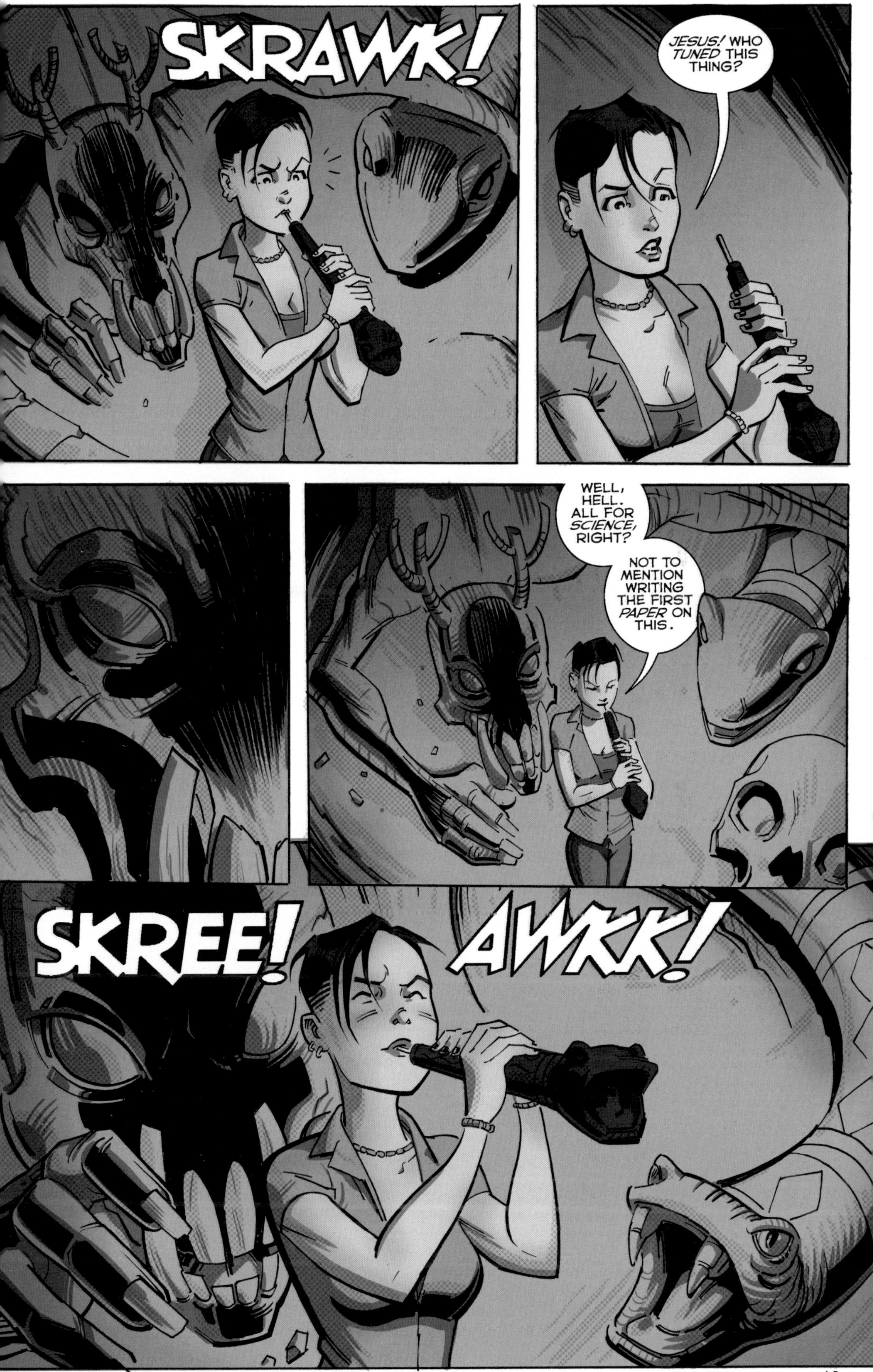
SKRAWK!
JESUS! WHO TUNED THIS THING?
WELL, HELL. ALL FOR SCIENCE, RIGHT?
NOT TO MENTION WRITING THE FIRST PAPER ON THIS.
SKREE!
AWKK!

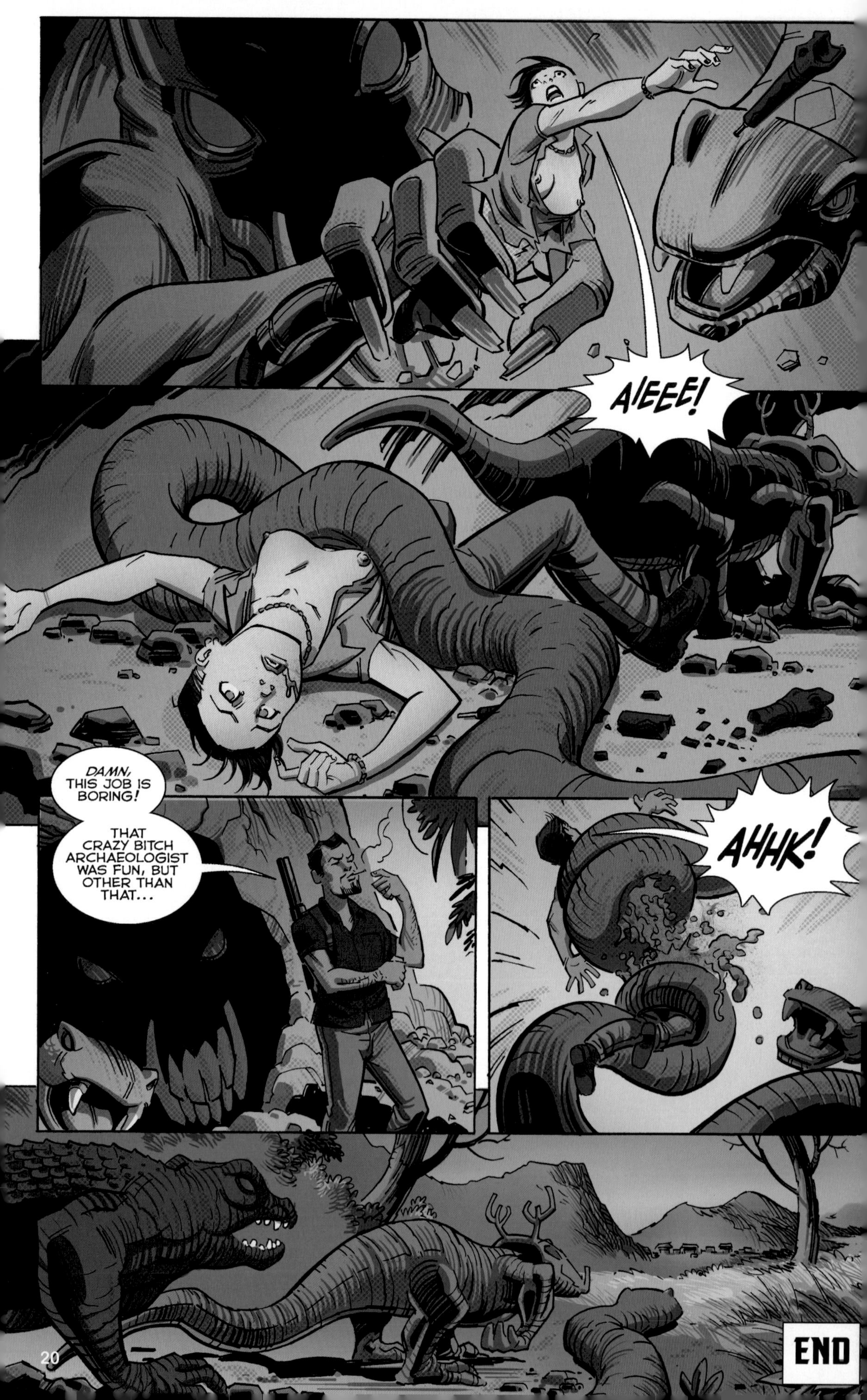

AIEEE!
DAMN, THIS JOB IS BORING!
THAT CRAZY BITCH ARCHAEOLOGIST WAS FUN, BUT OTHER THAN THAT...
AHHK!
END

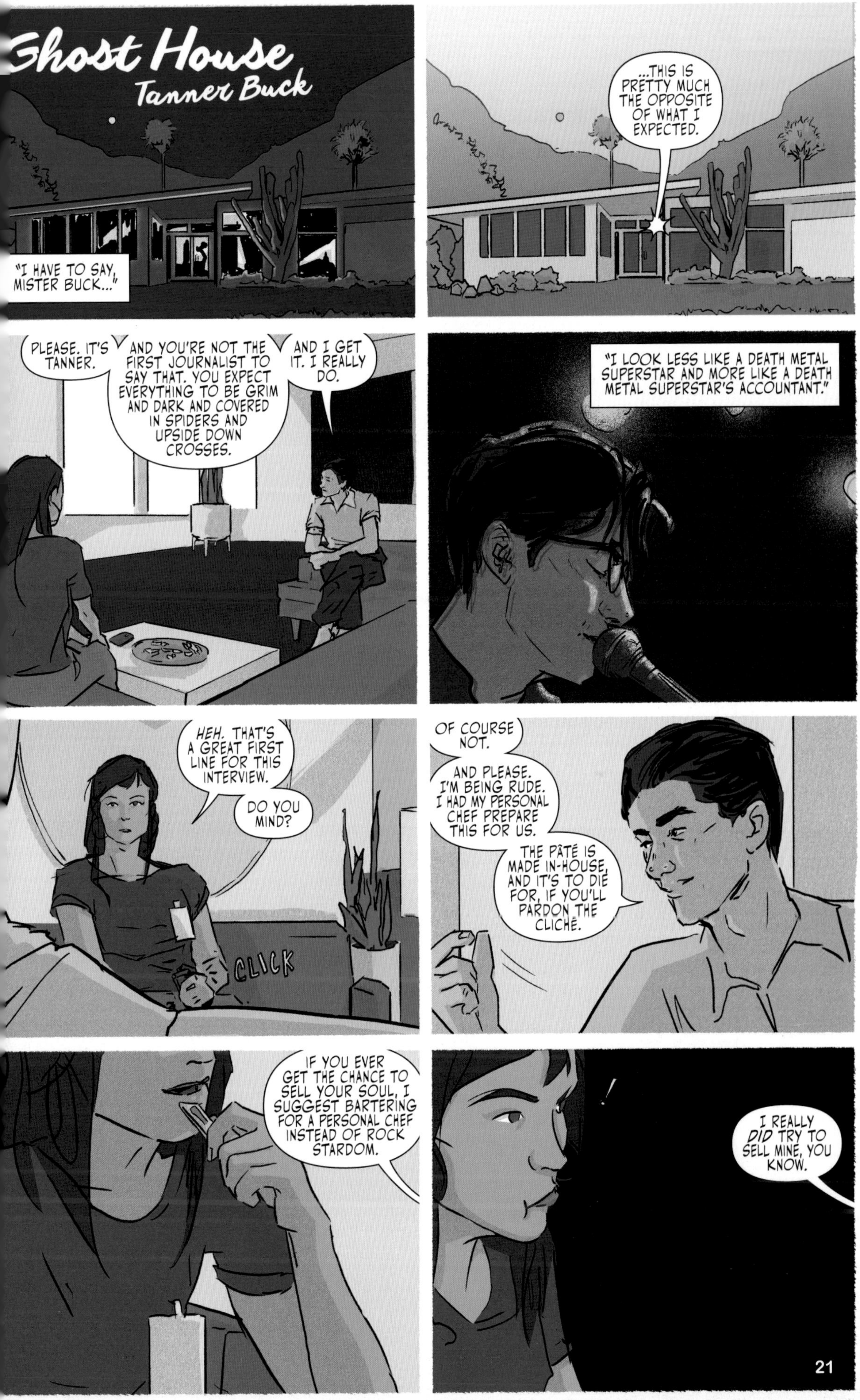

Ghost House
Tanner Buck
"I HAVE TO SAY, MISTER BUCK..."
...THIS IS PRETTY MUCH THE OPPOSITE OF WHAT I EXPECTED.
PLEASE. IT'S TANNER.
AND YOU'RE NOT THE FIRST JOURNALIST TO SAY THAT. YOU EXPECT EVERYTHING TO BE GRIM AND DARK AND COVERED IN SPIDERS AND UPSIDE DOWN CROSSES.
AND I GET IT. I REALLY DO.
"I LOOK LESS LIKE A DEATH METAL SUPERSTAR AND MORE LIKE A DEATH METAL SUPERSTAR'S ACCOUNTANT."
HEH. THAT'S A GREAT FIRST LINE FOR THIS INTERVIEW.
DO YOU MIND?
CLICK
OF COURSE NOT.
AND PLEASE. I'M BEING RUDE. I HAD MY PERSONAL CHEF PREPARE THIS FOR US.
THE PÂTÉ IS MADE IN-HOUSE, AND IT'S TO DIE FOR, IF YOU'LL PARDON THE CLICHÉ.
IF YOU EVER GET THE CHANCE TO SELL YOUR SOUL, I SUGGEST BARTERING FOR A PERSONAL CHEF INSTEAD OF ROCK STARDOM.
!
I REALLY *DID* TRY TO SELL MINE, YOU KNOW.

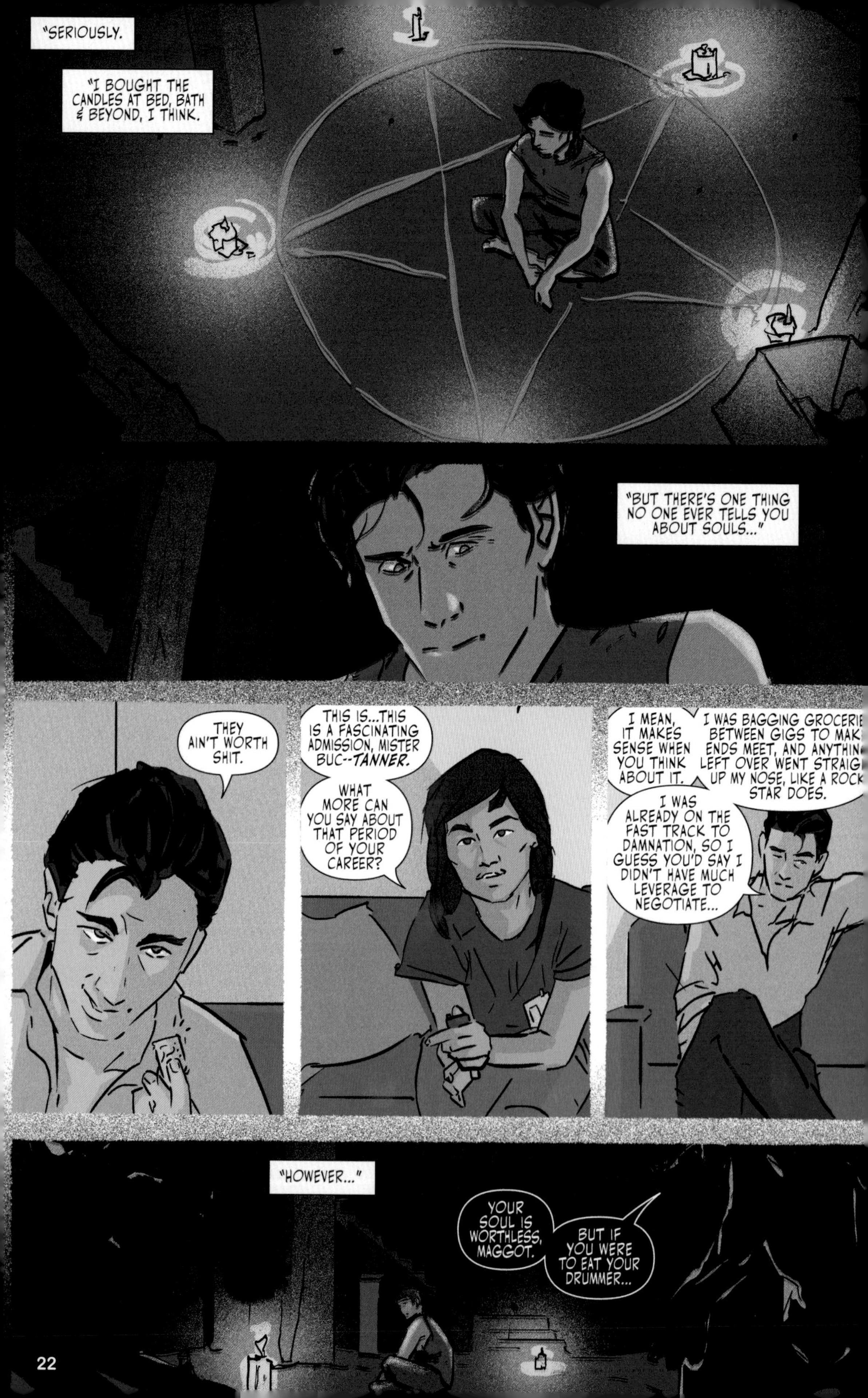
"SERIOUSLY.
"I BOUGHT THE CANDLES AT BED, BATH & BEYOND, I THINK.
"BUT THERE'S ONE THING NO ONE EVER TELLS YOU ABOUT SOULS..."
THEY AIN'T WORTH SHIT.
THIS IS...THIS IS A FASCINATING ADMISSION, MISTER BUC--*TANNER.*
WHAT MORE CAN YOU SAY ABOUT THAT PERIOD OF YOUR CAREER?
I MEAN, IT MAKES SENSE WHEN YOU THINK ABOUT IT.
I WAS BAGGING GROCERIE BETWEEN GIGS TO MAK ENDS MEET, AND ANYTHIN LEFT OVER WENT STRAIG UP MY NOSE, LIKE A ROCK STAR DOES.
I WAS ALREADY ON THE FAST TRACK TO DAMNATION, SO I GUESS YOU'D SAY I DIDN'T HAVE MUCH LEVERAGE TO NEGOTIATE...
"HOWEVER..."
YOUR SOUL IS WORTHLESS, MAGGOT.
BUT IF YOU WERE TO EAT YOUR DRUMMER...

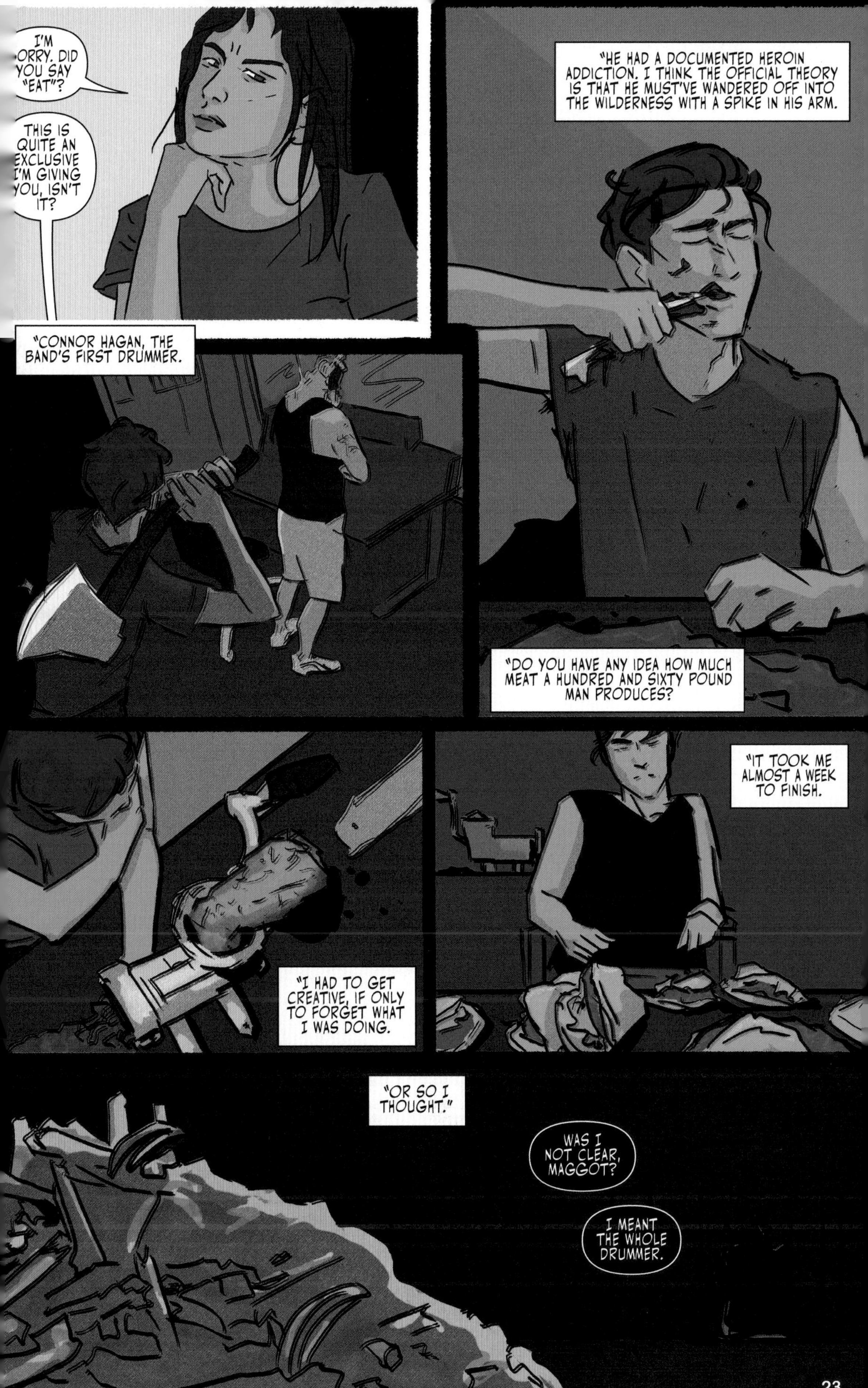
I'M SORRY. DID YOU SAY "EAT"?
THIS IS QUITE AN EXCLUSIVE I'M GIVING YOU, ISN'T IT?
"HE HAD A DOCUMENTED HEROIN ADDICTION. I THINK THE OFFICIAL THEORY IS THAT HE MUST'VE WANDERED OFF INTO THE WILDERNESS WITH A SPIKE IN HIS ARM.
"CONNOR HAGAN, THE BAND'S FIRST DRUMMER.
"DO YOU HAVE ANY IDEA HOW MUCH MEAT A HUNDRED AND SIXTY POUND MAN PRODUCES?
"I HAD TO GET CREATIVE, IF ONLY TO FORGET WHAT I WAS DOING.
"IT TOOK ME ALMOST A WEEK TO FINISH.
"OR SO I THOUGHT."
WAS I NOT CLEAR, MAGGOT?
I MEANT THE WHOLE DRUMMER.

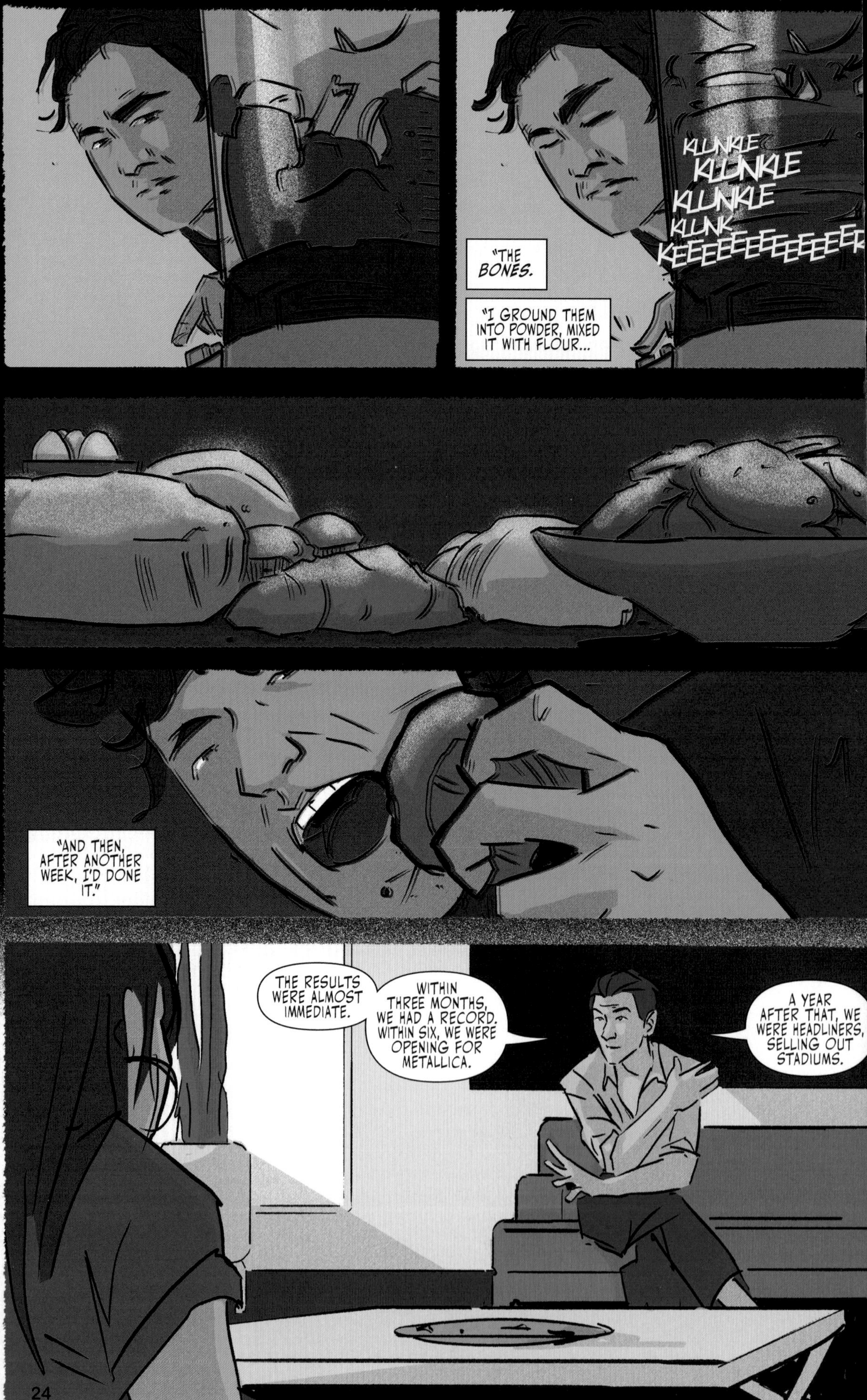
KLUNKLE
KLUNKLE
KLUNKLE
KLUNK
KEEEEEEEEEEEEER
"THE BONES.
"I GROUND THEM INTO POWDER, MIXED IT WITH FLOUR...
"AND THEN, AFTER ANOTHER WEEK, I'D DONE IT."
THE RESULTS WERE ALMOST IMMEDIATE.
WITHIN THREE MONTHS, WE HAD A RECORD. WITHIN SIX, WE WERE OPENING FOR METALLICA.
A YEAR AFTER THAT, WE WERE HEADLINERS, SELLING OUT STADIUMS.

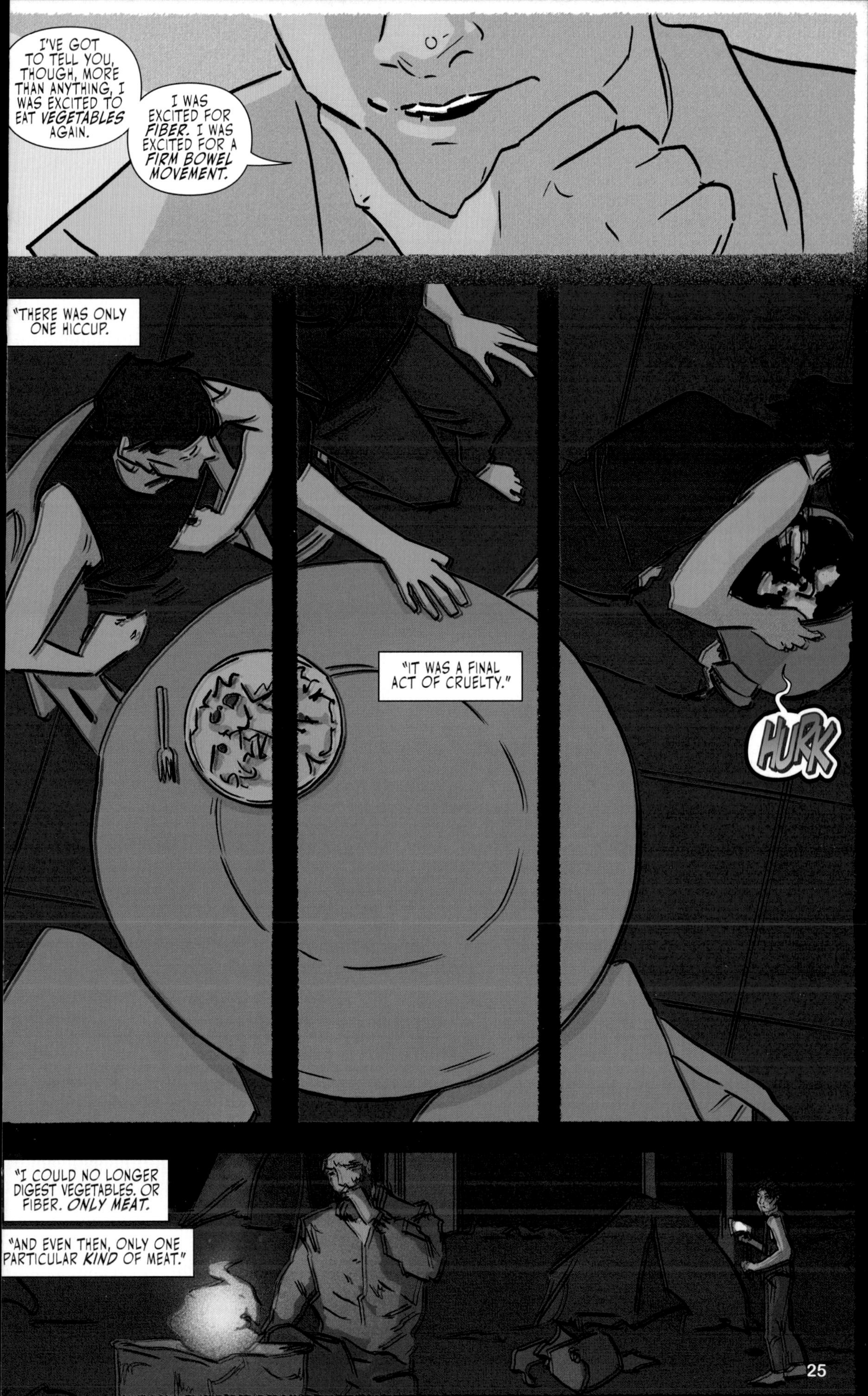
I'VE GOT TO TELL YOU, THOUGH, MORE THAN ANYTHING, I WAS EXCITED TO EAT *VEGETABLES* AGAIN.
I WAS EXCITED FOR *FIBER.* I WAS EXCITED FOR A *FIRM BOWEL MOVEMENT.*
"THERE WAS ONLY ONE HICCUP.
"IT WAS A FINAL ACT OF CRUELTY."
HURK
"I COULD NO LONGER DIGEST VEGETABLES. OR FIBER. *ONLY MEAT.*
"AND EVEN THEN, ONLY ONE PARTICULAR *KIND* OF MEAT."

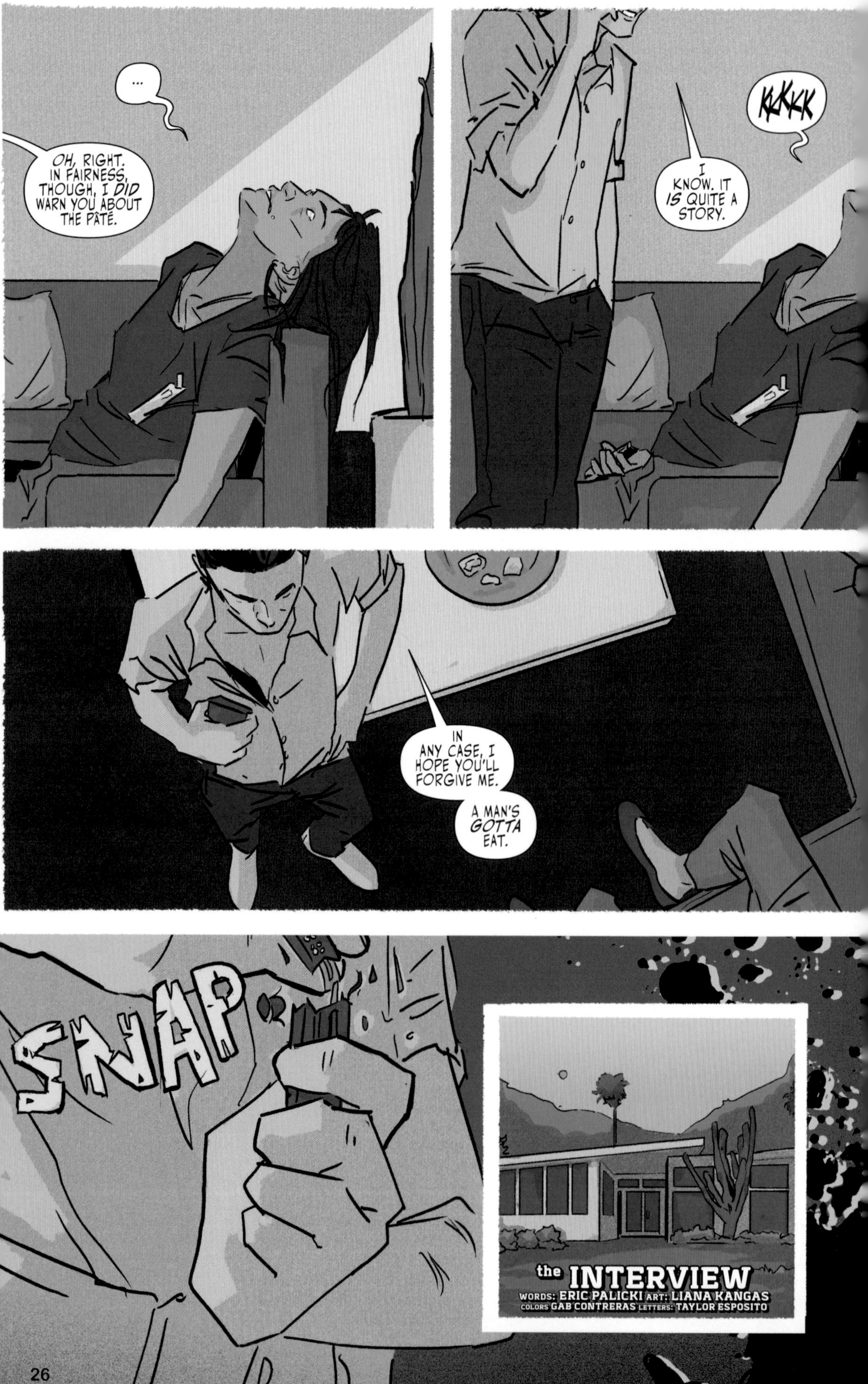
...
OH, RIGHT. IN FAIRNESS, THOUGH, I DID WARN YOU ABOUT THE PÂTÉ.
KKKKK
I KNOW. IT IS QUITE A STORY.
IN ANY CASE, I HOPE YOU'LL FORGIVE ME.
A MAN'S GOTTA EAT.
SNAP
the INTERVIEW
WORDS: ERIC PALICKI ART: LIANA KANGAS
COLORS GAB CONTRERAS LETTERS: TAYLOR ESPOSITO

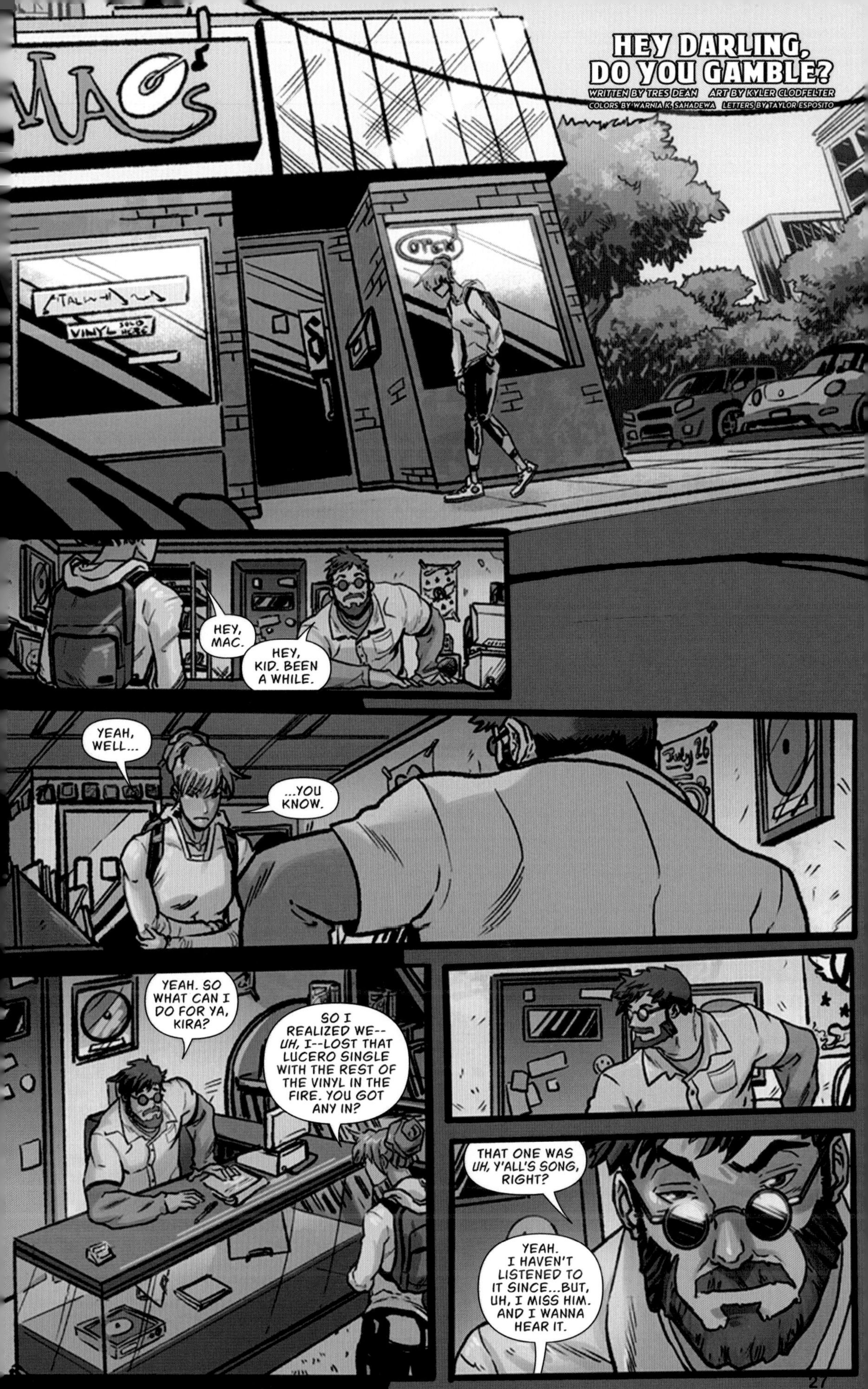
HEY DARLING, DO YOU GAMBLE?
WRITTEN BY TRES DEAN ART BY KYLER CLODFELTER
COLORS BY WARNIA K. SAHADEWA LETTERS BY TAYLOR ESPOSITO
HEY, MAC.
HEY, KID. BEEN A WHILE.
YEAH, WELL...
...YOU KNOW.
YEAH. SO WHAT CAN I DO FOR YA, KIRA?
SO I REALIZED WE--UH, I--LOST THAT LUCERO SINGLE WITH THE REST OF THE VINYL IN THE FIRE. YOU GOT ANY IN?
THAT ONE WAS UH, Y'ALL'S SONG, RIGHT?
YEAH. I HAVEN'T LISTENED TO IT SINCE...BUT, UH, I MISS HIM. AND I WANNA HEAR IT.

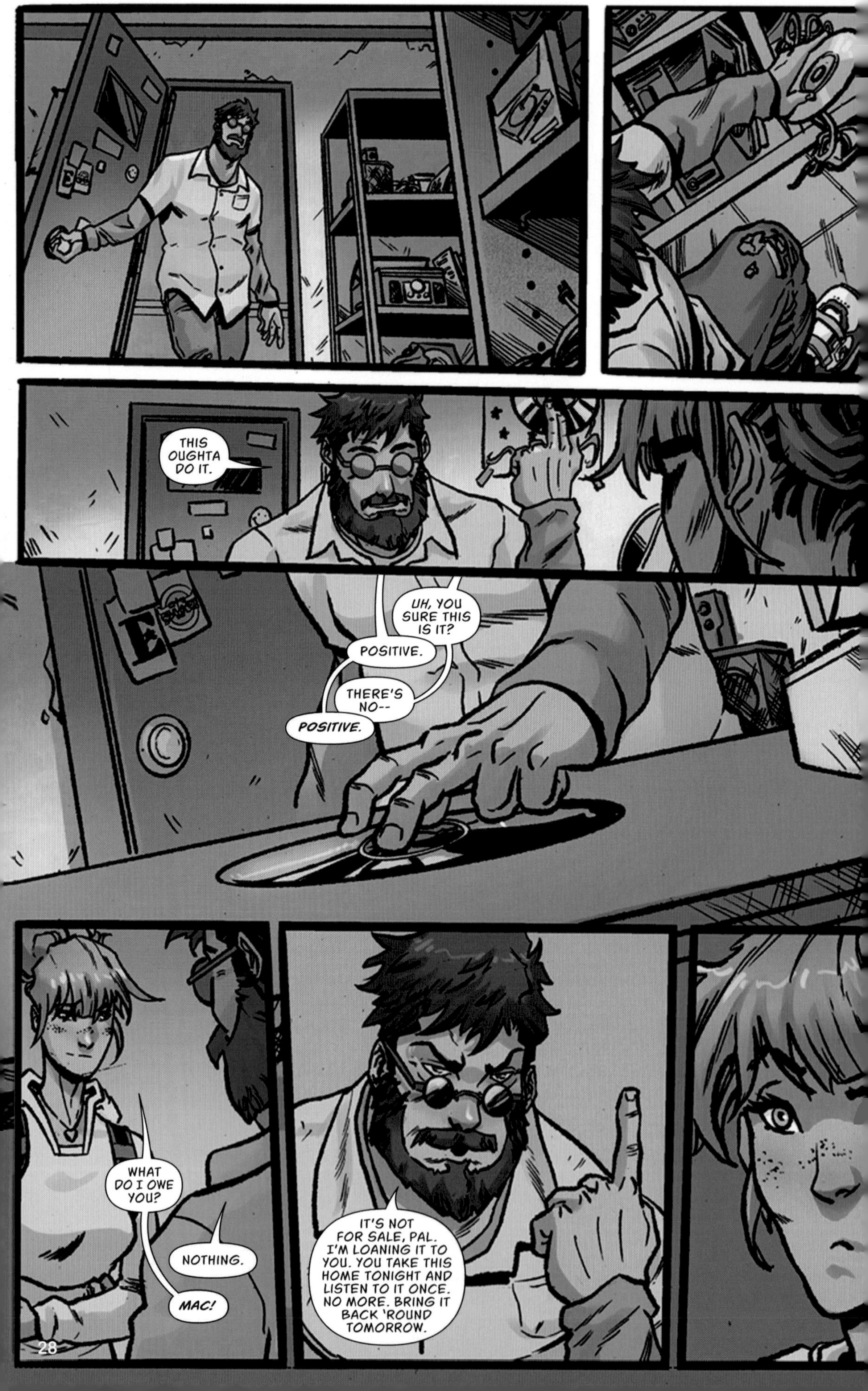
THIS OUGHTA DO IT.
UH, YOU SURE THIS IS IT?
POSITIVE.
THERE'S NO--
POSITIVE.
WHAT DO I OWE YOU?
NOTHING.
MAC!
IT'S NOT FOR SALE, PAL. I'M LOANING IT TO YOU. YOU TAKE THIS HOME TONIGHT AND LISTEN TO IT ONCE. NO MORE. BRING IT BACK 'ROUND TOMORROW.

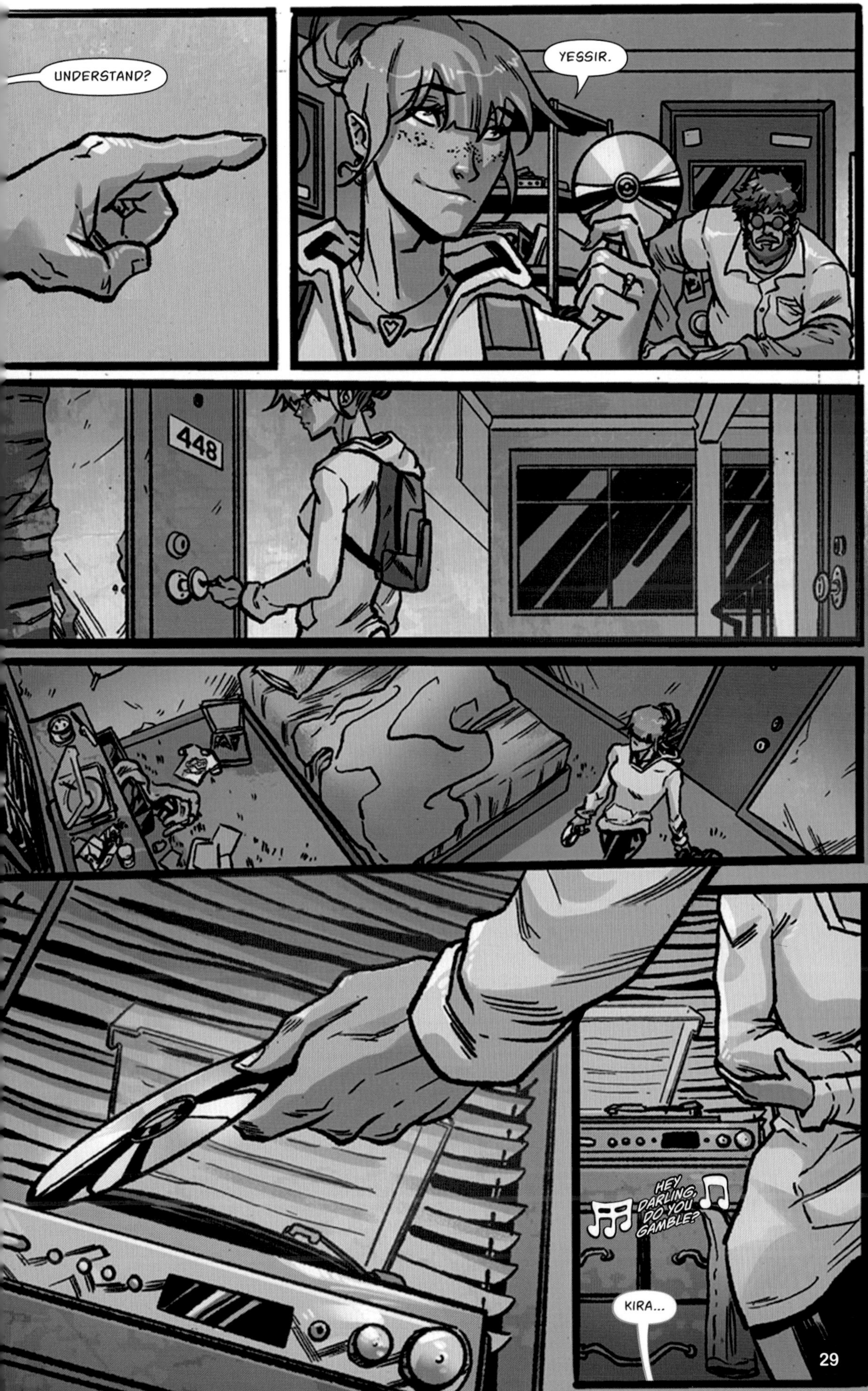
UNDERSTAND?
YESSIR.
448
HEY DARLING, DO YOU GAMBLE?
KIRA...

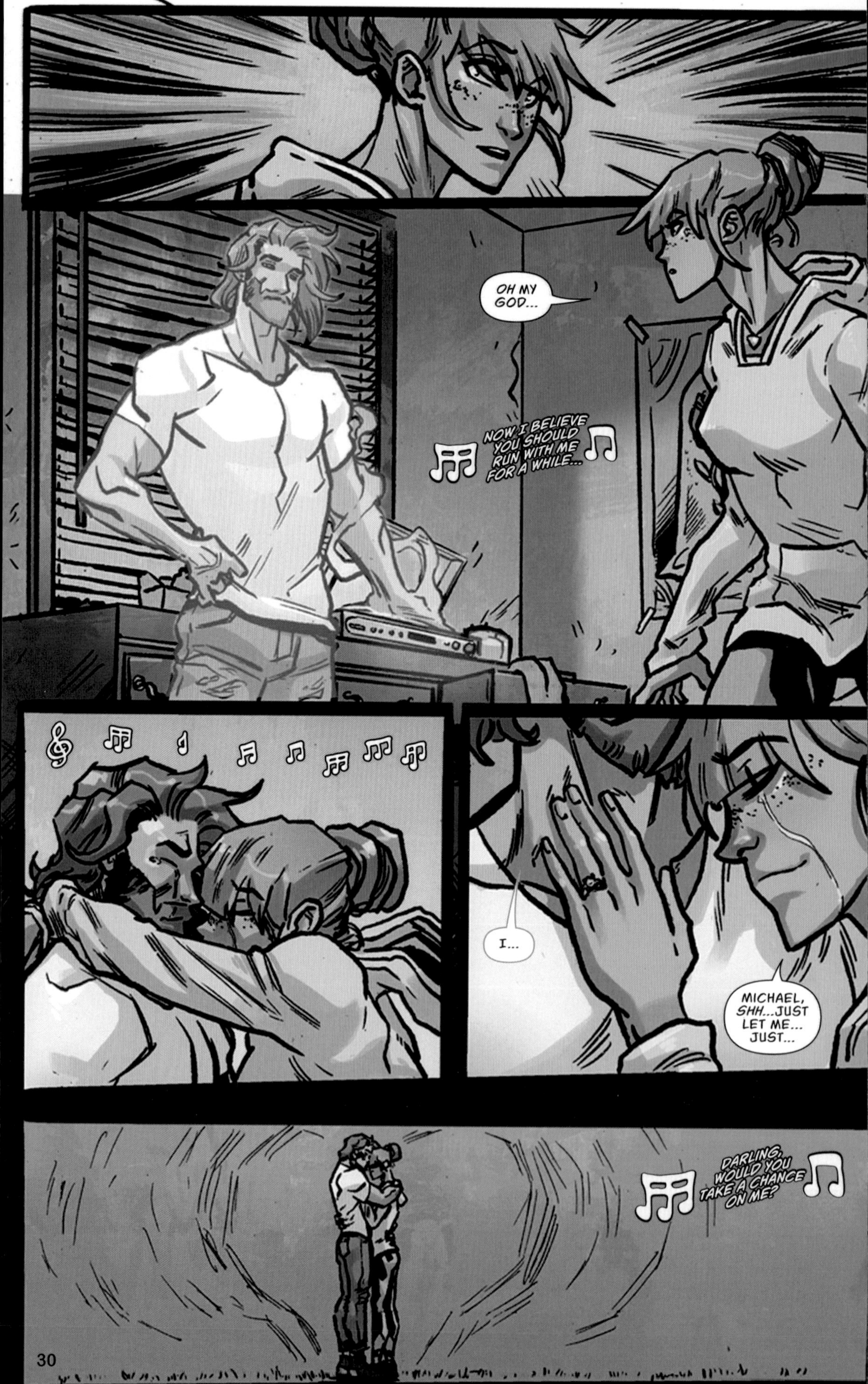
OH MY GOD...
NOW I BELIEVE YOU SHOULD RUN WITH ME FOR A WHILE...
I...
MICHAEL, SHH...JUST LET ME... JUST...
DARLING, WOULD YOU TAKE A CHANCE ON ME?

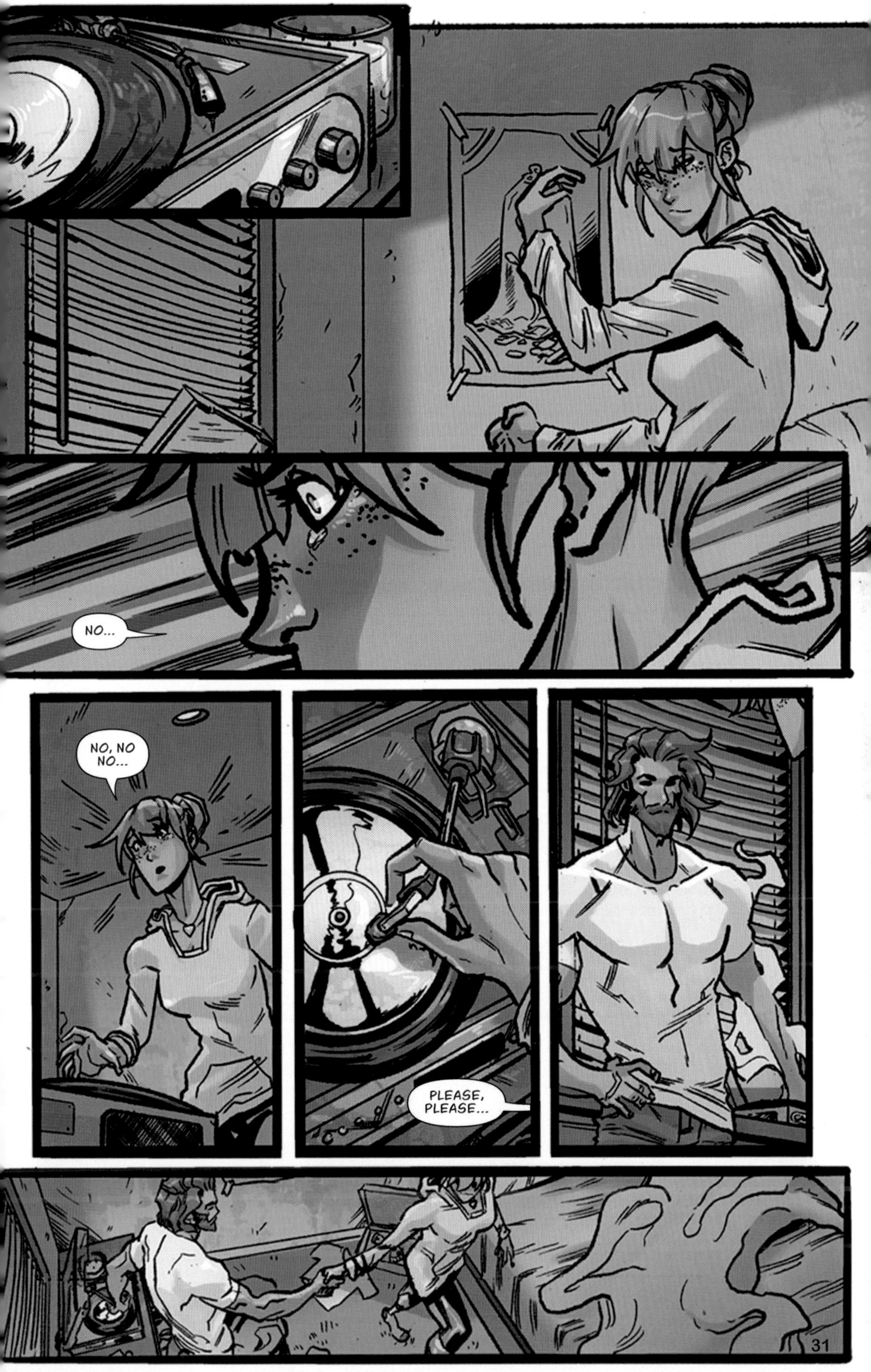
NO...
NO, NO NO...
PLEASE, PLEASE...

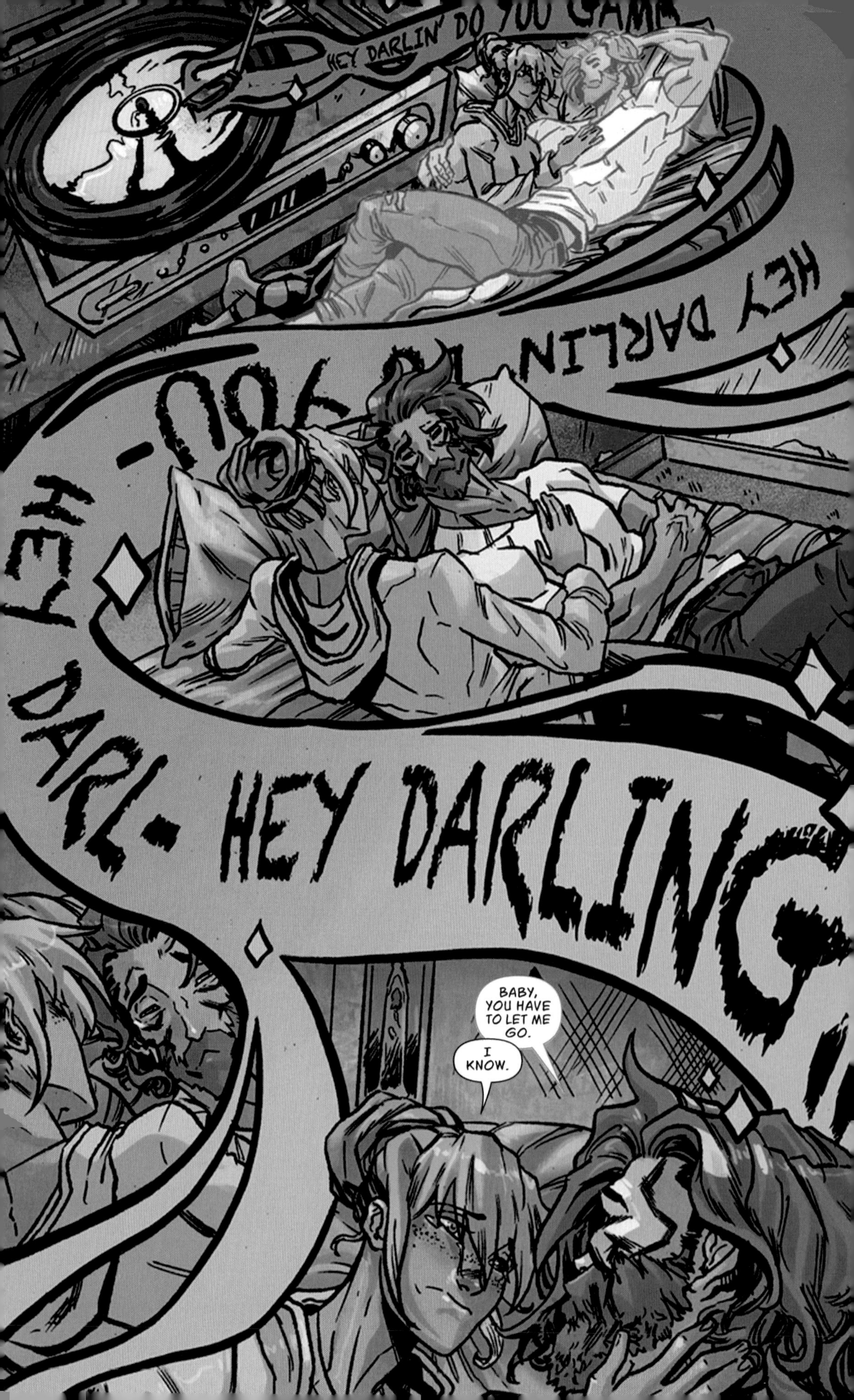
HEY DARLIN' DO YOU
HEY DARLIN
YOU-
HEY DARL-
HEY DARLING!!
BABY, YOU HAVE TO LET ME GO.
I KNOW.

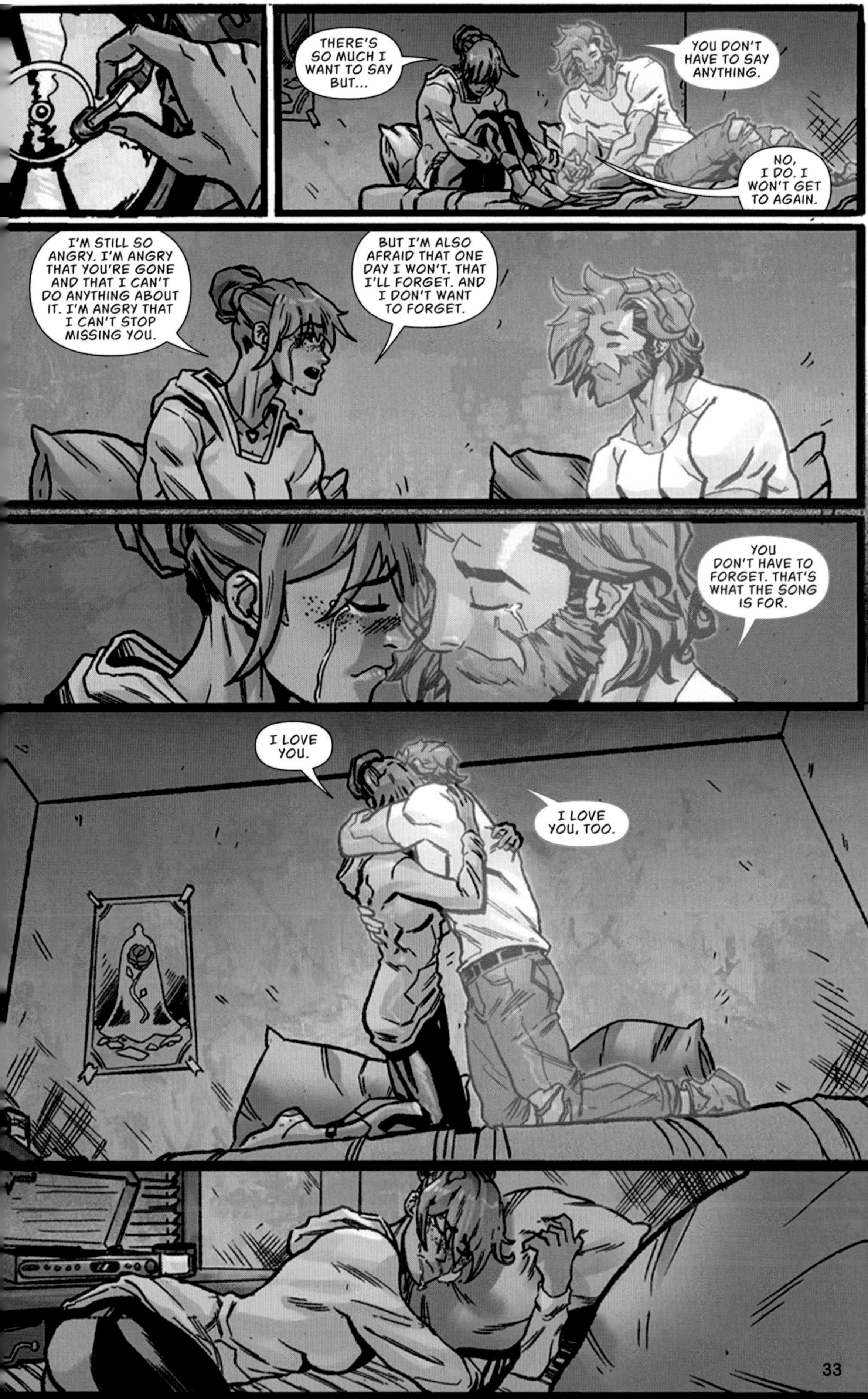
THERE'S SO MUCH I WANT TO SAY BUT...
YOU DON'T HAVE TO SAY ANYTHING.
NO, I DO. I WON'T GET TO AGAIN.
I'M STILL SO ANGRY. I'M ANGRY THAT YOU'RE GONE AND THAT I CAN'T DO ANYTHING ABOUT IT. I'M ANGRY THAT I CAN'T STOP MISSING YOU.
BUT I'M ALSO AFRAID THAT ONE DAY I WON'T. THAT I'LL FORGET. AND I DON'T WANT TO FORGET.
YOU DON'T HAVE TO FORGET. THAT'S WHAT THE SONG IS FOR.
I LOVE YOU.
I LOVE YOU, TOO.

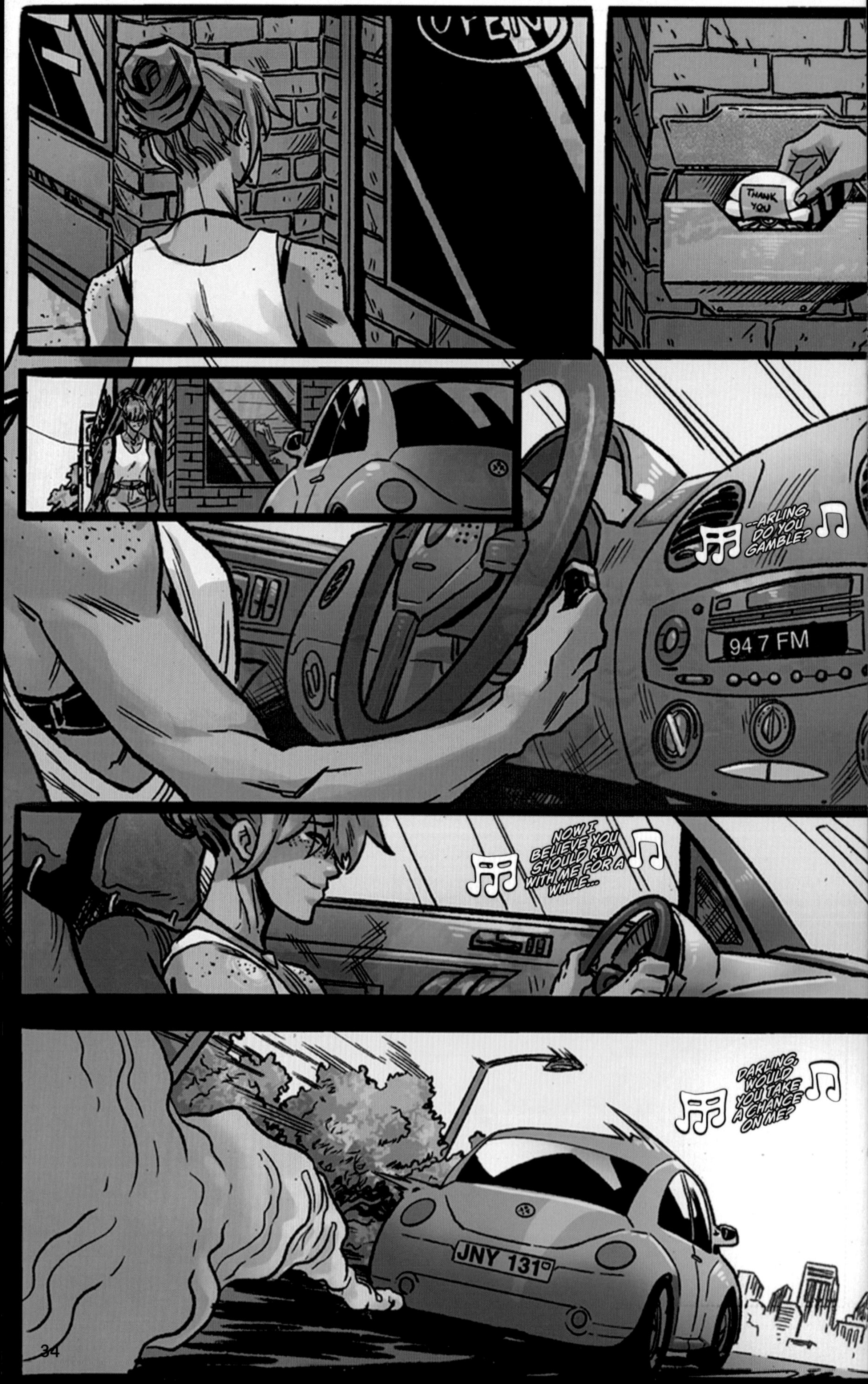
OPEN
THANK YOU
--ARLING, DO YOU GAMBLE?
94 7 FM
NOW I BELIEVE YOU SHOULD RUN WITH ME FOR A WHILE...
DARLING, WOULD YOU TAKE A CHANCE ON ME?
JNY 131

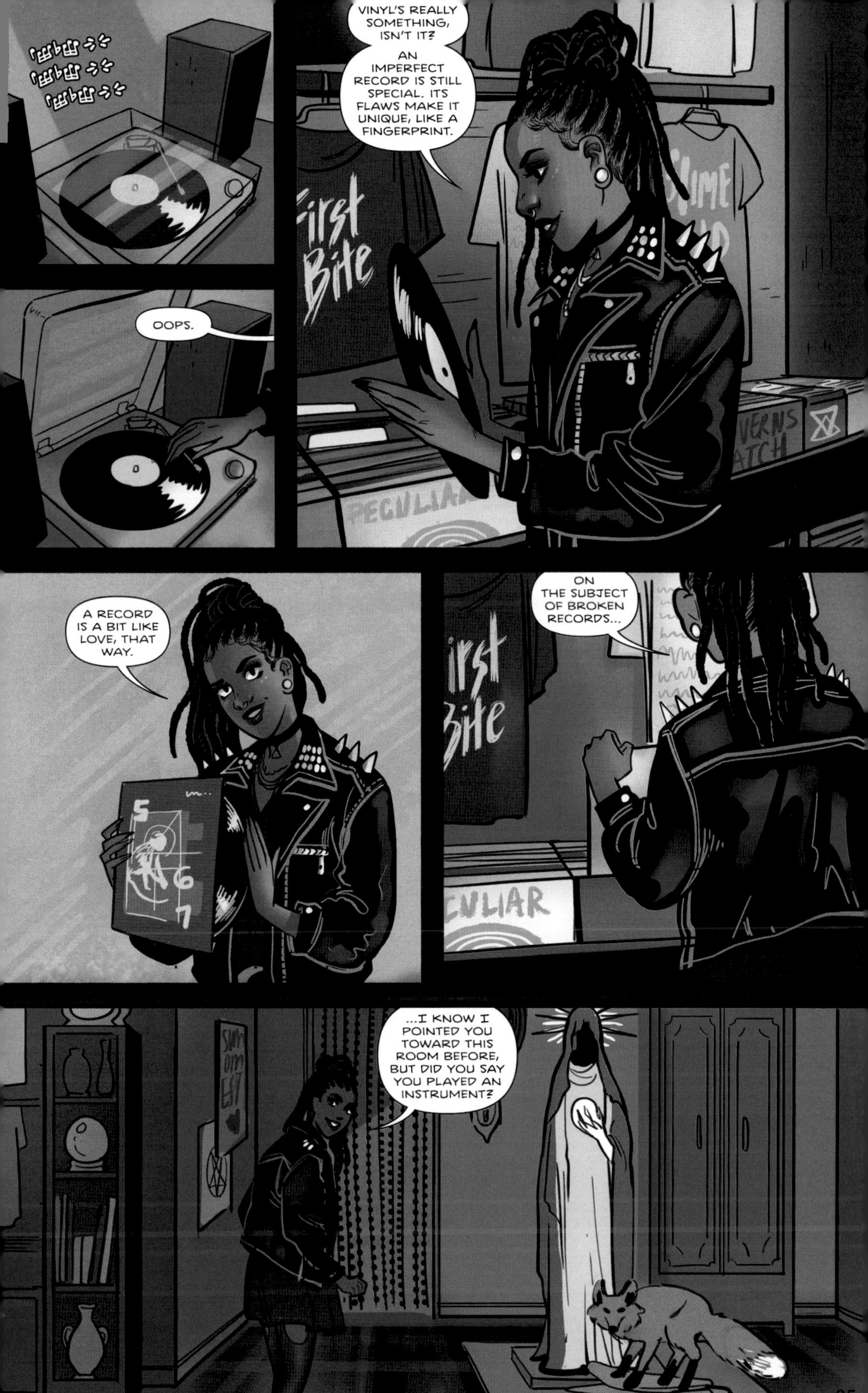
VINYL'S REALLY SOMETHING, ISN'T IT?
AN IMPERFECT RECORD IS STILL SPECIAL. ITS FLAWS MAKE IT UNIQUE, LIKE A FINGERPRINT.
OOPS.
A RECORD IS A BIT LIKE LOVE, THAT WAY.
ON THE SUBJECT OF BROKEN RECORDS...
...I KNOW I POINTED YOU TOWARD THIS ROOM BEFORE, BUT DID YOU SAY YOU PLAYED AN INSTRUMENT?

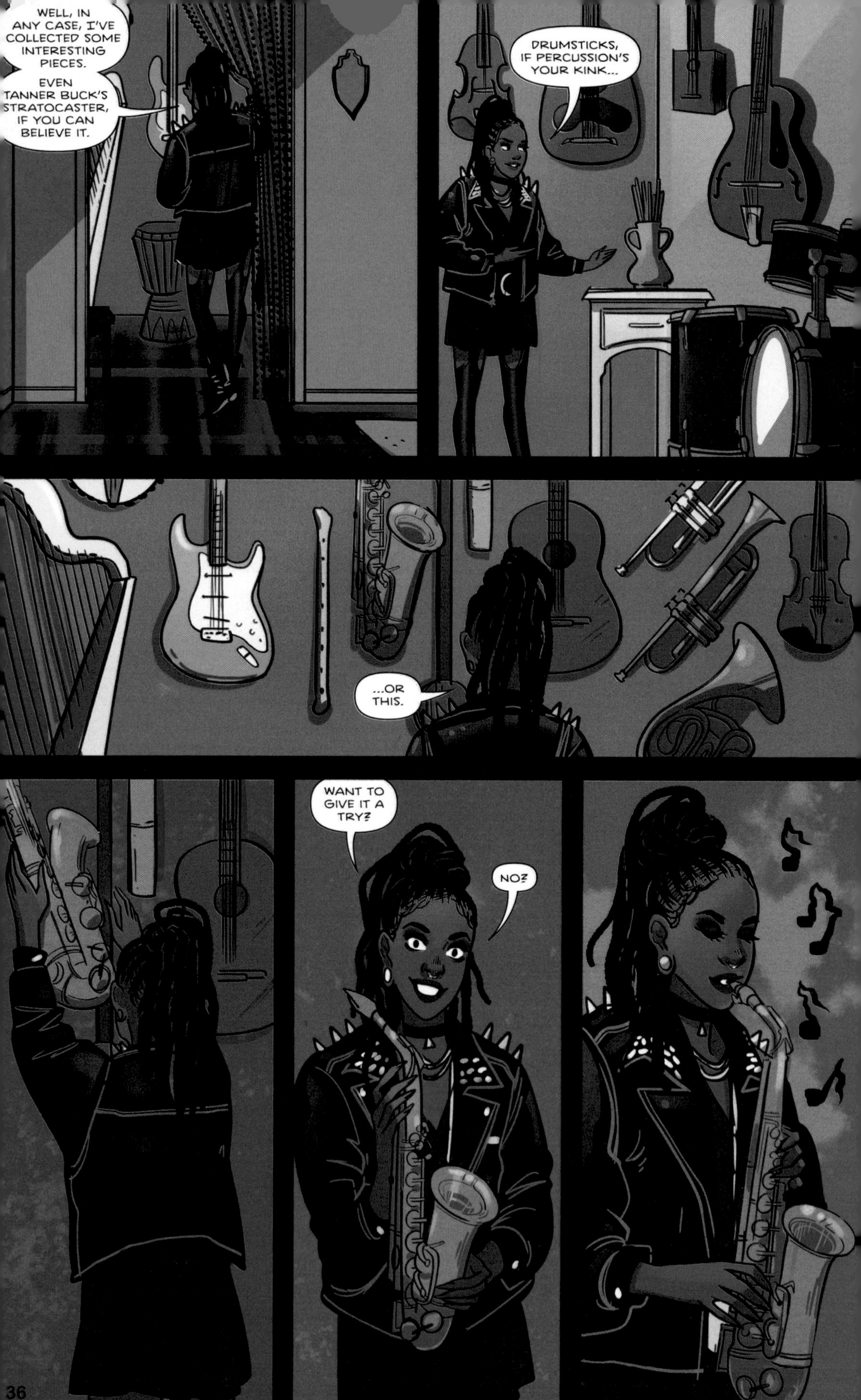
WELL, IN ANY CASE, I'VE COLLECTED SOME INTERESTING PIECES.
EVEN TANNER BUCK'S STRATOCASTER, IF YOU CAN BELIEVE IT.
DRUMSTICKS, IF PERCUSSION'S YOUR KINK...
...OR THIS.
WANT TO GIVE IT A TRY?
NO?

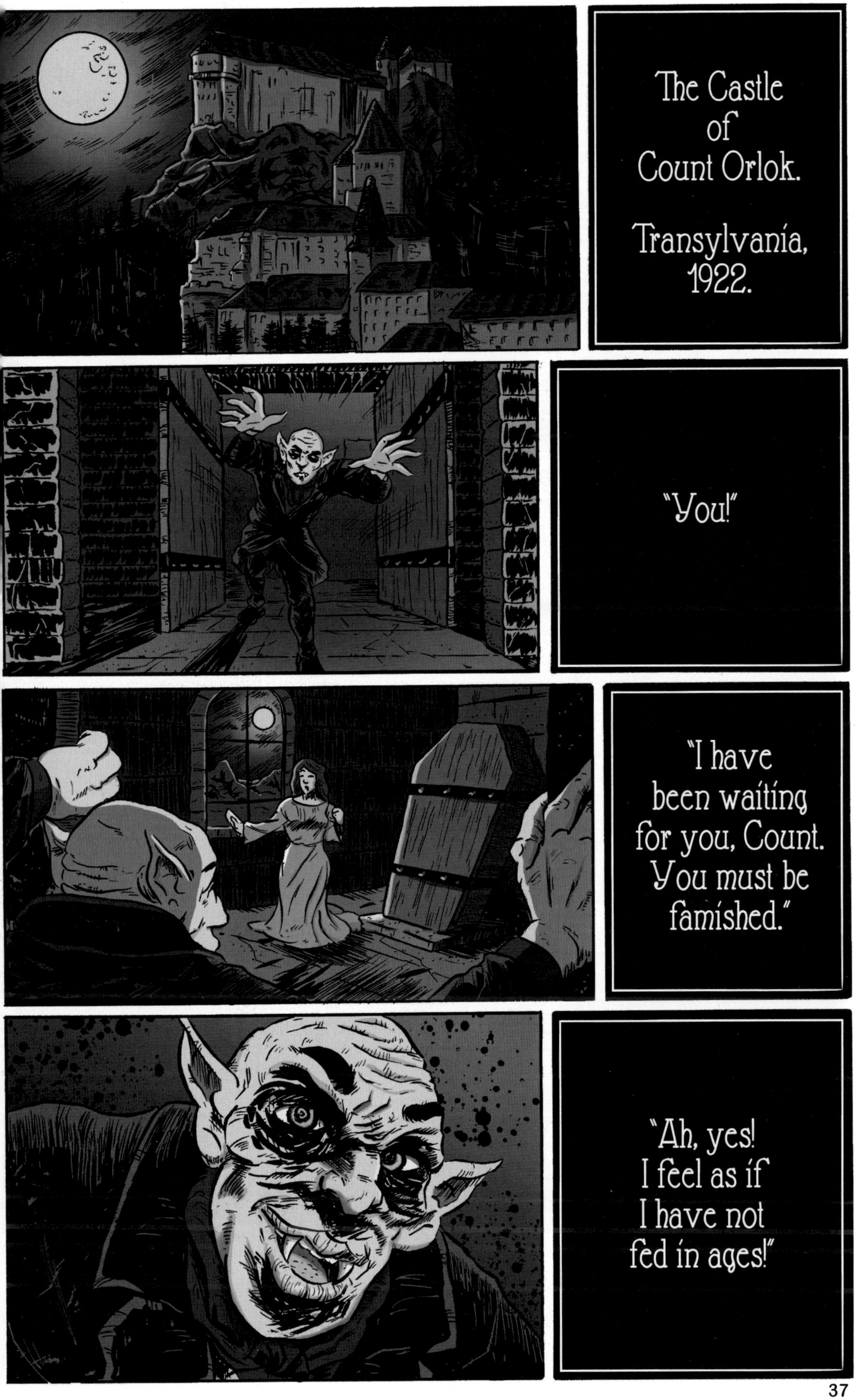
The Castle of Count Orlok.
Transylvania, 1922.
"You!"
"I have been waiting for you, Count. You must be famished."
"Ah, yes! I feel as if I have not fed in ages!"

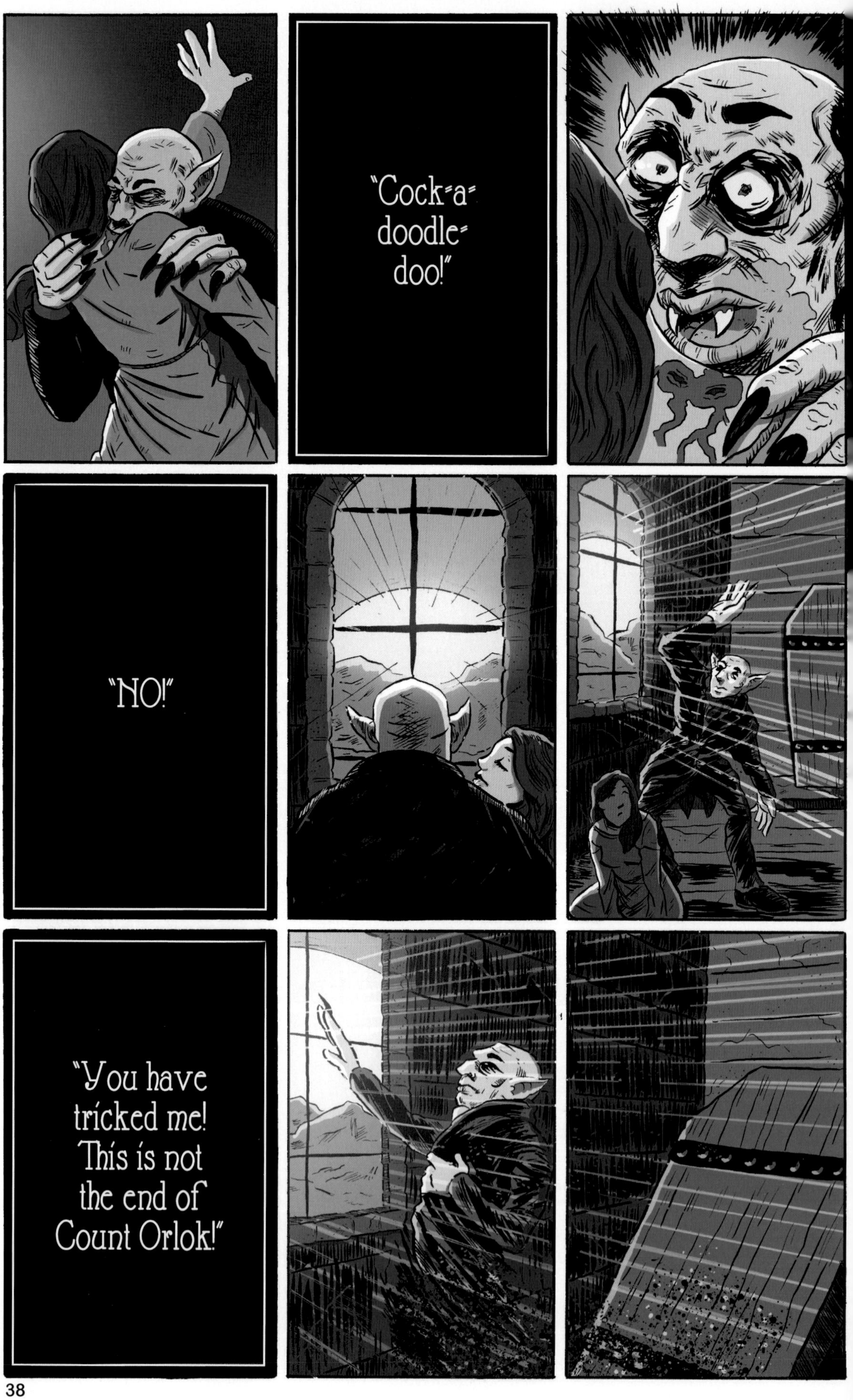
"Cock-a-doodle-doo!"
"NO!"
"You have tricked me! This is not the end of Count Orlok!"

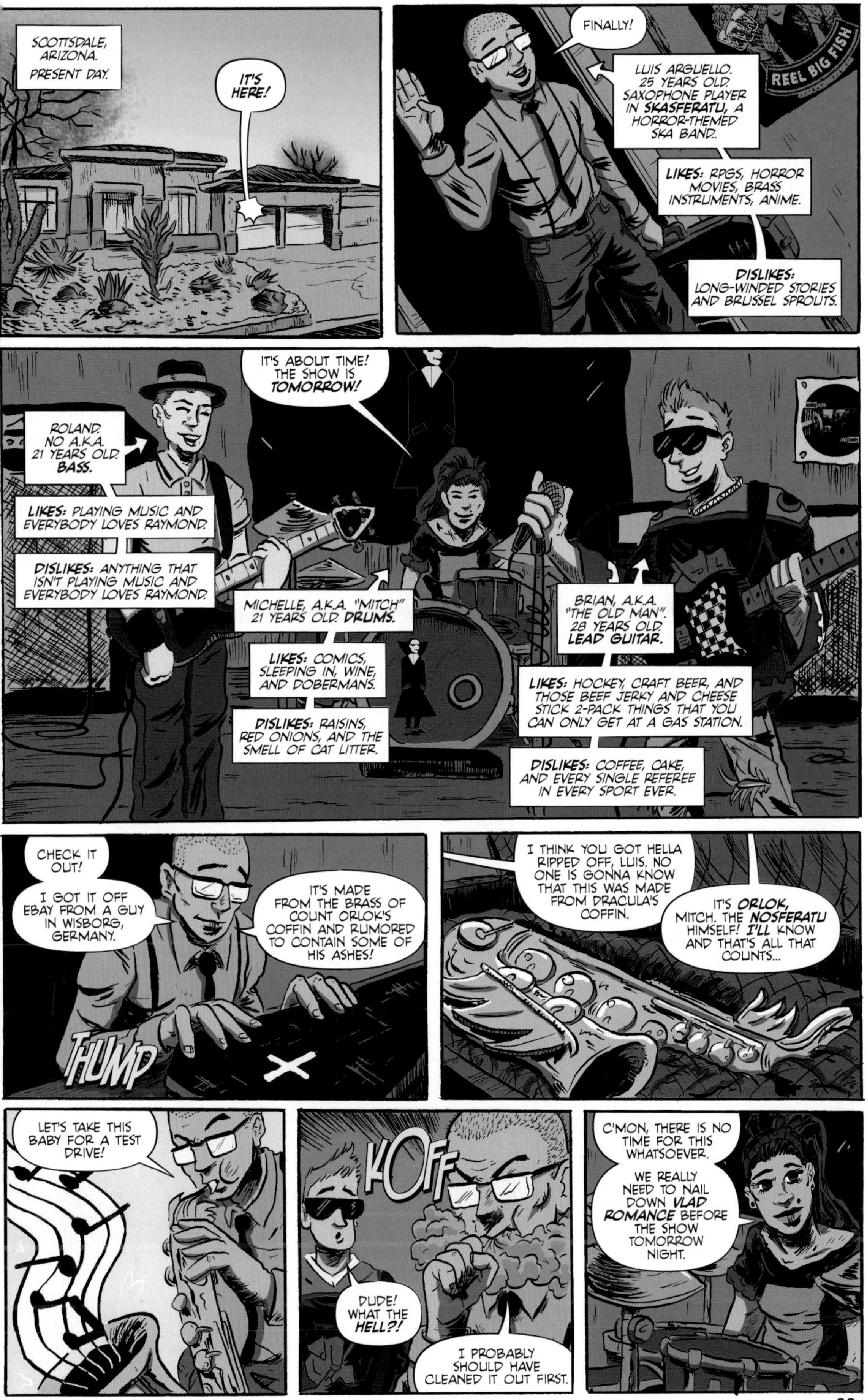
SCOTTSDALE, ARIZONA.
PRESENT DAY.
IT'S HERE!
FINALLY!
LUIS ARGUELLO. 25 YEARS OLD. SAXOPHONE PLAYER IN SKASFERATU, A HORROR-THEMED SKA BAND.
LIKES: RPGS, HORROR MOVIES, BRASS INSTRUMENTS, ANIME.
DISLIKES: LONG-WINDED STORIES AND BRUSSEL SPROUTS.
REEL BIG FISH
IT'S ABOUT TIME! THE SHOW IS TOMORROW!
ROLAND. NO A.K.A. 21 YEARS OLD. BASS.
LIKES: PLAYING MUSIC AND EVERYBODY LOVES RAYMOND.
DISLIKES: ANYTHING THAT ISN'T PLAYING MUSIC AND EVERYBODY LOVES RAYMOND.
MICHELLE, A.K.A. "MITCH" 21 YEARS OLD. DRUMS.
LIKES: COMICS, SLEEPING IN, WINE, AND DOBERMANS.
DISLIKES: RAISINS, RED ONIONS, AND THE SMELL OF CAT LITTER.
BRIAN, A.K.A. "THE OLD MAN". 28 YEARS OLD. LEAD GUITAR.
LIKES: HOCKEY, CRAFT BEER, AND THOSE BEEF JERKY AND CHEESE STICK 2-PACK THINGS THAT YOU CAN ONLY GET AT A GAS STATION.
DISLIKES: COFFEE, CAKE, AND EVERY SINGLE REFEREE IN EVERY SPORT EVER.
CHECK IT OUT!
I GOT IT OFF EBAY FROM A GUY IN WISBORG, GERMANY.
IT'S MADE FROM THE BRASS OF COUNT ORLOK'S COFFIN AND RUMORED TO CONTAIN SOME OF HIS ASHES!
THUMP
I THINK YOU GOT HELLA RIPPED OFF, LUIS. NO ONE IS GONNA KNOW THAT THIS WAS MADE FROM DRACULA'S COFFIN.
IT'S ORLOK, MITCH. THE NOSFERATU HIMSELF! I'LL KNOW AND THAT'S ALL THAT COUNTS...
LET'S TAKE THIS BABY FOR A TEST DRIVE!
KOFF
DUDE! WHAT THE HELL?!
I PROBABLY SHOULD HAVE CLEANED IT OUT FIRST.
C'MON, THERE IS NO TIME FOR THIS WHATSOEVER.
WE REALLY NEED TO NAIL DOWN VLAD ROMANCE BEFORE THE SHOW TOMORROW NIGHT.

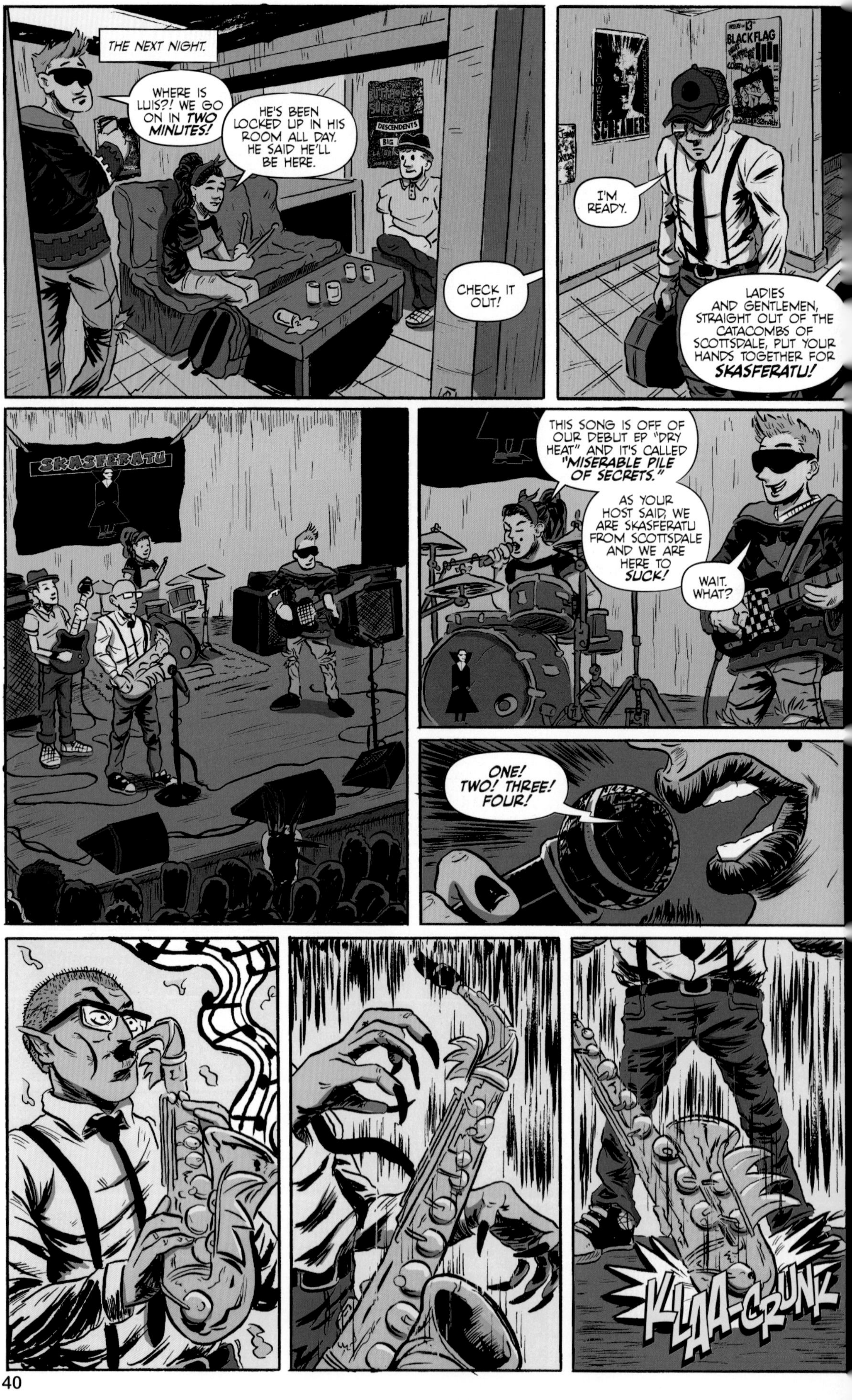
THE NEXT NIGHT.
WHERE IS LUIS?! WE GO ON IN *TWO MINUTES!*
HE'S BEEN LOCKED UP IN HIS ROOM ALL DAY. HE SAID HE'LL BE HERE.
DESCENDENTS
CHECK IT OUT!
SCREAMERS
BLACKFLAG
I'M READY.
LADIES AND GENTLEMEN, STRAIGHT OUT OF THE CATACOMBS OF SCOTTSDALE, PUT YOUR HANDS TOGETHER FOR **SKASFERATU!**
SKASFERATU
THIS SONG IS OFF OF OUR DEBUT EP "DRY HEAT" AND IT'S CALLED ***"MISERABLE PILE OF SECRETS."***
AS YOUR HOST SAID, WE ARE SKASFERATU FROM SCOTTSDALE AND WE ARE HERE TO ***SUCK!***
WAIT. WHAT?
ONE! TWO! THREE! FOUR!
KLAA-CRUNK

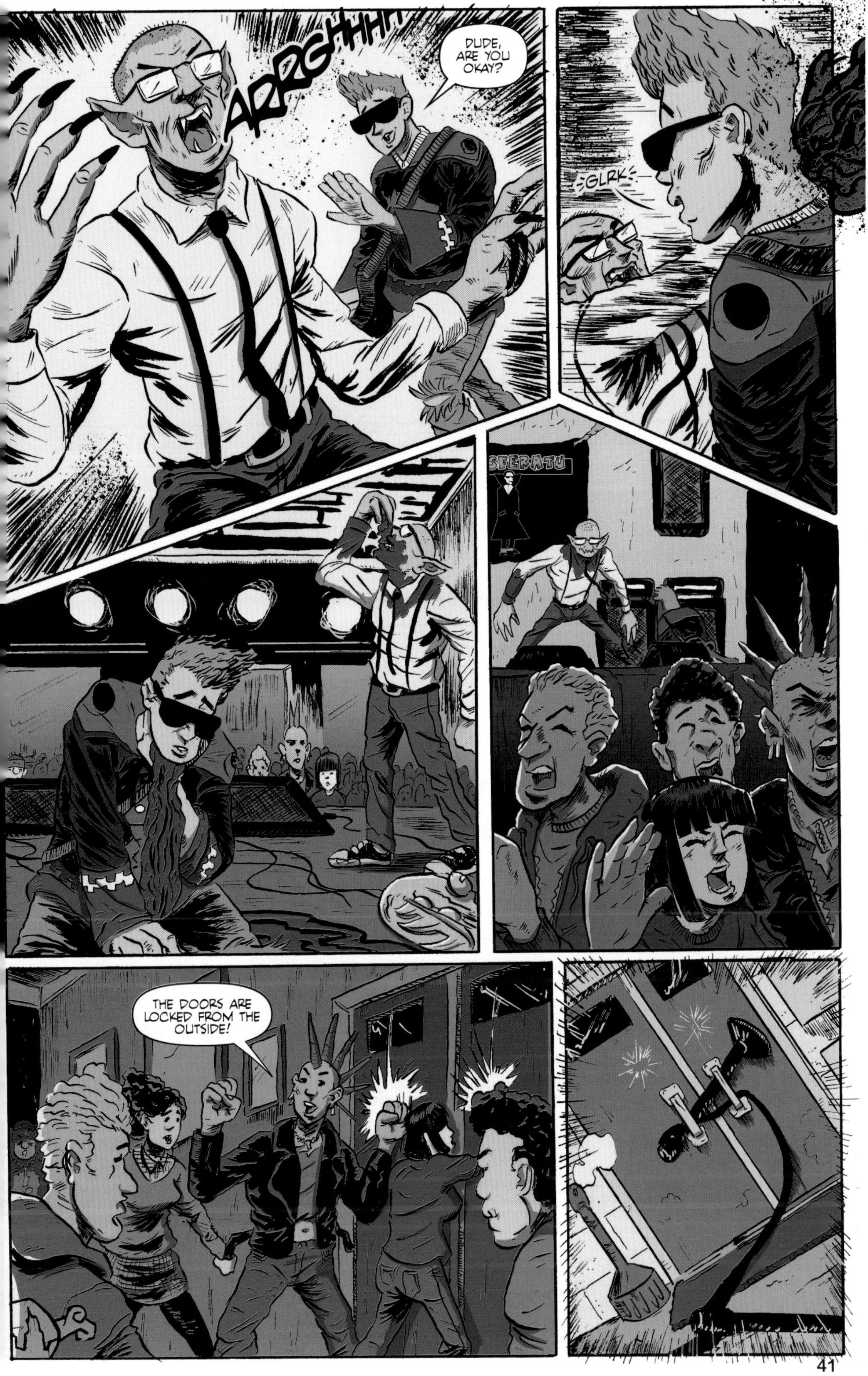
ARRGHHH
DUDE, ARE YOU OKAY?
GLRK
THE DOORS ARE LOCKED FROM THE OUTSIDE!

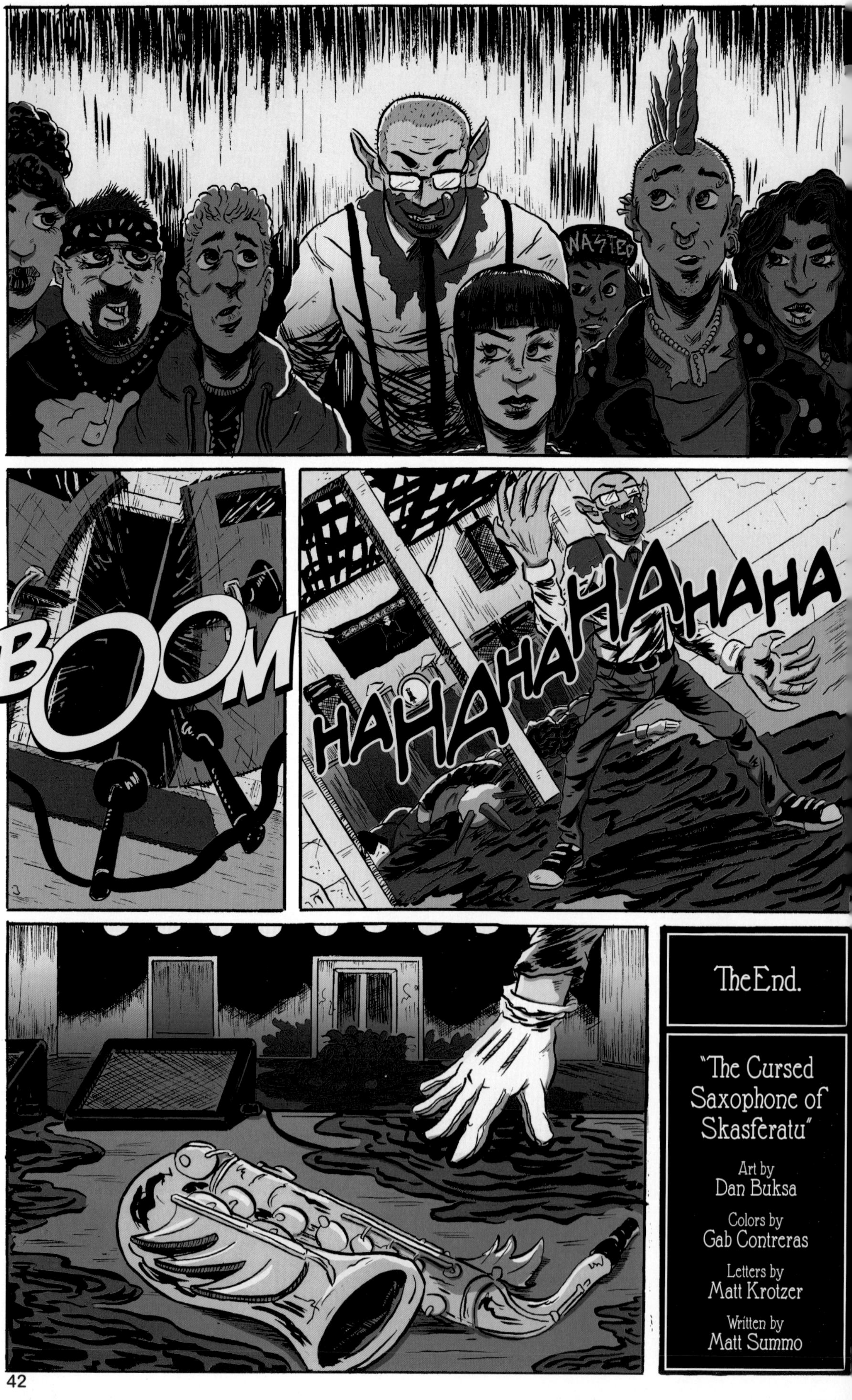

WASTED
BOOM
HAHAHAHAHAHAHA
The End.
"The Cursed Saxophone of Skasferatu"
Art by Dan Buksa
Colors by Gab Contreras
Letters by Matt Krotzer
Written by Matt Summo

LOVE IN A DARK CABIN

WORDS ALEXIS SARA
ART LEANNA CRUZ
COLORS GAB CONTRERAS
LETTERS TAYLOR ESPOSITO

WHAT IS HELL? IS HELL BEING HURT BY THE ONES YOU LOVE OVER AND OVER AGAIN? THEN MAYBE PEOPLE LIKE US WE LIVE IN HELL ALL THE TIME.

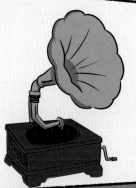

WHAT IS HELL? IS HELL BEING TRAPPED IN A SMALL BOX WATCHING SOMEONE'S "FRIENDS" TORTURE THEM FOR THE VERY REASON YOU BECAME A DEMON TO BEGIN WITH?

ALLY, WE FINISHED BREAKFAST. WE DON'T GET HOW TO WORK YOUR DISHWASHER, SO YOU CAN HANDLE IT, RIGHT HUN?

YES, TOBY WAS MESSY BUT I MEAN, *MEN* RIGHT?

LIKE YOU'RE ONE TO TALK LACY, I'M GLAD I'M DATING BAYLOR AND NOT YOU.

SORRY I DIDN'T MAKE YOU ANYTHING--

--BUT YOU KNOW IF YOU WANNA BE A REAL GIRL OR WHATEVER--

--WHATEVER YOU GOTTA MAKE SURE YOU TAKE CARE OF THAT BODY.

I AM SURE YOUR FOOD WOULD HAVE BEEN FANTASTIC BUT I'LL JUST GO MAKE SOMETHING.

REMEMBER, NO TOUCHING THE RECORD PLAYER, ALRIGHT?

GRANDMA ALWAYS SAID TO NEVER TOUCH IT.

WHATEVER. HEY BY THE WAY TOBY, YOU DIDN'T SAY YOU WERE GLAD THAT YOU WEREN'T DATING ALLY.

YOU'RE BEST FRIENDS SO SHOULD I BE JEALOUS?

LIKE I WOULD BE INTO ALLY!

I MEAN I KNEW HER BEFORE EVERYTHING AND SHE'S A NERD.

YEAH I GUESS YOU COULD NEVER SEE HEEEERRRR AS DESIRABLE. HEHE.

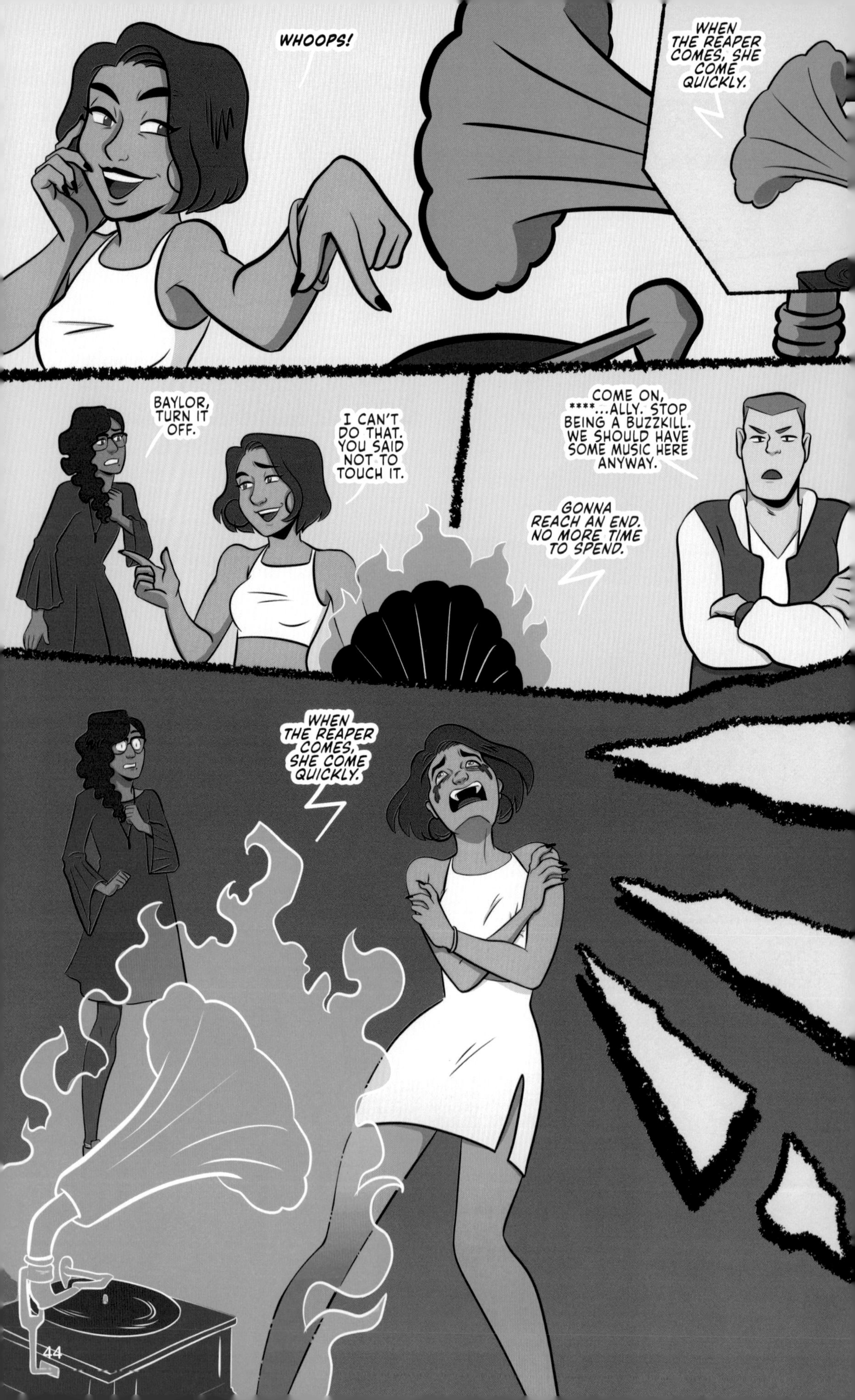
WHOOPS!
WHEN THE REAPER COMES, SHE COME QUICKLY.
BAYLOR, TURN IT OFF.
I CAN'T DO THAT. YOU SAID NOT TO TOUCH IT.
COME ON, ****...ALLY. STOP BEING A BUZZKILL. WE SHOULD HAVE SOME MUSIC HERE ANYWAY.
GONNA REACH AN END. NO MORE TIME TO SPEND.
WHEN THE REAPER COMES, SHE COME QUICKLY.

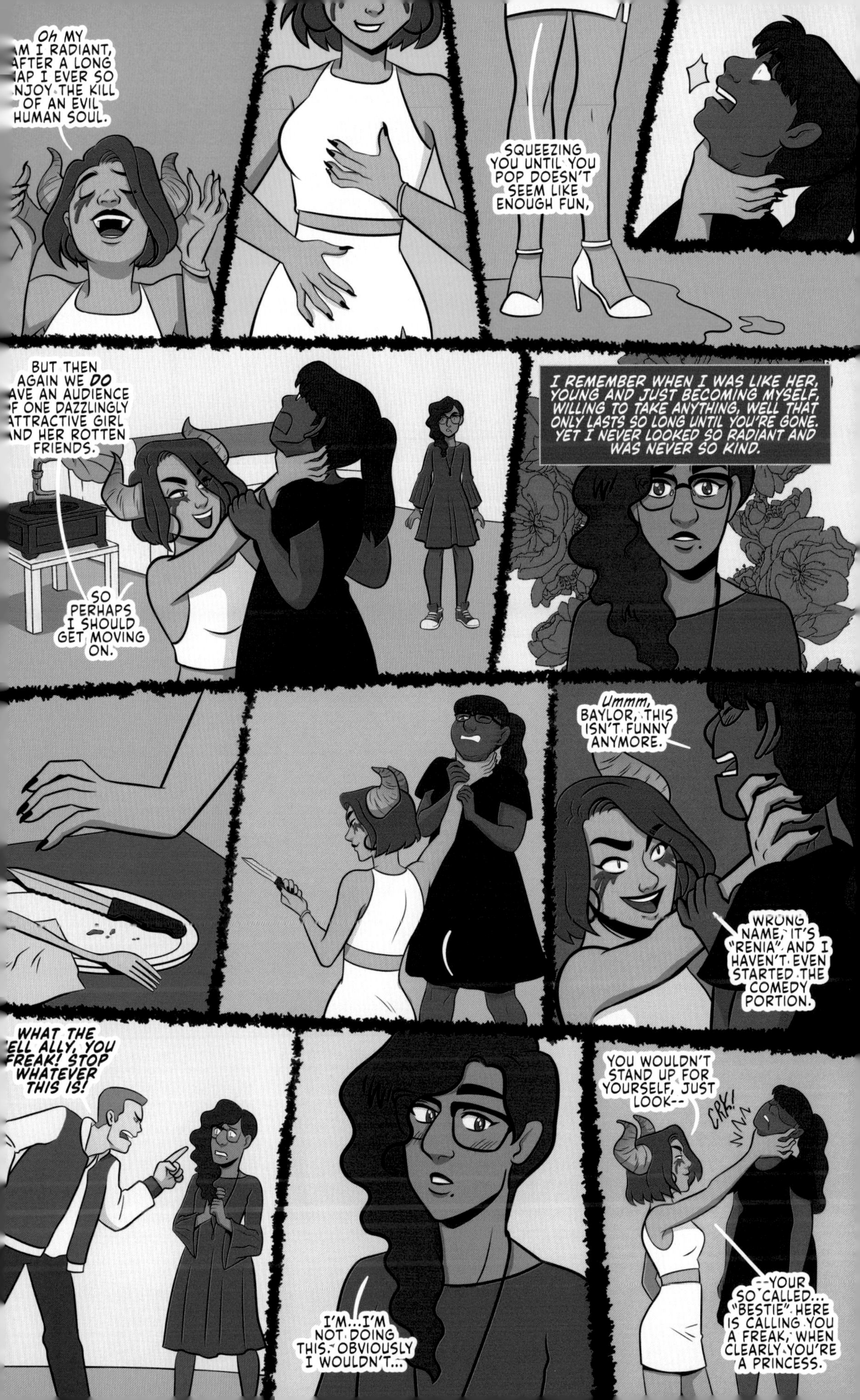
Oh MY
AM I RADIANT, AFTER A LONG NAP I EVER SO ENJOY THE KILL OF AN EVIL HUMAN SOUL.
SQUEEZING YOU UNTIL YOU POP DOESN'T SEEM LIKE ENOUGH FUN,
BUT THEN AGAIN WE DO HAVE AN AUDIENCE OF ONE DAZZLINGLY ATTRACTIVE GIRL AND HER ROTTEN FRIENDS.
SO PERHAPS I SHOULD GET MOVING ON.
I REMEMBER WHEN I WAS LIKE HER, YOUNG AND JUST BECOMING MYSELF, WILLING TO TAKE ANYTHING, WELL THAT ONLY LASTS SO LONG UNTIL YOU'RE GONE. YET I NEVER LOOKED SO RADIANT AND WAS NEVER SO KIND.
Ummm, BAYLOR, THIS ISN'T FUNNY ANYMORE.
WRONG NAME, IT'S "RENIA" AND I HAVEN'T EVEN STARTED THE COMEDY PORTION.
WHAT THE HELL ALLY, YOU FREAK! STOP WHATEVER THIS IS!
I'M...I'M NOT DOING THIS. OBVIOUSLY I WOULDN'T...
YOU WOULDN'T STAND UP FOR YOURSELF, JUST LOOK--
CRK!
--YOUR SO CALLED... "BESTIE" HERE IS CALLING YOU A FREAK, WHEN CLEARLY YOU'RE A PRINCESS.

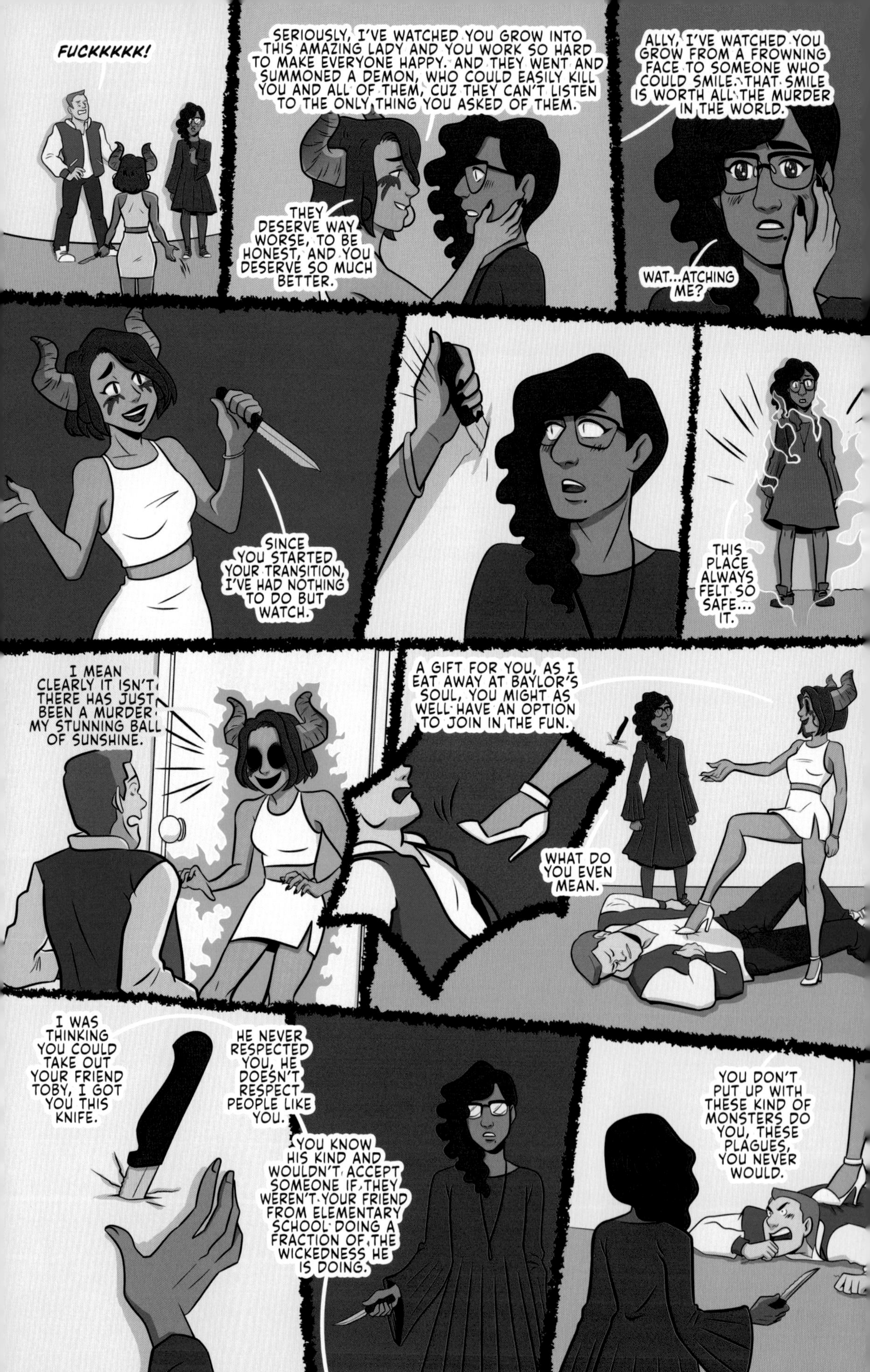
FUCKKKKK!
SERIOUSLY, I'VE WATCHED YOU GROW INTO THIS AMAZING LADY AND YOU WORK SO HARD TO MAKE EVERYONE HAPPY. AND THEY WENT AND SUMMONED A DEMON, WHO COULD EASILY KILL YOU AND ALL OF THEM, CUZ THEY CAN'T LISTEN TO THE ONLY THING YOU ASKED OF THEM.
THEY DESERVE WAY WORSE, TO BE HONEST, AND YOU DESERVE SO MUCH BETTER.
ALLY, I'VE WATCHED YOU GROW FROM A FROWNING FACE TO SOMEONE WHO COULD SMILE. THAT SMILE IS WORTH ALL THE MURDER IN THE WORLD.
WAT...ATCHING ME?
SINCE YOU STARTED YOUR TRANSITION, I'VE HAD NOTHING TO DO BUT WATCH.
THIS PLACE ALWAYS FELT SO SAFE... IT.
I MEAN CLEARLY IT ISN'T. THERE HAS JUST BEEN A MURDER MY STUNNING BALL OF SUNSHINE.
A GIFT FOR YOU, AS I EAT AWAY AT BAYLOR'S SOUL, YOU MIGHT AS WELL HAVE AN OPTION TO JOIN IN THE FUN.
WHAT DO YOU EVEN MEAN.
I WAS THINKING YOU COULD TAKE OUT YOUR FRIEND TOBY, I GOT YOU THIS KNIFE.
HE NEVER RESPECTED YOU, HE DOESN'T RESPECT PEOPLE LIKE YOU.
YOU KNOW HIS KIND AND WOULDN'T ACCEPT SOMEONE IF THEY WEREN'T YOUR FRIEND FROM ELEMENTARY SCHOOL DOING A FRACTION OF THE WICKEDNESS HE IS DOING.
YOU DON'T PUT UP WITH THESE KIND OF MONSTERS DO YOU, THESE PLAGUES, YOU NEVER WOULD.

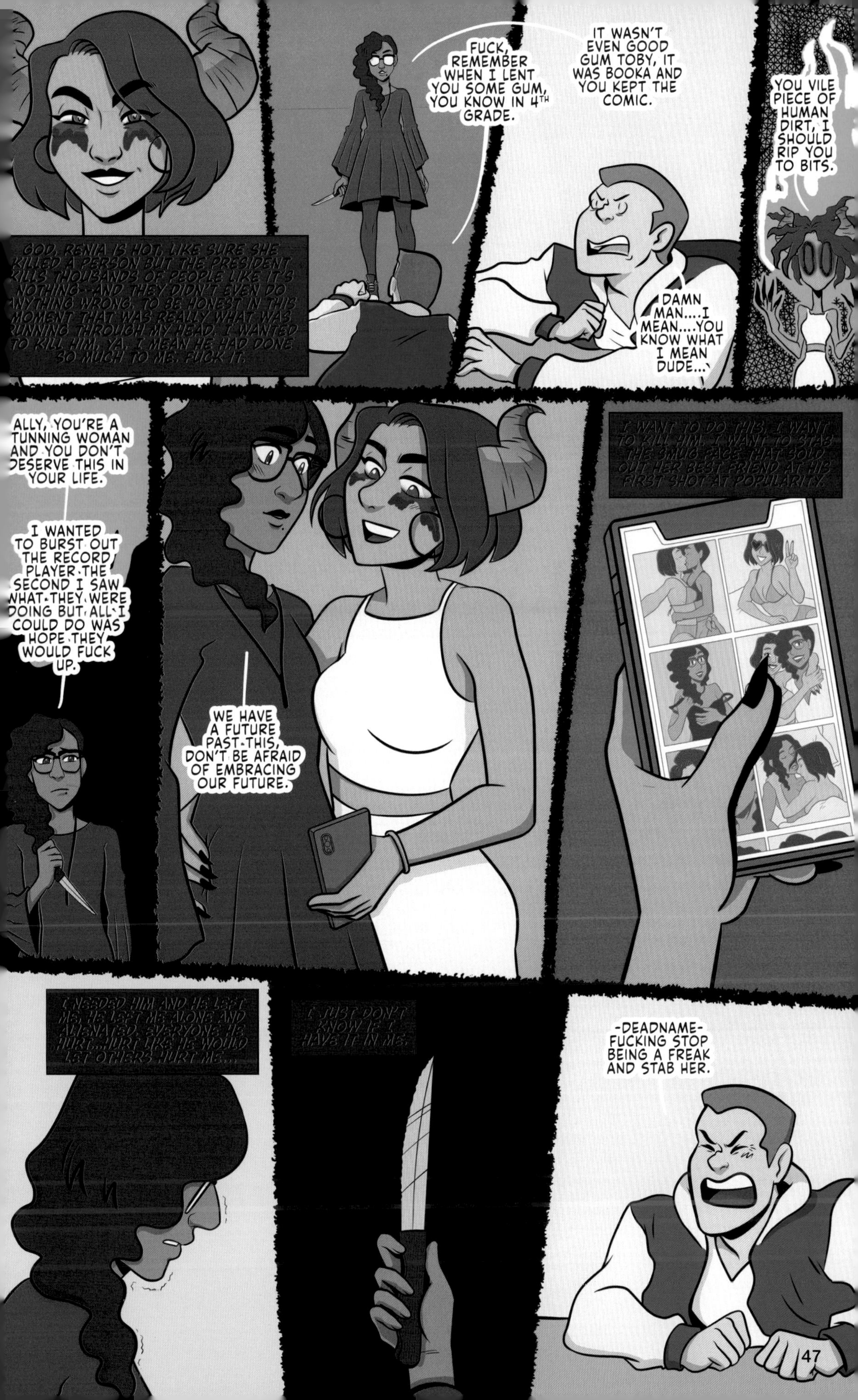
GOD, RENIA IS HOT, LIKE SURE SHE KILLED A PERSON BUT THE PRESIDENT KILLS THOUSANDS OF PEOPLE LIKE IT'S NOTHING--AND THEY DIDN'T EVEN DO ANYTHING WRONG. TO BE HONEST IN THIS MOMENT THAT WAS REALLY WHAT WAS RUNNING THROUGH MY HEAD. I WANTED TO KILL HIM, YA. I MEAN HE HAD DONE SO MUCH TO ME. FUCK IT.
FUCK, REMEMBER WHEN I LENT YOU SOME GUM, YOU KNOW IN 4TH GRADE.
IT WASN'T EVEN GOOD GUM TOBY, IT WAS BOOKA AND YOU KEPT THE COMIC.
DAMN MAN....I MEAN....YOU KNOW WHAT I MEAN DUDE...
YOU VILE PIECE OF HUMAN DIRT, I SHOULD RIP YOU TO BITS.
ALLY, YOU'RE A TUNNING WOMAN AND YOU DON'T DESERVE THIS IN YOUR LIFE.
I WANTED TO BURST OUT THE RECORD PLAYER THE SECOND I SAW WHAT THEY WERE DOING BUT ALL I COULD DO WAS HOPE THEY WOULD FUCK UP.
WE HAVE A FUTURE PAST THIS, DON'T BE AFRAID OF EMBRACING OUR FUTURE.
I WANT TO DO THIS. I WANT TO KILL HIM. I WANT TO STAB THE SMUG FACE THAT SOLD OUT HER BEST FRIEND AT HIS FIRST SHOT AT POPULARITY.
I NEEDED HIM AND HE LEFT ME. HE LEFT ME ALONE AND ALIENATED. EVERYONE HE HURT...HURT LIKE HE WOULD LET OTHERS HURT ME...
I JUST DON'T KNOW IF I HAVE IT IN ME.
-DEADNAME- FUCKING STOP BEING A FREAK AND STAB HER.

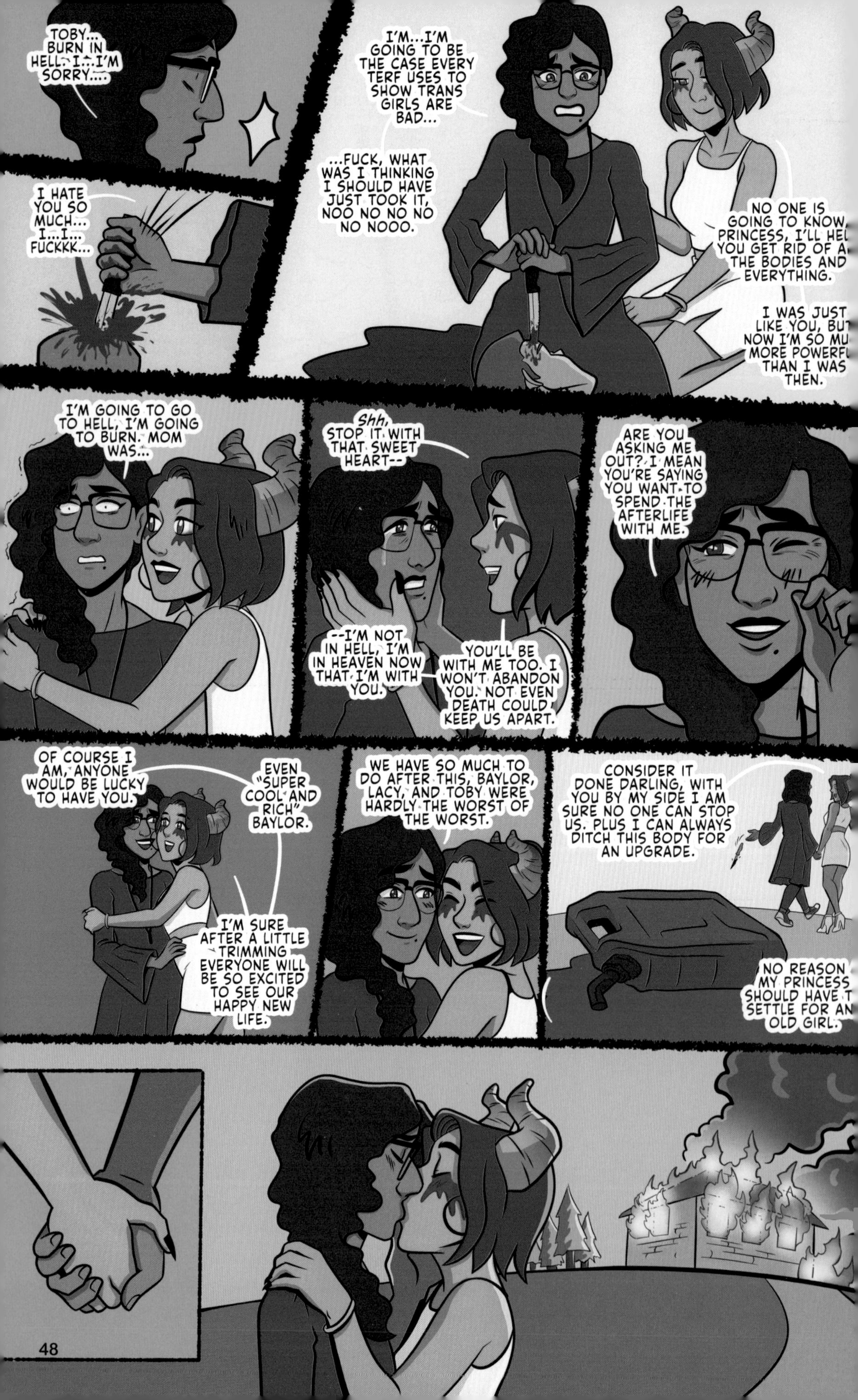
TOBY... BURN IN HELL. I...I'M SORRY....
I HATE YOU SO MUCH... I...I... FUCKKK...
I'M...I'M GOING TO BE THE CASE EVERY TERF USES TO SHOW TRANS GIRLS ARE BAD...
...FUCK, WHAT WAS I THINKING I SHOULD HAVE JUST TOOK IT, NOO NO NO NO NO NOOO.
NO ONE IS GOING TO KNOW, PRINCESS, I'LL HEL YOU GET RID OF A THE BODIES AND EVERYTHING.
I WAS JUST LIKE YOU, BUT NOW I'M SO MU MORE POWERF THAN I WAS THEN.
I'M GOING TO GO TO HELL, I'M GOING TO BURN. MOM WAS...
Shh, STOP IT WITH THAT SWEET HEART--
--I'M NOT IN HELL, I'M IN HEAVEN NOW THAT I'M WITH YOU.
YOU'LL BE WITH ME TOO. I WON'T ABANDON YOU. NOT EVEN DEATH COULD KEEP US APART.
ARE YOU ASKING ME OUT? I MEAN YOU'RE SAYING YOU WANT TO SPEND THE AFTERLIFE WITH ME.
OF COURSE I AM, ANYONE WOULD BE LUCKY TO HAVE YOU.
EVEN "SUPER COOL AND RICH" BAYLOR.
I'M SURE AFTER A LITTLE TRIMMING EVERYONE WILL BE SO EXCITED TO SEE OUR HAPPY NEW LIFE.
WE HAVE SO MUCH TO DO AFTER THIS, BAYLOR, LACY, AND TOBY WERE HARDLY THE WORST OF THE WORST.
CONSIDER IT DONE DARLING, WITH YOU BY MY SIDE I AM SURE NO ONE CAN STOP US. PLUS I CAN ALWAYS DITCH THIS BODY FOR AN UPGRADE.
NO REASON MY PRINCESS SHOULD HAVE T SETTLE FOR AN OLD GIRL.

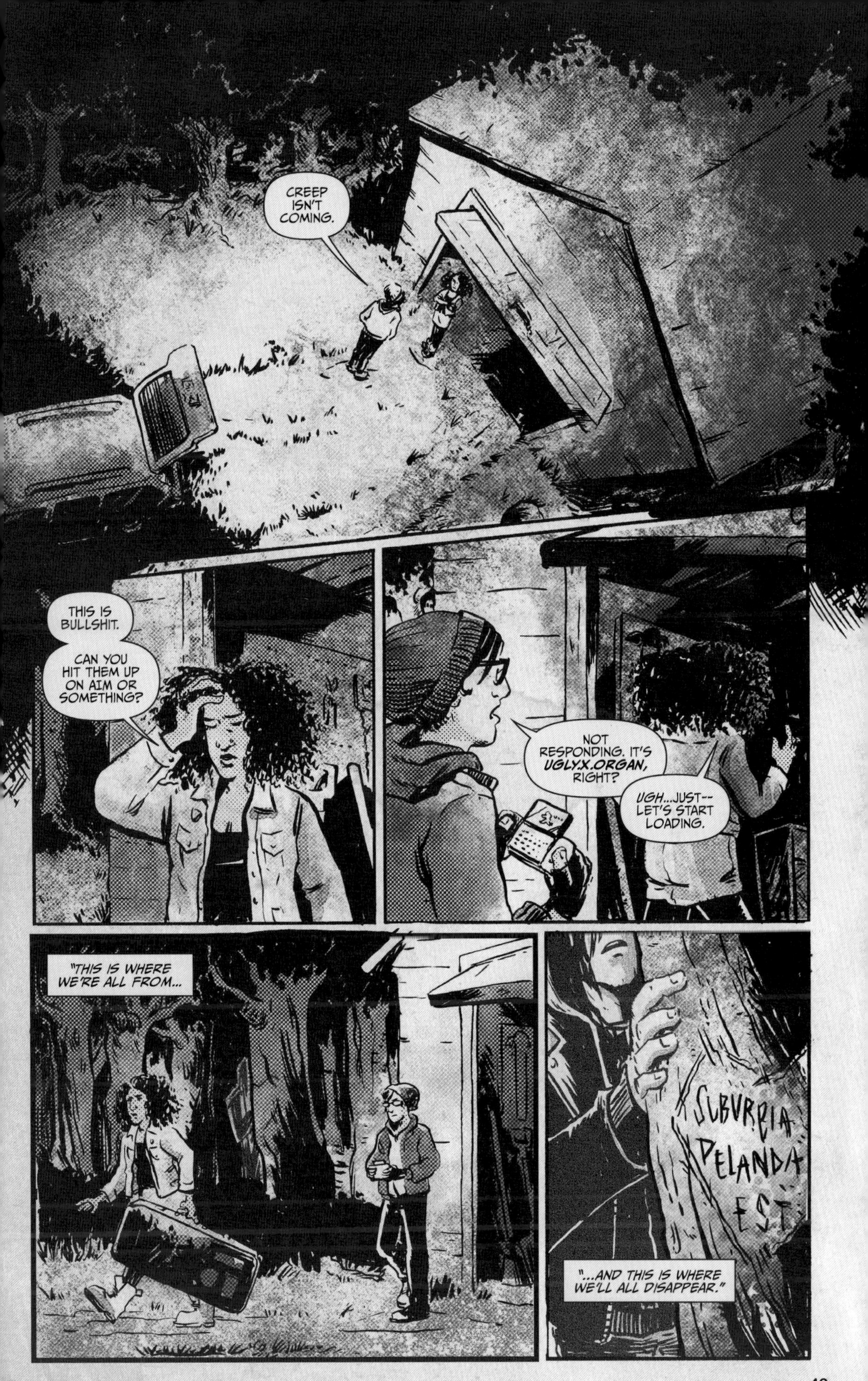
CREEP ISN'T COMING.
THIS IS BULLSHIT.
CAN YOU HIT THEM UP ON AIM OR SOMETHING?
NOT RESPONDING. IT'S UGLY.X.ORGAN, RIGHT?
UGH...JUST-- LET'S START LOADING.
"THIS IS WHERE WE'RE ALL FROM...
SUBURBIA DELANDA EST
"...AND THIS IS WHERE WE'LL ALL DISAPPEAR."

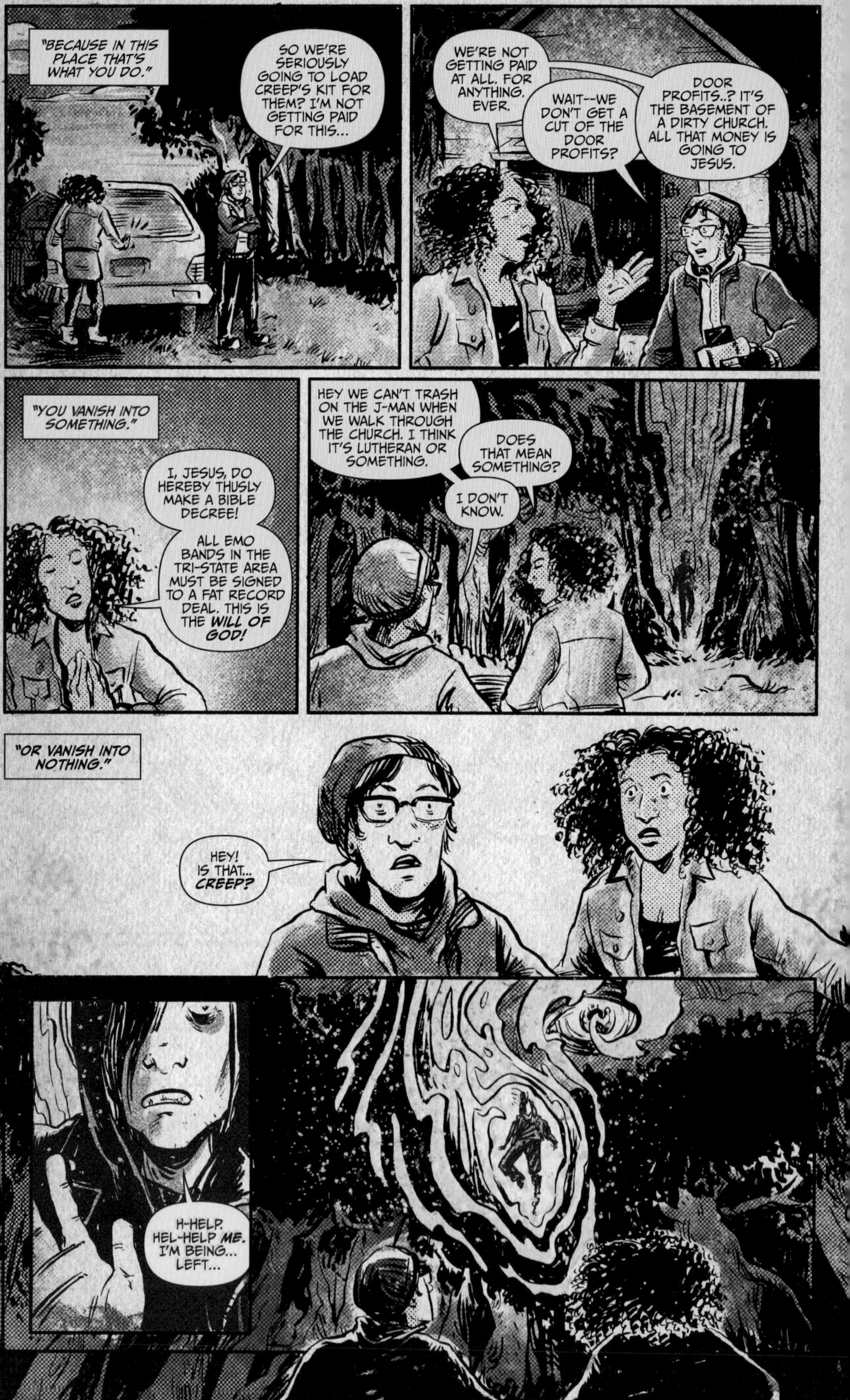
"BECAUSE IN THIS PLACE THAT'S WHAT YOU DO."
SO WE'RE SERIOUSLY GOING TO LOAD CREEP'S KIT FOR THEM? I'M NOT GETTING PAID FOR THIS...
WE'RE NOT GETTING PAID AT ALL. FOR ANYTHING. EVER.
WAIT--WE DON'T GET A CUT OF THE DOOR PROFITS?
DOOR PROFITS..? IT'S THE BASEMENT OF A DIRTY CHURCH. ALL THAT MONEY IS GOING TO JESUS.
"YOU VANISH INTO SOMETHING."
I, JESUS, DO HEREBY THUSLY MAKE A BIBLE DECREE!
ALL EMO BANDS IN THE TRI-STATE AREA MUST BE SIGNED TO A FAT RECORD DEAL. THIS IS THE WILL OF GOD!
HEY WE CAN'T TRASH ON THE J-MAN WHEN WE WALK THROUGH THE CHURCH. I THINK IT'S LUTHERAN OR SOMETHING.
DOES THAT MEAN SOMETHING?
I DON'T KNOW.
"OR VANISH INTO NOTHING."
HEY! IS THAT... CREEP?
H-HELP. HEL-HELP ME. I'M BEING... LEFT...

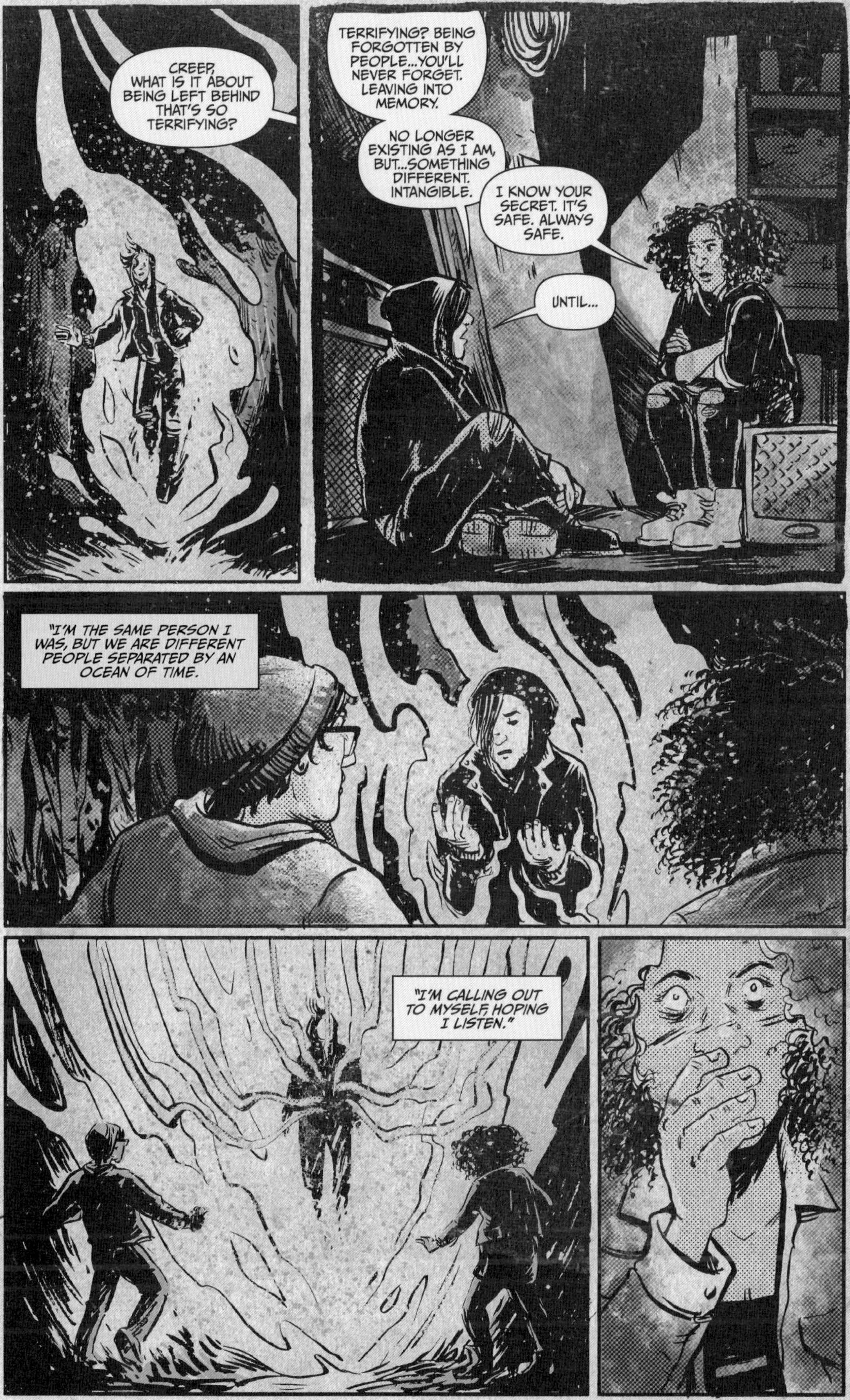
CREEP, WHAT IS IT ABOUT BEING LEFT BEHIND THAT'S SO TERRIFYING?
TERRIFYING? BEING FORGOTTEN BY PEOPLE...YOU'LL NEVER FORGET. LEAVING INTO MEMORY.
NO LONGER EXISTING AS I AM, BUT...SOMETHING DIFFERENT. INTANGIBLE.
I KNOW YOUR SECRET. IT'S SAFE. ALWAYS SAFE.
UNTIL...
"I'M THE SAME PERSON I WAS, BUT WE ARE DIFFERENT PEOPLE SEPARATED BY AN OCEAN OF TIME.
"I'M CALLING OUT TO MYSELF, HOPING I LISTEN."

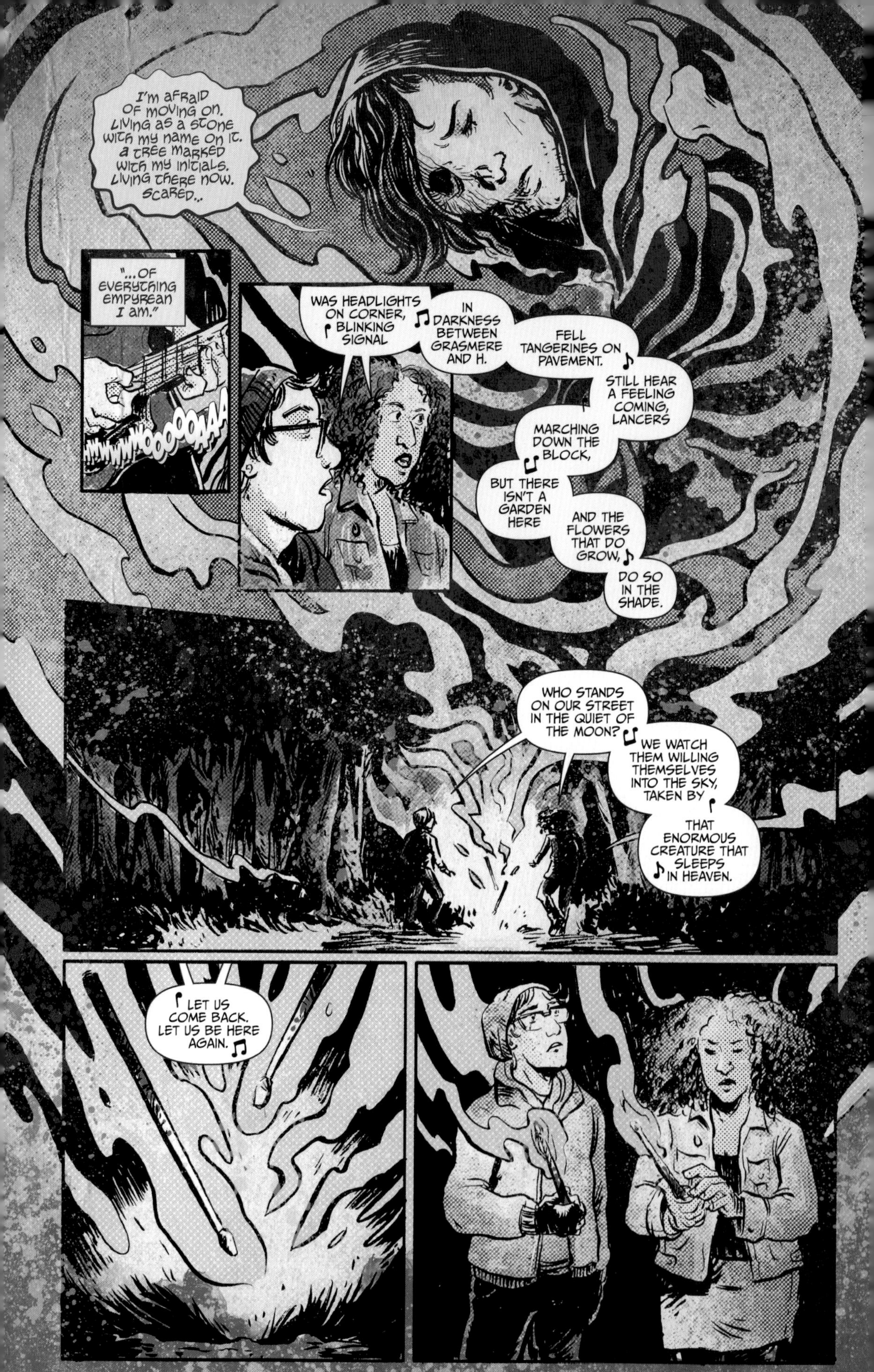

I'm afraid of moving on. Living as a stone with my name on it. a tree marked with my initials. Living there now. scared...
"...OF EVERYTHING EMPYREAN I AM."
HWWWWHOOOOOAAA
WAS HEADLIGHTS ON CORNER, BLINKING SIGNAL
IN DARKNESS BETWEEN GRASMERE AND H.
FELL TANGERINES ON PAVEMENT.
STILL HEAR A FEELING COMING, LANCERS
MARCHING DOWN THE BLOCK,
BUT THERE ISN'T A GARDEN HERE
AND THE FLOWERS THAT DO GROW,
DO SO IN THE SHADE.
WHO STANDS ON OUR STREET IN THE QUIET OF THE MOON?
WE WATCH THEM WILLING THEMSELVES INTO THE SKY, TAKEN BY
THAT ENORMOUS CREATURE THAT SLEEPS IN HEAVEN.
LET US COME BACK. LET US BE HERE AGAIN.

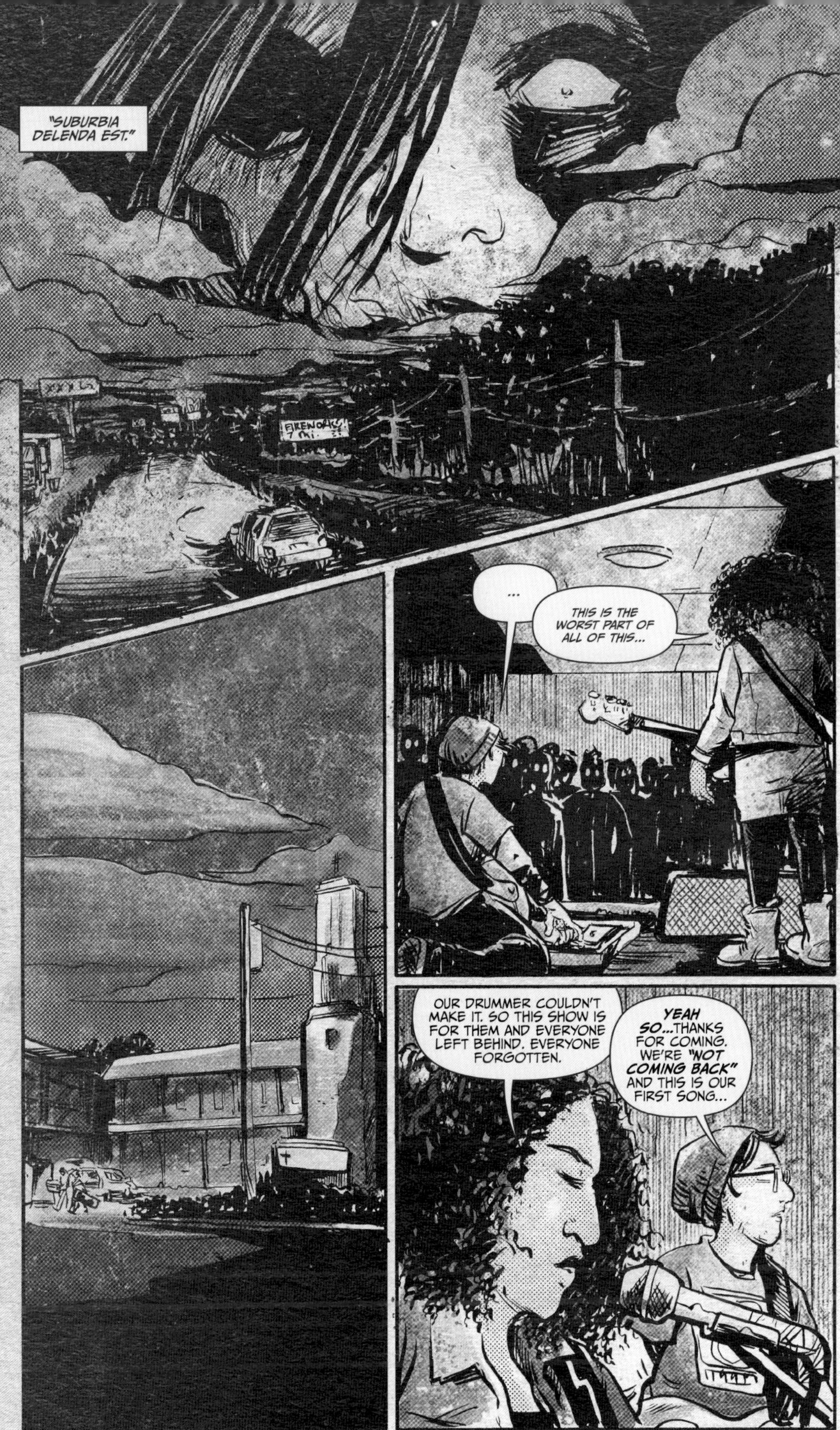
"SUBURBIA DELENDA EST."
FIREWORKS! 7 MI.
...
THIS IS THE WORST PART OF ALL OF THIS...
OUR DRUMMER COULDN'T MAKE IT. SO THIS SHOW IS FOR THEM AND EVERYONE LEFT BEHIND. EVERYONE FORGOTTEN.
YEAH SO...THANKS FOR COMING. WE'RE "NOT COMING BACK" AND THIS IS OUR FIRST SONG...

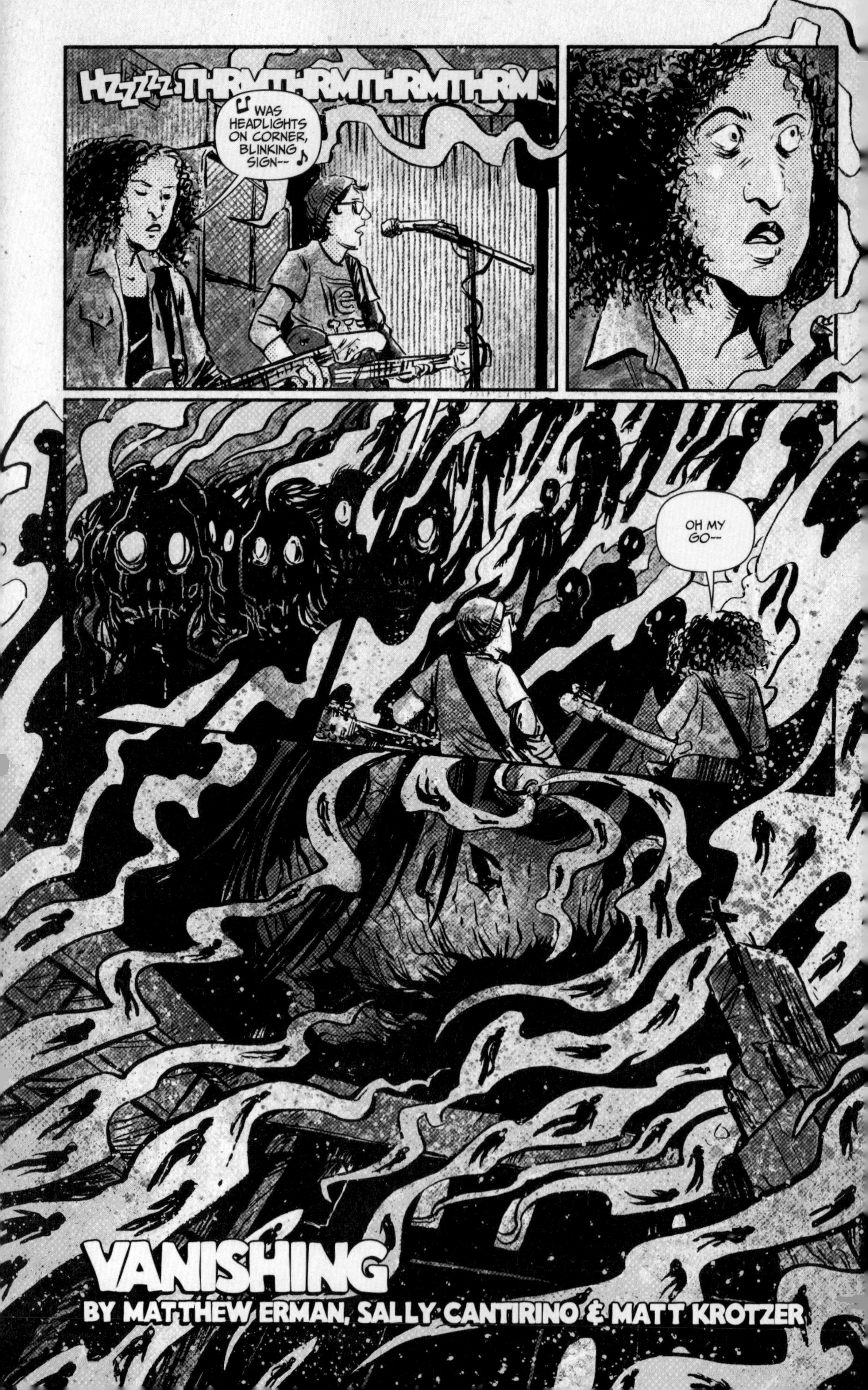
HZZZZZ-THRMTHRMTHRMTHRM
♪ WAS HEADLIGHTS ON CORNER, BLINKING SIGN-- ♪
OH MY GO--

VANISHING

BY MATTHEW ERMAN, SALLY CANTIRINO & MATT KROTZER

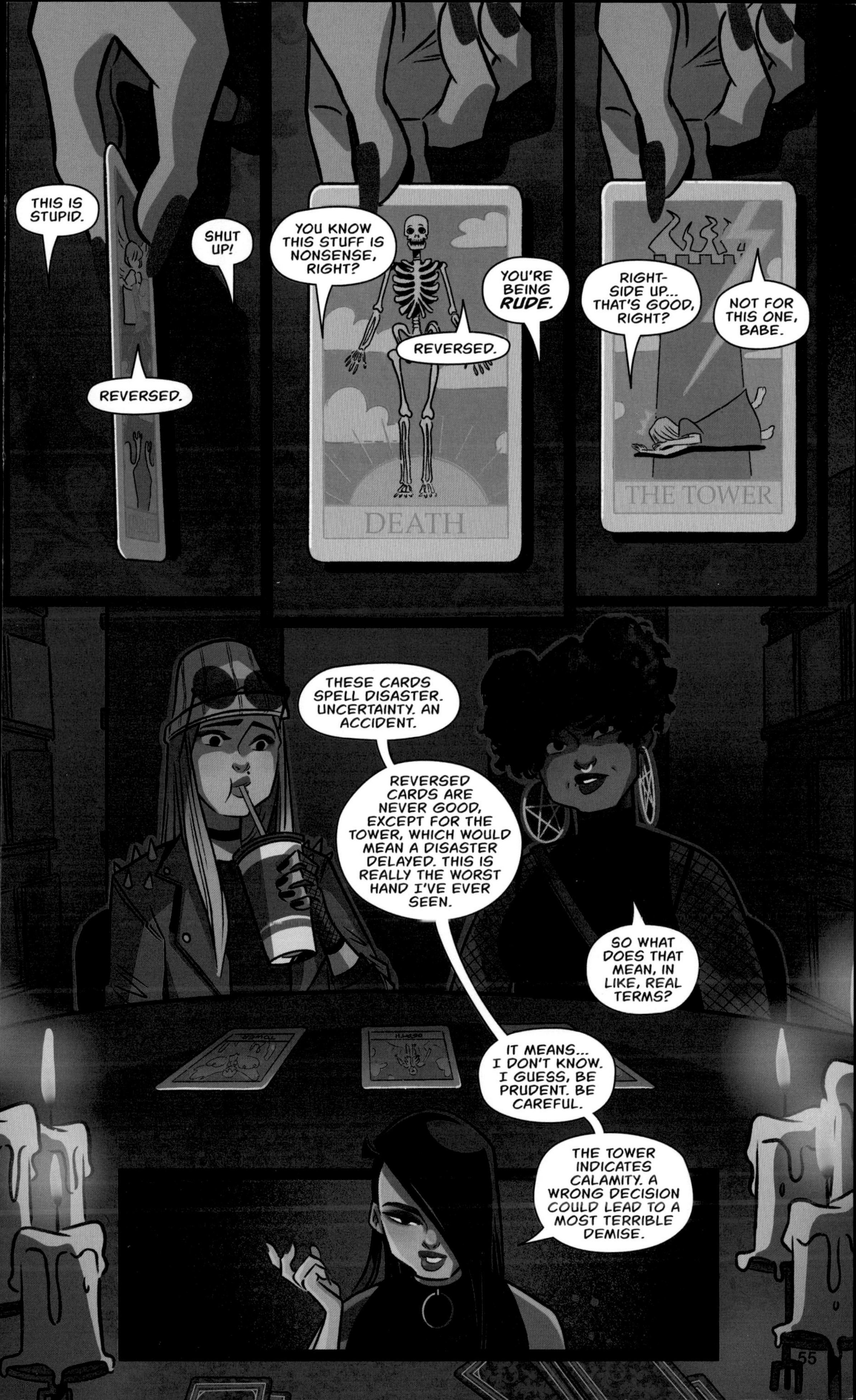
THIS IS STUPID.
SHUT UP!
REVERSED.
YOU KNOW THIS STUFF IS NONSENSE, RIGHT?
DEATH
REVERSED.
YOU'RE BEING **RUDE**.
THE TOWER
RIGHT-SIDE UP... THAT'S GOOD, RIGHT?
NOT FOR THIS ONE, BABE.
THESE CARDS SPELL DISASTER. UNCERTAINTY. AN ACCIDENT.
REVERSED CARDS ARE NEVER GOOD, EXCEPT FOR THE TOWER, WHICH WOULD MEAN A DISASTER DELAYED. THIS IS REALLY THE WORST HAND I'VE EVER SEEN.
SO WHAT DOES THAT MEAN, IN LIKE, REAL TERMS?
IT MEANS... I DON'T KNOW. I GUESS, BE PRUDENT. BE CAREFUL.
THE TOWER INDICATES CALAMITY. A WRONG DECISION COULD LEAD TO A MOST TERRIBLE DEMISE.

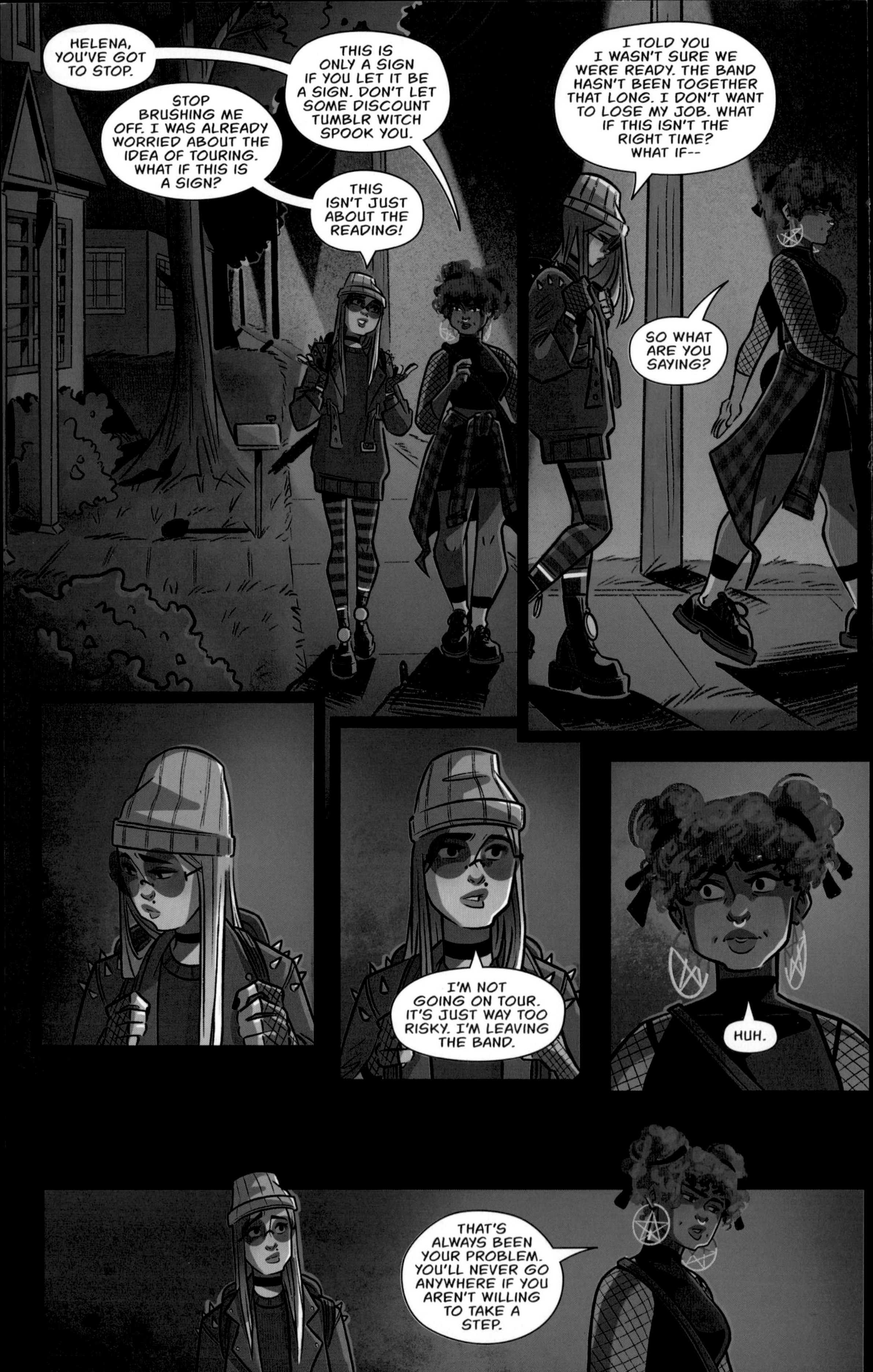

HELENA, YOU'VE GOT TO STOP.
STOP BRUSHING ME OFF. I WAS ALREADY WORRIED ABOUT THE IDEA OF TOURING. WHAT IF THIS IS A SIGN?
THIS IS ONLY A SIGN IF YOU LET IT BE A SIGN. DON'T LET SOME DISCOUNT TUMBLR WITCH SPOOK YOU.
THIS ISN'T JUST ABOUT THE READING!
I TOLD YOU I WASN'T SURE WE WERE READY. THE BAND HASN'T BEEN TOGETHER THAT LONG. I DON'T WANT TO LOSE MY JOB. WHAT IF THIS ISN'T THE RIGHT TIME? WHAT IF--
SO WHAT ARE YOU SAYING?
I'M NOT GOING ON TOUR. IT'S JUST WAY TOO RISKY. I'M LEAVING THE BAND.
HUH.
THAT'S ALWAYS BEEN YOUR PROBLEM. YOU'LL NEVER GO ANYWHERE IF YOU AREN'T WILLING TO TAKE A STEP.

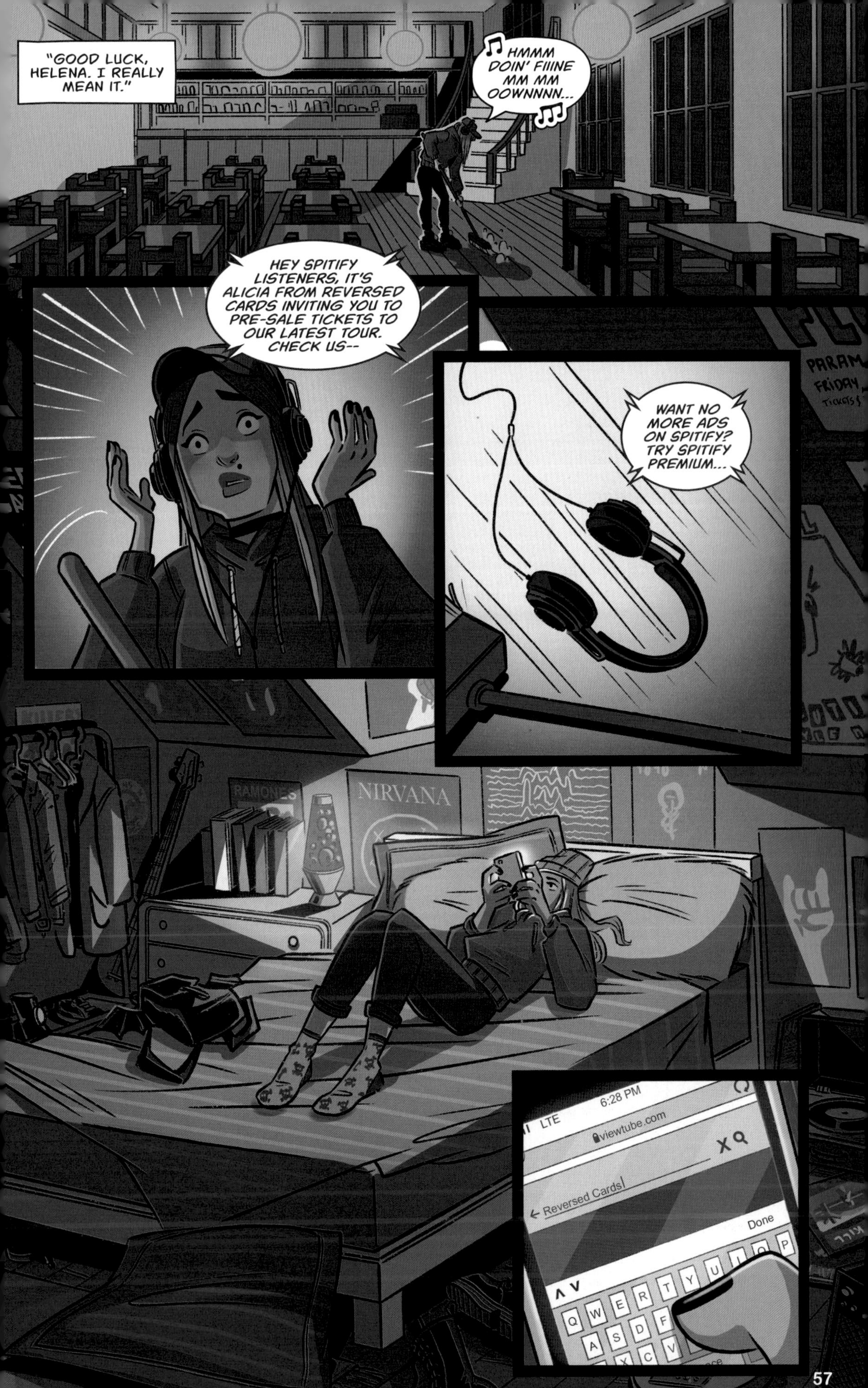
"GOOD LUCK, HELENA. I REALLY MEAN IT."
HMMM DOIN' FIIINE MM MM OOWNNNN...
HEY SPITIFY LISTENERS, IT'S ALICIA FROM REVERSED CARDS INVITING YOU TO PRE-SALE TICKETS TO OUR LATEST TOUR. CHECK US--
WANT NO MORE ADS ON SPITIFY? TRY SPITIFY PREMIUM...
RAMONES
NIRVANA
6:28 PM
LTE
viewtube.com
Reversed Cards
Done

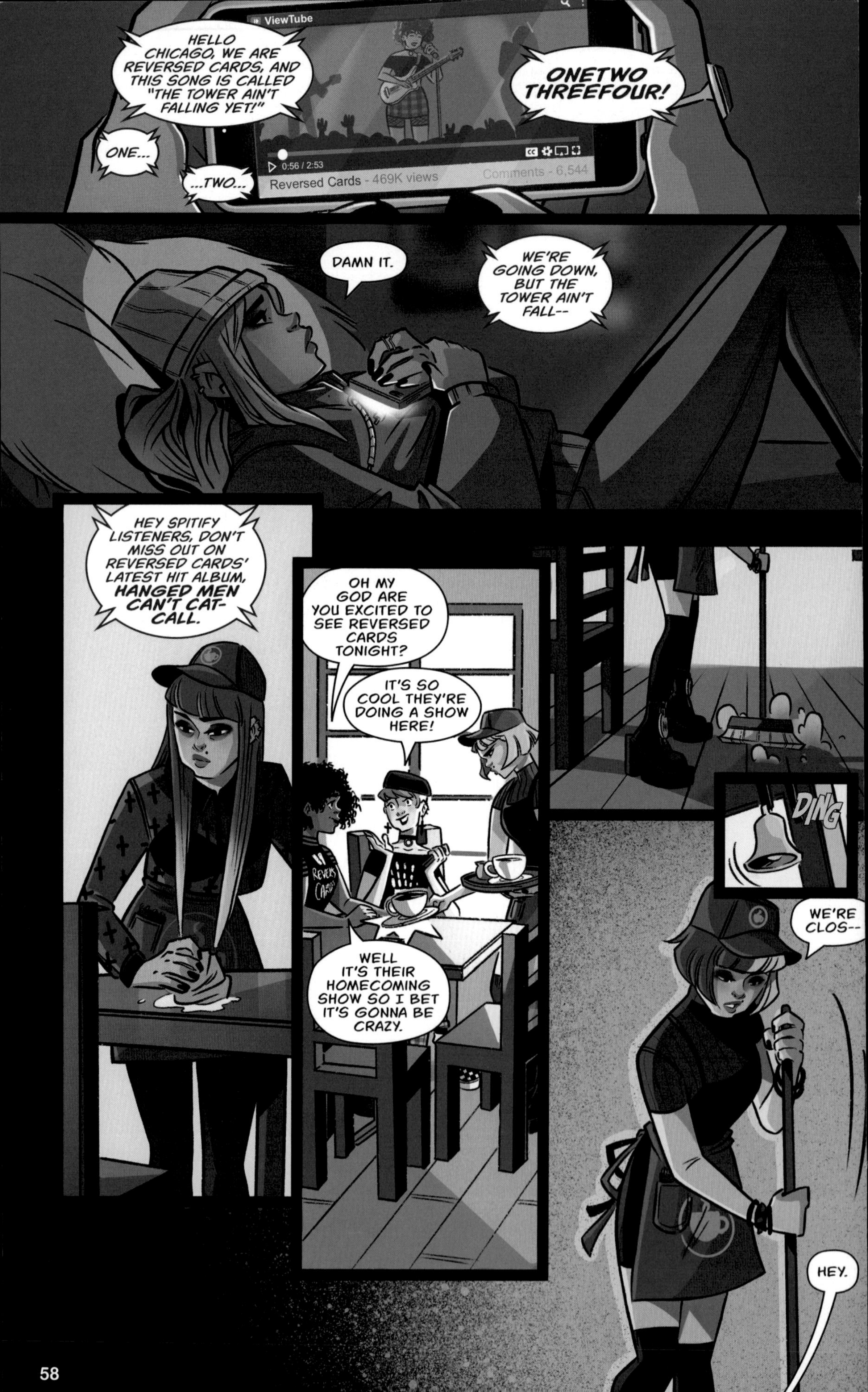
ViewTube
HELLO CHICAGO, WE ARE REVERSED CARDS, AND THIS SONG IS CALLED "THE TOWER AIN'T FALLING YET!"
ONETWO THREEFOUR!
ONE...
...TWO...
0:56 / 2:53
Reversed Cards - 469K views
Comments - 6,544
DAMN IT.
WE'RE GOING DOWN, BUT THE TOWER AIN'T FALL--
HEY SPITIFY LISTENERS, DON'T MISS OUT ON REVERSED CARDS' LATEST HIT ALBUM, HANGED MEN CAN'T CAT-CALL.
OH MY GOD ARE YOU EXCITED TO SEE REVERSED CARDS TONIGHT?
IT'S SO COOL THEY'RE DOING A SHOW HERE!
WELL IT'S THEIR HOMECOMING SHOW SO I BET IT'S GONNA BE CRAZY.
DING
WE'RE CLOS--
HEY.

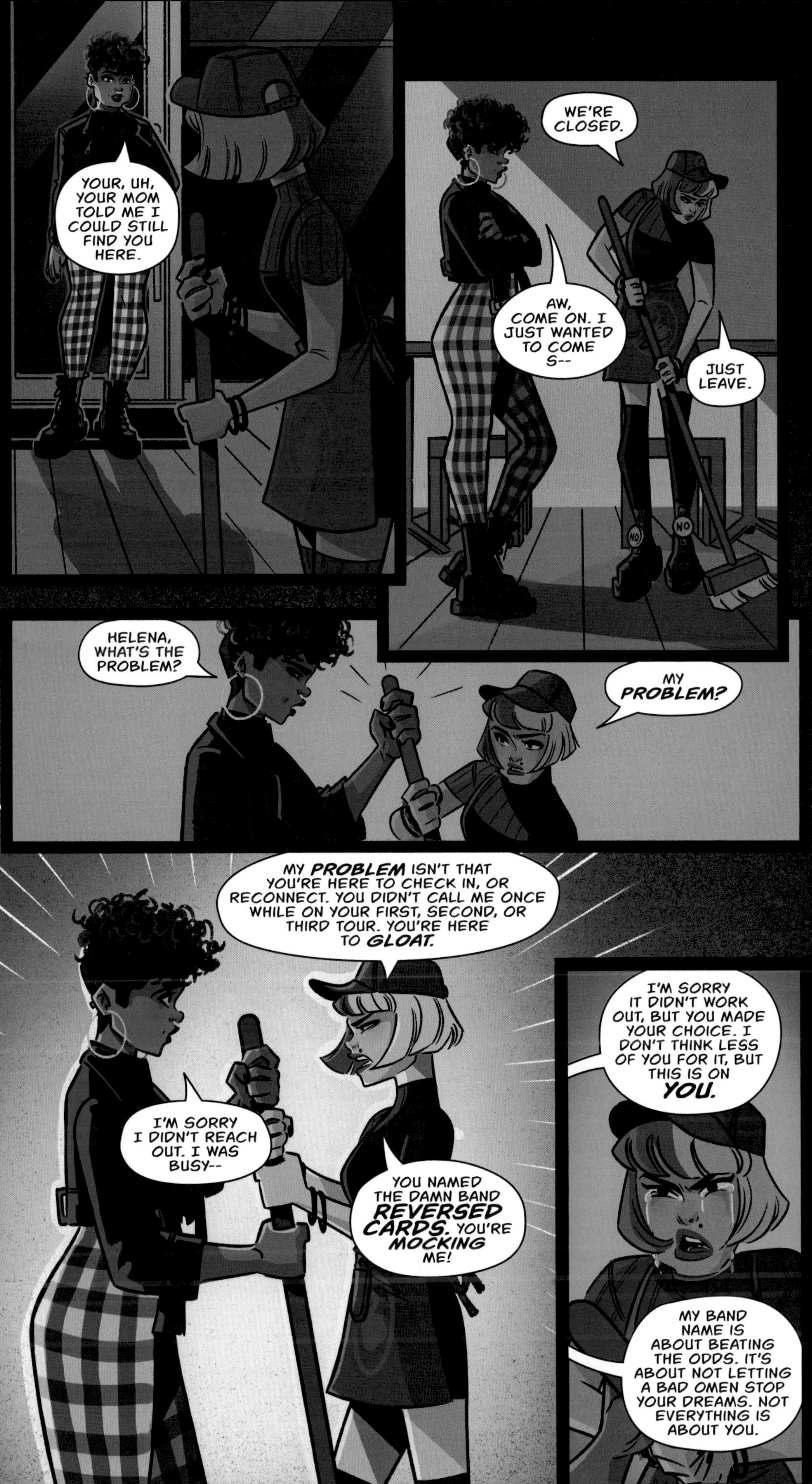
YOUR, UH, YOUR MOM TOLD ME I COULD STILL FIND YOU HERE.
WE'RE CLOSED.
AW, COME ON. I JUST WANTED TO COME S--
JUST LEAVE.
HELENA, WHAT'S THE PROBLEM?
MY PROBLEM?
MY PROBLEM ISN'T THAT YOU'RE HERE TO CHECK IN, OR RECONNECT. YOU DIDN'T CALL ME ONCE WHILE ON YOUR FIRST, SECOND, OR THIRD TOUR. YOU'RE HERE TO GLOAT.
I'M SORRY I DIDN'T REACH OUT. I WAS BUSY--
YOU NAMED THE DAMN BAND REVERSED CARDS. YOU'RE MOCKING ME!
I'M SORRY IT DIDN'T WORK OUT, BUT YOU MADE YOUR CHOICE. I DON'T THINK LESS OF YOU FOR IT, BUT THIS IS ON YOU.
MY BAND NAME IS ABOUT BEATING THE ODDS. IT'S ABOUT NOT LETTING A BAD OMEN STOP YOUR DREAMS. NOT EVERYTHING IS ABOUT YOU.
NO
NO

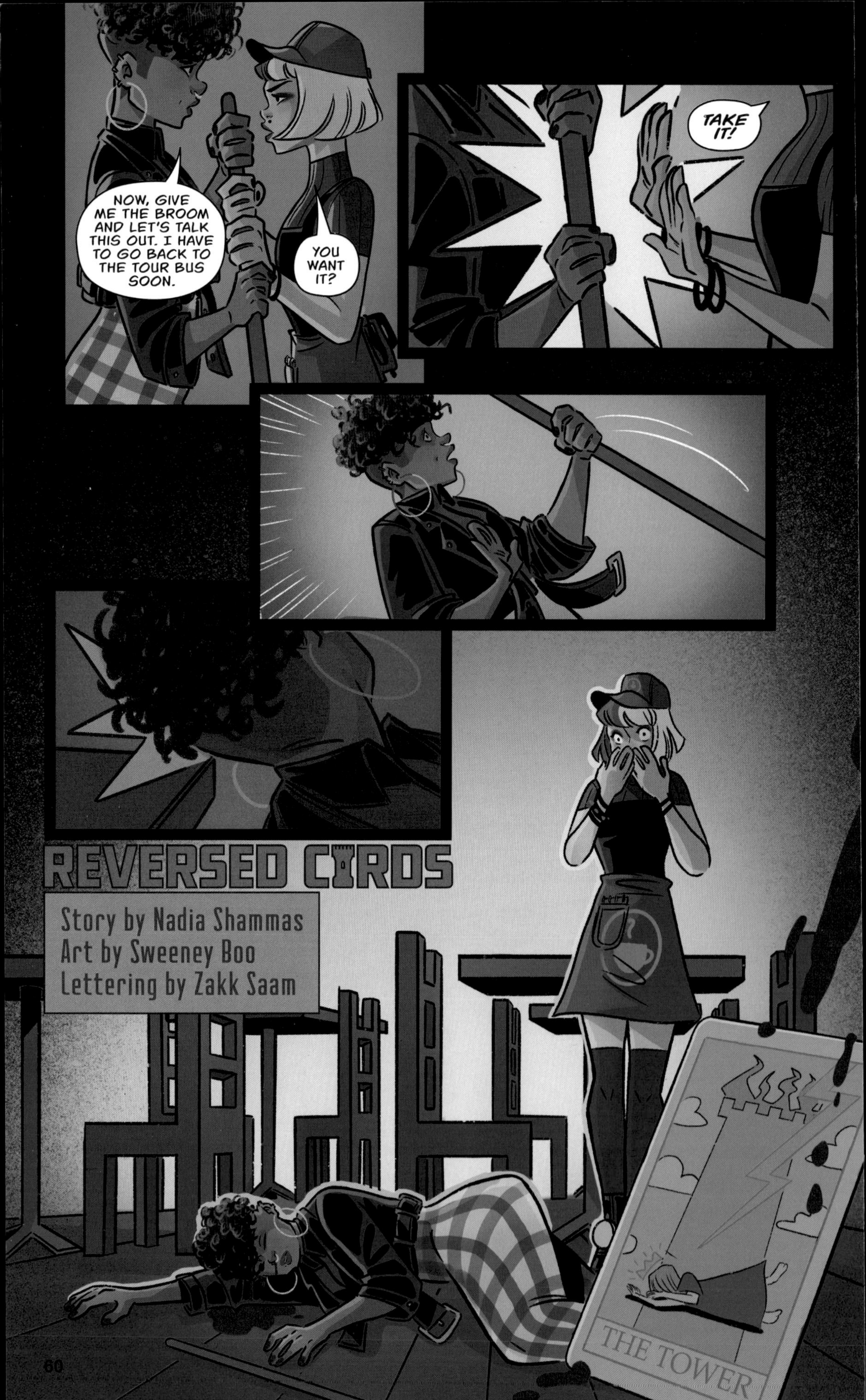
NOW, GIVE ME THE BROOM AND LET'S TALK THIS OUT. I HAVE TO GO BACK TO THE TOUR BUS SOON.
YOU WANT IT?
TAKE IT!
REVERSED CARDS
Story by Nadia Shammas
Art by Sweeney Boo
Lettering by Zakk Saam
THE TOWER

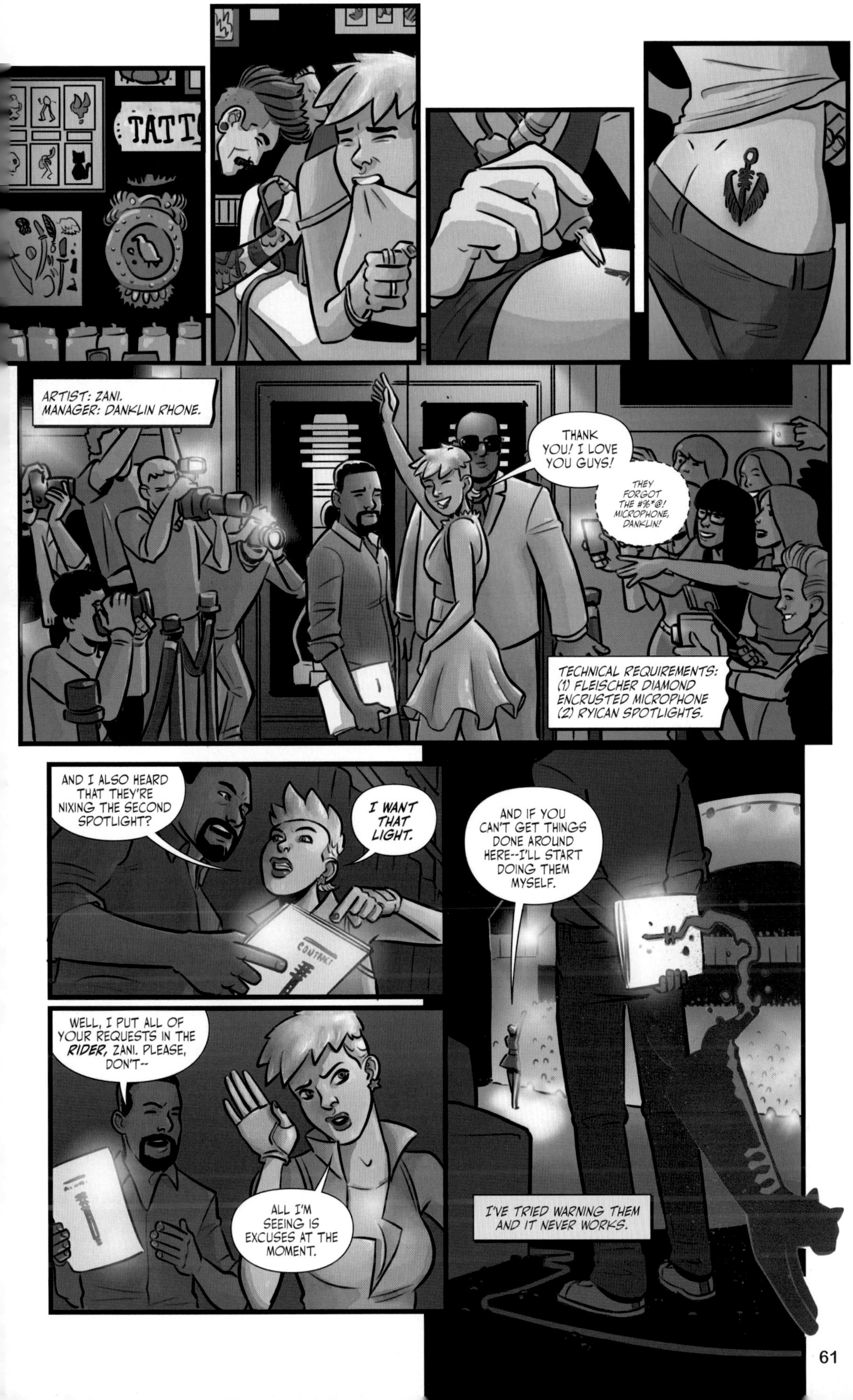
TATT
ARTIST: ZANI.
MANAGER: DANKLIN RHONE.
THANK YOU! I LOVE YOU GUYS!
THEY FORGOT THE #%*@! MICROPHONE, DANKLIN!
TECHNICAL REQUIREMENTS: (1) FLEISCHER DIAMOND ENCRUSTED MICROPHONE (2) RYICAN SPOTLIGHTS.
AND I ALSO HEARD THAT THEY'RE NIXING THE SECOND SPOTLIGHT?
I WANT THAT LIGHT.
CONTRACT
WELL, I PUT ALL OF YOUR REQUESTS IN THE RIDER, ZANI. PLEASE, DON'T--
ALL I'M SEEING IS EXCUSES AT THE MOMENT.
AND IF YOU CAN'T GET THINGS DONE AROUND HERE--I'LL START DOING THEM MYSELF.
I'VE TRIED WARNING THEM AND IT NEVER WORKS.

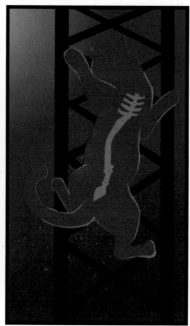

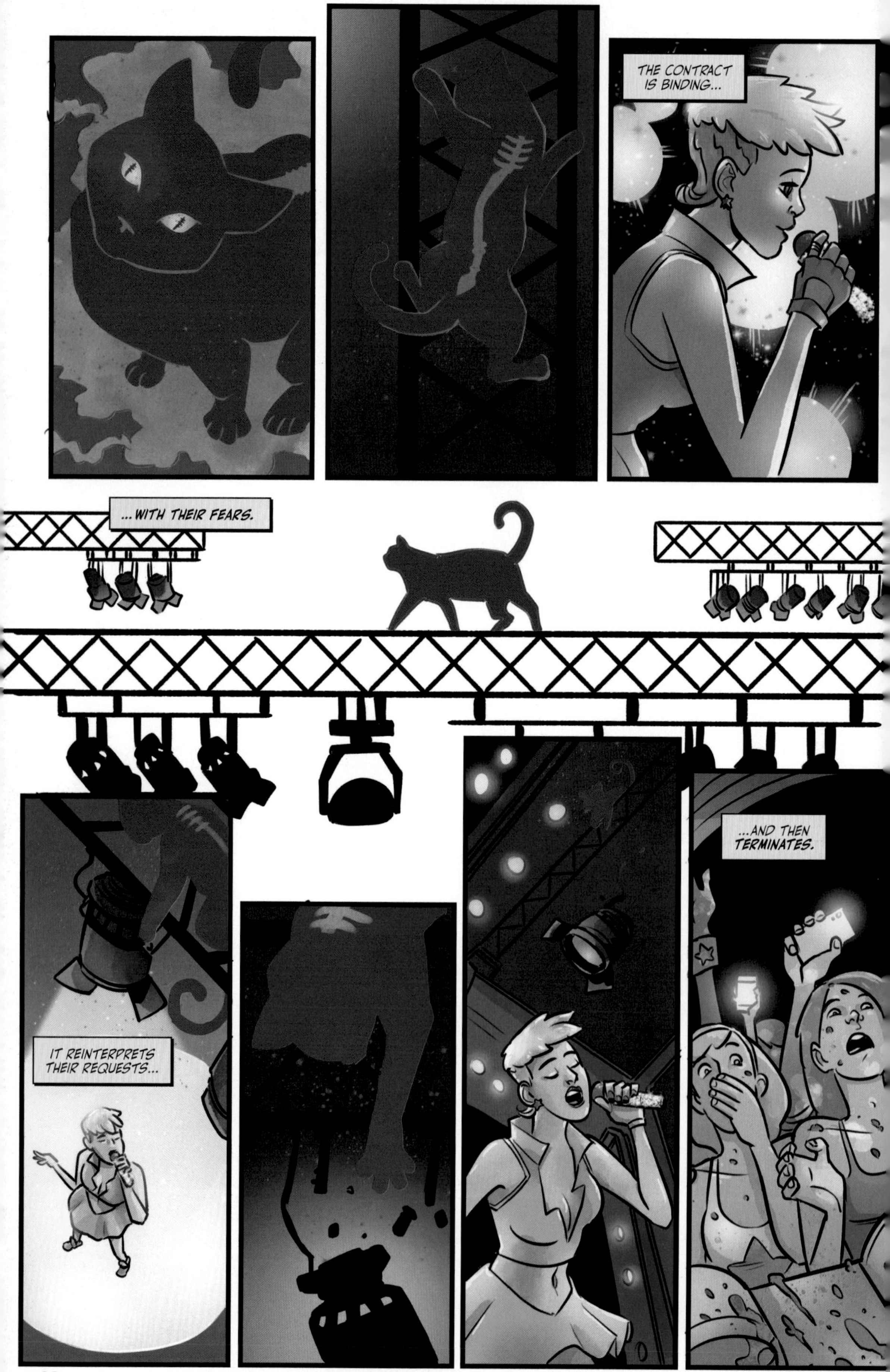
THE CONTRACT IS BINDING...
...WITH THEIR FEARS.
IT REINTERPRETS THEIR REQUESTS...
...AND THEN TERMINATES.

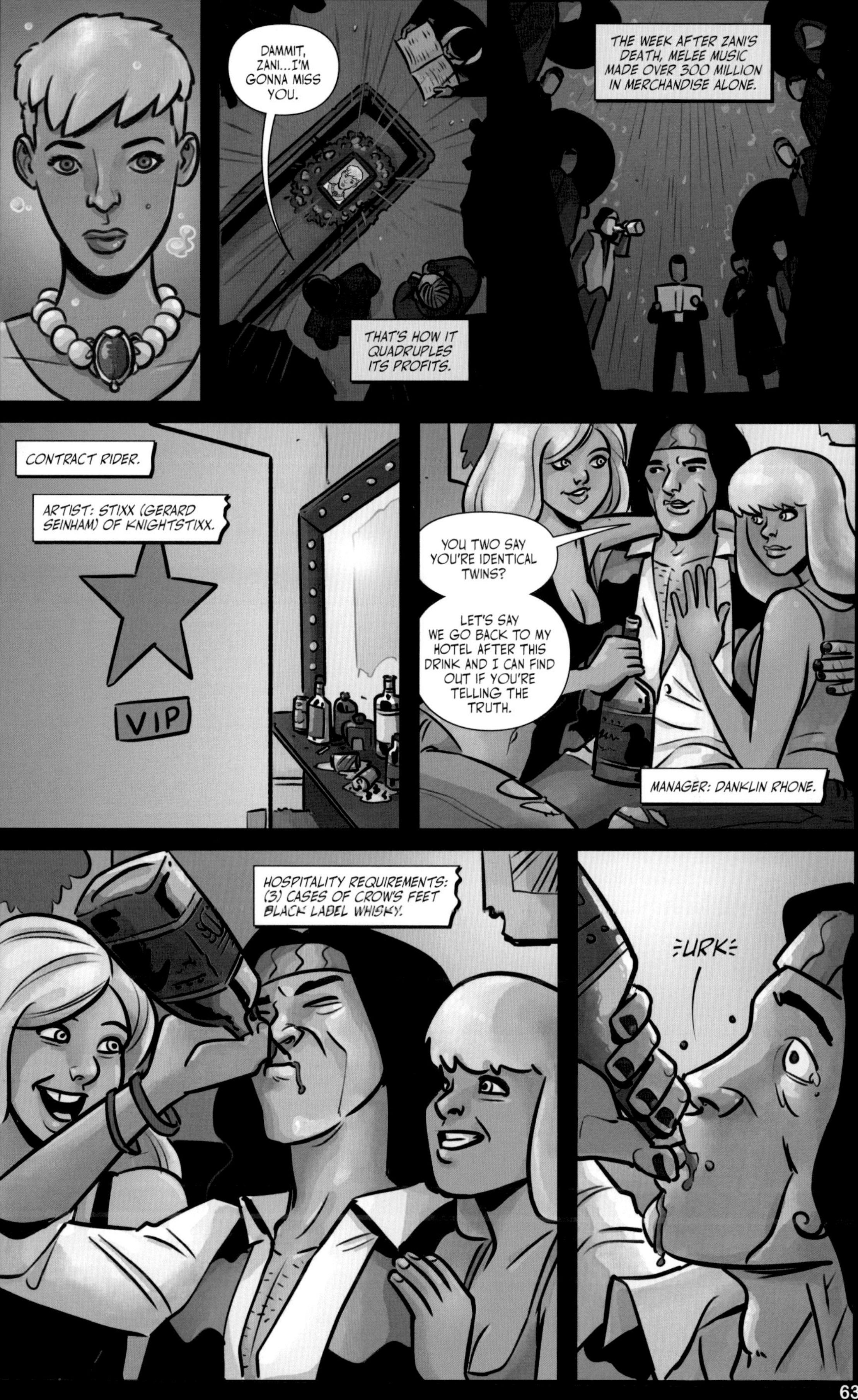
DAMMIT, ZANI...I'M GONNA MISS YOU.
THAT'S HOW IT QUADRUPLES ITS PROFITS.
THE WEEK AFTER ZANI'S DEATH, MELEE MUSIC MADE OVER 300 MILLION IN MERCHANDISE ALONE.
CONTRACT RIDER.
ARTIST: STIXX (GERARD SEINHAM) OF KNIGHTSTIXX.
VIP
YOU TWO SAY YOU'RE IDENTICAL TWINS?
LET'S SAY WE GO BACK TO MY HOTEL AFTER THIS DRINK AND I CAN FIND OUT IF YOU'RE TELLING THE TRUTH.
MANAGER: DANKLIN RHONE.
HOSPITALITY REQUIREMENTS: (3) CASES OF CROW'S FEET BLACK LABEL WHISKY.
URK

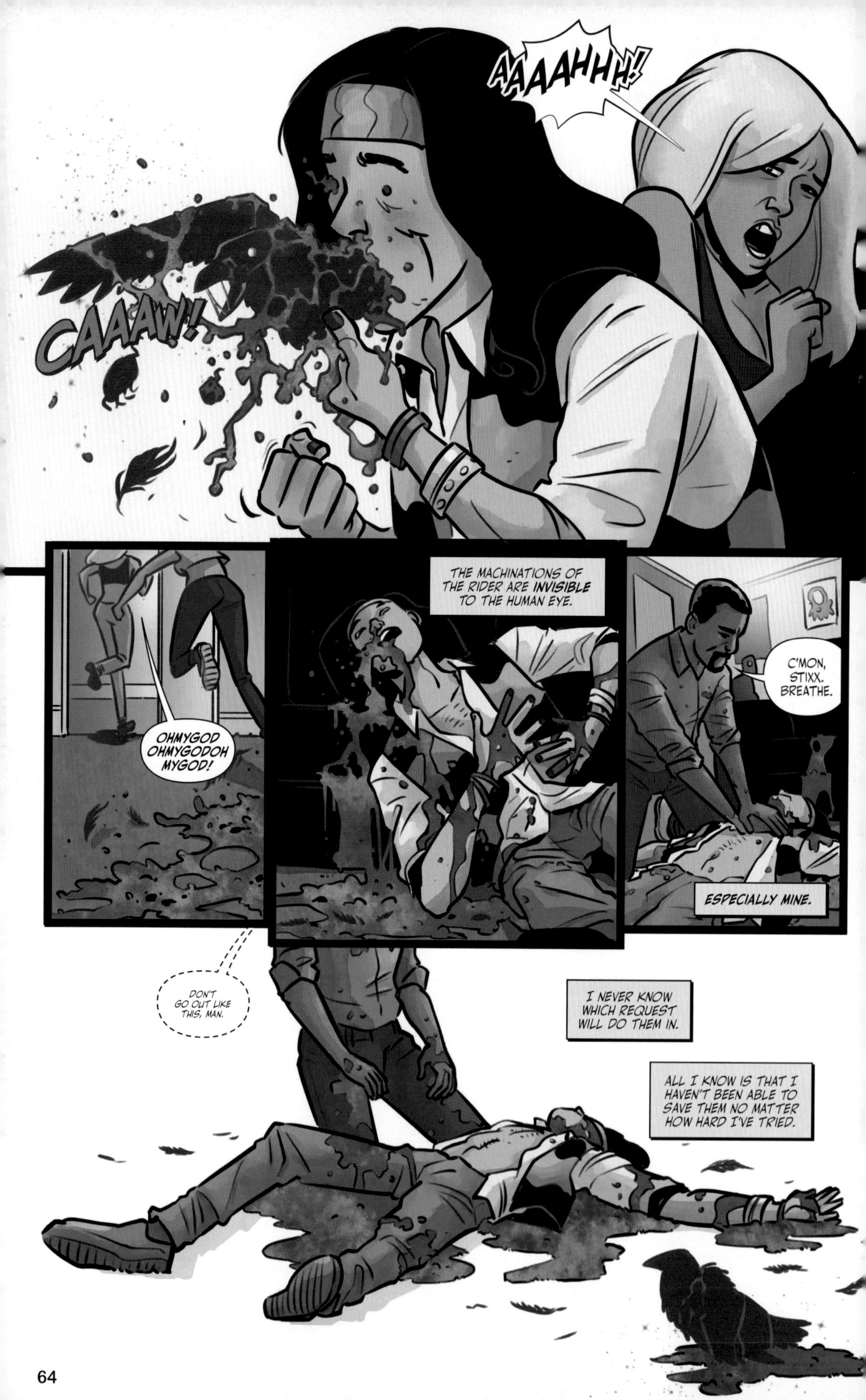
AAAAHHH!
CAAAW!
OHMYGOD OHMYGODOH MYGOD!
THE MACHINATIONS OF THE RIDER ARE INVISIBLE TO THE HUMAN EYE.
C'MON, STIXX. BREATHE.
ESPECIALLY MINE.
DON'T GO OUT LIKE THIS, MAN.
I NEVER KNOW WHICH REQUEST WILL DO THEM IN.
ALL I KNOW IS THAT I HAVEN'T BEEN ABLE TO SAVE THEM NO MATTER HOW HARD I'VE TRIED.

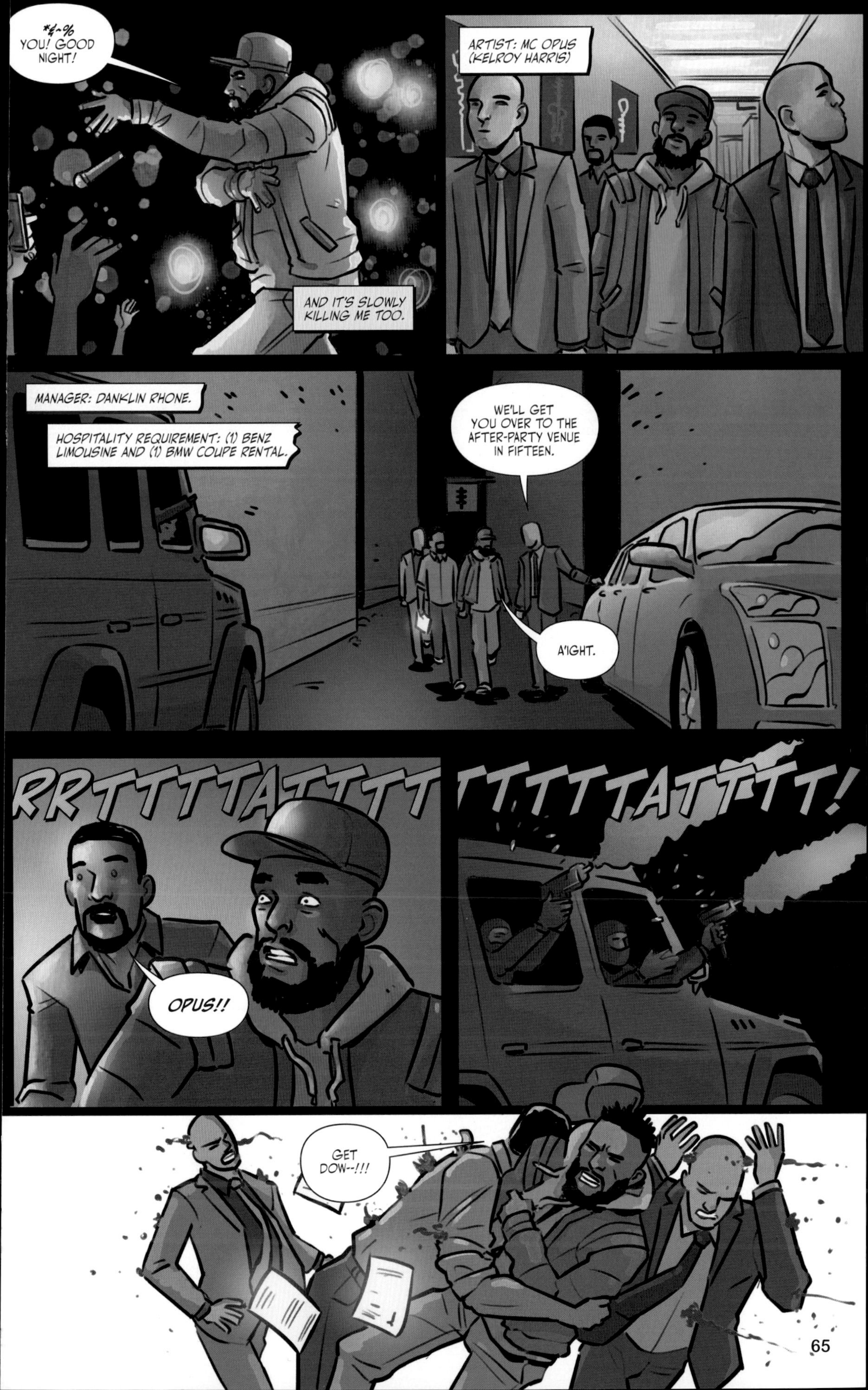
*&-% YOU! GOOD NIGHT!
AND IT'S SLOWLY KILLING ME TOO.
ARTIST: MC OPUS (KELROY HARRIS)
MANAGER: DANKLIN RHONE.
HOSPITALITY REQUIREMENT: (1) BENZ LIMOUSINE AND (1) BMW COUPE RENTAL.
WE'LL GET YOU OVER TO THE AFTER-PARTY VENUE IN FIFTEEN.
A'IGHT.
RRTTTTATTTTTTTTTTTATTTTT!
OPUS!!
GET DOW--!!!

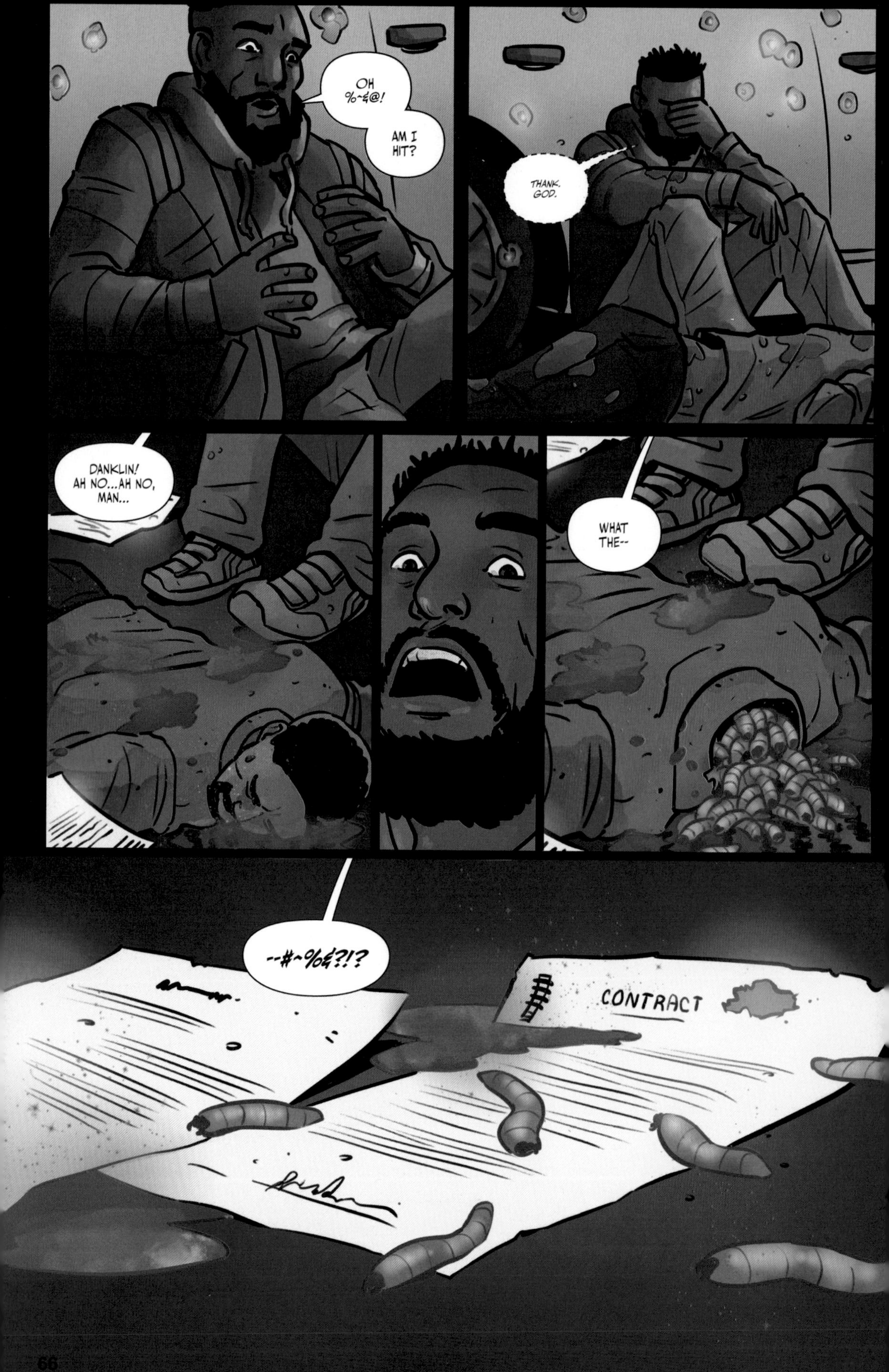
OH %~$@!
AM I HIT?
THANK. GOD.
DANKLIN! AH NO...AH NO, MAN...
WHAT THE--
--#~%$?!?
CONTRACT

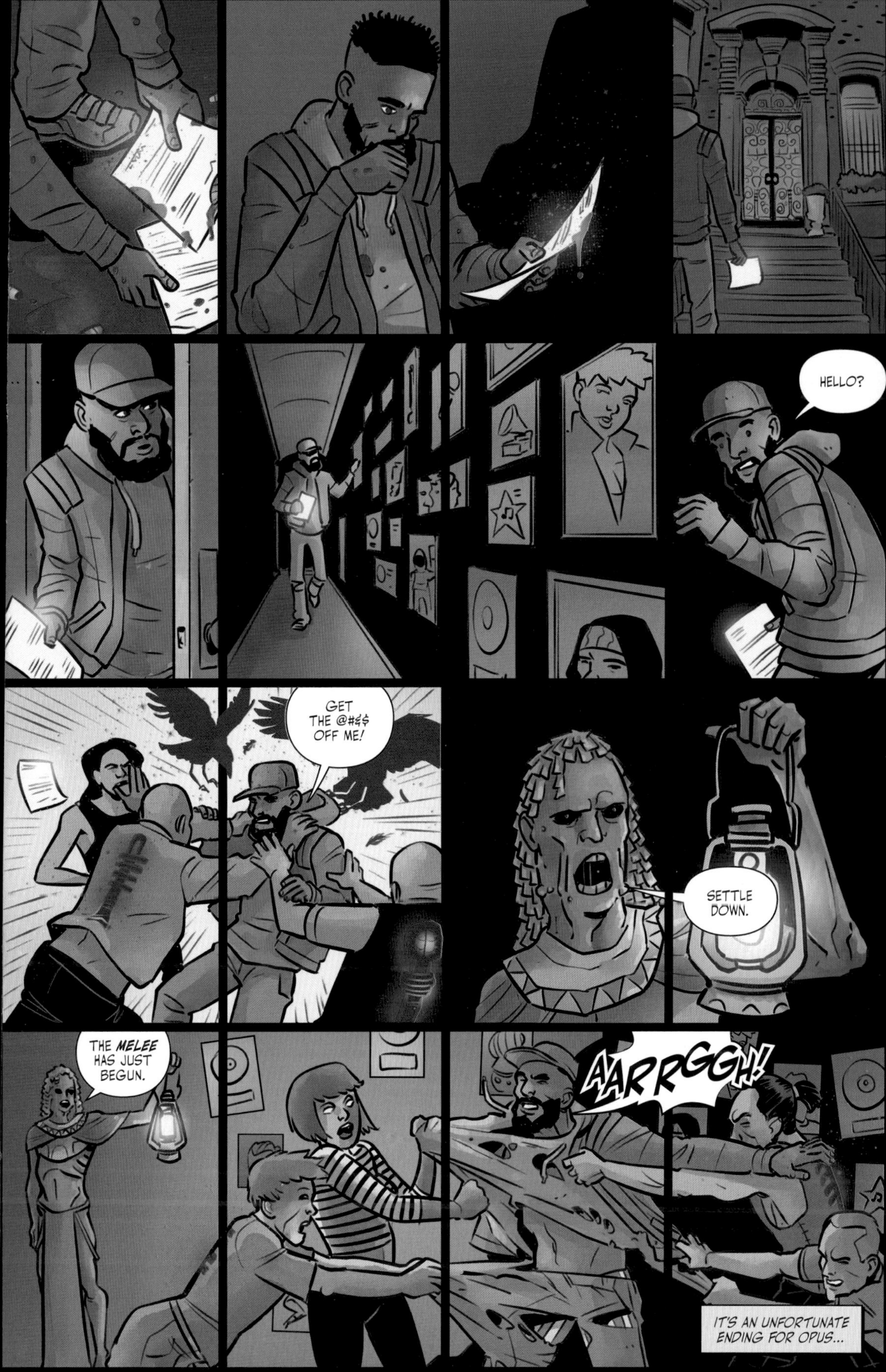
HELLO?
GET THE @#$$ OFF ME!
SETTLE DOWN.
THE MELEE HAS JUST BEGUN.
AARRGGH!
IT'S AN UNFORTUNATE ENDING FOR OPUS...

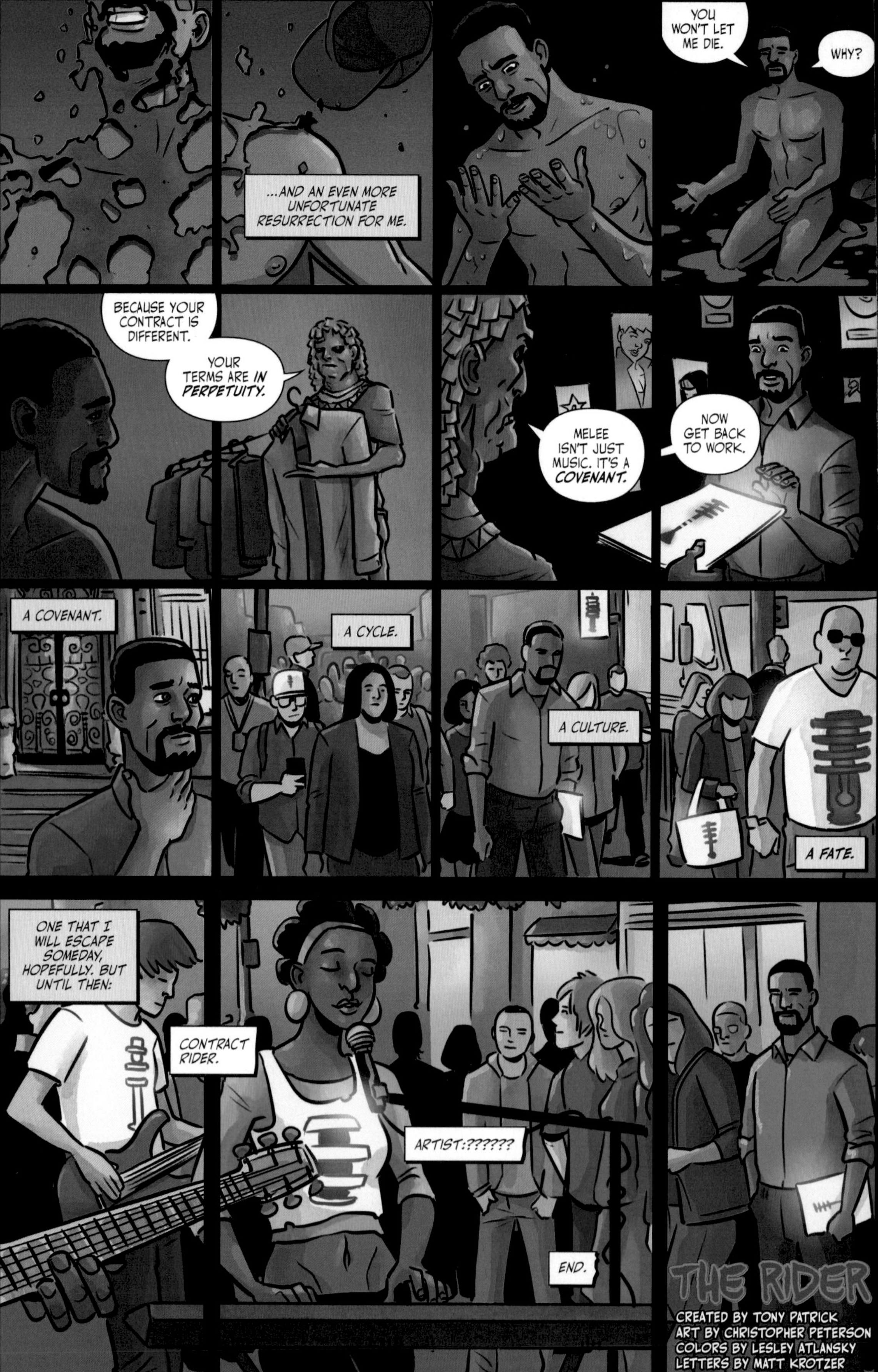
...AND AN EVEN MORE UNFORTUNATE RESURRECTION FOR ME.
YOU WON'T LET ME DIE.
WHY?
BECAUSE YOUR CONTRACT IS DIFFERENT.
YOUR TERMS ARE IN PERPETUITY.
MELEE ISN'T JUST MUSIC. IT'S A COVENANT.
NOW GET BACK TO WORK.
A COVENANT.
A CYCLE.
A CULTURE.
A FATE.
ONE THAT I WILL ESCAPE SOMEDAY, HOPEFULLY. BUT UNTIL THEN:
CONTRACT RIDER.
ARTIST:??????
END.
THE RIDER
CREATED BY TONY PATRICK
ART BY CHRISTOPHER PETERSON
COLORS BY LESLEY ATLANSKY
LETTERS BY MATT KROTZER

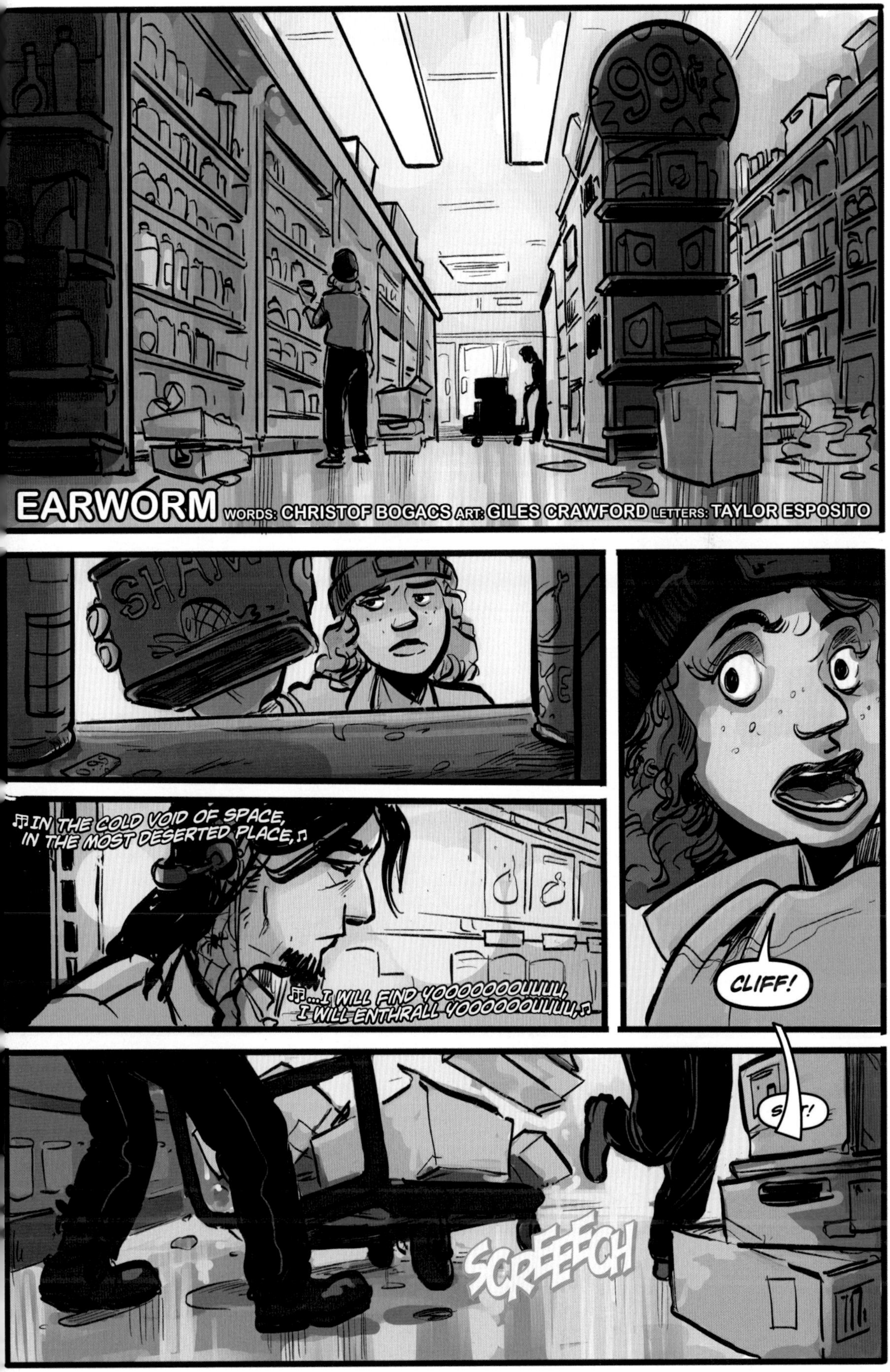
EARWORM WORDS: CHRISTOF BOGACS ART: GILES CRAWFORD LETTERS: TAYLOR ESPOSITO
99¢
♬IN THE COLD VOID OF SPACE, IN THE MOST DESERTED PLACE,♫
♬...I WILL FIND YOOOOOOOUUUU, I WILL ENTHRALL YOOOOOOUUUU,♫
CLIFF!
SCREEECH

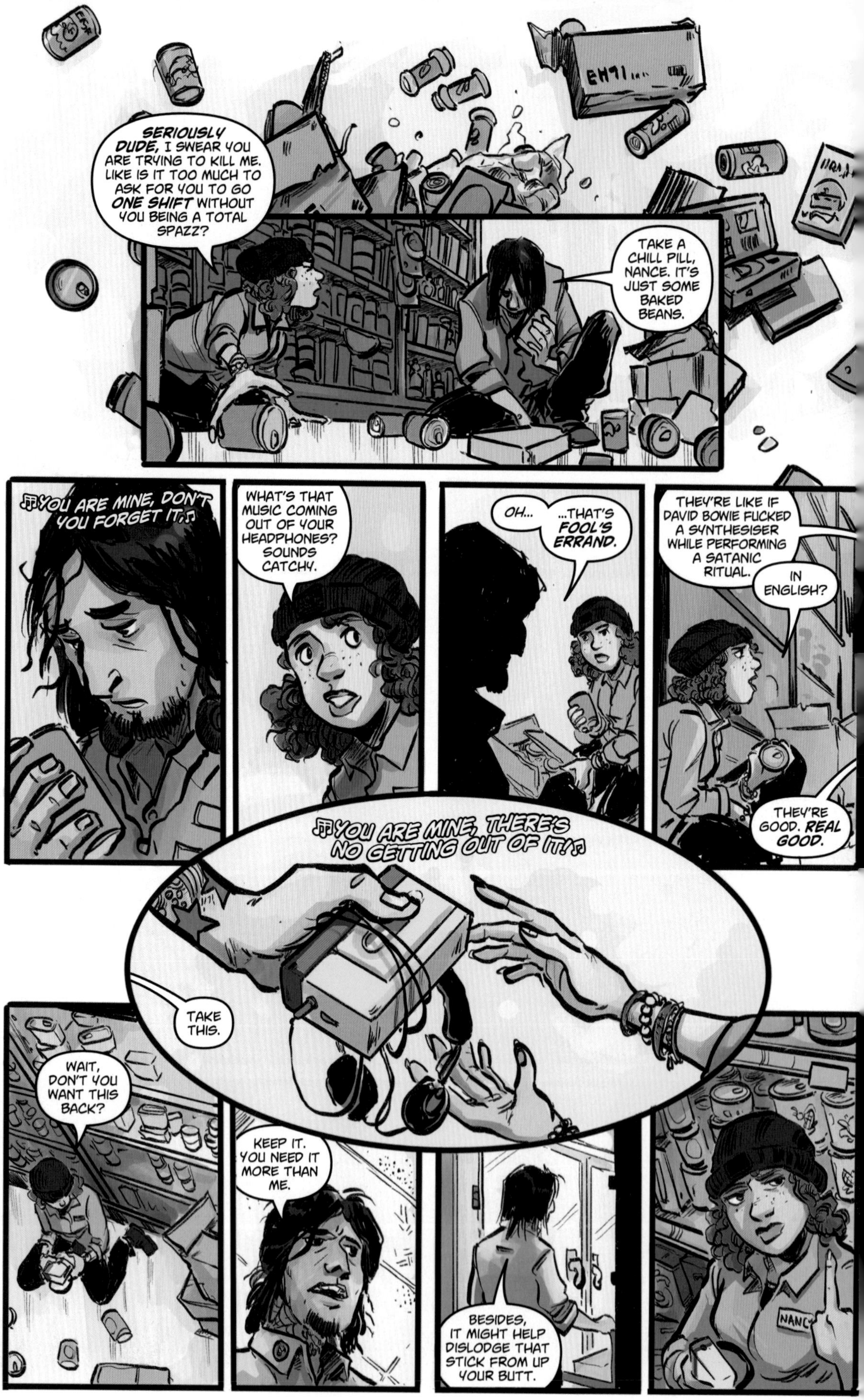

SERIOUSLY DUDE, I SWEAR YOU ARE TRYING TO KILL ME. LIKE IS IT TOO MUCH TO ASK FOR YOU TO GO ONE SHIFT WITHOUT YOU BEING A TOTAL SPAZZ?
TAKE A CHILL PILL, NANCE. IT'S JUST SOME BAKED BEANS.
♫YOU ARE MINE, DON'T YOU FORGET IT,♫
WHAT'S THAT MUSIC COMING OUT OF YOUR HEADPHONES? SOUNDS CATCHY.
OH...
...THAT'S FOOL'S ERRAND.
THEY'RE LIKE IF DAVID BOWIE FUCKED A SYNTHESISER WHILE PERFORMING A SATANIC RITUAL.
IN ENGLISH?
THEY'RE GOOD. REAL GOOD.
♫YOU ARE MINE, THERE'S NO GETTING OUT OF IT!♫
TAKE THIS.
WAIT, DON'T YOU WANT THIS BACK?
KEEP IT. YOU NEED IT MORE THAN ME.
BESIDES, IT MIGHT HELP DISLODGE THAT STICK FROM UP YOUR BUTT.
NANC

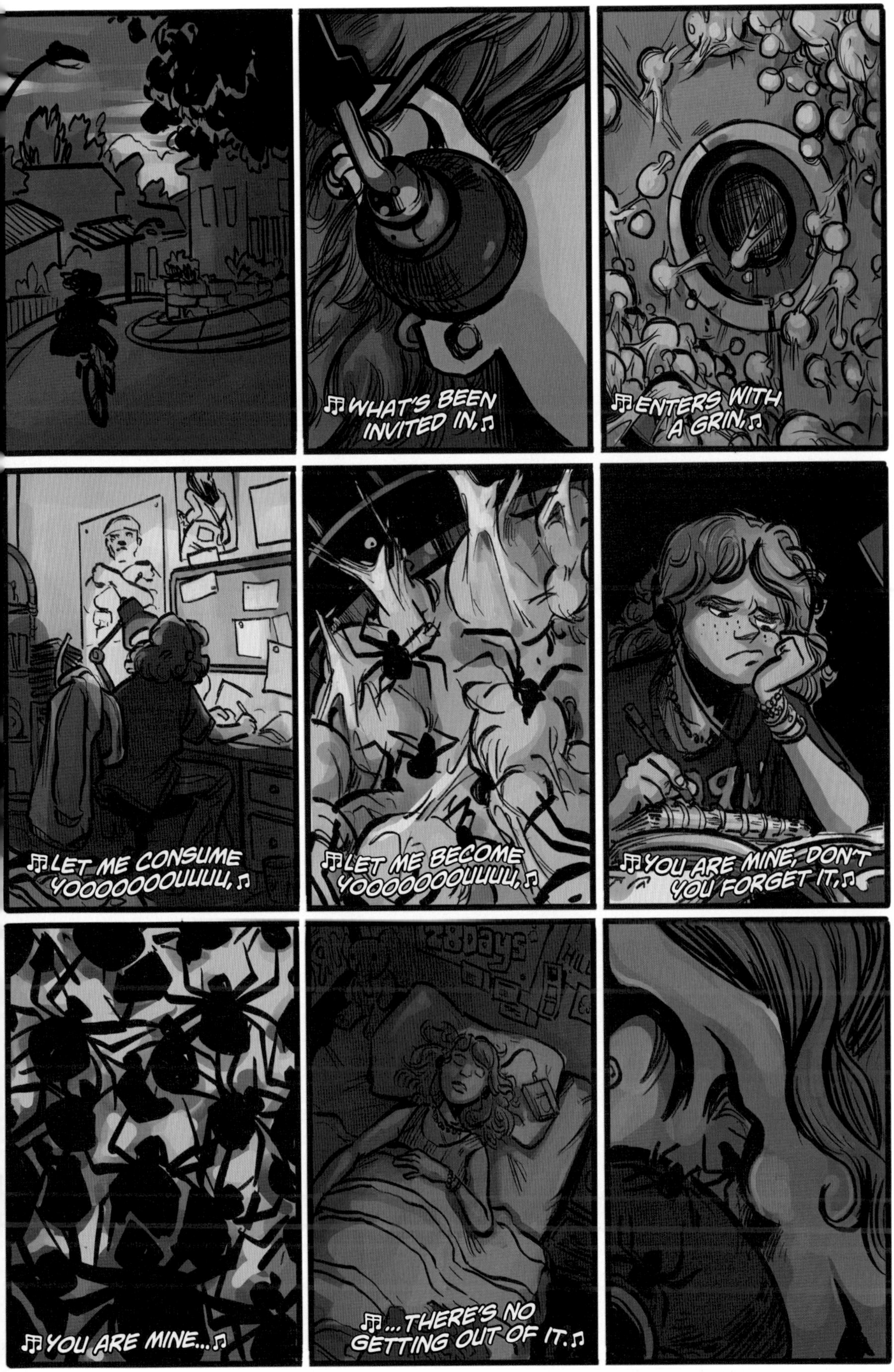
♬ WHAT'S BEEN INVITED IN, ♫
♬ ENTERS WITH A GRIN, ♫
♬ LET ME CONSUME YOOOOOOOOUUUU, ♫
♬ LET ME BECOME YOOOOOOOOUUUU, ♫
♬ YOU ARE MINE, DON'T YOU FORGET IT, ♫
♬ YOU ARE MINE... ♫
♬ ...THERE'S NO GETTING OUT OF IT. ♫

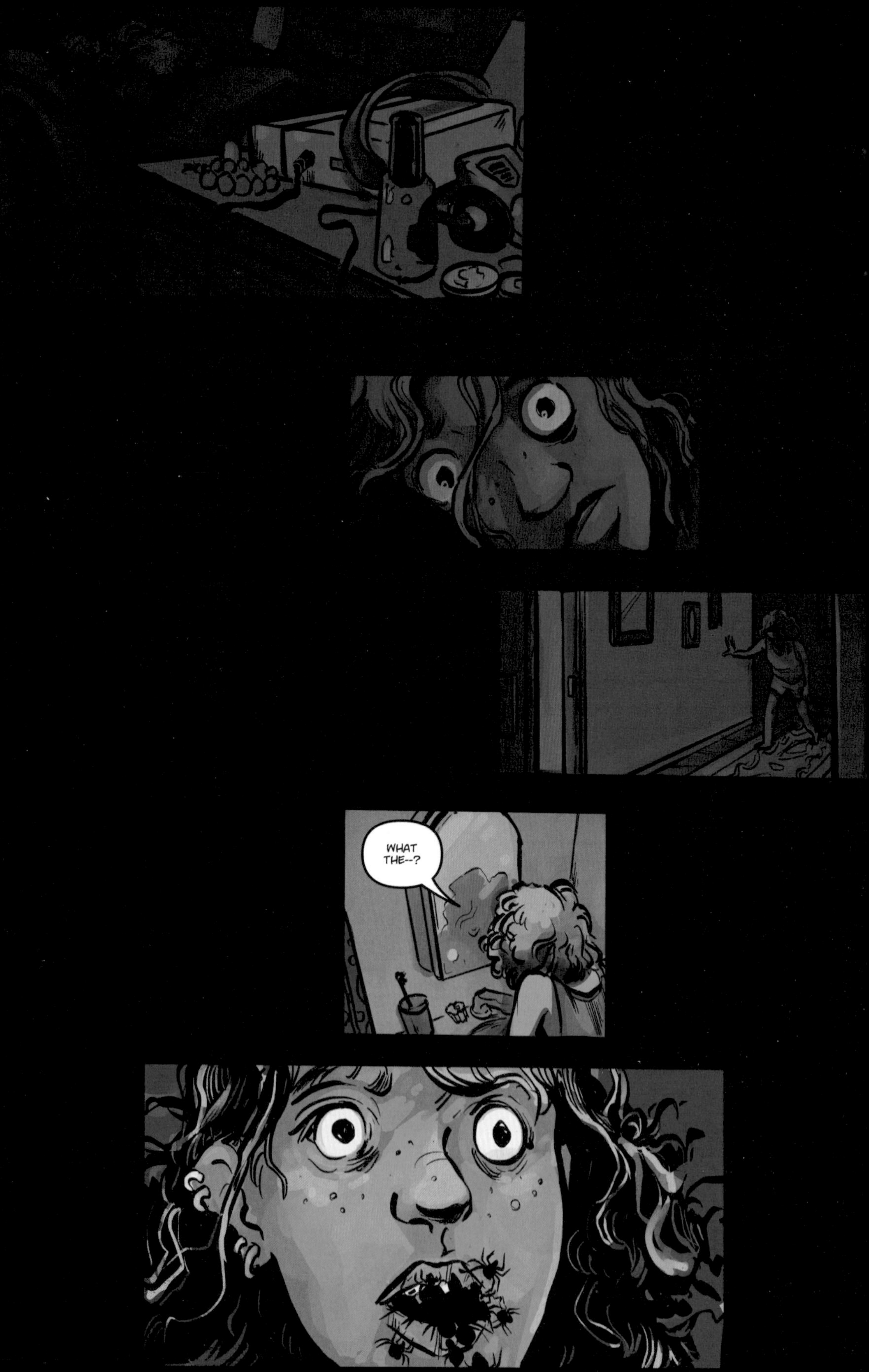
WHAT THE--?

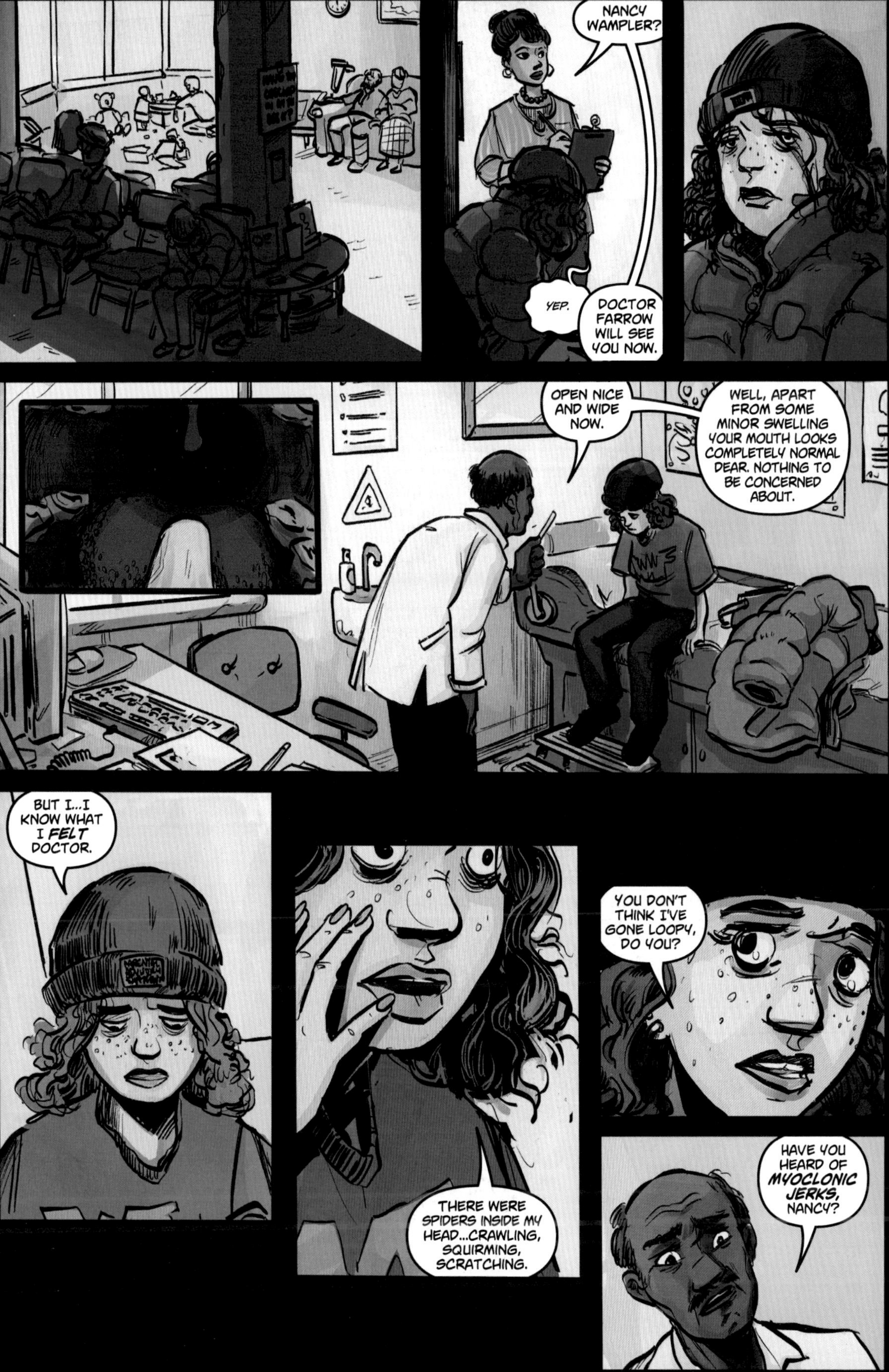
NANCY WAMPLER?
YEP.
DOCTOR FARROW WILL SEE YOU NOW.
OPEN NICE AND WIDE NOW.
WELL, APART FROM SOME MINOR SWELLING YOUR MOUTH LOOKS COMPLETELY NORMAL DEAR. NOTHING TO BE CONCERNED ABOUT.
BUT I...I KNOW WHAT I *FELT* DOCTOR.
THERE WERE SPIDERS INSIDE MY HEAD...CRAWLING, SQUIRMING, SCRATCHING.
YOU DON'T THINK I'VE GONE LOOPY, DO YOU?
HAVE YOU HEARD OF *MYOCLONIC JERKS*, NANCY?

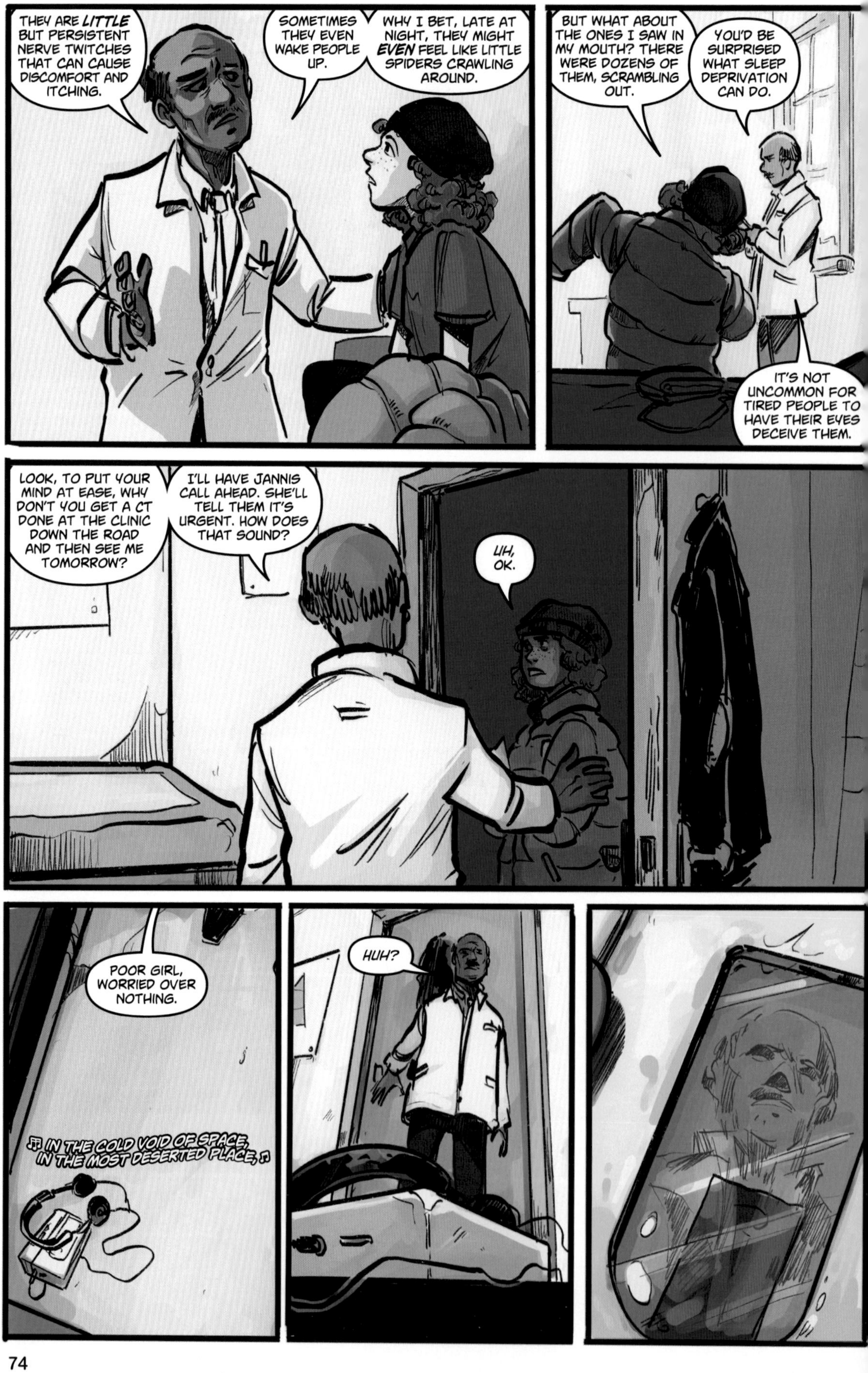
THEY ARE LITTLE BUT PERSISTENT NERVE TWITCHES THAT CAN CAUSE DISCOMFORT AND ITCHING.
SOMETIMES THEY EVEN WAKE PEOPLE UP.
WHY I BET, LATE AT NIGHT, THEY MIGHT EVEN FEEL LIKE LITTLE SPIDERS CRAWLING AROUND.
BUT WHAT ABOUT THE ONES I SAW IN MY MOUTH? THERE WERE DOZENS OF THEM, SCRAMBLING OUT.
YOU'D BE SURPRISED WHAT SLEEP DEPRIVATION CAN DO.
IT'S NOT UNCOMMON FOR TIRED PEOPLE TO HAVE THEIR EYES DECEIVE THEM.
LOOK, TO PUT YOUR MIND AT EASE, WHY DON'T YOU GET A CT DONE AT THE CLINIC DOWN THE ROAD AND THEN SEE ME TOMORROW?
I'LL HAVE JANNIS CALL AHEAD. SHE'LL TELL THEM IT'S URGENT. HOW DOES THAT SOUND?
UH, OK.
POOR GIRL, WORRIED OVER NOTHING.
♫ IN THE COLD VOID OF SPACE, IN THE MOST DESERTED PLACE, ♫
HUH?

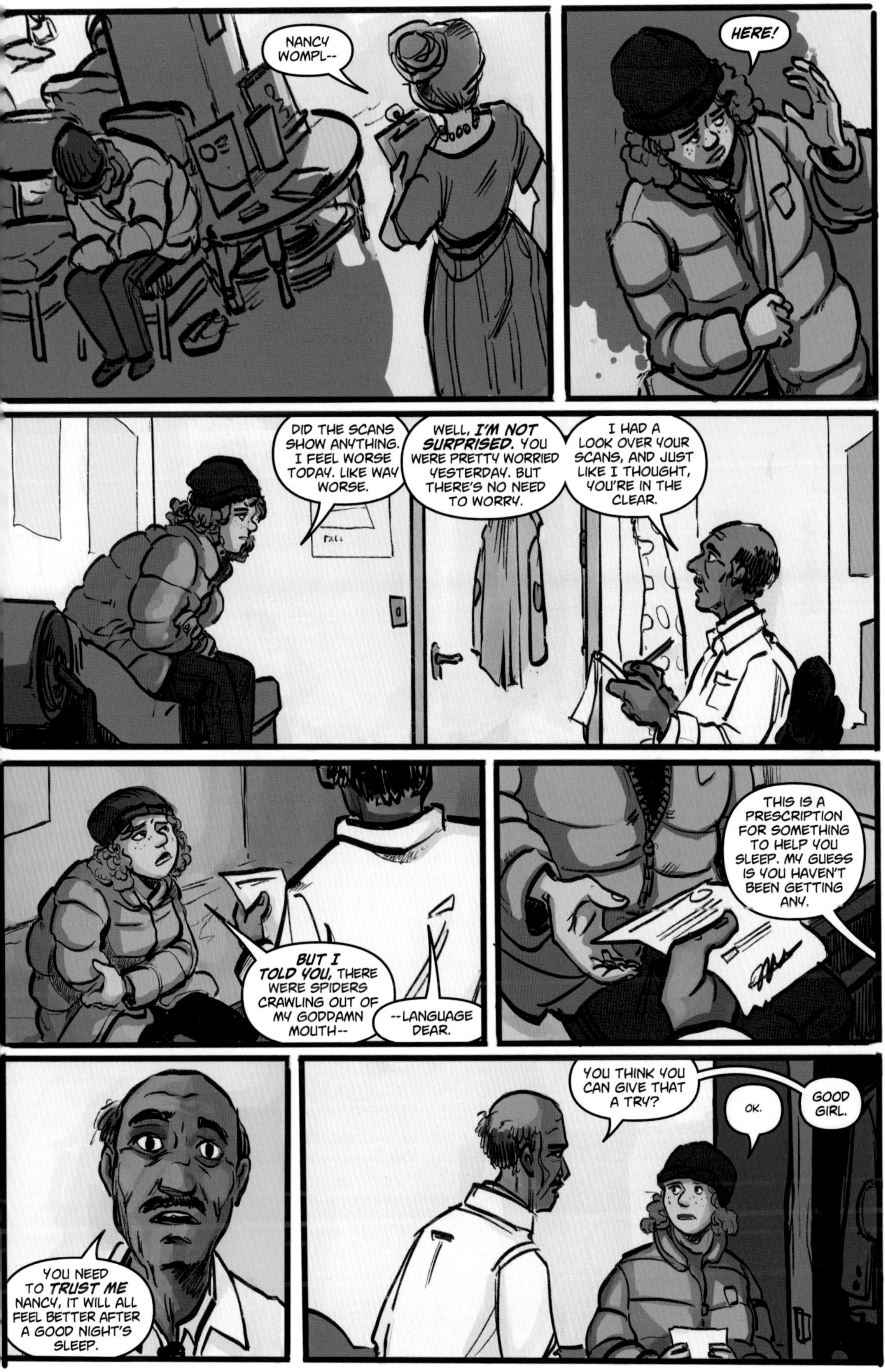
NANCY WOMPL--
HERE!
DID THE SCANS SHOW ANYTHING. I FEEL WORSE TODAY. LIKE WAY WORSE.
WELL, I'M NOT SURPRISED. YOU WERE PRETTY WORRIED YESTERDAY. BUT THERE'S NO NEED TO WORRY.
I HAD A LOOK OVER YOUR SCANS, AND JUST LIKE I THOUGHT, YOU'RE IN THE CLEAR.
BUT I TOLD YOU, THERE WERE SPIDERS CRAWLING OUT OF MY GODDAMN MOUTH--
--LANGUAGE DEAR.
THIS IS A PRESCRIPTION FOR SOMETHING TO HELP YOU SLEEP. MY GUESS IS YOU HAVEN'T BEEN GETTING ANY.
YOU NEED TO TRUST ME NANCY, IT WILL ALL FEEL BETTER AFTER A GOOD NIGHT'S SLEEP.
YOU THINK YOU CAN GIVE THAT A TRY?
OK.
GOOD GIRL.

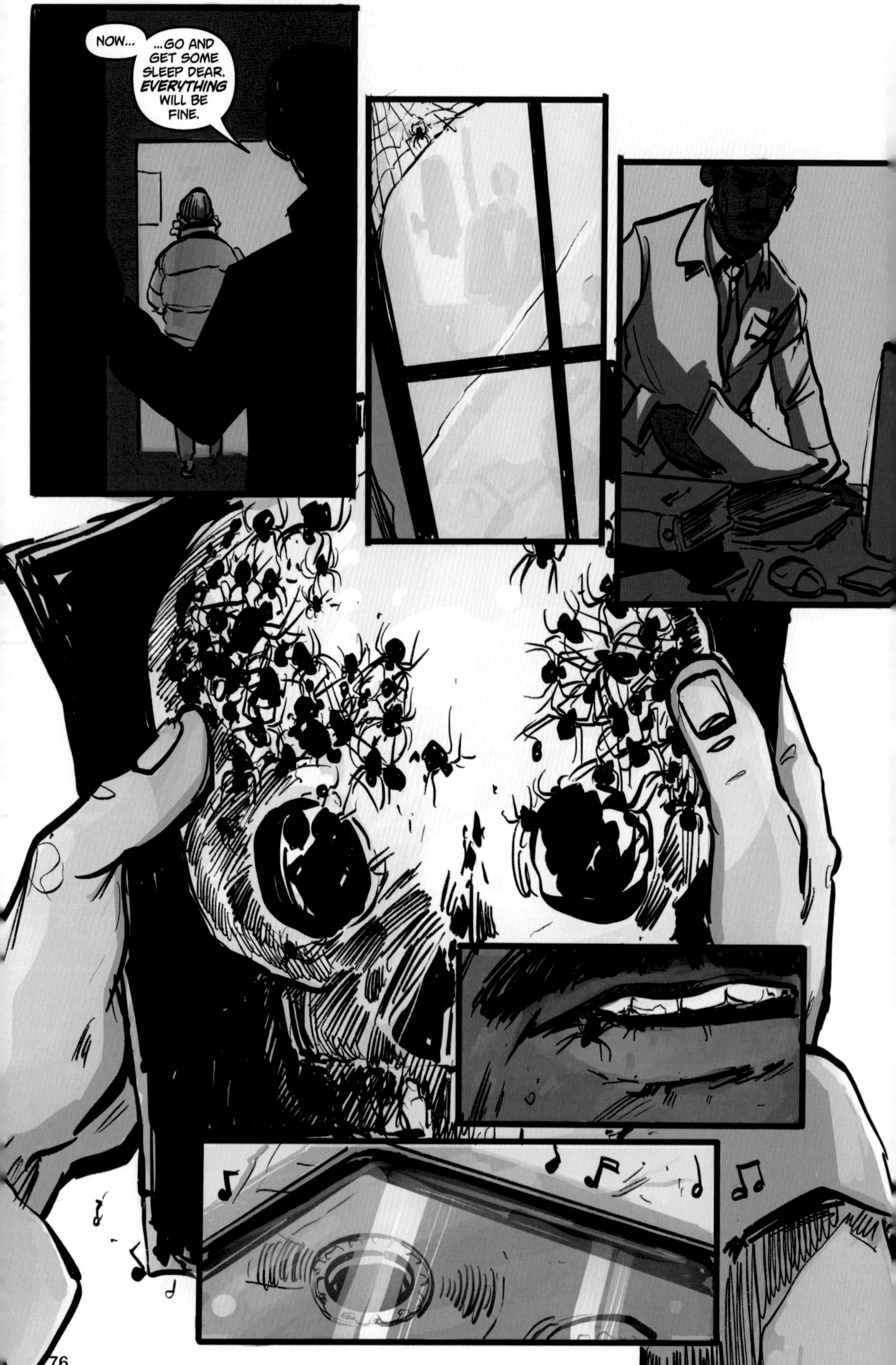
NOW...
...GO AND GET SOME SLEEP DEAR. EVERYTHING WILL BE FINE.

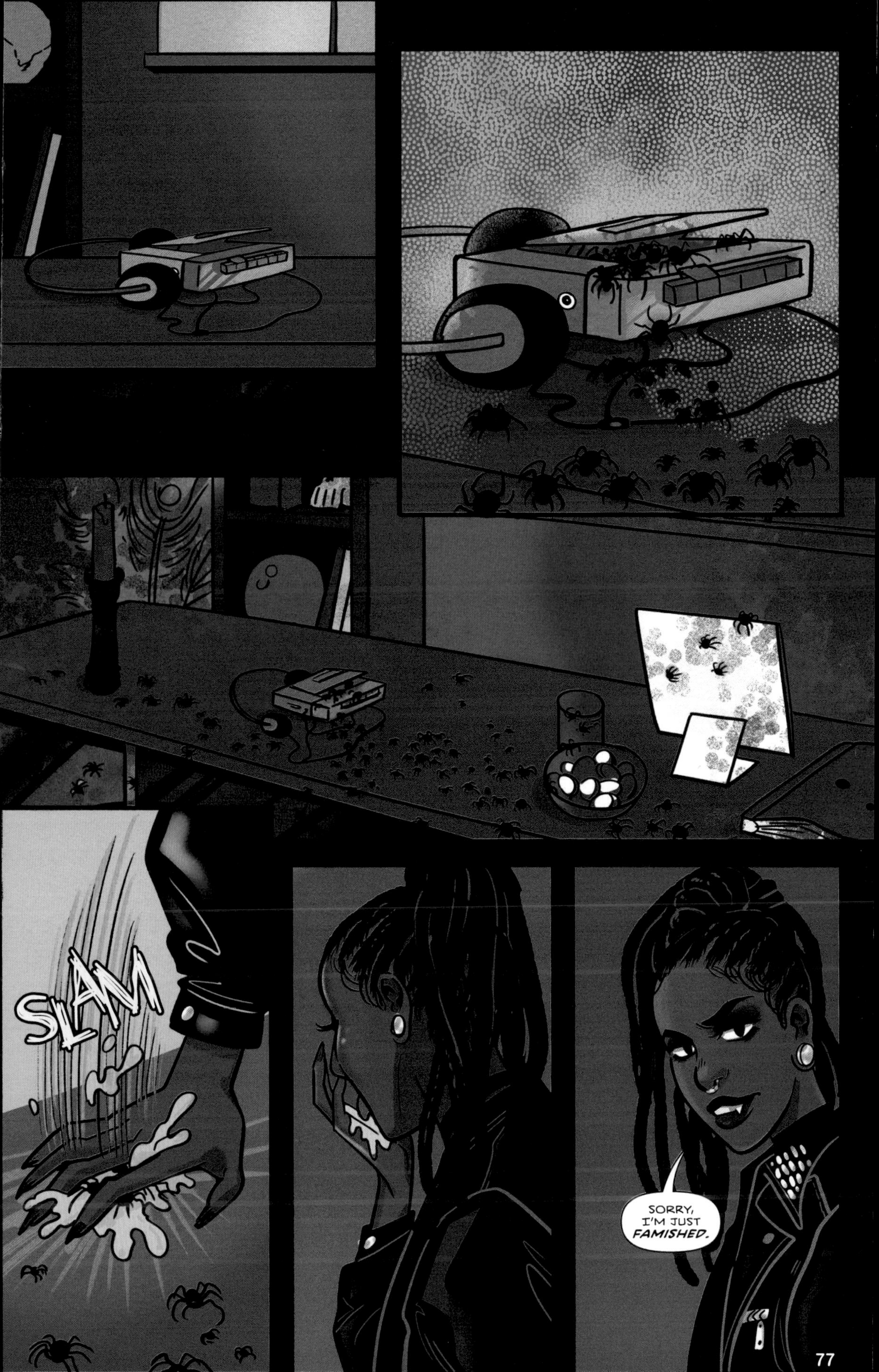
SLAM
SORRY, I'M JUST *FAMISHED.*

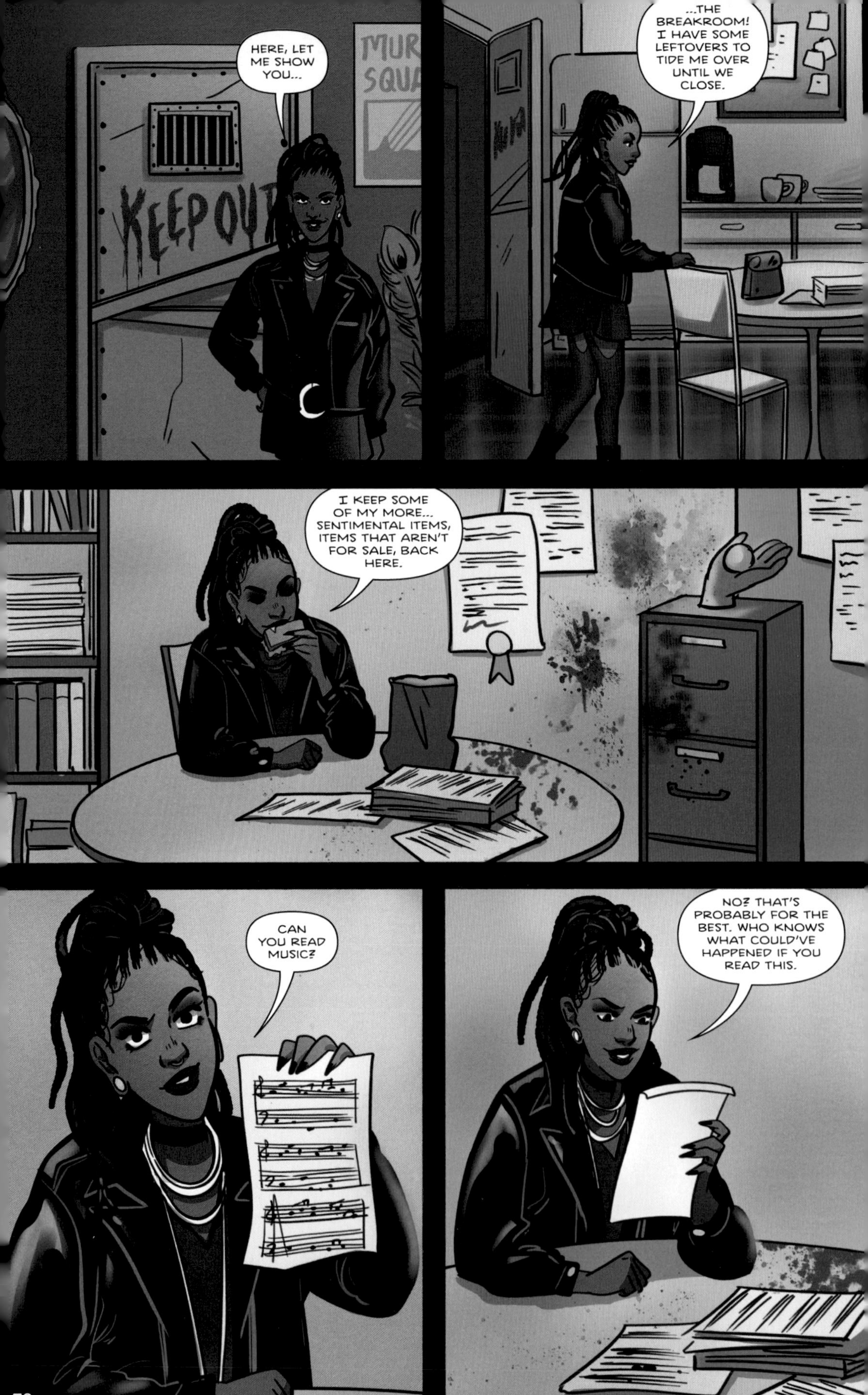
HERE, LET ME SHOW YOU...
...THE BREAKROOM! I HAVE SOME LEFTOVERS TO TIDE ME OVER UNTIL WE CLOSE.
I KEEP SOME OF MY MORE... SENTIMENTAL ITEMS, ITEMS THAT AREN'T FOR SALE, BACK HERE.
CAN YOU READ MUSIC?
NO? THAT'S PROBABLY FOR THE BEST. WHO KNOWS WHAT COULD'VE HAPPENED IF YOU READ THIS.

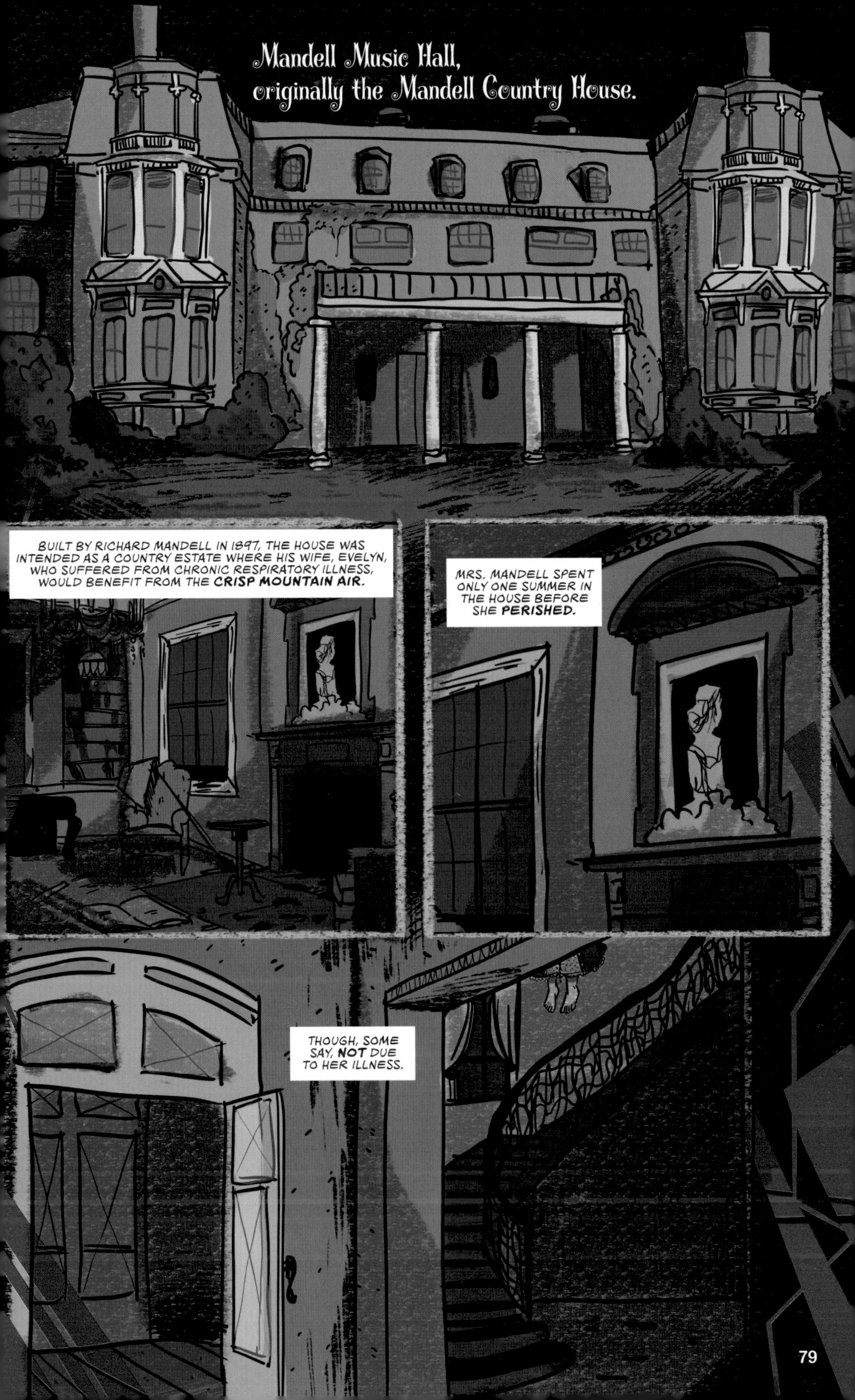
Mandell Music Hall,
originally the Mandell Country House.
BUILT BY RICHARD MANDELL IN 1897, THE HOUSE WAS INTENDED AS A COUNTRY ESTATE WHERE HIS WIFE, EVELYN, WHO SUFFERED FROM CHRONIC RESPIRATORY ILLNESS, WOULD BENEFIT FROM THE CRISP MOUNTAIN AIR.
MRS. MANDELL SPENT ONLY ONE SUMMER IN THE HOUSE BEFORE SHE PERISHED.
THOUGH, SOME SAY, NOT DUE TO HER ILLNESS.

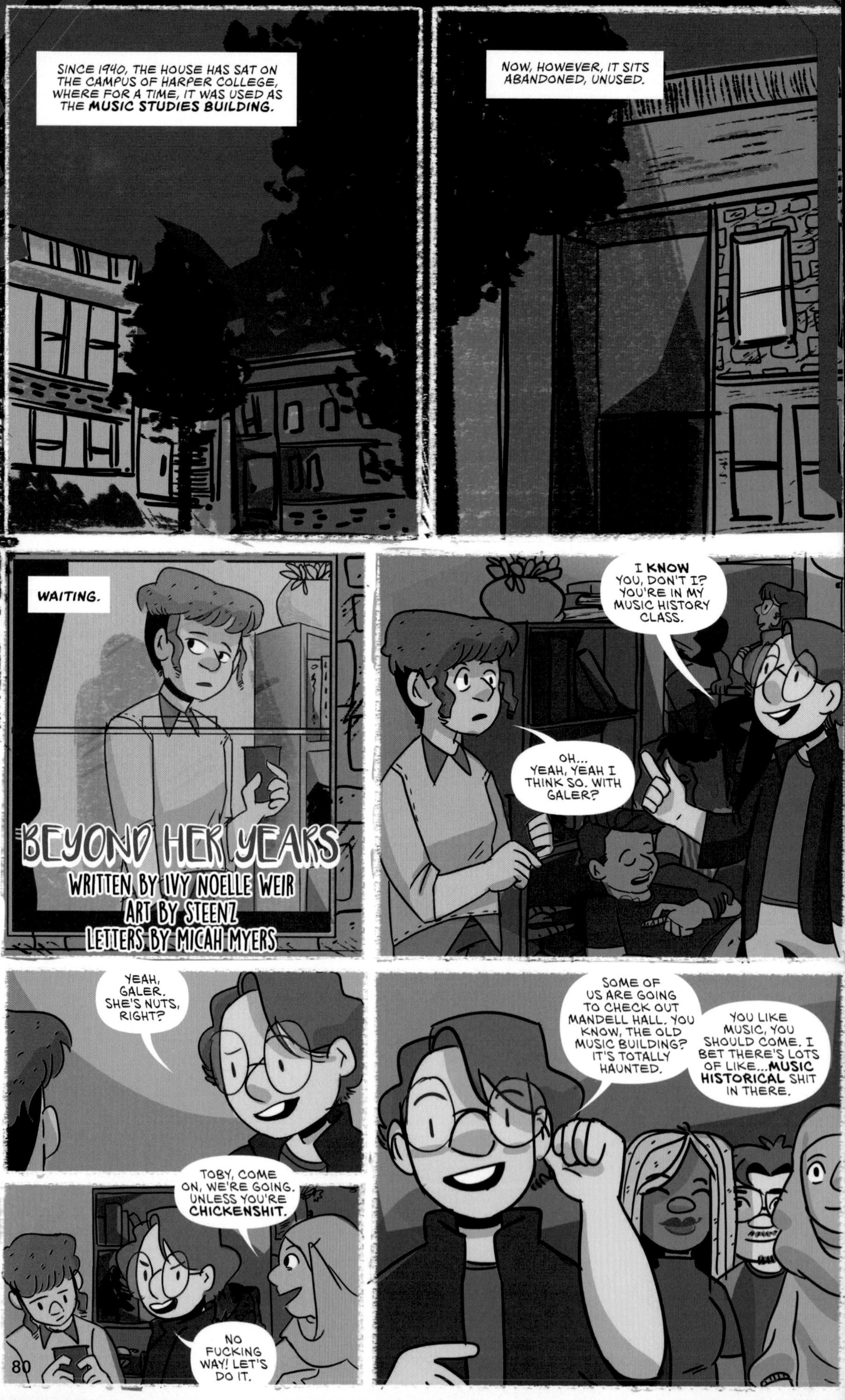

SINCE 1940, THE HOUSE HAS SAT ON THE CAMPUS OF HARPER COLLEGE, WHERE FOR A TIME, IT WAS USED AS THE **MUSIC STUDIES BUILDING.**
NOW, HOWEVER, IT SITS ABANDONED, UNUSED.
WAITING.
BEYOND HER YEARS
WRITTEN BY IVY NOELLE WEIR
ART BY STEENZ
LETTERS BY MICAH MYERS
I **KNOW** YOU, DON'T I? YOU'RE IN MY MUSIC HISTORY CLASS.
OH... YEAH, YEAH I THINK SO. WITH GALER?
YEAH, GALER. SHE'S NUTS, RIGHT?
SOME OF US ARE GOING TO CHECK OUT MANDELL HALL. YOU KNOW, THE OLD MUSIC BUILDING? IT'S TOTALLY HAUNTED.
YOU LIKE MUSIC, YOU SHOULD COME. I BET THERE'S LOTS OF LIKE... **MUSIC HISTORICAL** SHIT IN THERE.
TOBY, COME ON, WE'RE GOING. UNLESS YOU'RE **CHICKENSHIT.**
NO FUCKING WAY! LET'S DO IT.

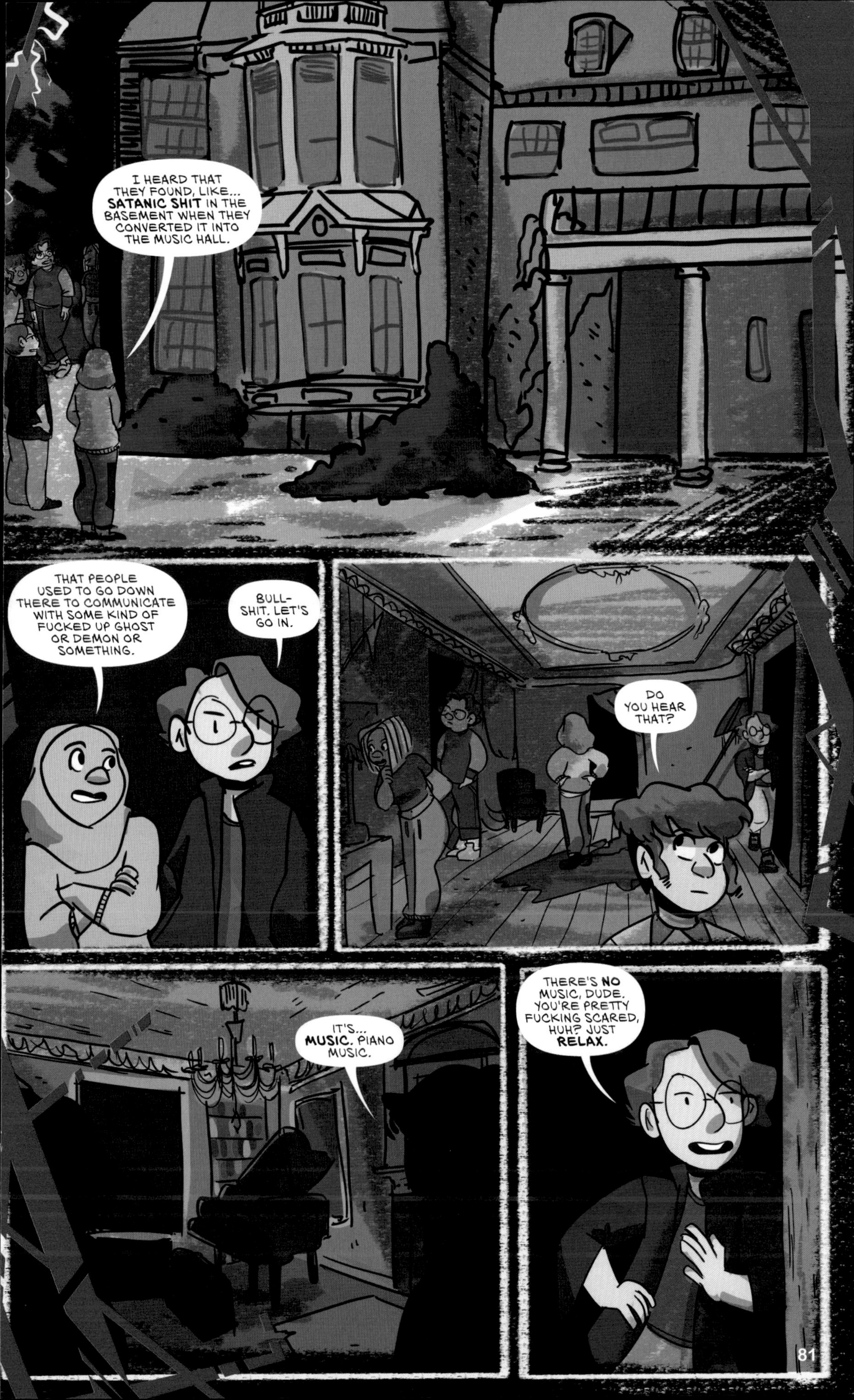
I HEARD THAT THEY FOUND, LIKE... SATANIC SHIT IN THE BASEMENT WHEN THEY CONVERTED IT INTO THE MUSIC HALL.
THAT PEOPLE USED TO GO DOWN THERE TO COMMUNICATE WITH SOME KIND OF FUCKED UP GHOST OR DEMON OR SOMETHING.
BULL-SHIT. LET'S GO IN.
DO YOU HEAR THAT?
IT'S... MUSIC. PIANO MUSIC.
THERE'S NO MUSIC, DUDE. YOU'RE PRETTY FUCKING SCARED, HUH? JUST RELAX.

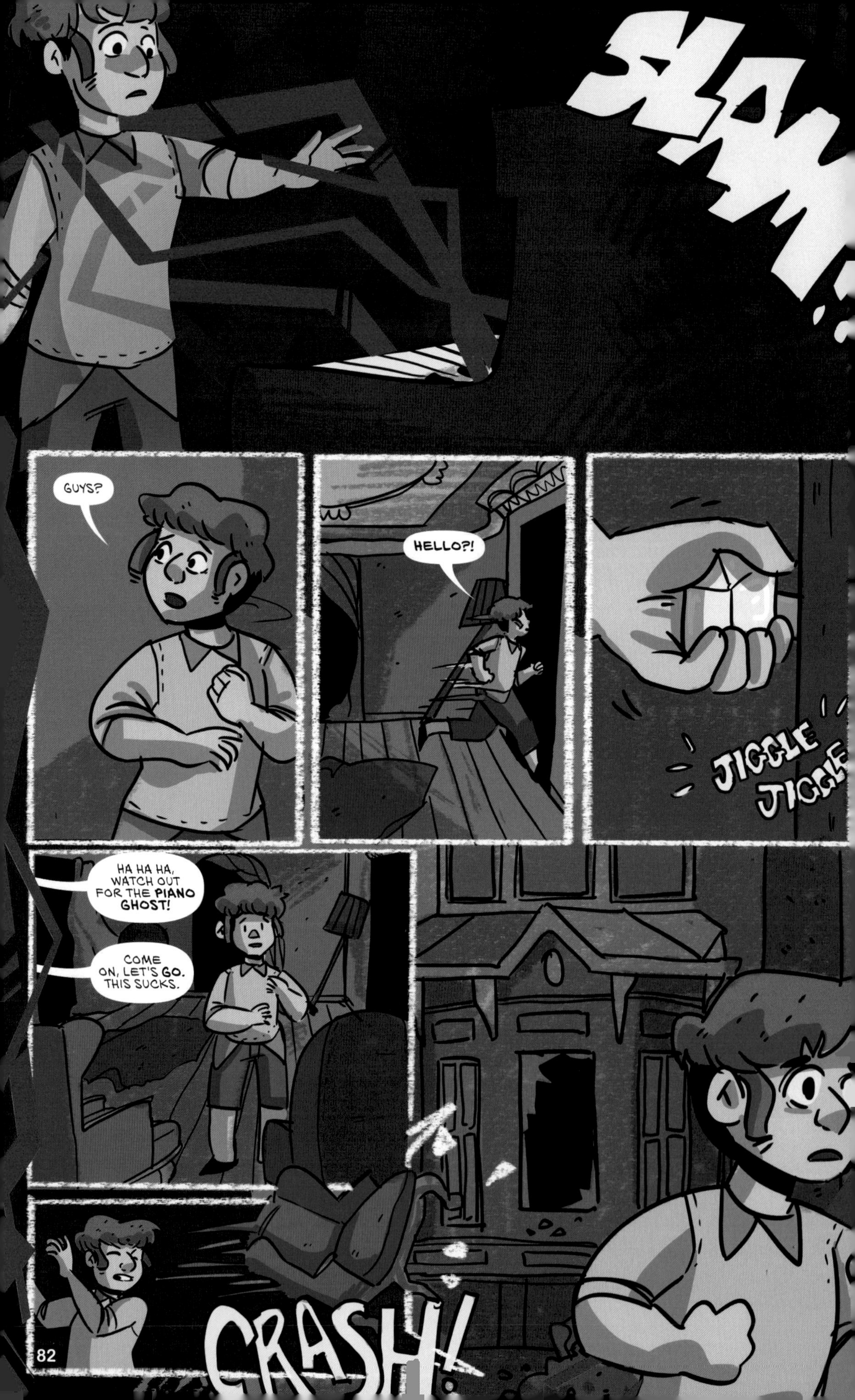
SLAM!!
GUYS?
HELLO?!
JIGGLE JIGGLE
HA HA HA, WATCH OUT FOR THE PIANO GHOST!
COME ON, LET'S GO. THIS SUCKS.
CRASH!

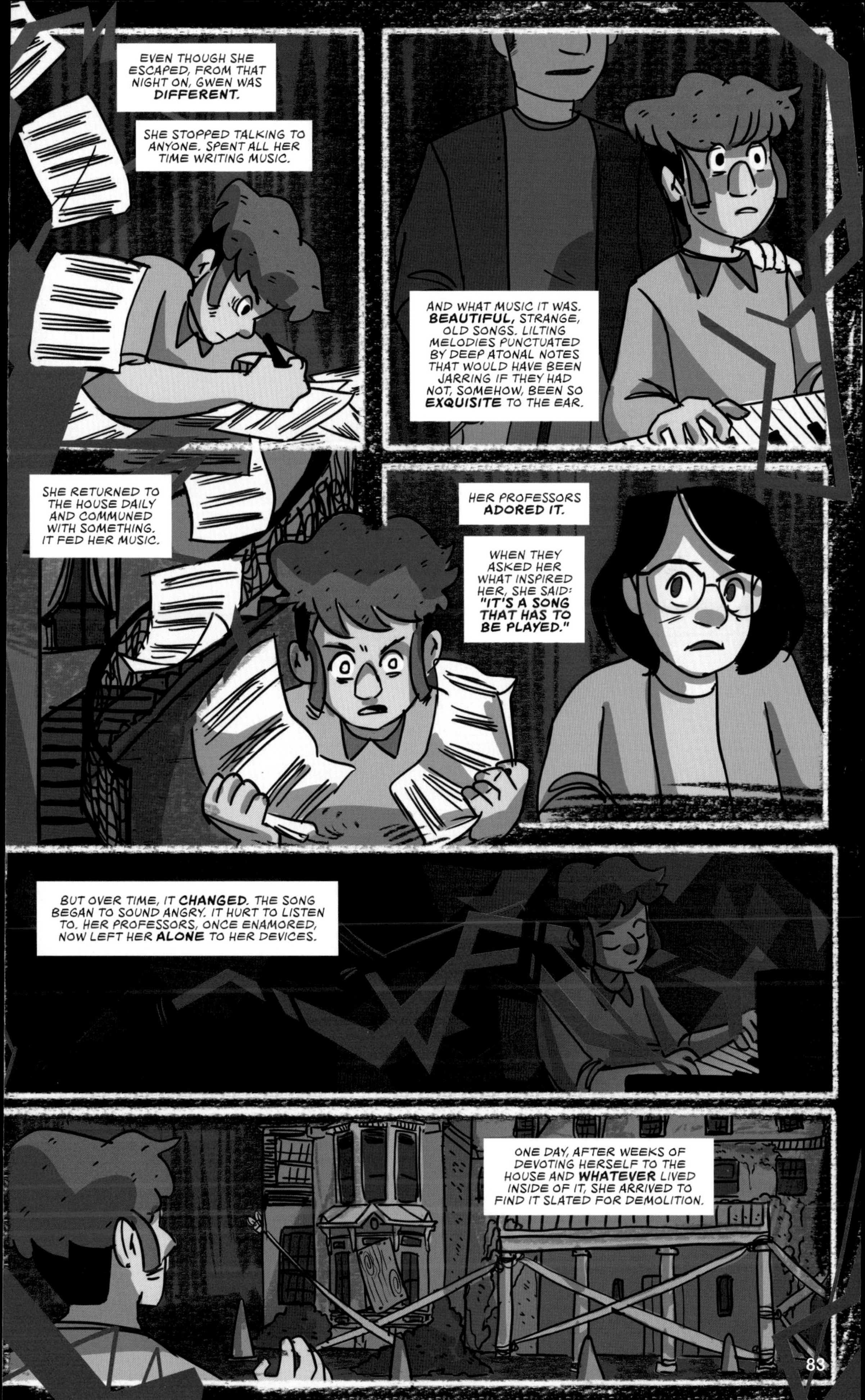
EVEN THOUGH SHE ESCAPED, FROM THAT NIGHT ON, GWEN WAS DIFFERENT.
SHE STOPPED TALKING TO ANYONE. SPENT ALL HER TIME WRITING MUSIC.
AND WHAT MUSIC IT WAS. BEAUTIFUL, STRANGE, OLD SONGS. LILTING MELODIES PUNCTUATED BY DEEP ATONAL NOTES THAT WOULD HAVE BEEN JARRING IF THEY HAD NOT, SOMEHOW, BEEN SO EXQUISITE TO THE EAR.
SHE RETURNED TO THE HOUSE DAILY AND COMMUNED WITH SOMETHING. IT FED HER MUSIC.
HER PROFESSORS ADORED IT.
WHEN THEY ASKED HER WHAT INSPIRED HER, SHE SAID: "IT'S A SONG THAT HAS TO BE PLAYED."
BUT OVER TIME, IT CHANGED. THE SONG BEGAN TO SOUND ANGRY. IT HURT TO LISTEN TO. HER PROFESSORS, ONCE ENAMORED, NOW LEFT HER ALONE TO HER DEVICES.
ONE DAY, AFTER WEEKS OF DEVOTING HERSELF TO THE HOUSE AND WHATEVER LIVED INSIDE OF IT, SHE ARRIVED TO FIND IT SLATED FOR DEMOLITION.

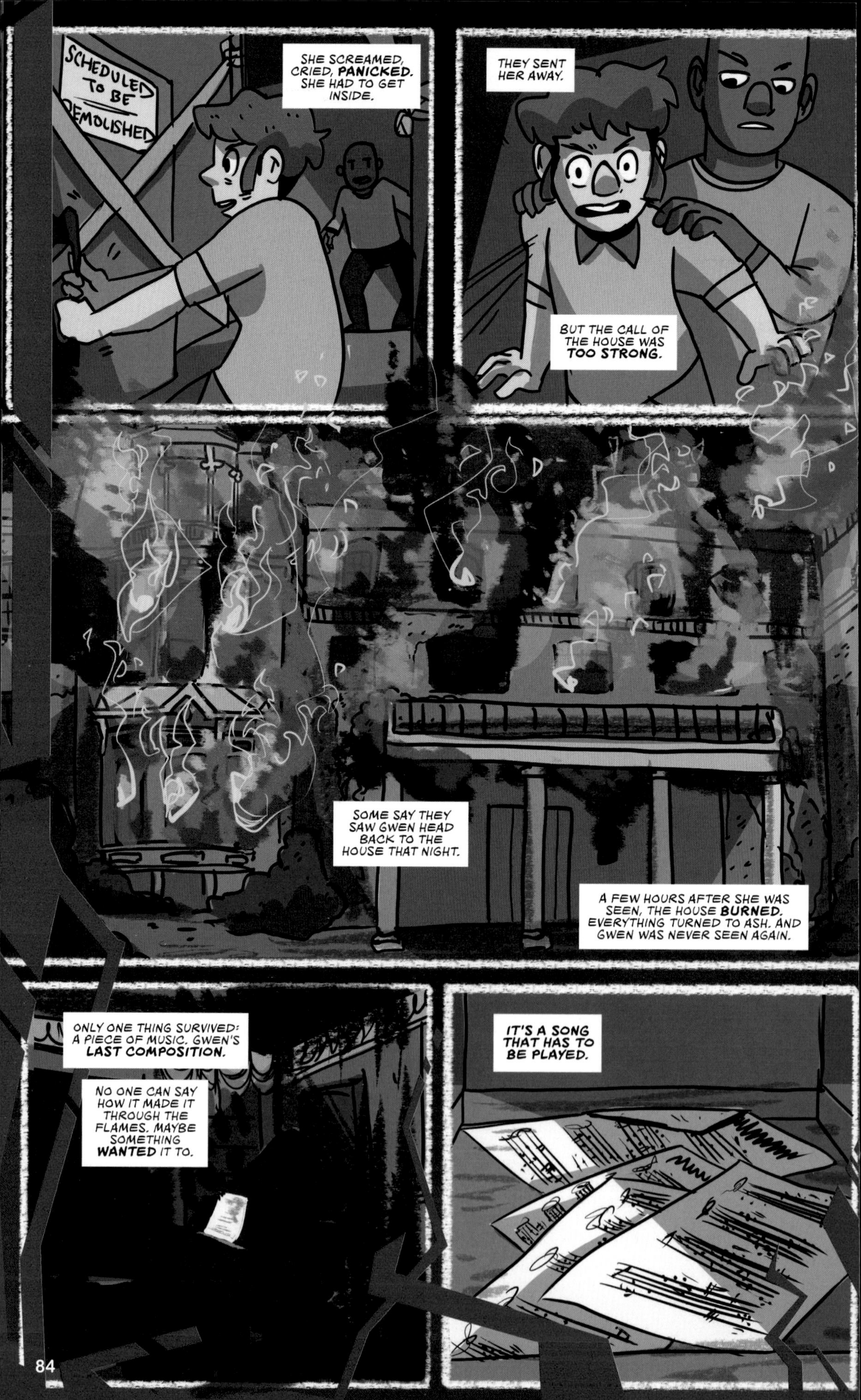
SCHEDULED TO BE DEMOLISHED
SHE SCREAMED, CRIED, **PANICKED.** SHE HAD TO GET INSIDE.
THEY SENT HER AWAY.
BUT THE CALL OF THE HOUSE WAS **TOO STRONG.**
SOME SAY THEY SAW GWEN HEAD BACK TO THE HOUSE THAT NIGHT.
A FEW HOURS AFTER SHE WAS SEEN, THE HOUSE **BURNED.** EVERYTHING TURNED TO ASH. AND GWEN WAS NEVER SEEN AGAIN.
ONLY ONE THING SURVIVED: A PIECE OF MUSIC. GWEN'S **LAST COMPOSITION.**
NO ONE CAN SAY HOW IT MADE IT THROUGH THE FLAMES. MAYBE SOMETHING **WANTED** IT TO.
IT'S A SONG THAT HAS TO BE PLAYED.

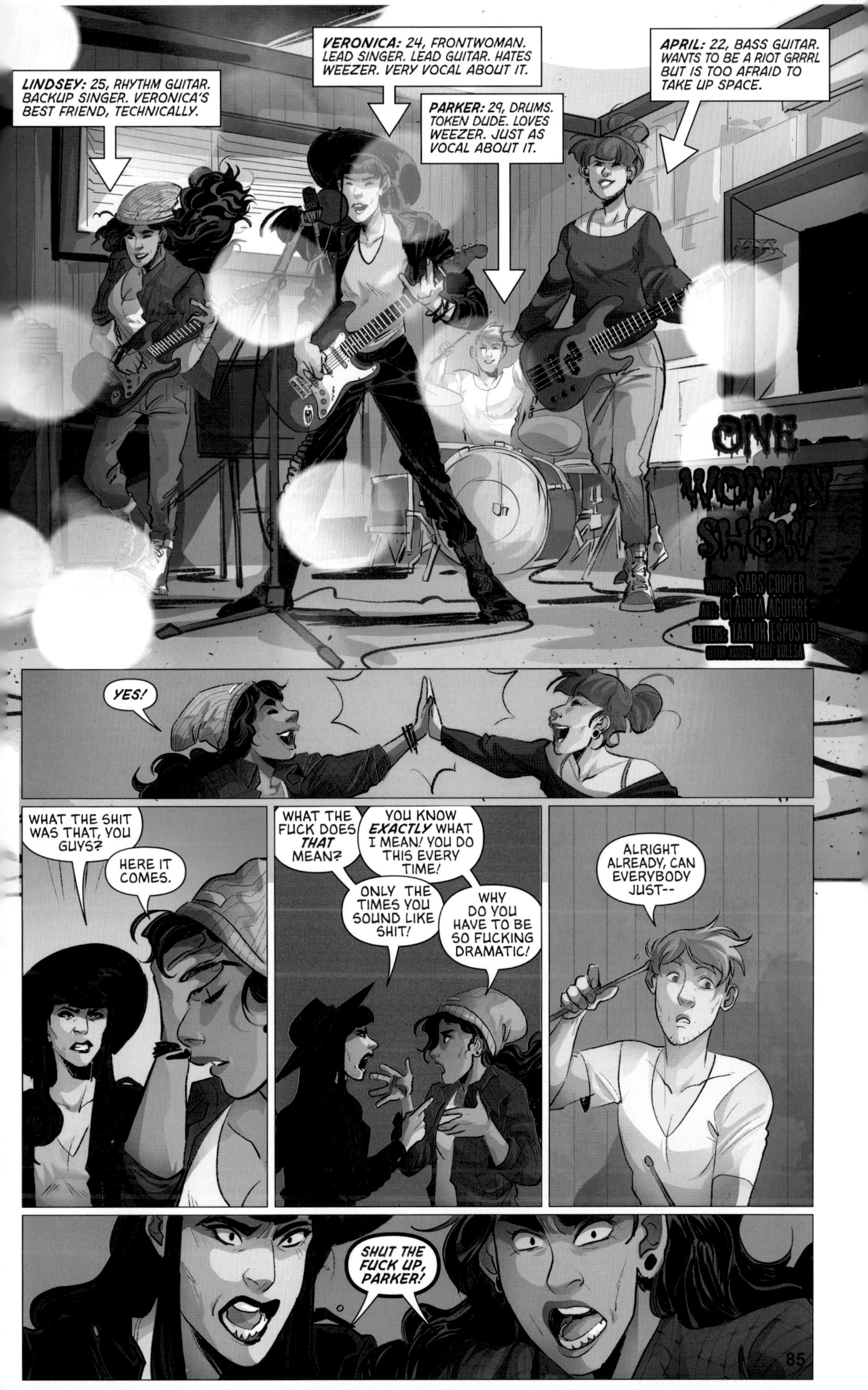
VERONICA: 24, FRONTWOMAN. LEAD SINGER. LEAD GUITAR. HATES WEEZER. VERY VOCAL ABOUT IT.
APRIL: 22, BASS GUITAR. WANTS TO BE A RIOT GRRRL BUT IS TOO AFRAID TO TAKE UP SPACE.
LINDSEY: 25, RHYTHM GUITAR. BACKUP SINGER. VERONICA'S BEST FRIEND, TECHNICALLY.
PARKER: 29, DRUMS. TOKEN DUDE. LOVES WEEZER. JUST AS VOCAL ABOUT IT.
ONE WOMAN SHOW
WORDS: SABS COOPER
ART: CLAUDIA AGUIRRE
LETTERS: TAYLOR ESPOSITO
LETTER ASSISTS: PIXIE KOLESA
YES!
WHAT THE SHIT WAS THAT, YOU GUYS?
HERE IT COMES.
WHAT THE FUCK DOES THAT MEAN?
YOU KNOW EXACTLY WHAT I MEAN! YOU DO THIS EVERY TIME!
ONLY THE TIMES YOU SOUND LIKE SHIT!
WHY DO YOU HAVE TO BE SO FUCKING DRAMATIC!
ALRIGHT ALREADY, CAN EVERYBODY JUST--
SHUT THE FUCK UP, PARKER!

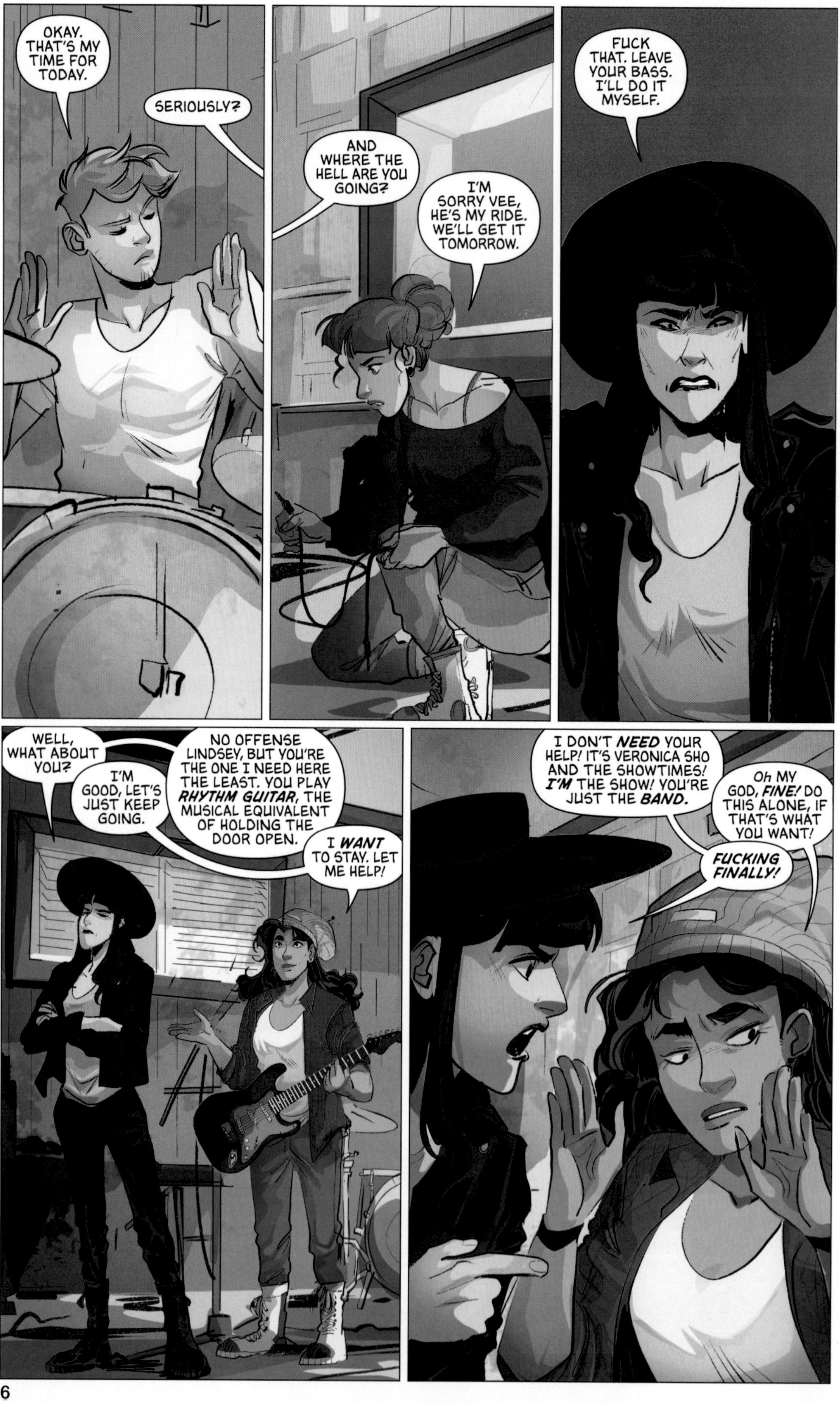
OKAY. THAT'S MY TIME FOR TODAY.
SERIOUSLY?
AND WHERE THE HELL ARE YOU GOING?
I'M SORRY VEE, HE'S MY RIDE. WE'LL GET IT TOMORROW.
FUCK THAT. LEAVE YOUR BASS. I'LL DO IT MYSELF.
WELL, WHAT ABOUT YOU?
I'M GOOD, LET'S JUST KEEP GOING.
NO OFFENSE LINDSEY, BUT YOU'RE THE ONE I NEED HERE THE LEAST. YOU PLAY RHYTHM GUITAR, THE MUSICAL EQUIVALENT OF HOLDING THE DOOR OPEN.
I WANT TO STAY. LET ME HELP!
I DON'T NEED YOUR HELP! IT'S VERONICA SHO AND THE SHOWTIMES! I'M THE SHOW! YOU'RE JUST THE BAND.
Oh MY GOD, FINE! DO THIS ALONE, IF THAT'S WHAT YOU WANT!
FUCKING FINALLY!

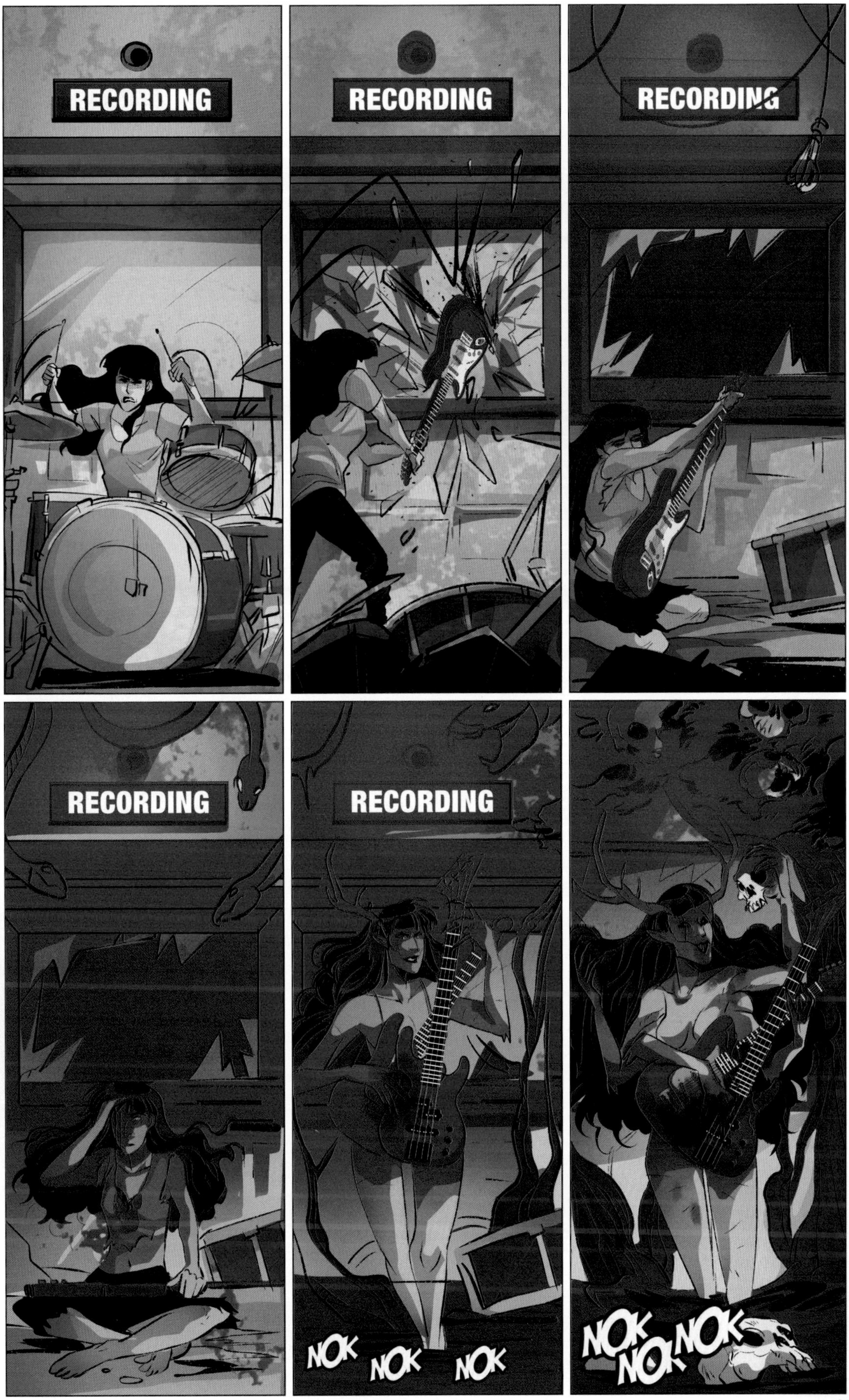
RECORDING
RECORDING
RECORDING
RECORDING
RECORDING
NOK
NOK
NOK
NOK
NOK
NOK

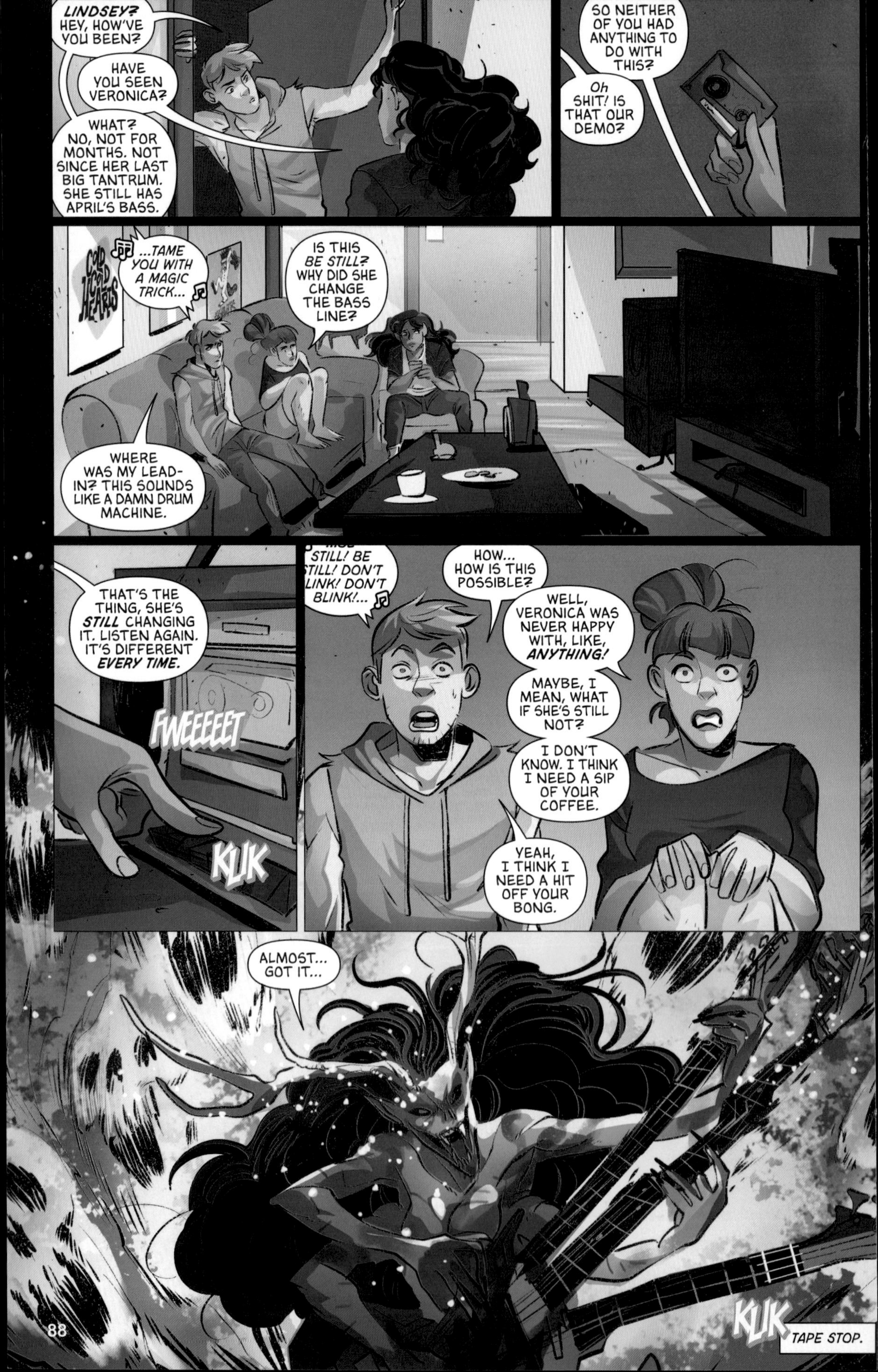
LINDSEY? HEY, HOW'VE YOU BEEN?
HAVE YOU SEEN VERONICA?
WHAT? NO, NOT FOR MONTHS. NOT SINCE HER LAST BIG TANTRUM. SHE STILL HAS APRIL'S BASS.
SO NEITHER OF YOU HAD ANYTHING TO DO WITH THIS?
Oh SHIT! IS THAT OUR DEMO?
COLD COLD HEARTS
...TAME YOU WITH A MAGIC TRICK...
IS THIS BE STILL? WHY DID SHE CHANGE THE BASS LINE?
WHERE WAS MY LEAD-IN? THIS SOUNDS LIKE A DAMN DRUM MACHINE.
THAT'S THE THING, SHE'S STILL CHANGING IT. LISTEN AGAIN. IT'S DIFFERENT EVERY TIME.
FWEEEEET
KLIK
STILL! BE STILL! DON'T BLINK! DON'T BLINK!...
HOW... HOW IS THIS POSSIBLE?
WELL, VERONICA WAS NEVER HAPPY WITH, LIKE, ANYTHING!
MAYBE, I MEAN, WHAT IF SHE'S STILL NOT?
I DON'T KNOW. I THINK I NEED A SIP OF YOUR COFFEE.
YEAH, I THINK I NEED A HIT OFF YOUR BONG.
ALMOST... GOT IT...
KLIK
TAPE STOP.

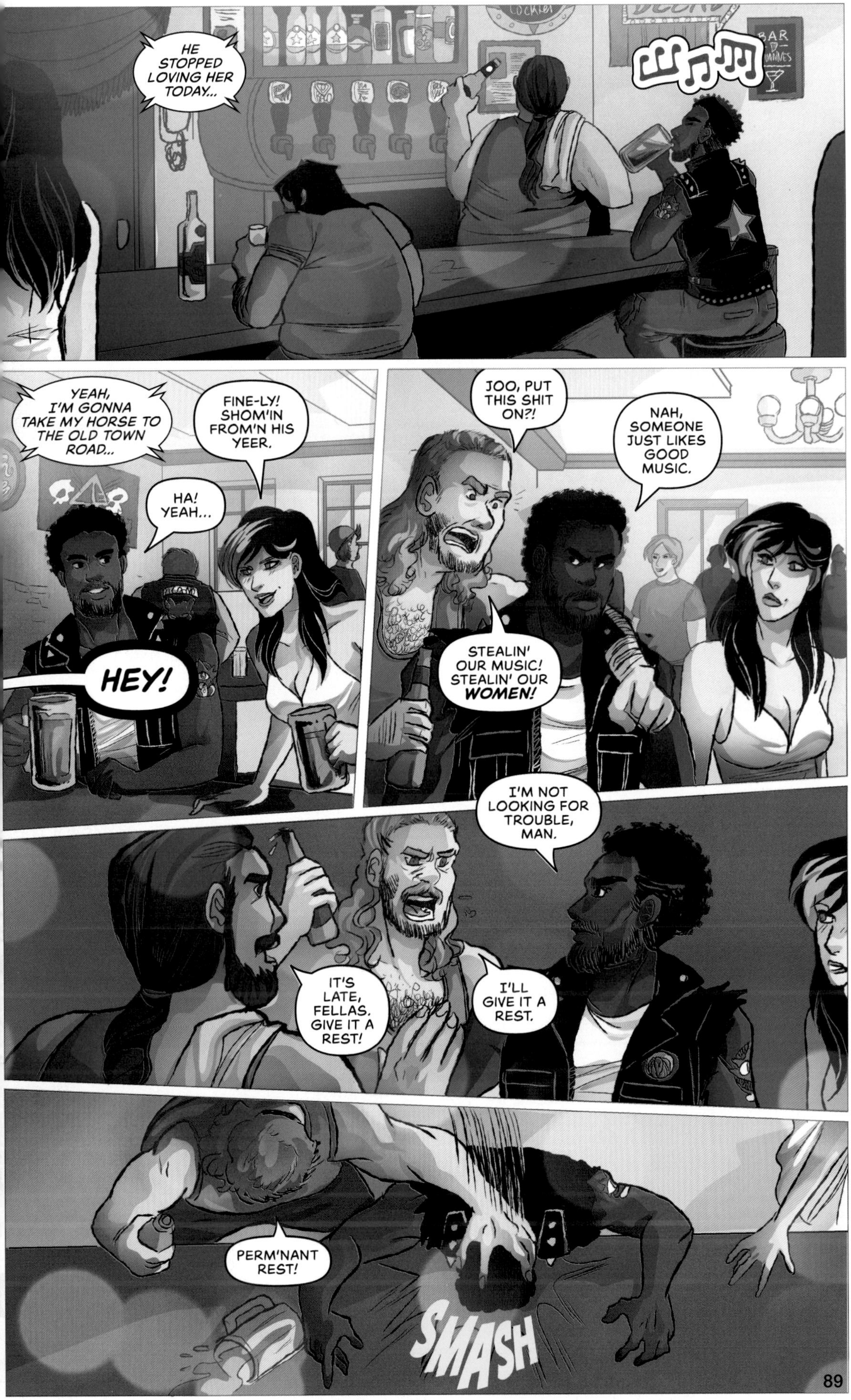
HE STOPPED LOVING HER TODAY...
YEAH, I'M GONNA TAKE MY HORSE TO THE OLD TOWN ROAD...
FINE-LY! SHOM'IN FROM'N HIS YEER.
HA! YEAH...
HEY!
JOO, PUT THIS SHIT ON?!
NAH, SOMEONE JUST LIKES GOOD MUSIC.
STEALIN' OUR MUSIC! STEALIN' OUR WOMEN!
I'M NOT LOOKING FOR TROUBLE, MAN.
IT'S LATE, FELLAS. GIVE IT A REST!
I'LL GIVE IT A REST.
PERM'NANT REST!
SMASH

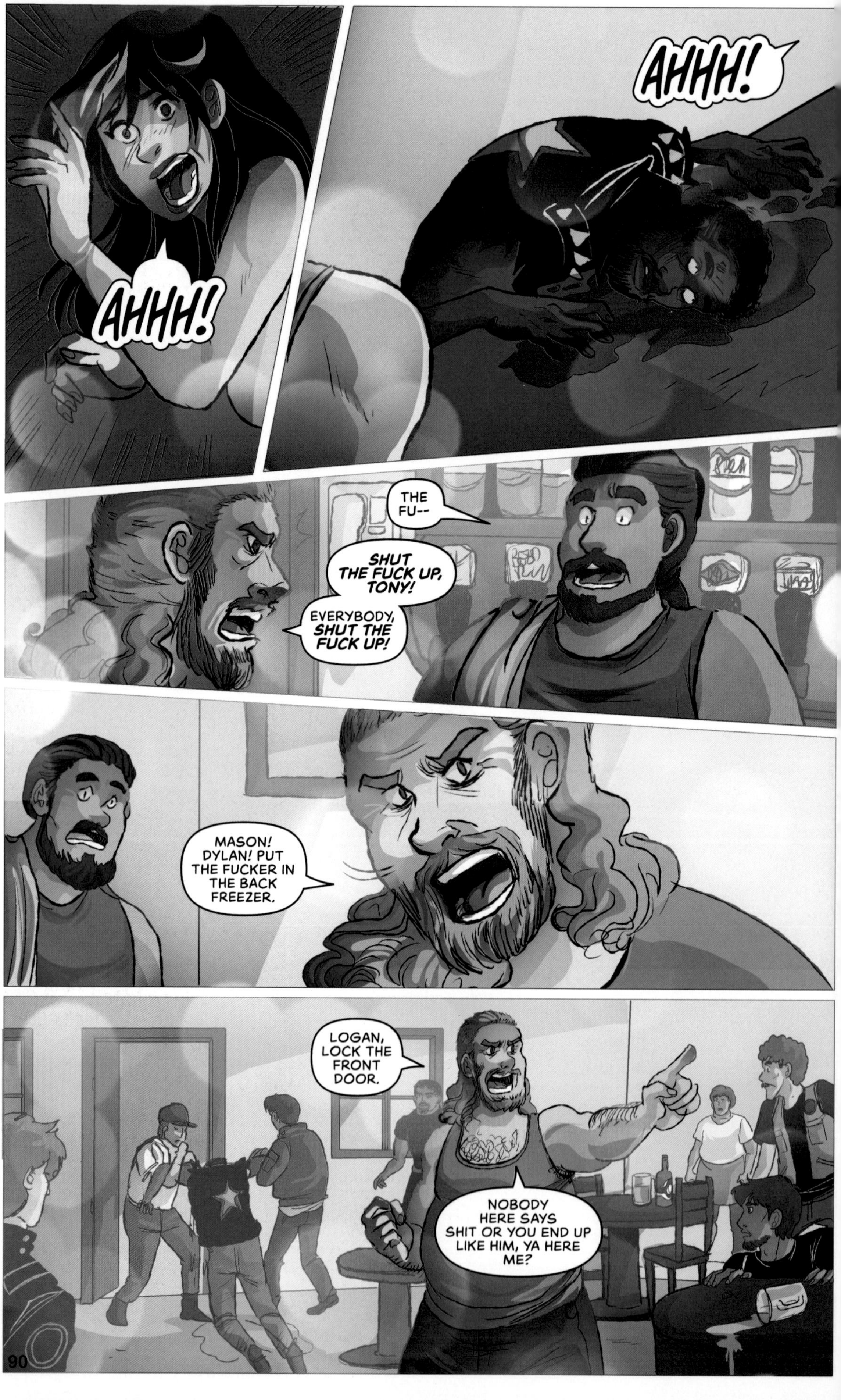
AHHH!
AHHH!
THE FU--
SHUT THE FUCK UP, TONY!
EVERYBODY, SHUT THE FUCK UP!
MASON! DYLAN! PUT THE FUCKER IN THE BACK FREEZER.
LOGAN, LOCK THE FRONT DOOR.
NOBODY HERE SAYS SHIT OR YOU END UP LIKE HIM, YA HERE ME?

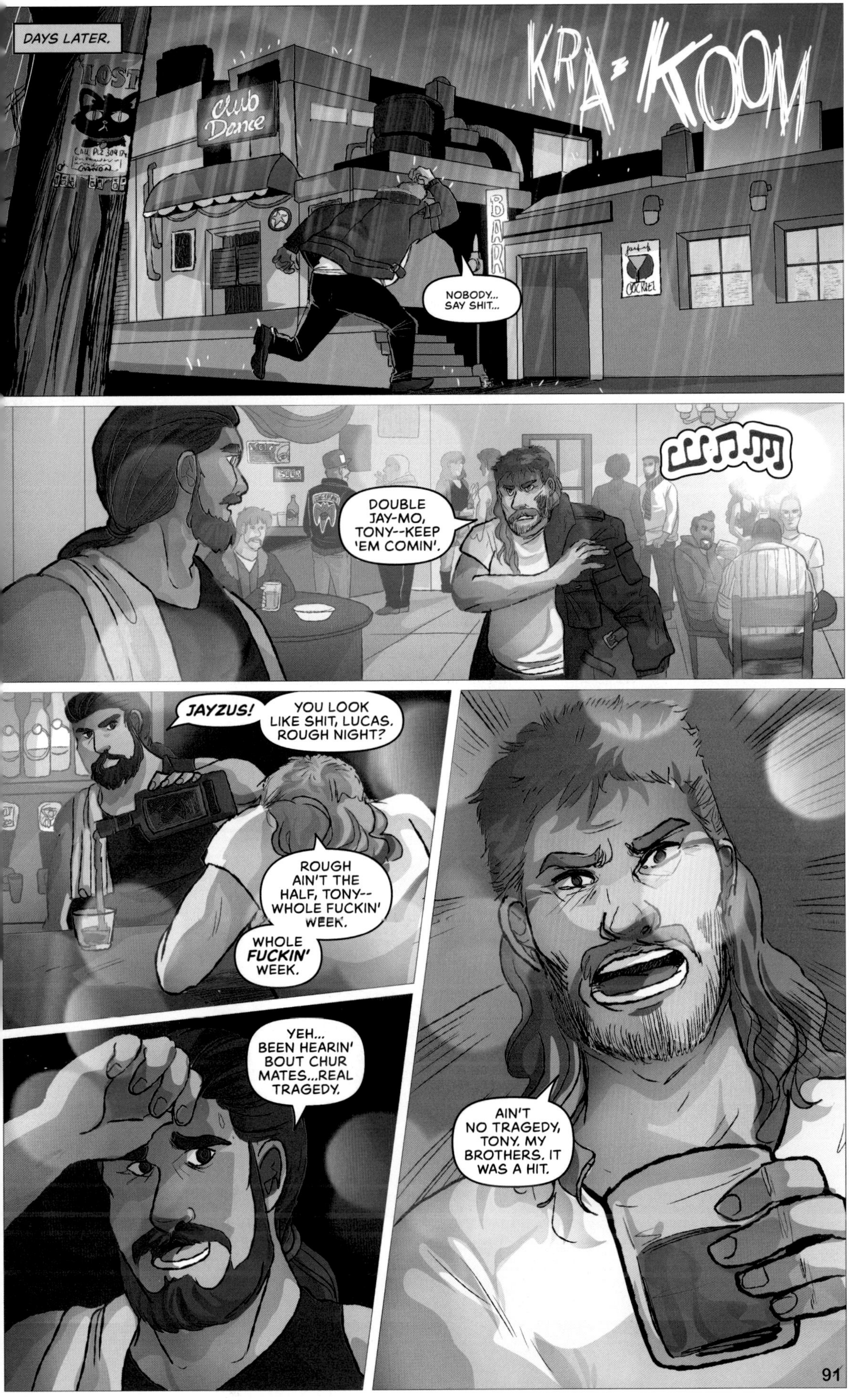
DAYS LATER.
KRA-KOOM
Club Dance
BAR
LOST
NOBODY... SAY SHIT...
DOUBLE JAY-MO, TONY--KEEP 'EM COMIN'.
JAYZUS!
YOU LOOK LIKE SHIT, LUCAS. ROUGH NIGHT?
ROUGH AIN'T THE HALF, TONY-- WHOLE FUCKIN' WEEK.
WHOLE *FUCKIN'* WEEK.
YEH... BEEN HEARIN' BOUT CHUR MATES...REAL TRAGEDY.
AIN'T NO TRAGEDY, TONY. MY BROTHERS. IT WAS A HIT.

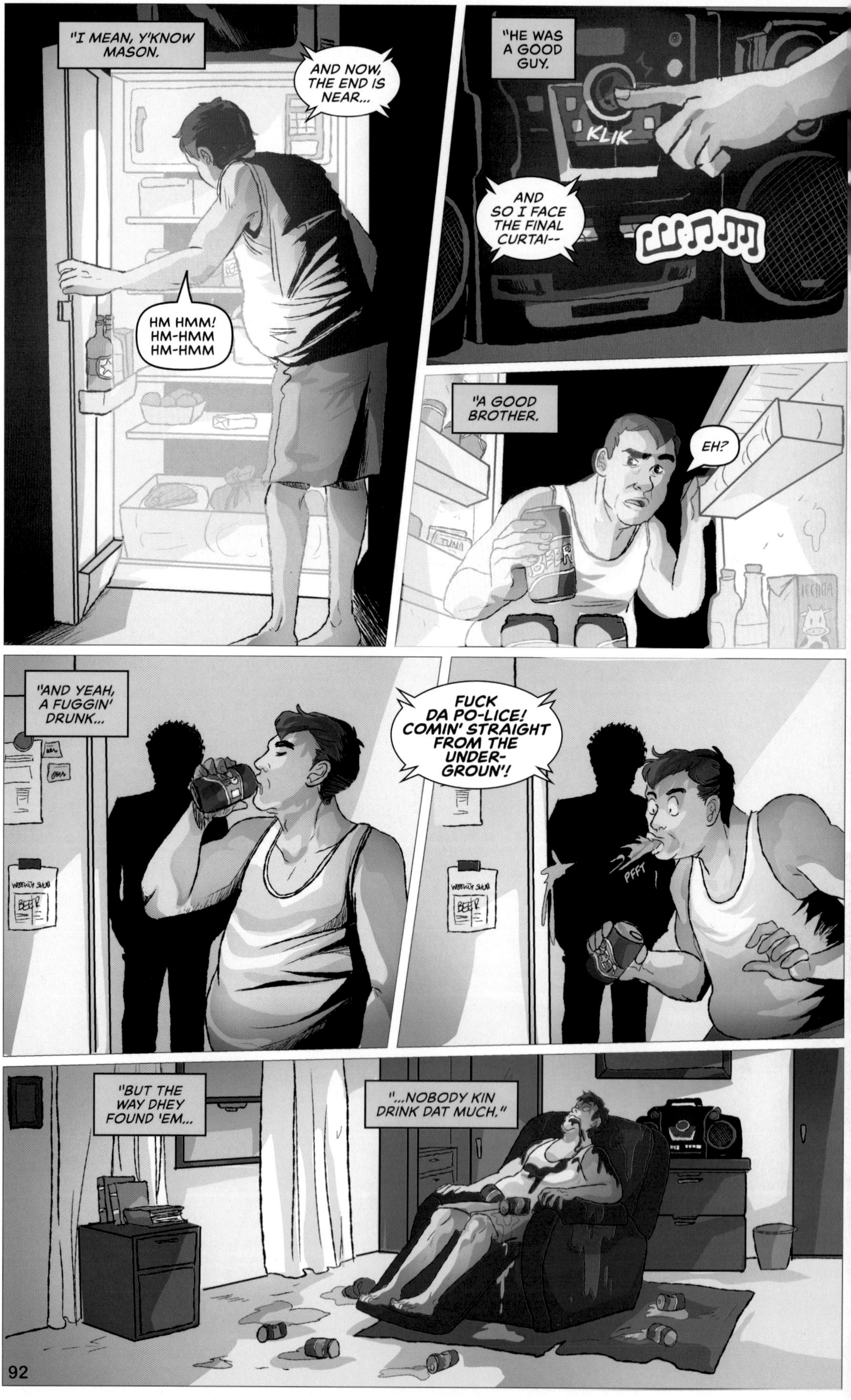
"I MEAN, Y'KNOW MASON.
AND NOW, THE END IS NEAR...
HM HMM! HM-HMM HM-HMM
"HE WAS A GOOD GUY.
KLIK
AND SO I FACE THE FINAL CURTAI--
"A GOOD BROTHER.
EH?
BEER
TUNA
"AND YEAH, A FUGGIN' DRUNK...
FUCK DA PO-LICE! COMIN' STRAIGHT FROM THE UNDER-GROUN'!
PFFT
"BUT THE WAY DHEY FOUND 'EM...
"...NOBODY KIN DRINK DAT MUCH."

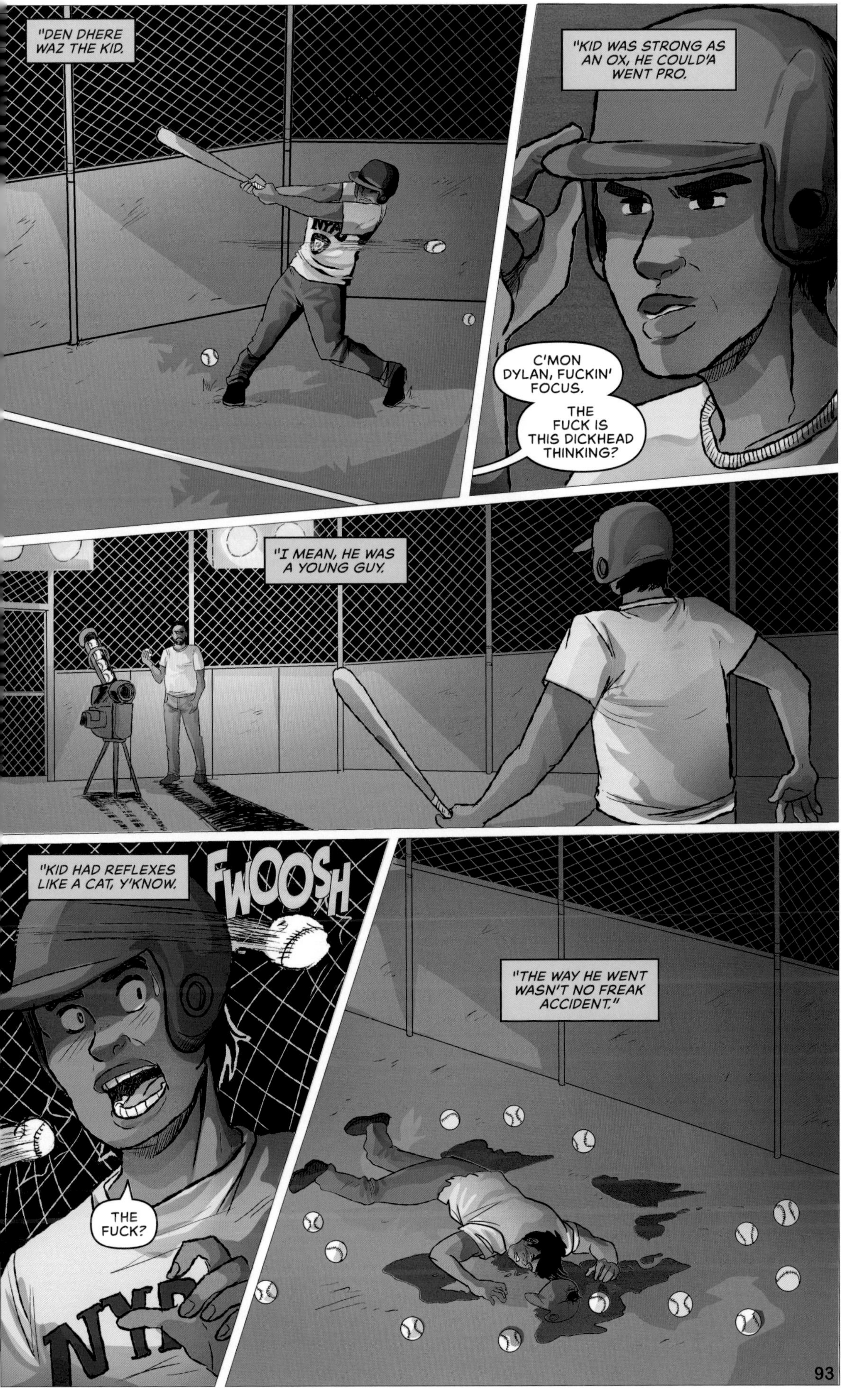
"DEN DHERE WAZ THE KID.
"KID WAS STRONG AS AN OX, HE COULD'A WENT PRO.
C'MON DYLAN, FUCKIN' FOCUS.
THE FUCK IS THIS DICKHEAD THINKING?
"I MEAN, HE WAS A YOUNG GUY.
"KID HAD REFLEXES LIKE A CAT, Y'KNOW.
FWOOSH
THE FUCK?
"THE WAY HE WENT WASN'T NO FREAK ACCIDENT."

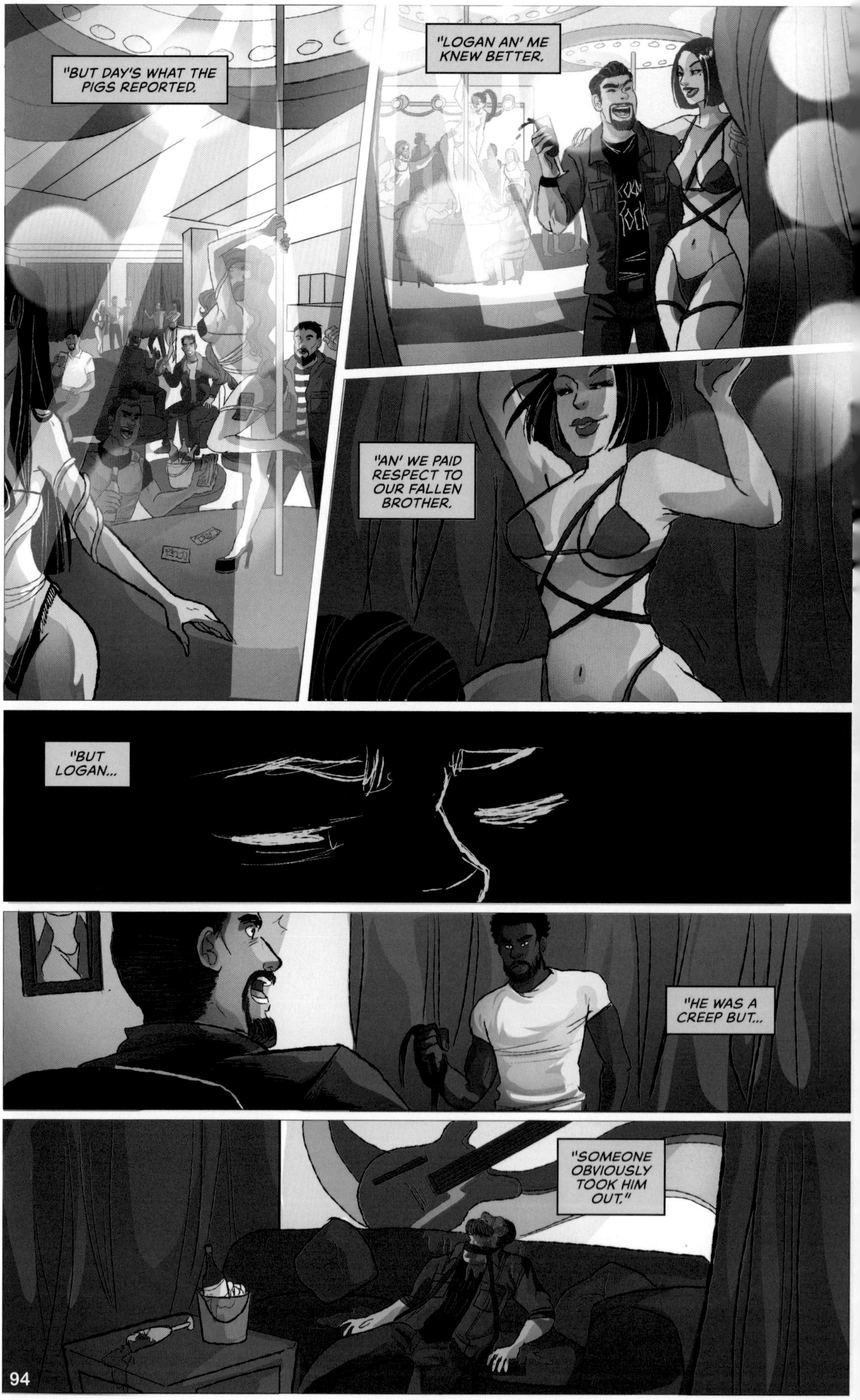
"BUT DAY'S WHAT THE PIGS REPORTED.
"LOGAN AN' ME KNEW BETTER.
"AN' WE PAID RESPECT TO OUR FALLEN BROTHER.
"BUT LOGAN...
"HE WAS A CREEP BUT...
"SOMEONE OBVIOUSLY TOOK HIM OUT."

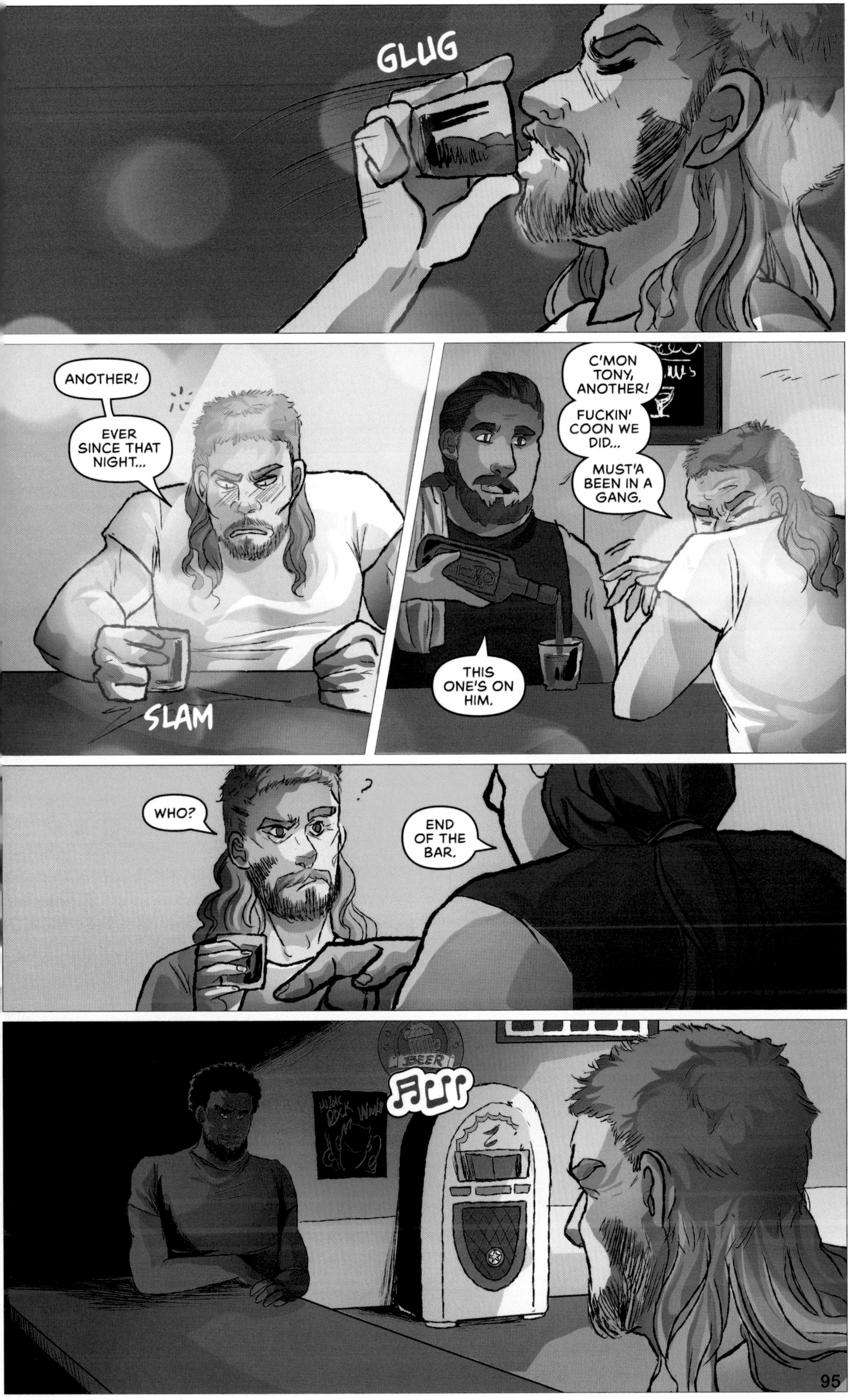
GLUG
ANOTHER!
EVER SINCE THAT NIGHT...
SLAM
C'MON TONY, ANOTHER!
FUCKIN' COON WE DID...
MUST'A BEEN IN A GANG.
THIS ONE'S ON HIM.
WHO?
END OF THE BAR.
BEER

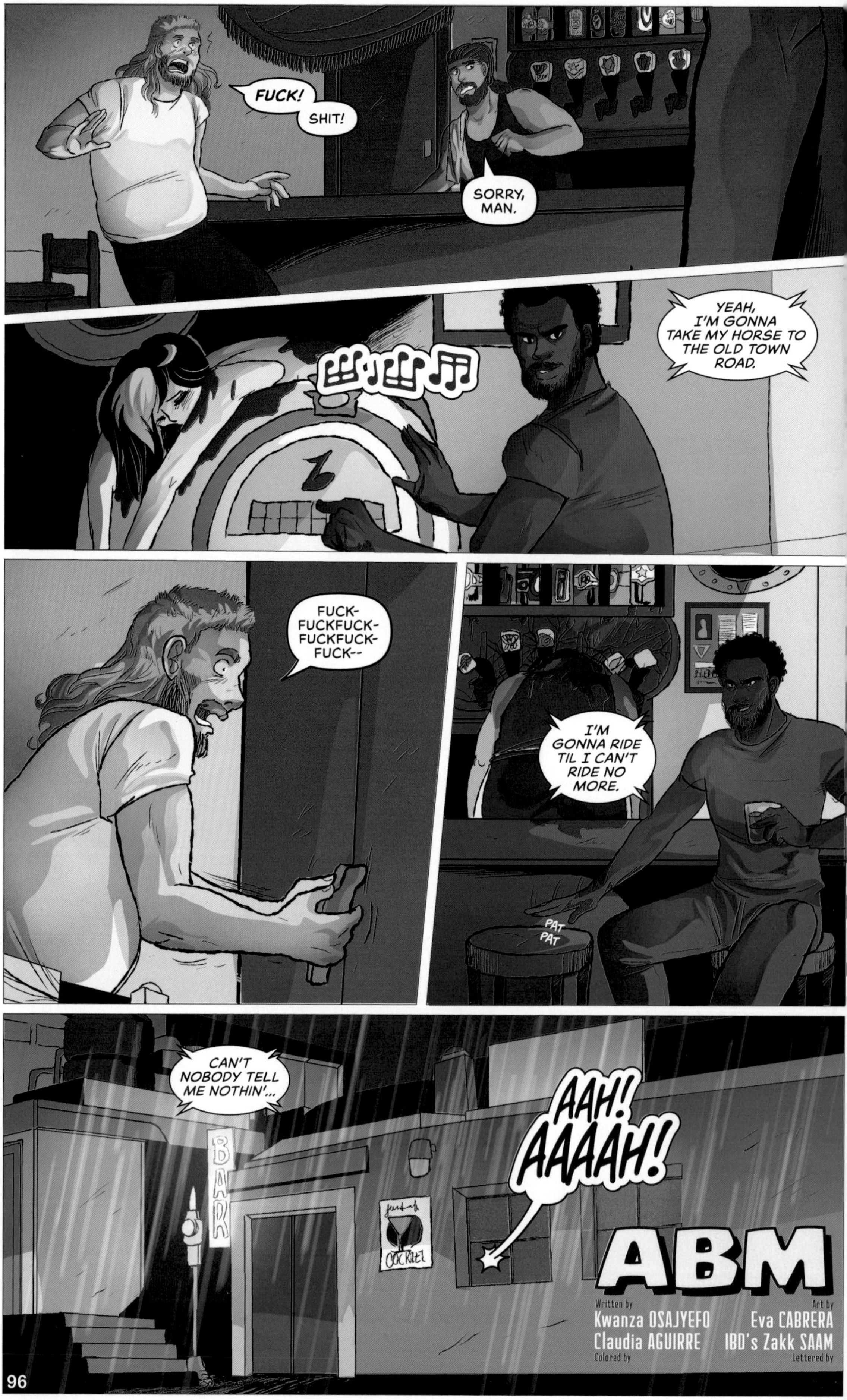
FUCK!
SHIT!
SORRY, MAN.
YEAH, I'M GONNA TAKE MY HORSE TO THE OLD TOWN ROAD.
FUCK-FUCKFUCK-FUCKFUCK-FUCK--
I'M GONNA RIDE TIL I CAN'T RIDE NO MORE.
PAT PAT
CAN'T NOBODY TELL ME NOTHIN'...
AAH! AAAAH!
BAR
ABM
Written by
Kwanza OSAJYEFO
Art by
Eva CABRERA
Claudia AGUIRRE
Colored by
IBD's Zakk SAAM
Lettered by

WE INTERRUPT THIS ANTHOLOGY FOR AN IMPORTANT PUBLIC SERVICE ANNOUNCEMENT.

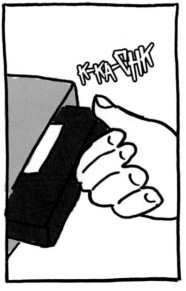

K-KA-CHK

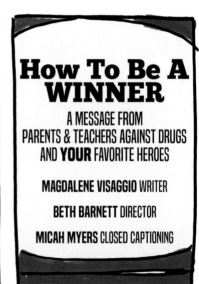

How To Be A WINNER

A MESSAGE FROM PARENTS & TEACHERS AGAINST DRUGS AND **YOUR** FAVORITE HEROES

MAGDALENE VISAGGIO WRITER

BETH BARNETT DIRECTOR

MICAH MYERS CLOSED CAPTIONING

THAT TEST TODAY WAS **SO** HARD, JENNY!

I DON'T EVEN KNOW WHAT I'M EVER GONNA USE **FRACTIONS** FOR.

IT'S ENOUGH TO MAKE ME WANT TO **THROW MY LIFE AWAY** BY QUITTING SCHOOL!

YOU'RE **RIGHT**, TIM! I'VE HAD ENOUGH OF THAT PATRIARCHAL, RACIST EDUCATIONAL SYSTEM THAT DEMANDS I UPHOLD IMPERIALISTIC CAPITALISM!

PSSSST. HEY, KIDS.

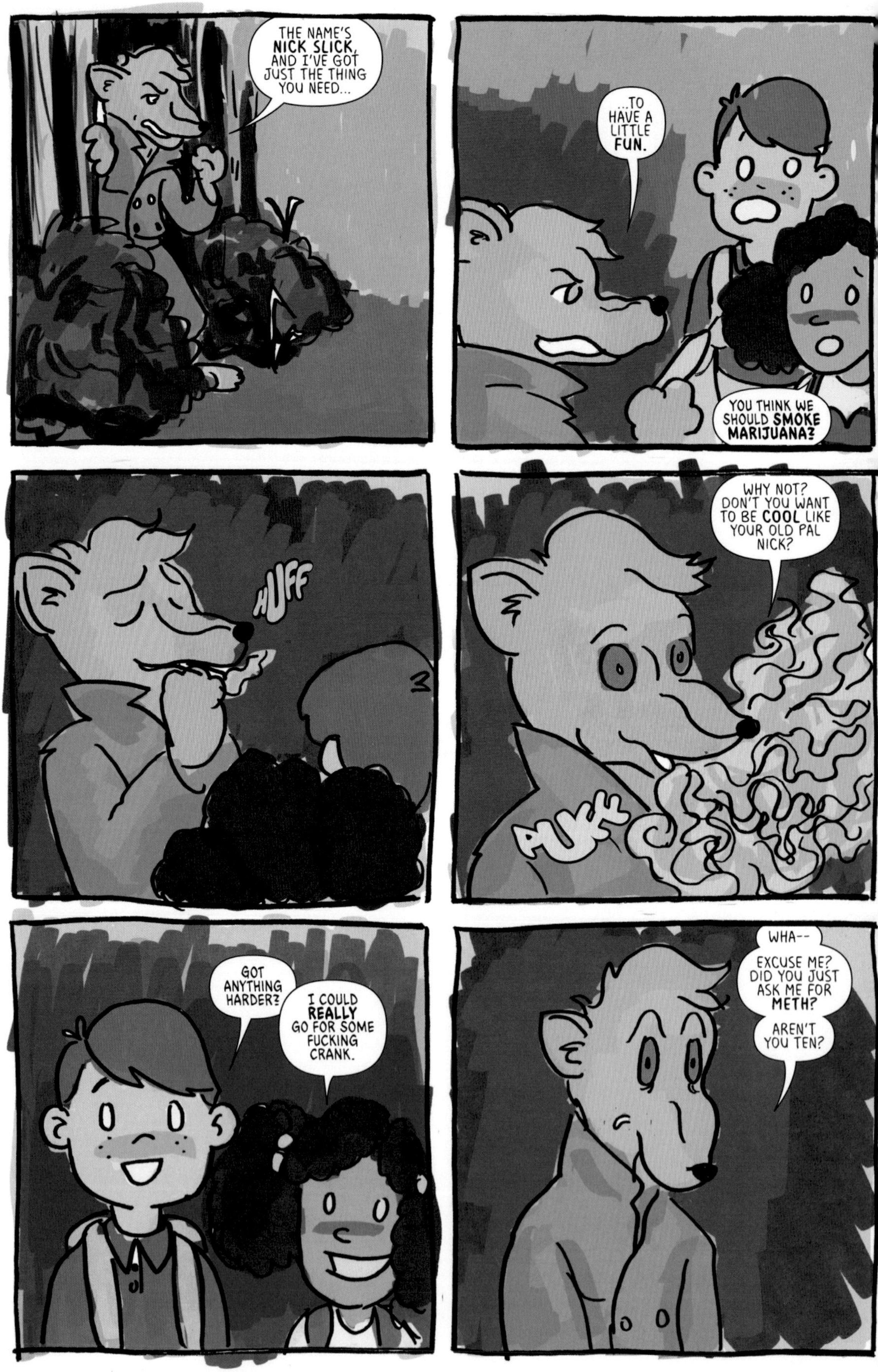
THE NAME'S **NICK SLICK,** AND I'VE GOT JUST THE THING YOU NEED...
...TO HAVE A LITTLE **FUN.**
YOU THINK WE SHOULD **SMOKE MARIJUANA?**
HUFF
WHY NOT? DON'T YOU WANT TO BE **COOL** LIKE YOUR OLD PAL NICK?
PUFF
GOT ANYTHING HARDER?
I COULD **REALLY** GO FOR SOME FUCKING CRANK.
WHA--
EXCUSE ME? DID YOU JUST ASK ME FOR **METH?**
AREN'T YOU TEN?

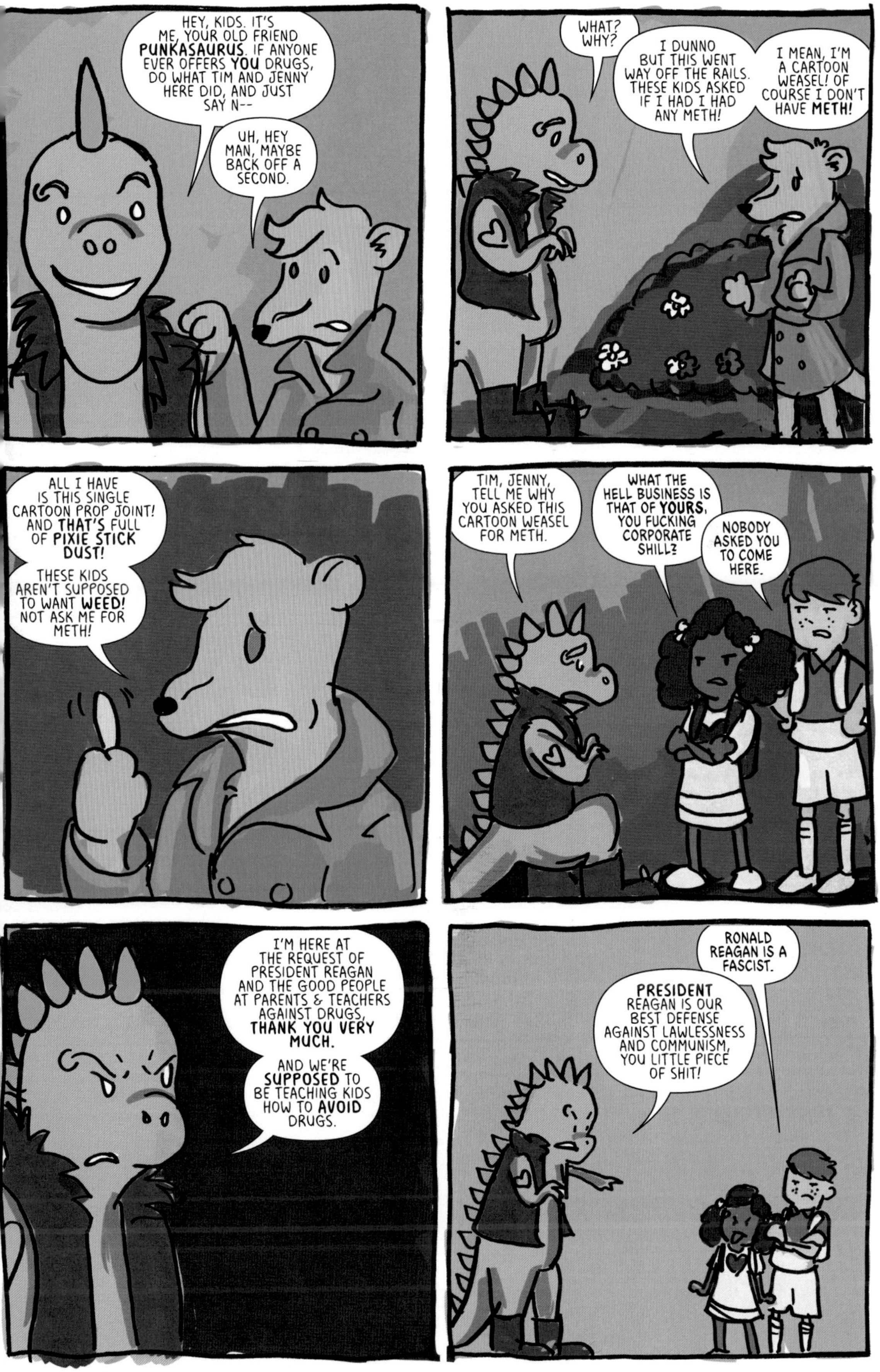
HEY, KIDS. IT'S ME, YOUR OLD FRIEND **PUNKASAURUS**. IF ANYONE EVER OFFERS **YOU** DRUGS, DO WHAT TIM AND JENNY HERE DID, AND JUST SAY N--
UH, HEY MAN, MAYBE BACK OFF A SECOND.
WHAT? WHY?
I DUNNO BUT THIS WENT WAY OFF THE RAILS. THESE KIDS ASKED IF I HAD I HAD ANY METH!
I MEAN, I'M A CARTOON WEASEL! OF COURSE I DON'T HAVE **METH!**
ALL I HAVE IS THIS SINGLE CARTOON PROP JOINT! AND **THAT'S** FULL OF **PIXIE STICK DUST!**
THESE KIDS AREN'T SUPPOSED TO WANT **WEED!** NOT ASK ME FOR METH!
TIM, JENNY, TELL ME WHY YOU ASKED THIS CARTOON WEASEL FOR METH.
WHAT THE HELL BUSINESS IS THAT OF **YOURS**, YOU FUCKING CORPORATE SHILL?
NOBODY ASKED YOU TO COME HERE.
I'M HERE AT THE REQUEST OF PRESIDENT REAGAN AND THE GOOD PEOPLE AT PARENTS & TEACHERS AGAINST DRUGS, **THANK YOU VERY MUCH.**
AND WE'RE **SUPPOSED** TO BE TEACHING KIDS HOW TO **AVOID** DRUGS.
RONALD REAGAN IS A FASCIST.
PRESIDENT REAGAN IS OUR BEST DEFENSE AGAINST LAWLESSNESS AND COMMUNISM, YOU LITTLE PIECE OF SHIT!

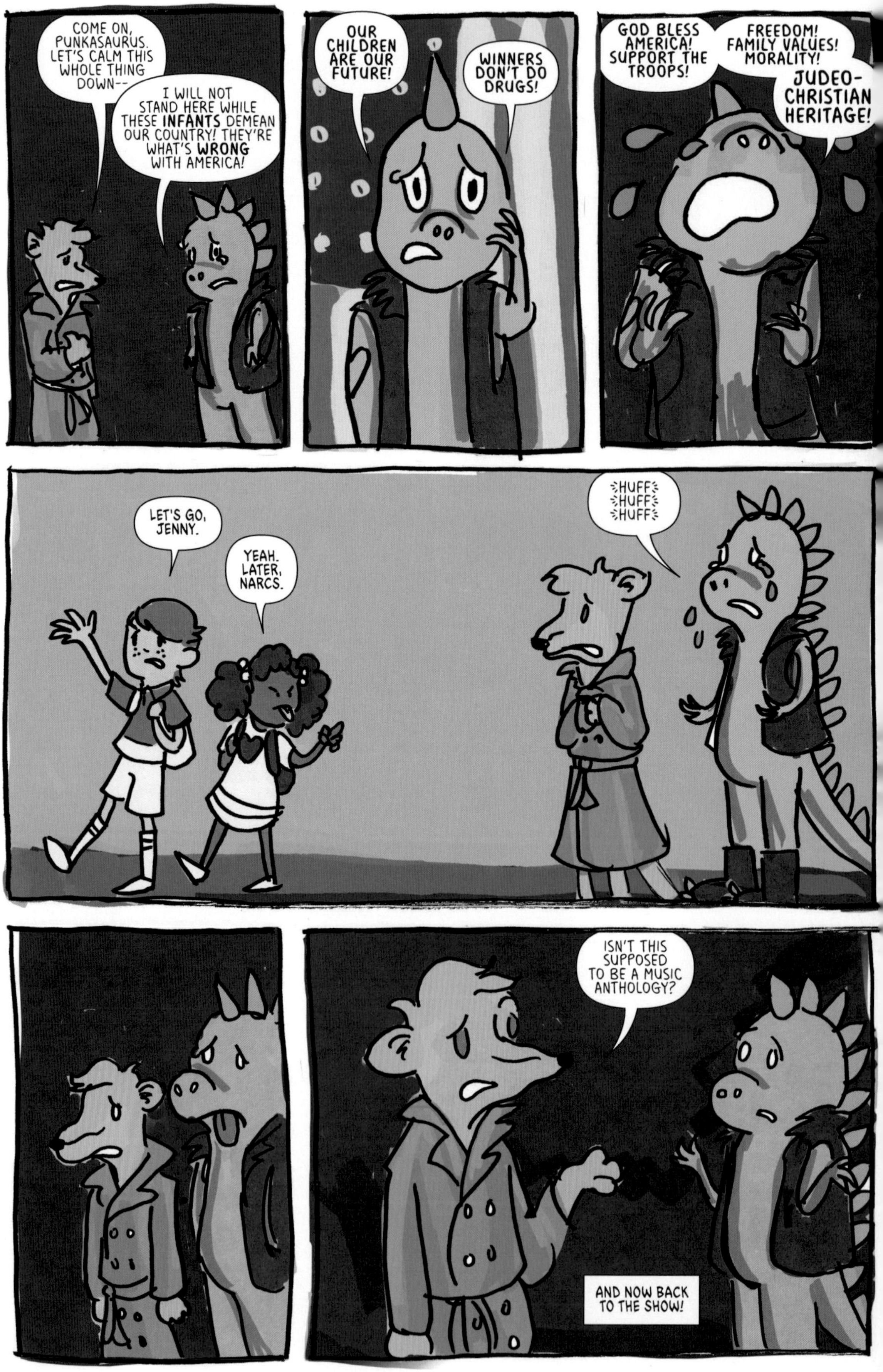
COME ON, PUNKASAURUS. LET'S CALM THIS WHOLE THING DOWN--
I WILL NOT STAND HERE WHILE THESE **INFANTS** DEMEAN OUR COUNTRY! THEY'RE WHAT'S **WRONG** WITH AMERICA!
OUR CHILDREN ARE OUR FUTURE!
WINNERS DON'T DO DRUGS!
GOD BLESS AMERICA! SUPPORT THE TROOPS!
FREEDOM! FAMILY VALUES! MORALITY!
JUDEO-CHRISTIAN HERITAGE!
LET'S GO, JENNY.
YEAH. LATER, NARCS.
HUFF HUFF HUFF
ISN'T THIS SUPPOSED TO BE A MUSIC ANTHOLOGY?
AND NOW BACK TO THE SHOW!

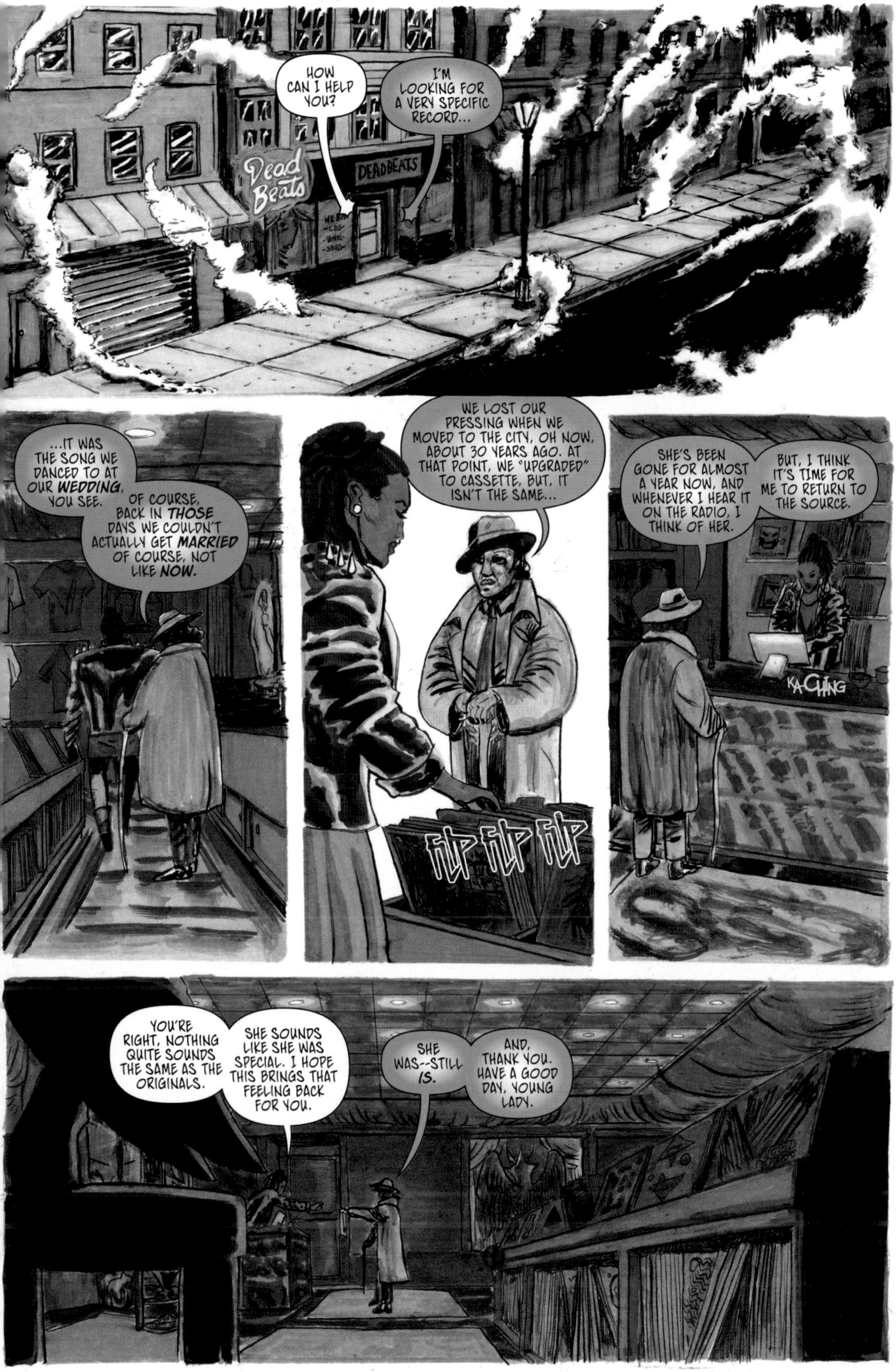
Dead Beats
DEADBEATS
WE BUY CDS VINYL
HOW CAN I HELP YOU?
I'M LOOKING FOR A VERY SPECIFIC RECORD...
...IT WAS THE SONG WE DANCED TO AT OUR WEDDING, YOU SEE.
OF COURSE, BACK IN THOSE DAYS WE COULDN'T ACTUALLY GET MARRIED OF COURSE, NOT LIKE NOW.
WE LOST OUR PRESSING WHEN WE MOVED TO THE CITY, OH NOW, ABOUT 30 YEARS AGO. AT THAT POINT, WE "UPGRADED" TO CASSETTE, BUT, IT ISN'T THE SAME...
FLIP FLIP FLIP
SHE'S BEEN GONE FOR ALMOST A YEAR NOW, AND WHENEVER I HEAR IT ON THE RADIO, I THINK OF HER.
BUT, I THINK IT'S TIME FOR ME TO RETURN TO THE SOURCE.
KA-CHING
YOU'RE RIGHT, NOTHING QUITE SOUNDS THE SAME AS THE ORIGINALS.
SHE SOUNDS LIKE SHE WAS SPECIAL. I HOPE THIS BRINGS THAT FEELING BACK FOR YOU.
SHE WAS--STILL IS.
AND, THANK YOU. HAVE A GOOD DAY, YOUNG LADY.

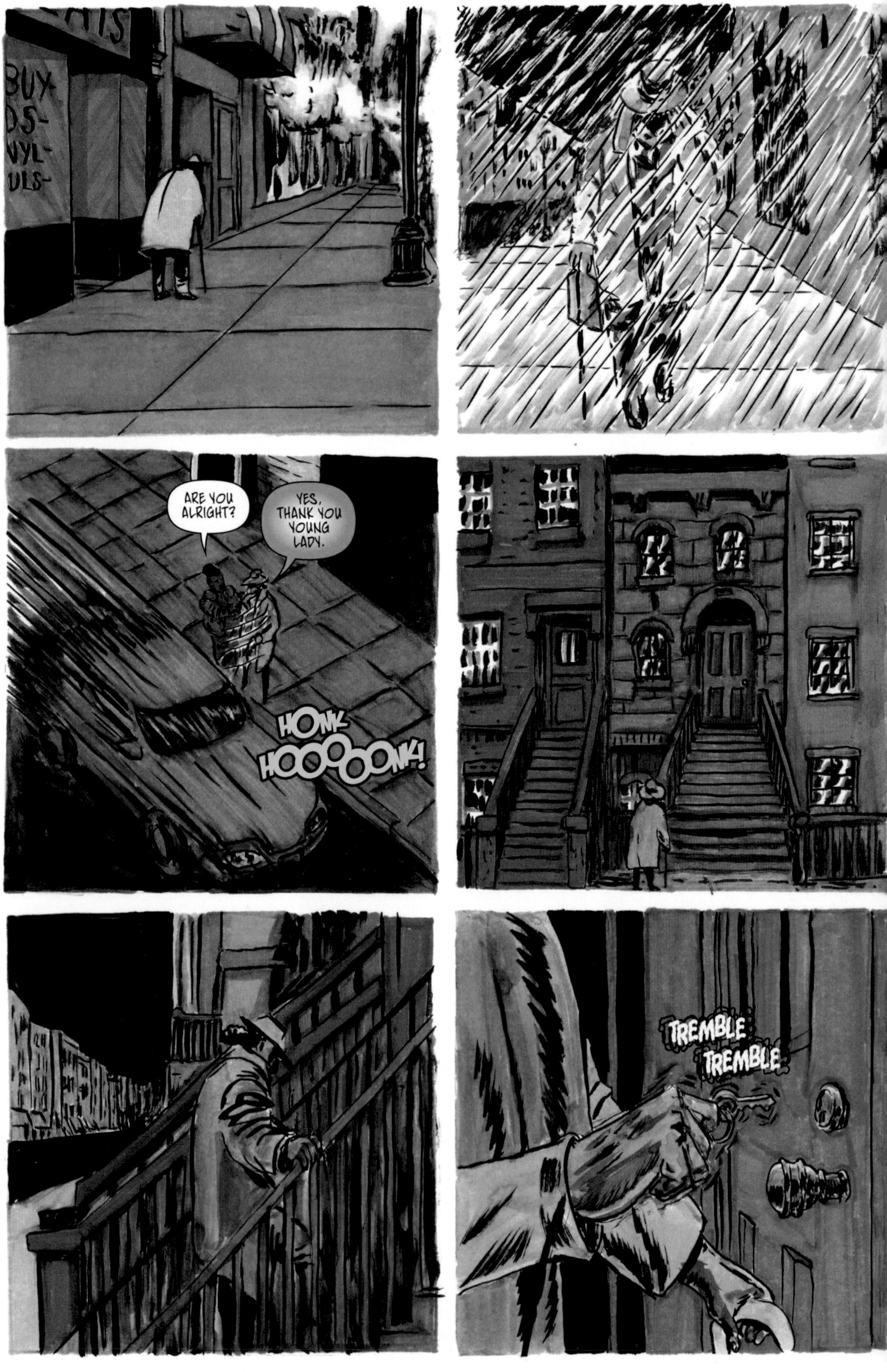
BUY
ARE YOU ALRIGHT?
YES, THANK YOU YOUNG LADY.
HONK
HOOOOONK!
TREMBLE
TREMBLE

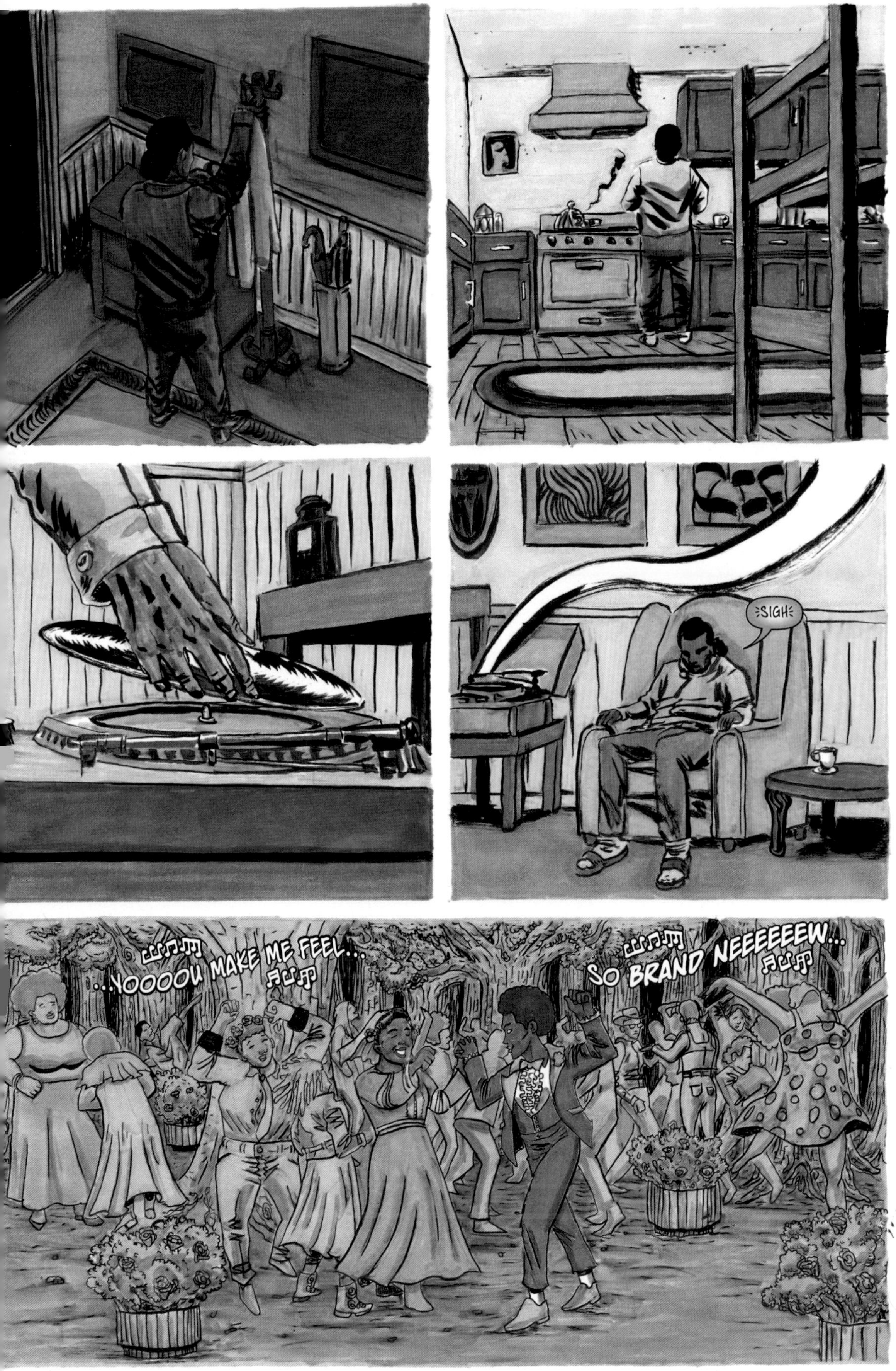
SIGH
...YOOOOU MAKE ME FEEL...
SO BRAND NEEEEEEW...

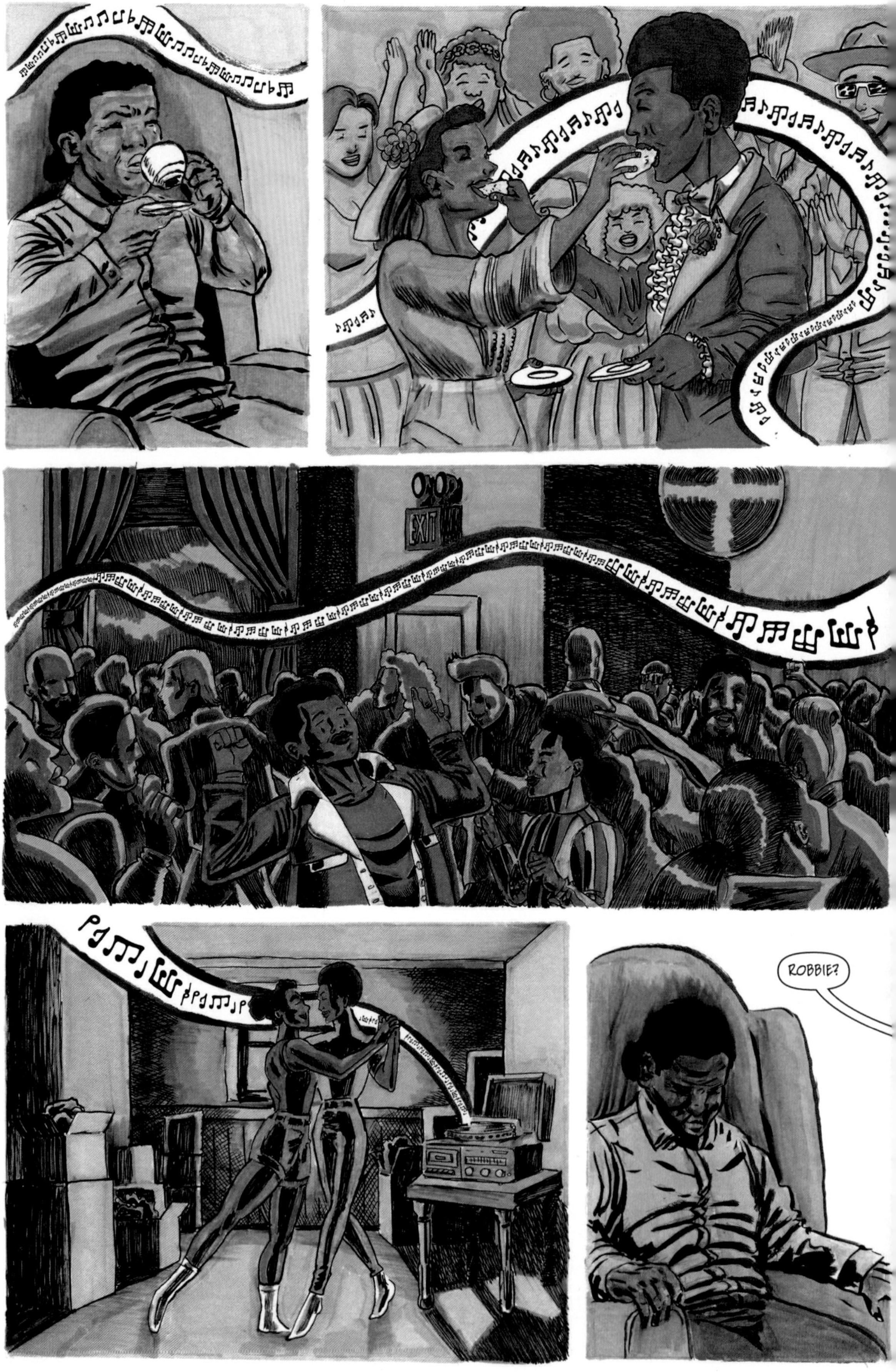
ROBBIE?

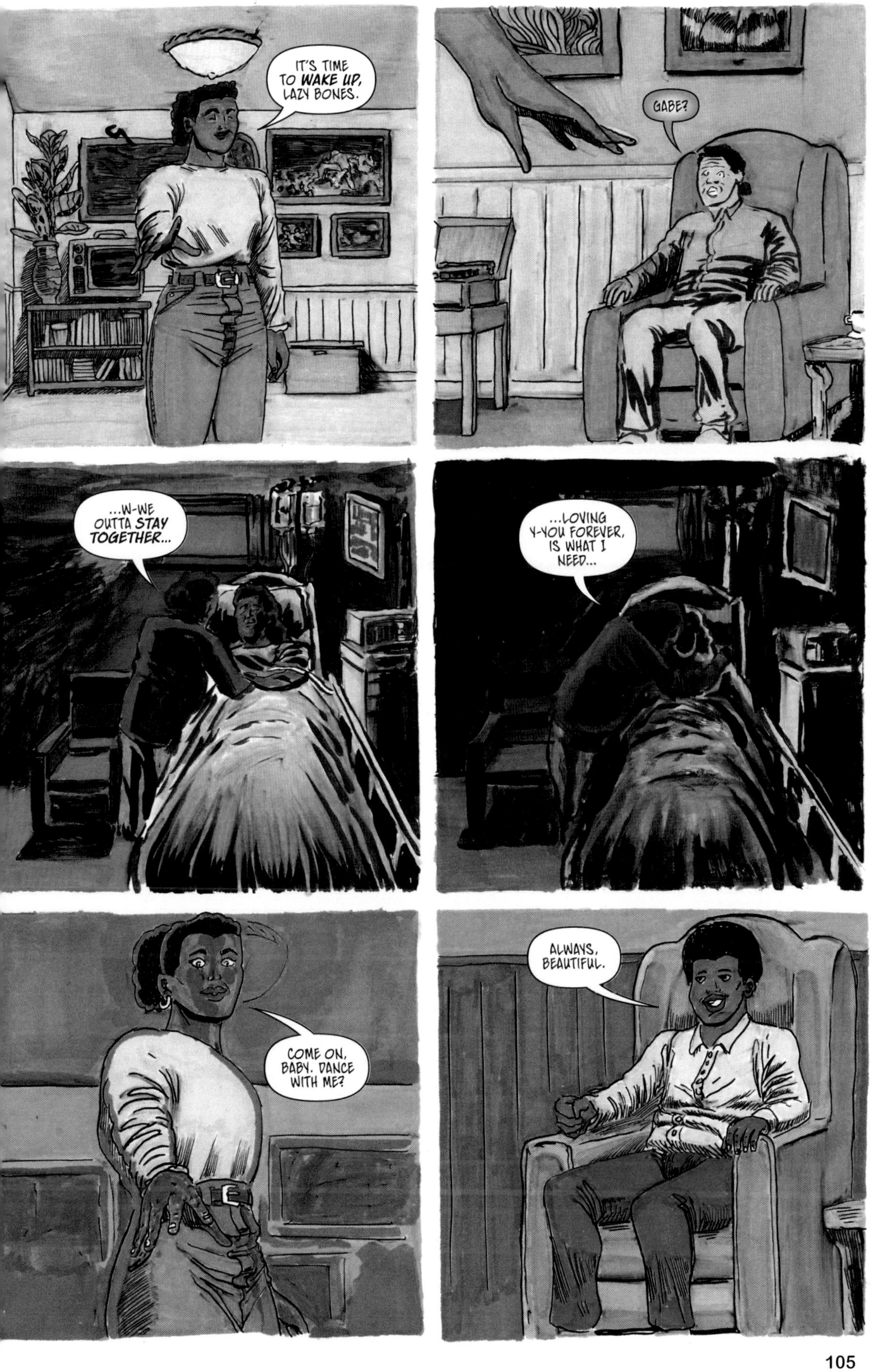
IT'S TIME TO **WAKE UP,** LAZY BONES.
GABE?
...W-WE OUTTA **STAY TOGETHER...**
...LOVING Y-YOU FOREVER, IS WHAT I NEED...
COME ON, BABY. DANCE WITH ME?
ALWAYS, BEAUTIFUL.

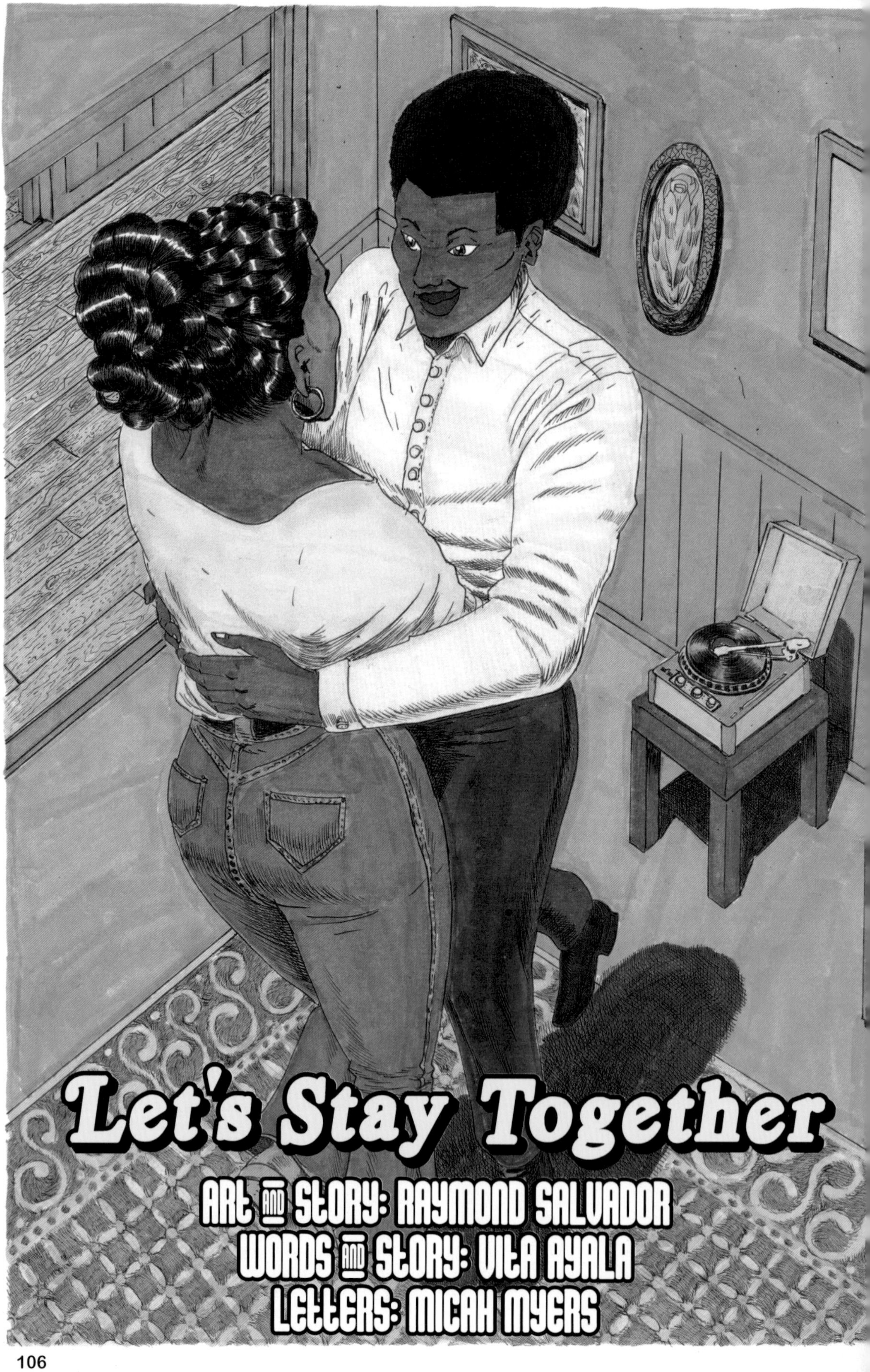
Let's Stay Together
ART AND STORY: RAYMOND SALVADOR
WORDS AND STORY: VITA AYALA
LETTERS: MICAH MYERS

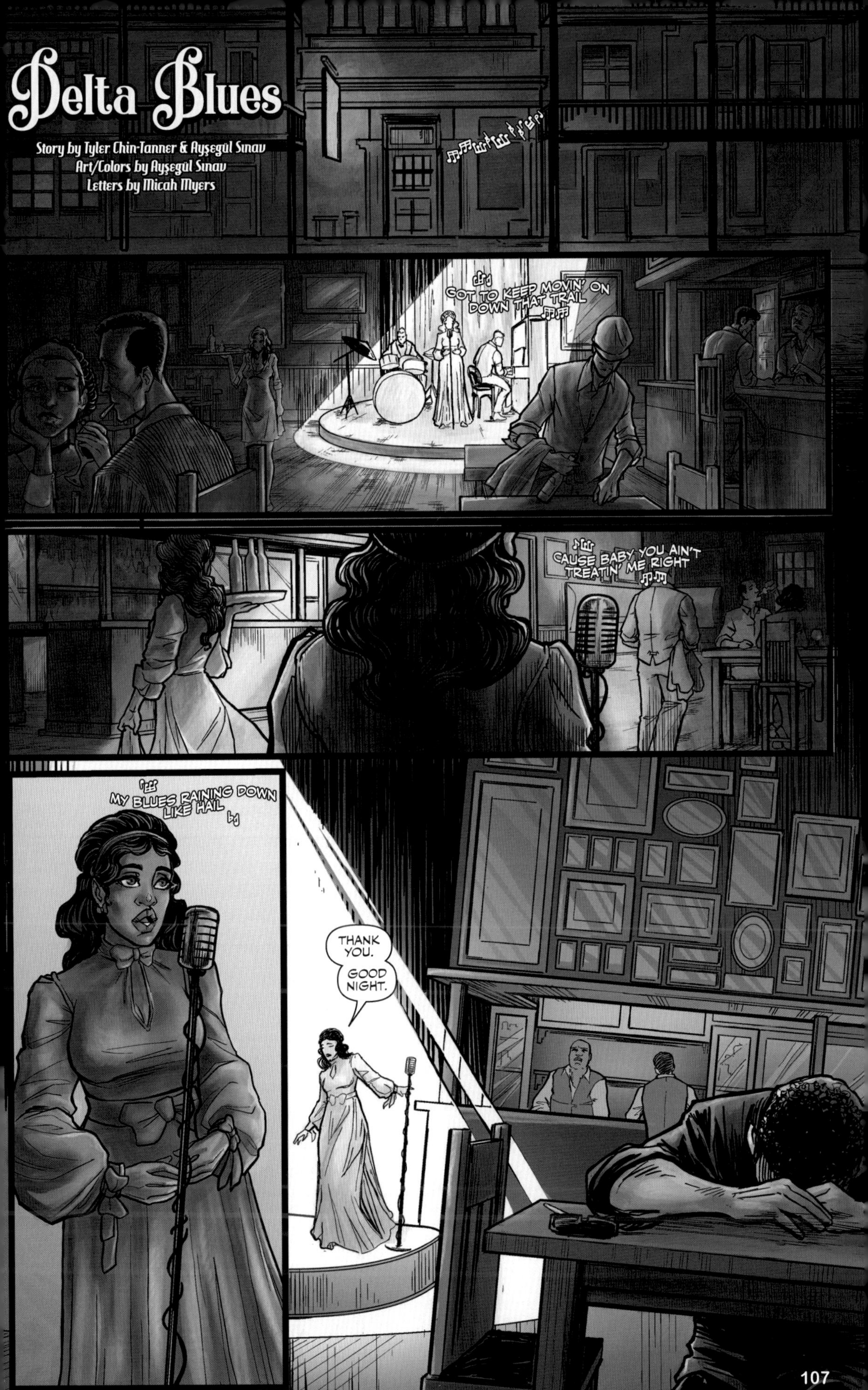

Delta Blues
Story by Tyler Chin-Tanner & Ayşegül Sınav
Art/Colors by Ayşegül Sınav
Letters by Micah Myers
GOT TO KEEP MOVIN' ON DOWN THAT TRAIL
CAUSE BABY YOU AIN'T TREATIN' ME RIGHT
MY BLUES RAINING DOWN LIKE HAIL
THANK YOU. GOOD NIGHT.

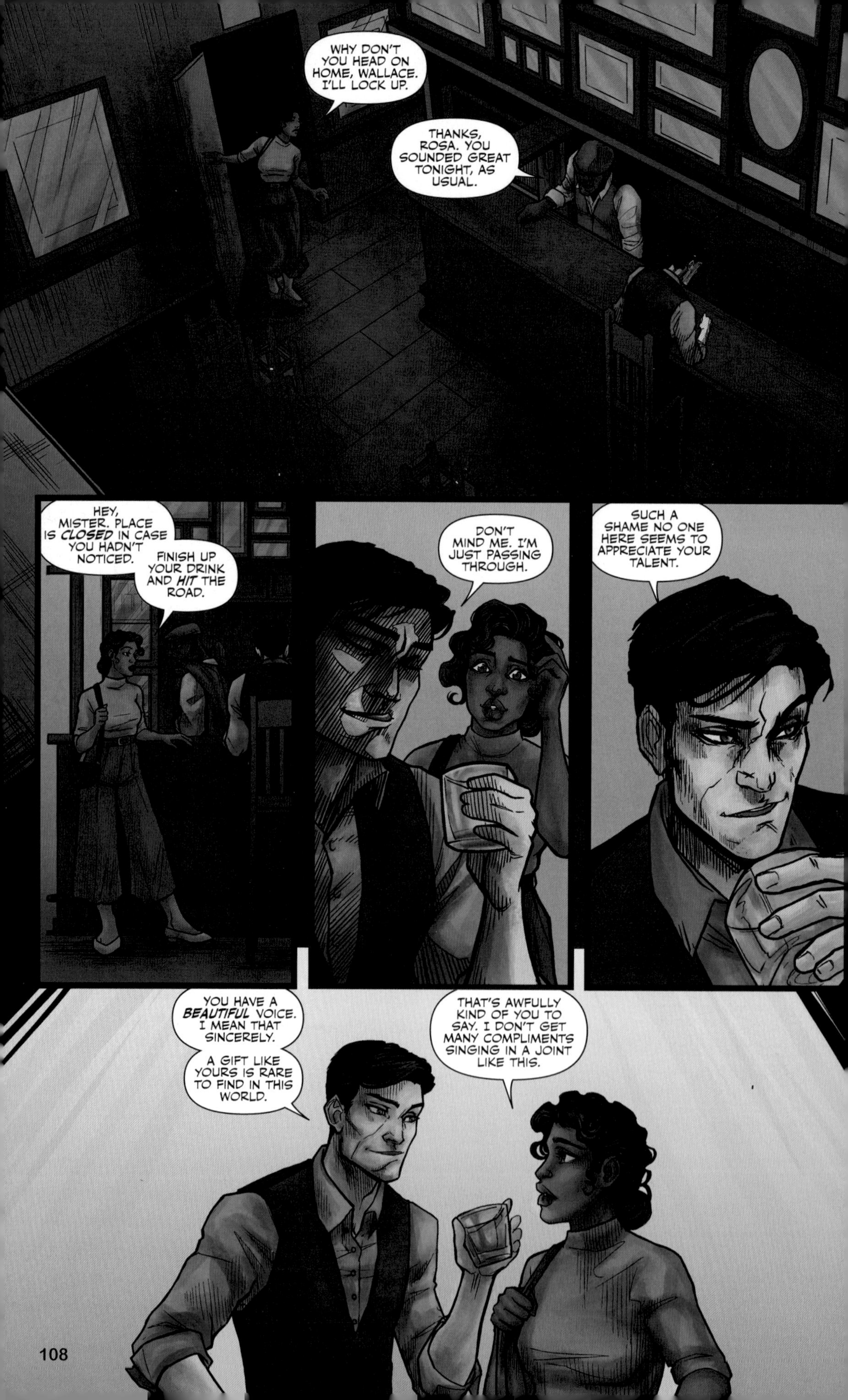
WHY DON'T YOU HEAD ON HOME, WALLACE. I'LL LOCK UP.
THANKS, ROSA. YOU SOUNDED GREAT TONIGHT, AS USUAL.
HEY, MISTER. PLACE IS *CLOSED* IN CASE YOU HADN'T NOTICED.
FINISH UP YOUR DRINK AND *HIT* THE ROAD.
DON'T MIND ME. I'M JUST PASSING THROUGH.
SUCH A SHAME NO ONE HERE SEEMS TO APPRECIATE YOUR TALENT.
YOU HAVE A *BEAUTIFUL* VOICE. I MEAN THAT SINCERELY.
A GIFT LIKE YOURS IS RARE TO FIND IN THIS WORLD.
THAT'S AWFULLY KIND OF YOU TO SAY. I DON'T GET MANY COMPLIMENTS SINGING IN A JOINT LIKE THIS.

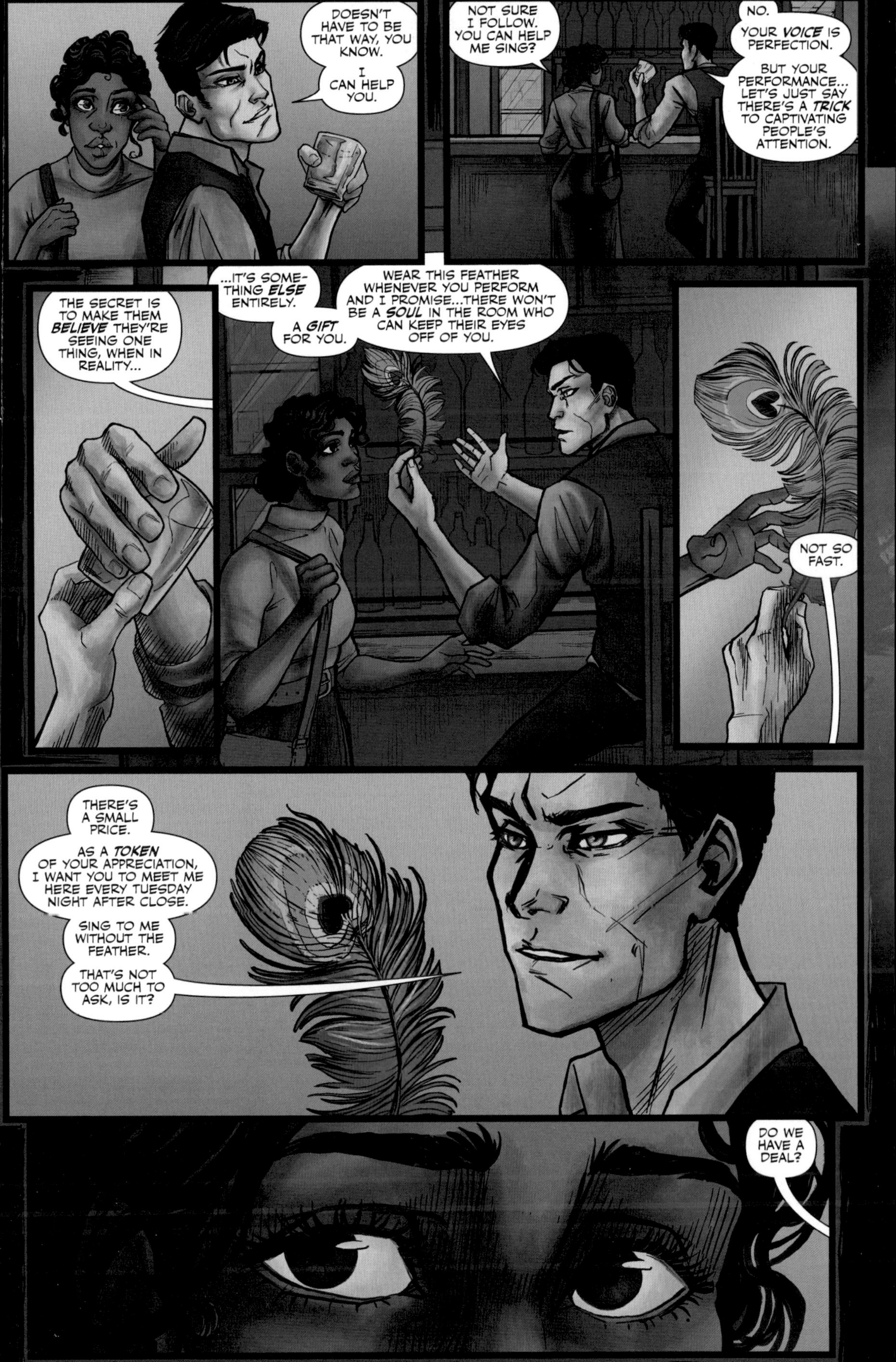
DOESN'T HAVE TO BE THAT WAY, YOU KNOW.
I CAN HELP YOU.
NOT SURE I FOLLOW. YOU CAN HELP ME SING?
NO.
YOUR VOICE IS PERFECTION.
BUT YOUR PERFORMANCE... LET'S JUST SAY THERE'S A TRICK TO CAPTIVATING PEOPLE'S ATTENTION.
THE SECRET IS TO MAKE THEM BELIEVE THEY'RE SEEING ONE THING, WHEN IN REALITY...
...IT'S SOMETHING ELSE ENTIRELY.
A GIFT FOR YOU.
WEAR THIS FEATHER WHENEVER YOU PERFORM AND I PROMISE...THERE WON'T BE A SOUL IN THE ROOM WHO CAN KEEP THEIR EYES OFF OF YOU.
NOT SO FAST.
THERE'S A SMALL PRICE.
AS A TOKEN OF YOUR APPRECIATION, I WANT YOU TO MEET ME HERE EVERY TUESDAY NIGHT AFTER CLOSE.
SING TO ME WITHOUT THE FEATHER.
THAT'S NOT TOO MUCH TO ASK, IS IT?
DO WE HAVE A DEAL?

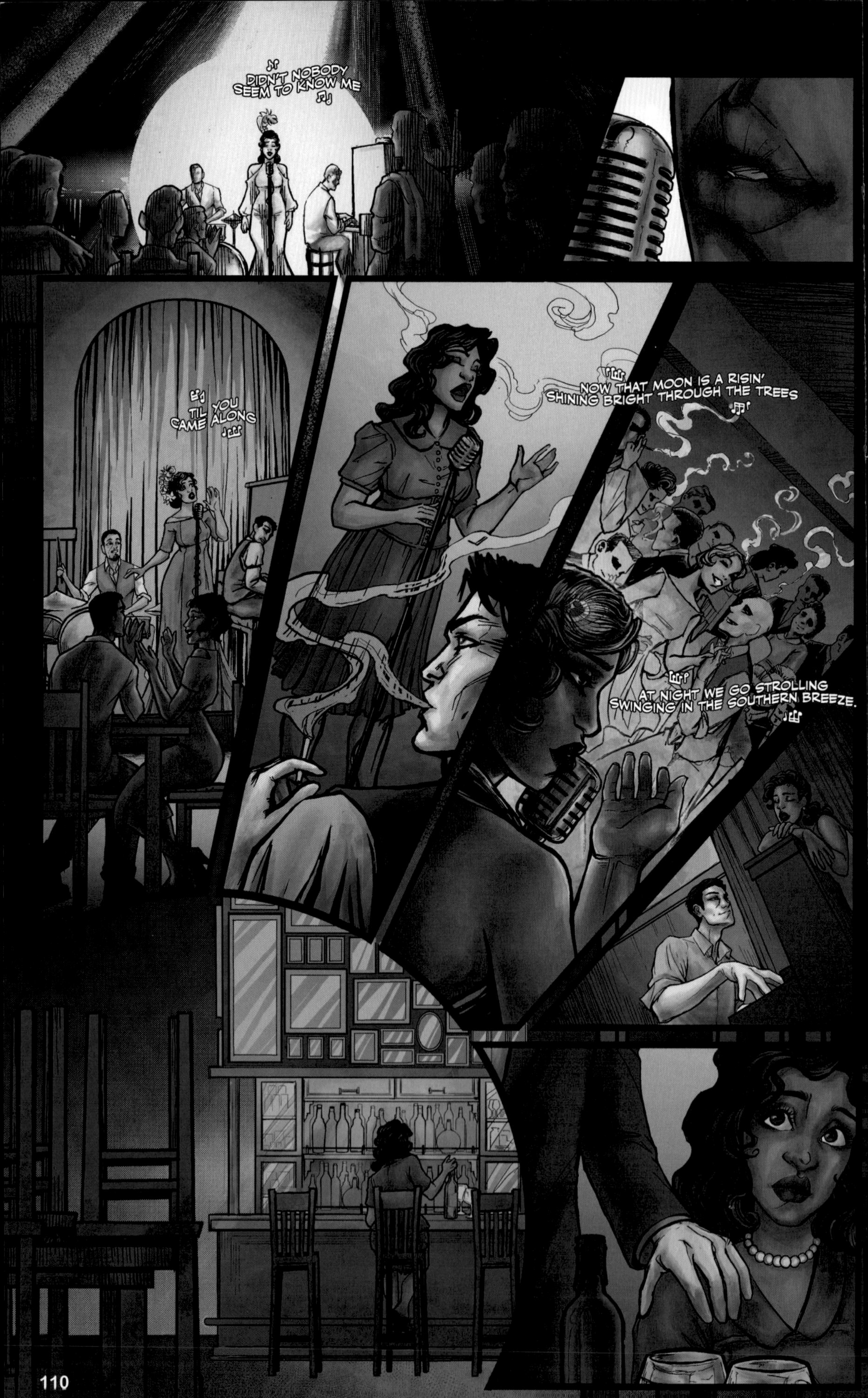
DIDN'T NOBODY SEEM TO KNOW ME
TIL YOU CAME ALONG
NOW THAT MOON IS A RISIN' SHINING BRIGHT THROUGH THE TREES
AT NIGHT WE GO STROLLING SWINGING IN THE SOUTHERN BREEZE.

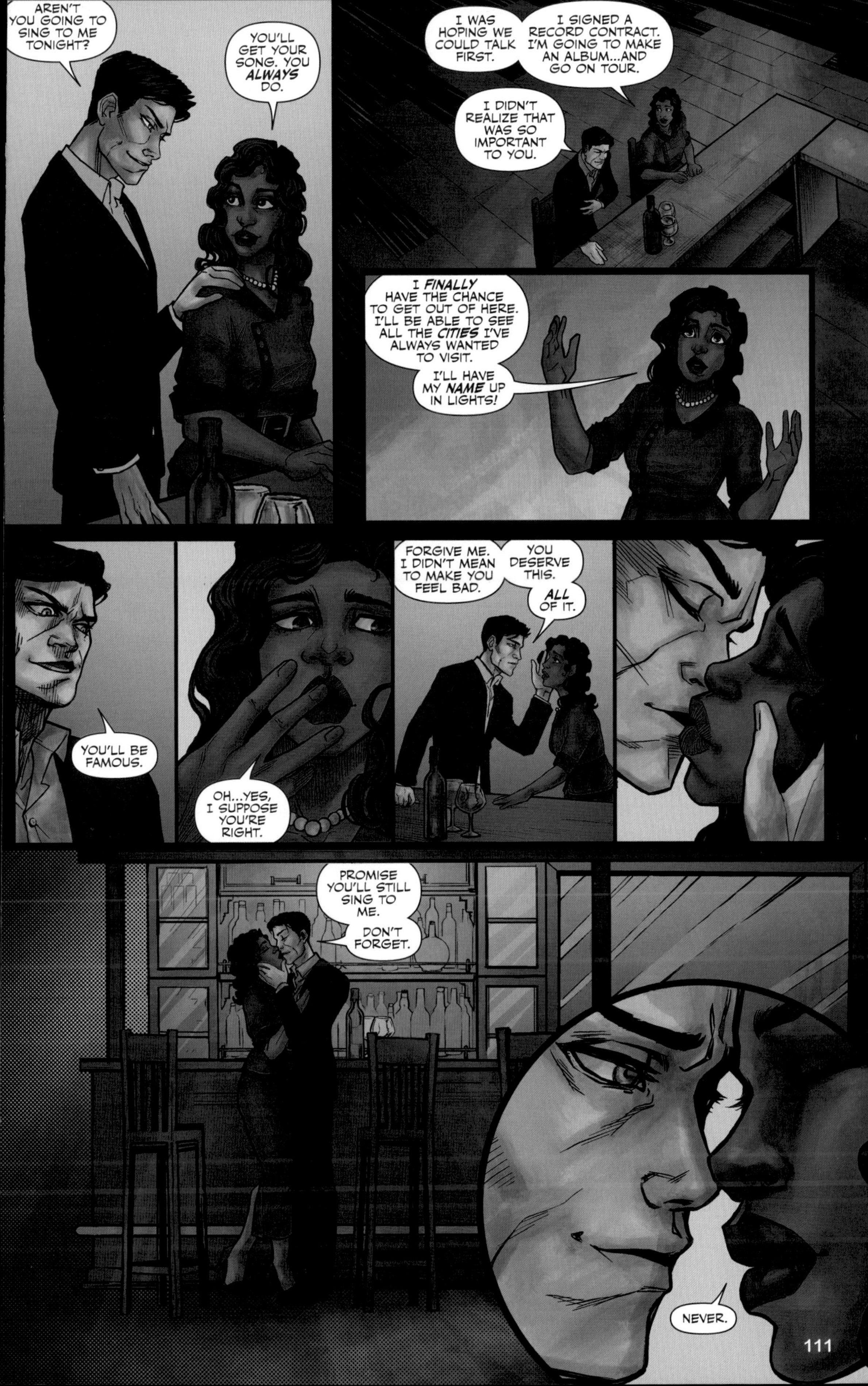
AREN'T YOU GOING TO SING TO ME TONIGHT?
YOU'LL GET YOUR SONG. YOU ALWAYS DO.
I WAS HOPING WE COULD TALK FIRST.
I SIGNED A RECORD CONTRACT. I'M GOING TO MAKE AN ALBUM...AND GO ON TOUR.
I DIDN'T REALIZE THAT WAS SO IMPORTANT TO YOU.
I FINALLY HAVE THE CHANCE TO GET OUT OF HERE. I'LL BE ABLE TO SEE ALL THE CITIES I'VE ALWAYS WANTED TO VISIT.
I'LL HAVE MY NAME UP IN LIGHTS!
YOU'LL BE FAMOUS.
OH...YES, I SUPPOSE YOU'RE RIGHT.
FORGIVE ME. I DIDN'T MEAN TO MAKE YOU FEEL BAD.
YOU DESERVE THIS.
ALL OF IT.
PROMISE YOU'LL STILL SING TO ME.
DON'T FORGET.
NEVER.

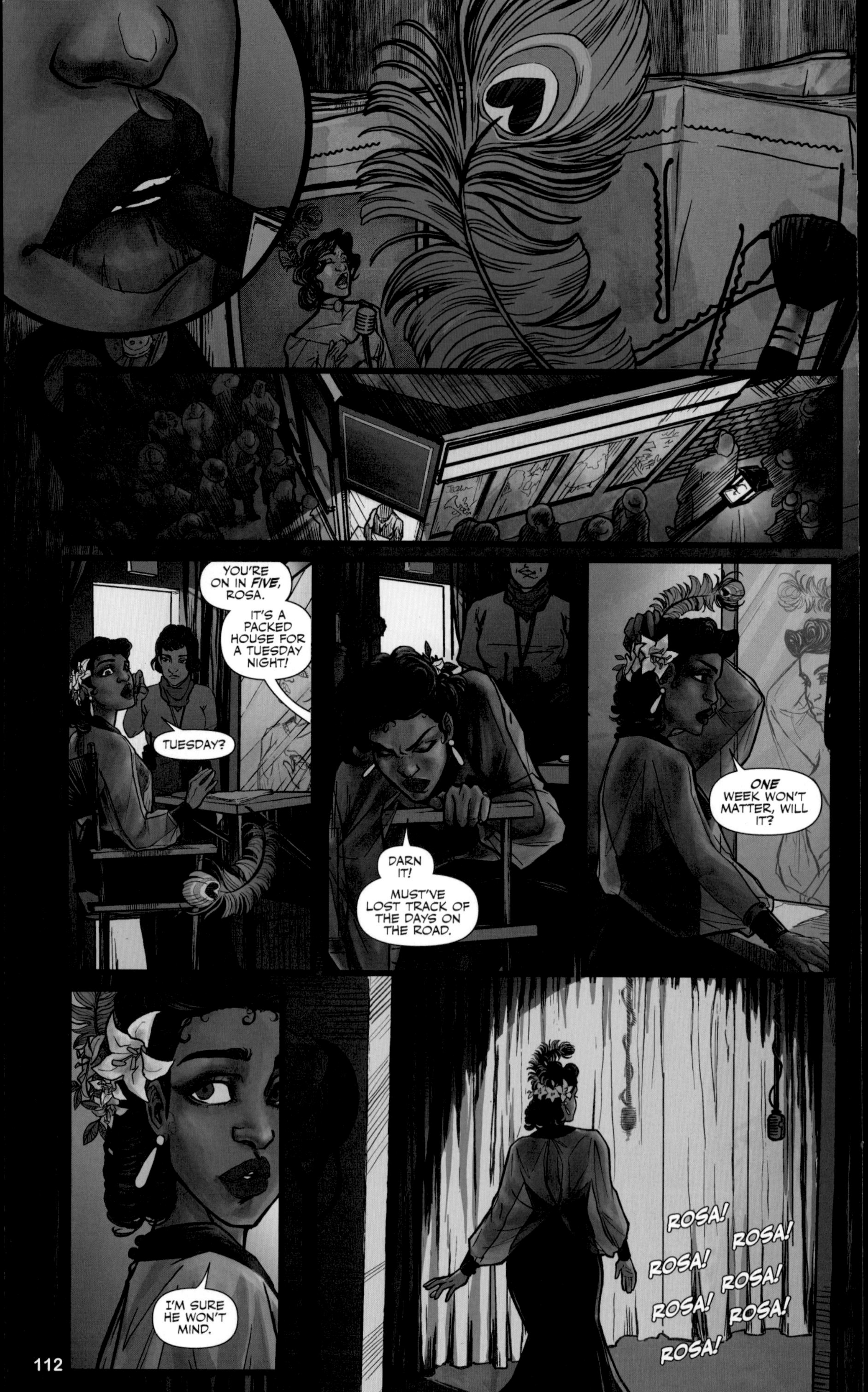
YOU'RE ON IN *FIVE*, ROSA.
IT'S A PACKED HOUSE FOR A TUESDAY NIGHT!
TUESDAY?
DARN IT!
MUST'VE LOST TRACK OF THE DAYS ON THE ROAD.
ONE WEEK WON'T MATTER, WILL IT?
I'M SURE HE WON'T MIND.
ROSA! ROSA! ROSA! ROSA! ROSA! ROSA! ROSA!

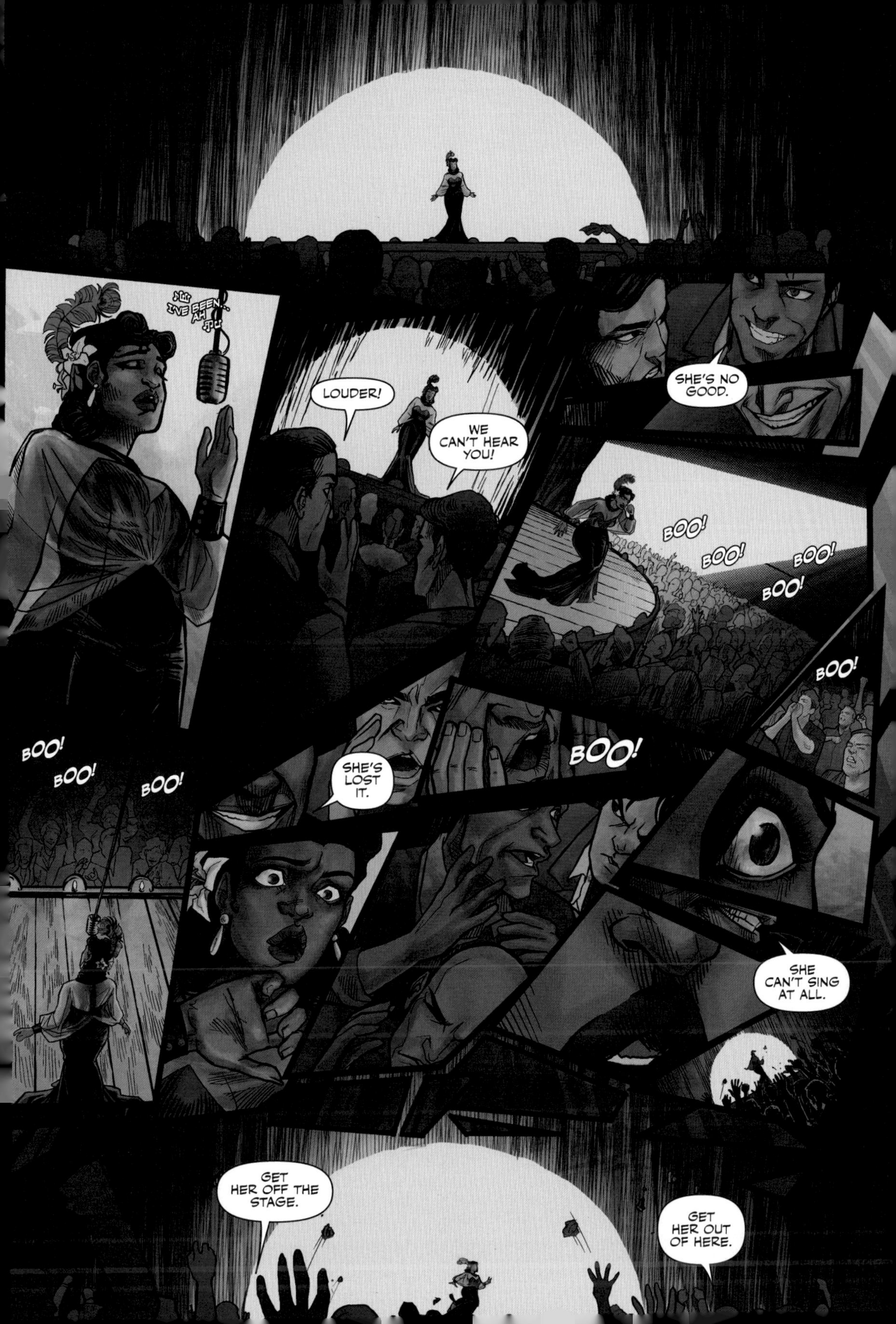
♪ I'VE BEEN... AH ♫
LOUDER!
WE CAN'T HEAR YOU!
SHE'S NO GOOD.
BOO!
BOO!
BOO!
BOO!
BOO!
BOO!
BOO!
BOO!
BOO!
SHE'S LOST IT.
SHE CAN'T SING AT ALL.
GET HER OFF THE STAGE.
GET HER OUT OF HERE.

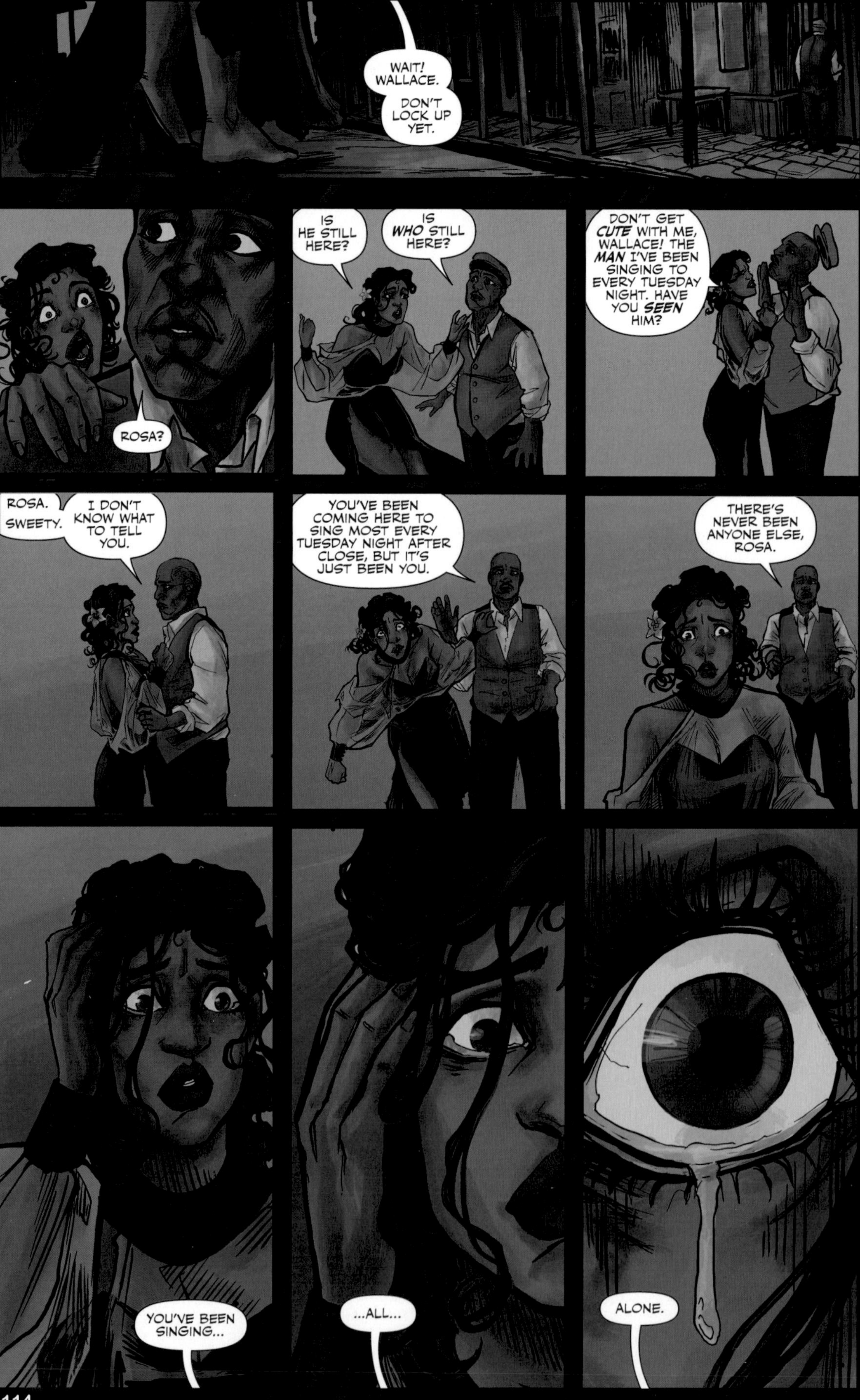
WAIT! WALLACE.
DON'T LOCK UP YET.
ROSA?
IS HE STILL HERE?
IS WHO STILL HERE?
DON'T GET CUTE WITH ME, WALLACE! THE MAN I'VE BEEN SINGING TO EVERY TUESDAY NIGHT. HAVE YOU SEEN HIM?
ROSA. SWEETY.
I DON'T KNOW WHAT TO TELL YOU.
YOU'VE BEEN COMING HERE TO SING MOST EVERY TUESDAY NIGHT AFTER CLOSE, BUT IT'S JUST BEEN YOU.
THERE'S NEVER BEEN ANYONE ELSE, ROSA.
YOU'VE BEEN SINGING...
...ALL...
ALONE.

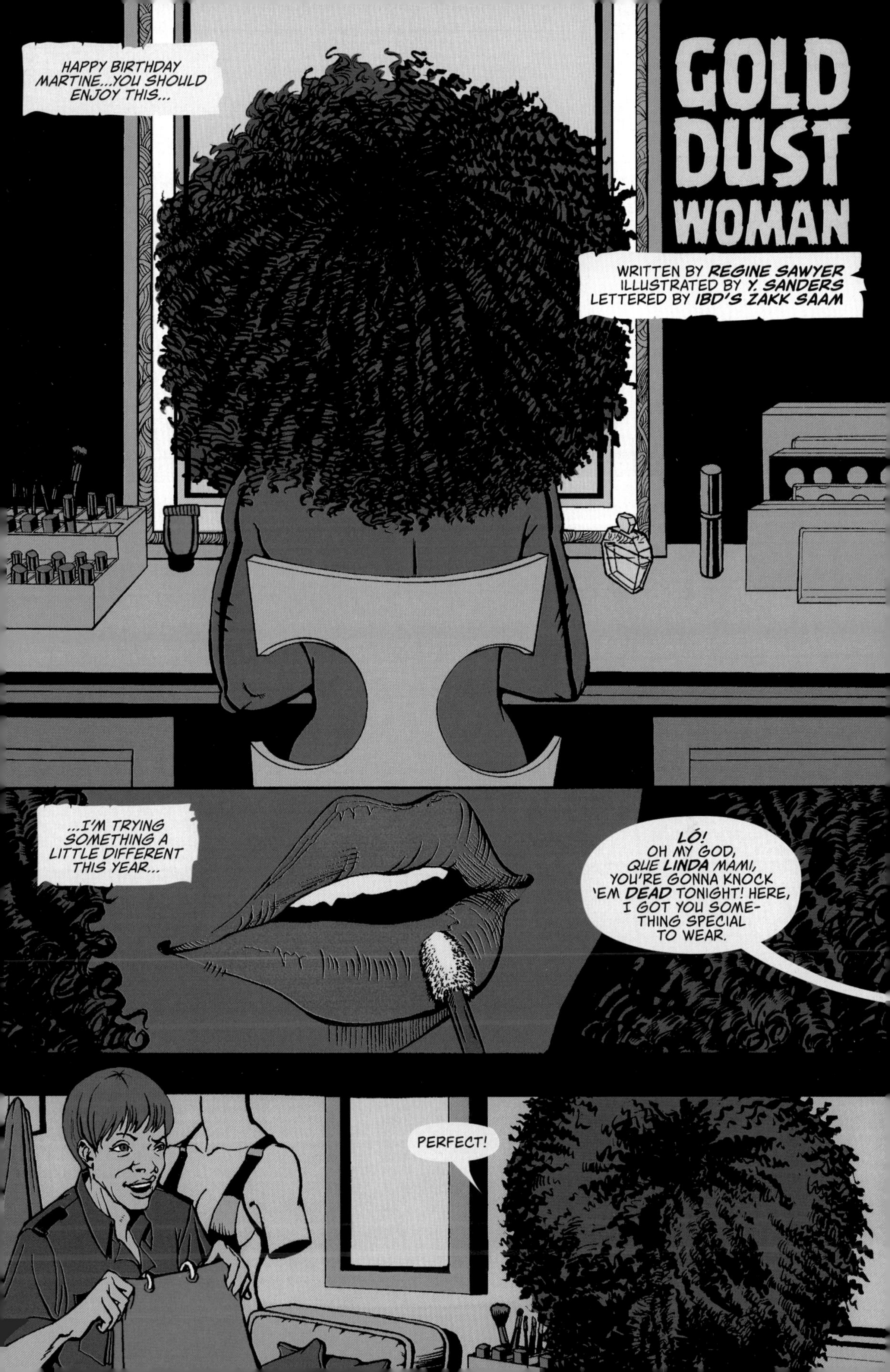
HAPPY BIRTHDAY MARTINE...YOU SHOULD ENJOY THIS...
GOLD DUST WOMAN
WRITTEN BY REGINE SAWYER
ILLUSTRATED BY Y. SANDERS
LETTERED BY IBD'S ZAKK SAAM
...I'M TRYING SOMETHING A LITTLE DIFFERENT THIS YEAR...
LÓ! OH MY GOD, QUE LINDA MAMI, YOU'RE GONNA KNOCK 'EM DEAD TONIGHT! HERE, I GOT YOU SOMETHING SPECIAL TO WEAR.
PERFECT!

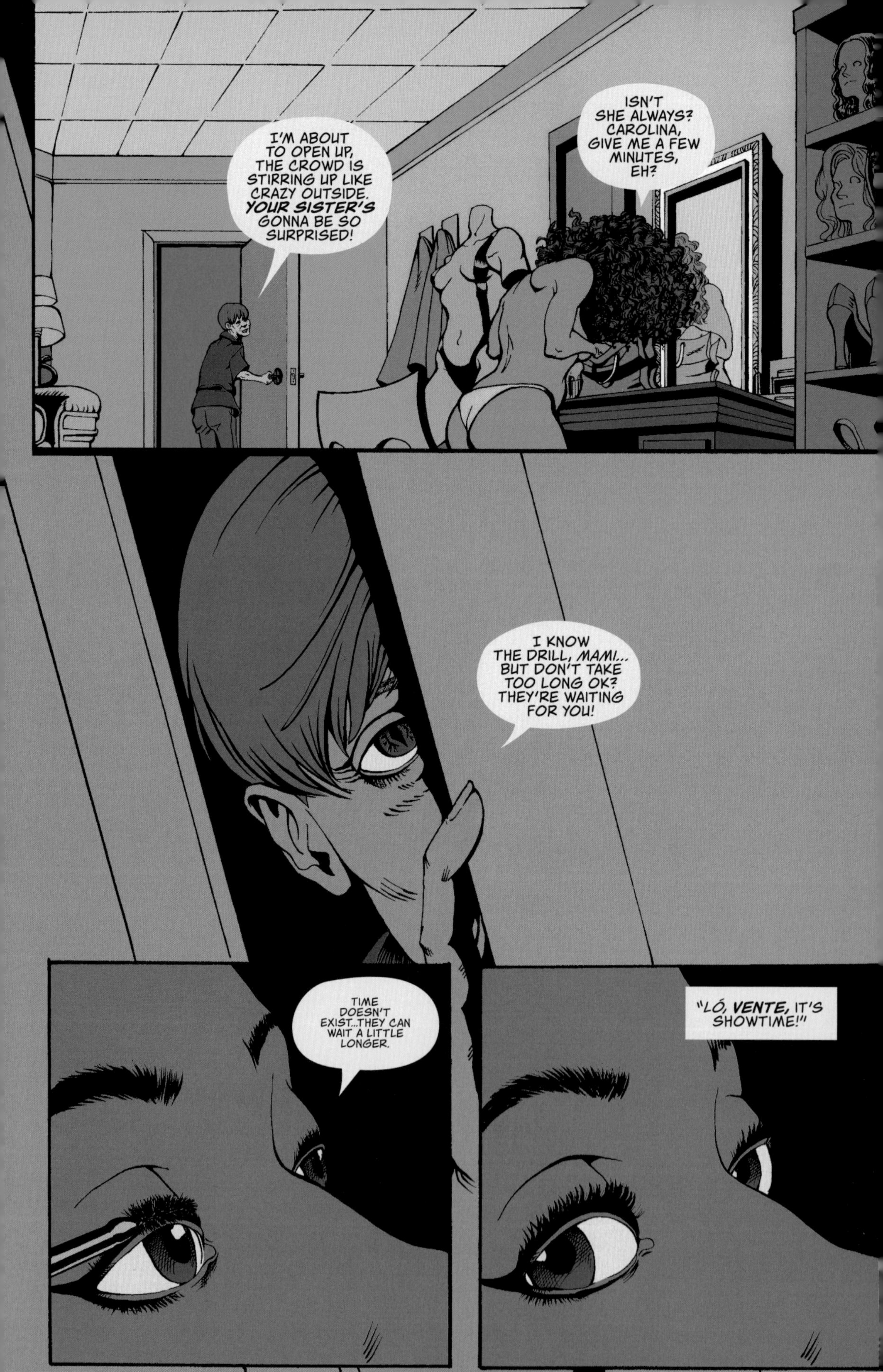
I'M ABOUT TO OPEN UP, THE CROWD IS STIRRING UP LIKE CRAZY OUTSIDE. YOUR SISTER'S GONNA BE SO SURPRISED!
ISN'T SHE ALWAYS? CAROLINA, GIVE ME A FEW MINUTES, EH?
I KNOW THE DRILL, MAMI... BUT DON'T TAKE TOO LONG OK? THEY'RE WAITING FOR YOU!
TIME DOESN'T EXIST...THEY CAN WAIT A LITTLE LONGER.
"LÓ, VENTE, IT'S SHOWTIME!"

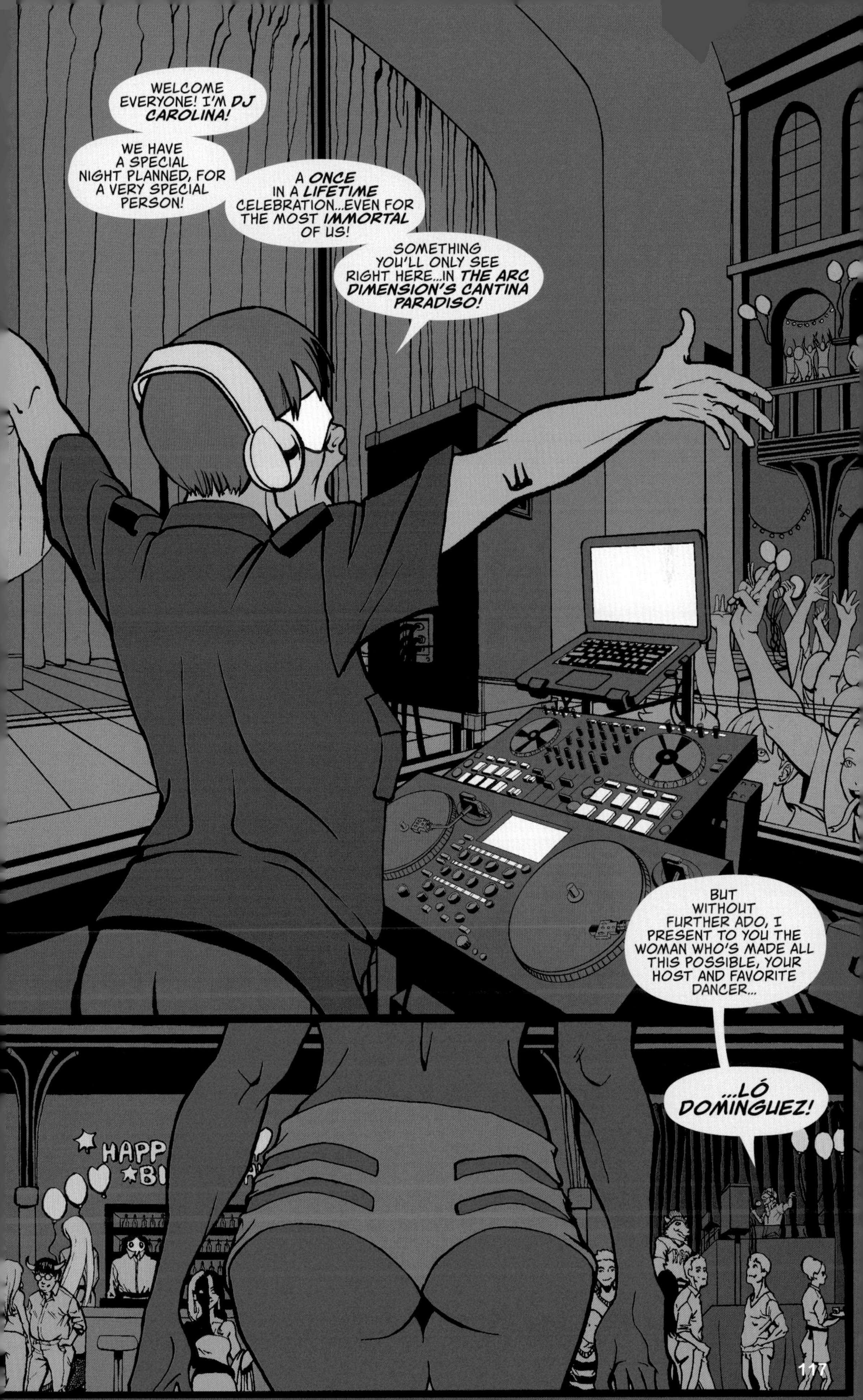

WELCOME EVERYONE! I'M DJ CAROLINA!
WE HAVE A SPECIAL NIGHT PLANNED, FOR A VERY SPECIAL PERSON!
A ONCE IN A LIFETIME CELEBRATION...EVEN FOR THE MOST IMMORTAL OF US!
SOMETHING YOU'LL ONLY SEE RIGHT HERE...IN THE ARC DIMENSION'S CANTINA PARADISO!
BUT WITHOUT FURTHER ADO, I PRESENT TO YOU THE WOMAN WHO'S MADE ALL THIS POSSIBLE, YOUR HOST AND FAVORITE DANCER...
...LÓ DOMÍNGUEZ!

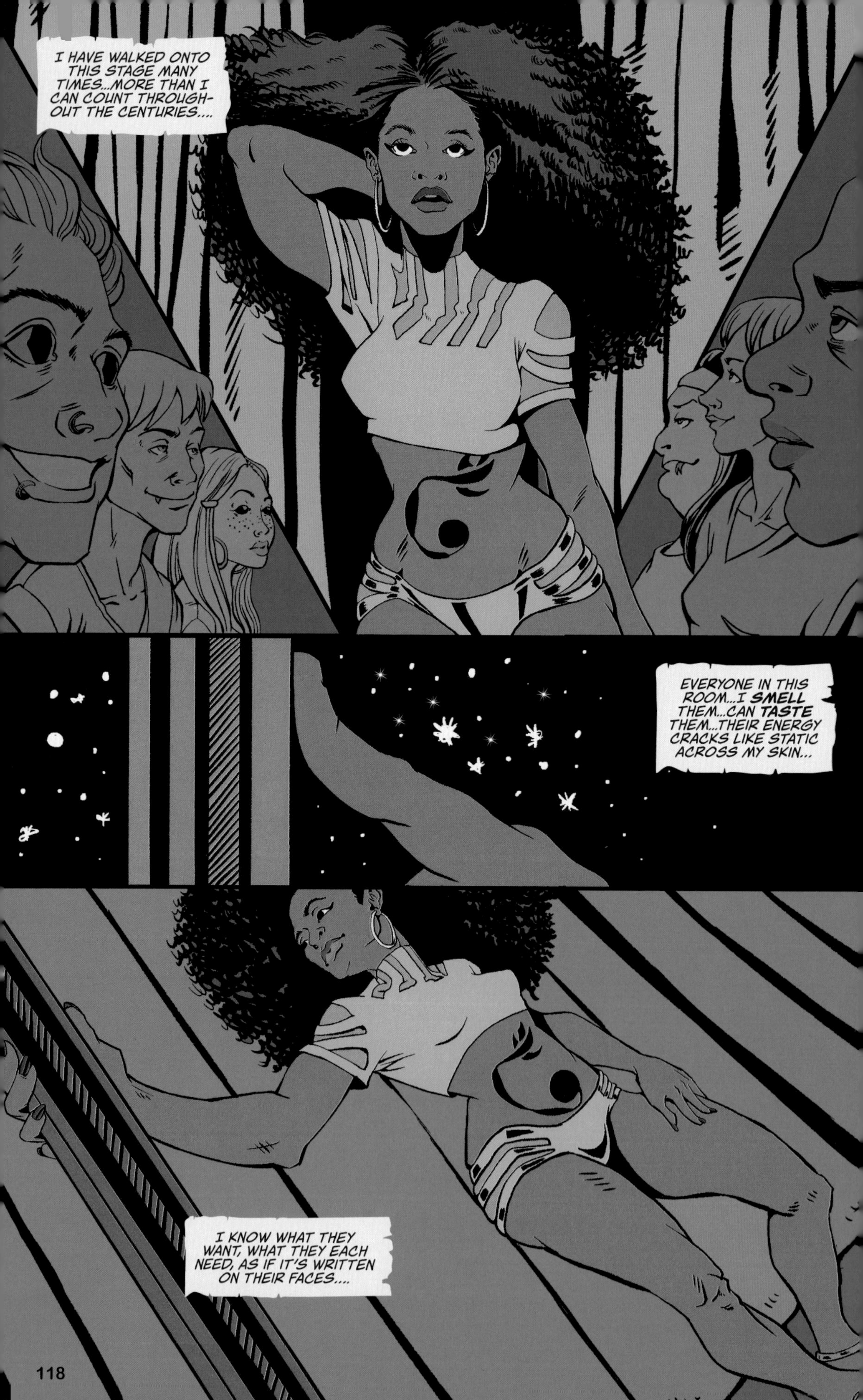
I HAVE WALKED ONTO THIS STAGE MANY TIMES...MORE THAN I CAN COUNT THROUGH-OUT THE CENTURIES....
EVERYONE IN THIS ROOM...I **SMELL** THEM...CAN **TASTE** THEM...THEIR ENERGY CRACKS LIKE STATIC ACROSS MY SKIN...
I KNOW WHAT THEY WANT, WHAT THEY EACH NEED, AS IF IT'S WRITTEN ON THEIR FACES....

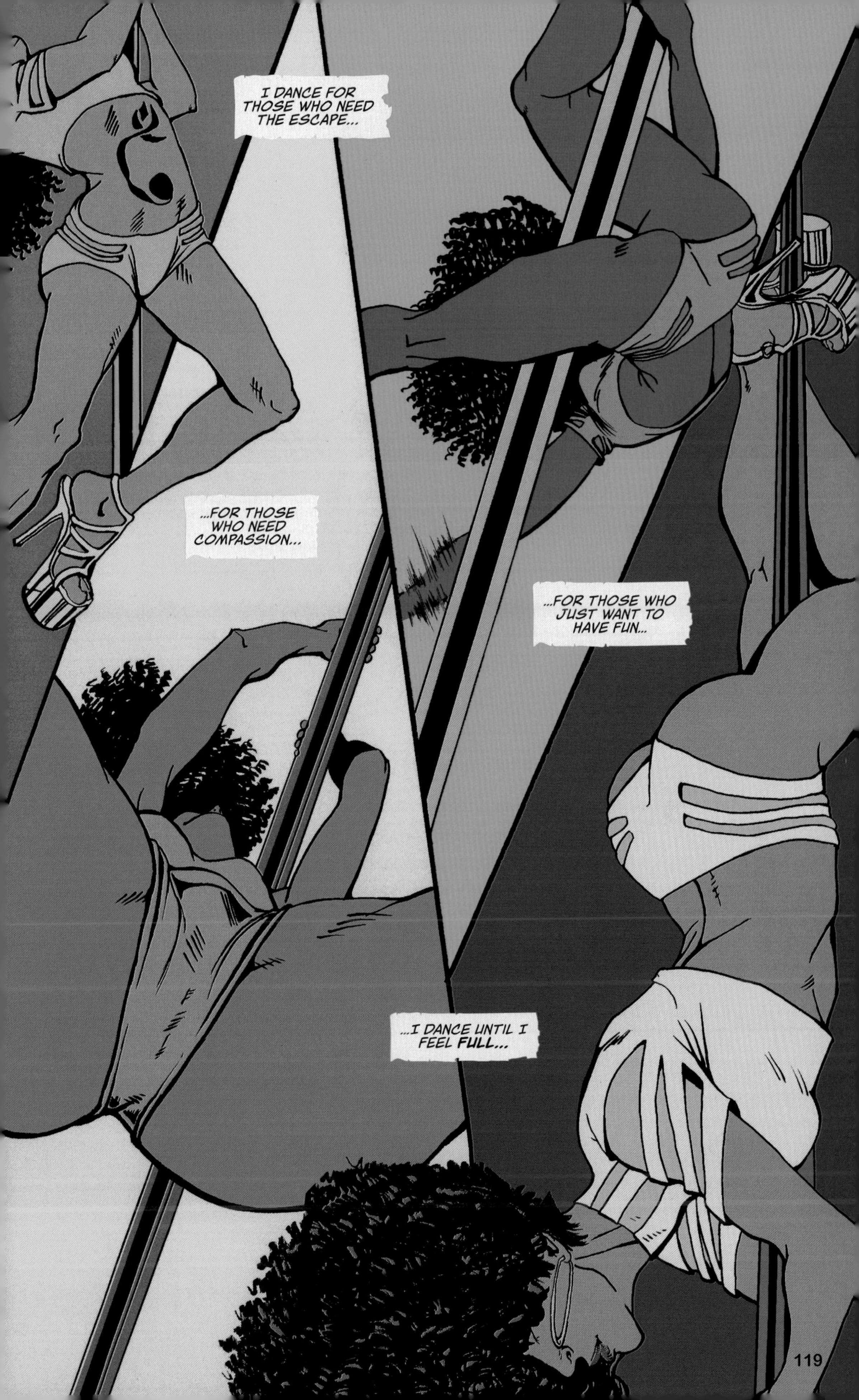
I DANCE FOR THOSE WHO NEED THE ESCAPE...
...FOR THOSE WHO NEED COMPASSION...
...FOR THOSE WHO JUST WANT TO HAVE FUN...
...I DANCE UNTIL I FEEL **FULL...**

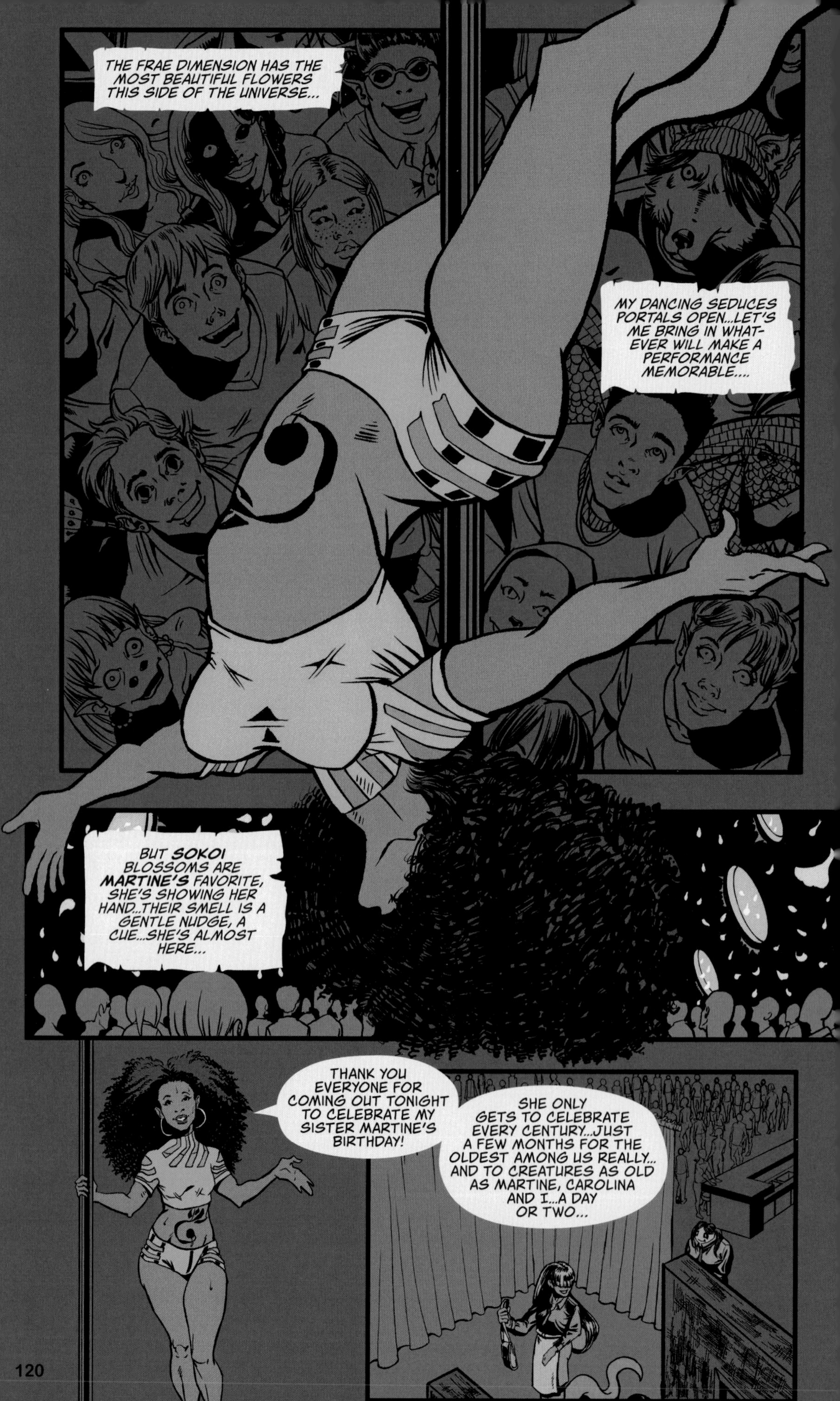
THE FRAE DIMENSION HAS THE MOST BEAUTIFUL FLOWERS THIS SIDE OF THE UNIVERSE...
MY DANCING SEDUCES PORTALS OPEN...LET'S ME BRING IN WHAT-EVER WILL MAKE A PERFORMANCE MEMORABLE....
BUT **SOKOI** BLOSSOMS ARE **MARTINE'S** FAVORITE, SHE'S SHOWING HER HAND...THEIR SMELL IS A GENTLE NUDGE, A CUE...SHE'S ALMOST HERE...
THANK YOU EVERYONE FOR COMING OUT TONIGHT TO CELEBRATE MY SISTER MARTINE'S BIRTHDAY!
SHE ONLY GETS TO CELEBRATE EVERY CENTURY...JUST A FEW MONTHS FOR THE OLDEST AMONG US REALLY... AND TO CREATURES AS OLD AS MARTINE, CAROLINA AND I...A DAY OR TWO...

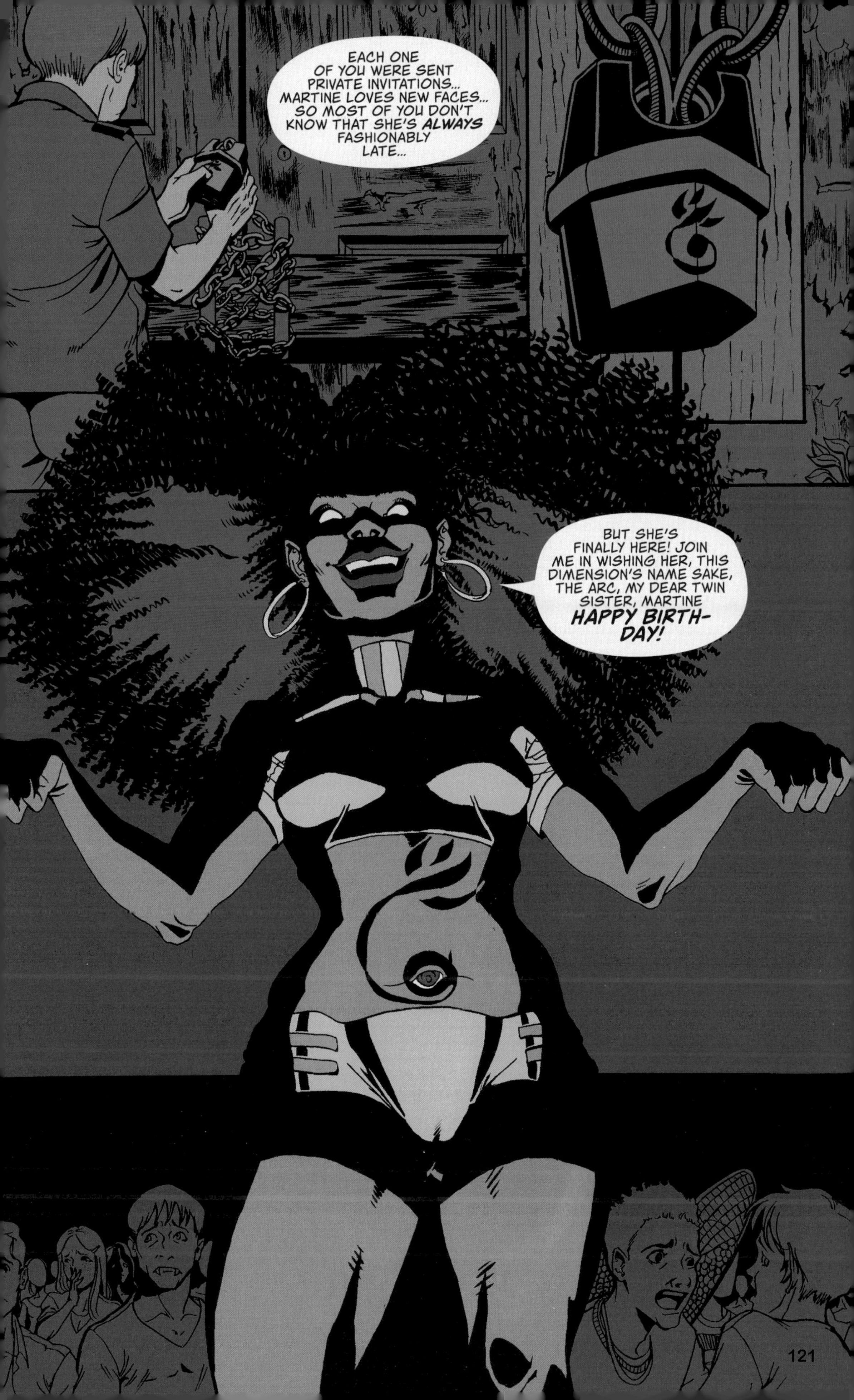
EACH ONE OF YOU WERE SENT PRIVATE INVITATIONS... MARTINE LOVES NEW FACES... SO MOST OF YOU DON'T KNOW THAT SHE'S *ALWAYS* FASHIONABLY LATE...
BUT SHE'S FINALLY HERE! JOIN ME IN WISHING HER, THIS DIMENSION'S NAME SAKE, THE ARC, MY DEAR TWIN SISTER, MARTINE ***HAPPY BIRTH-DAY!***

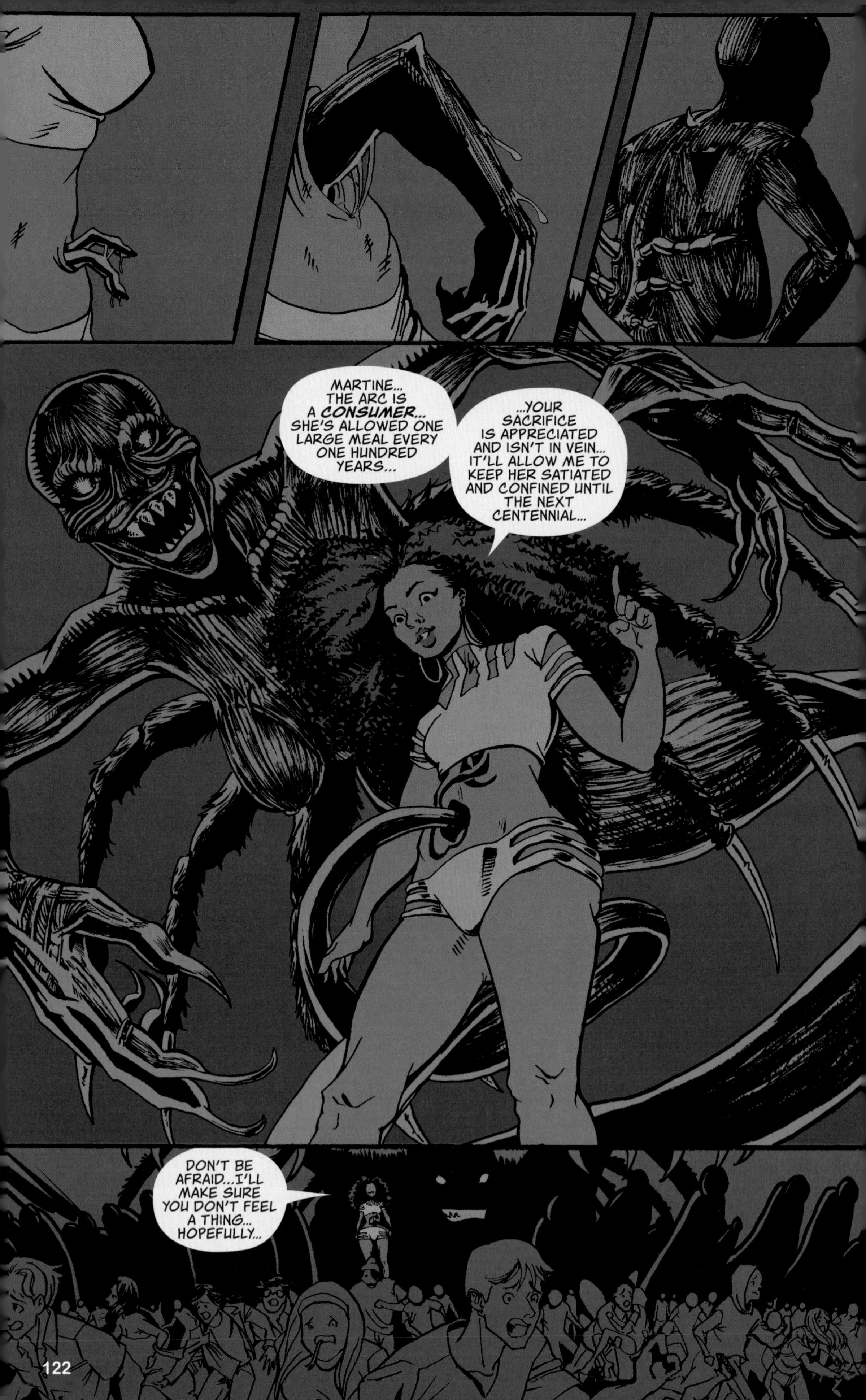
MARTINE... THE ARC IS A *CONSUMER*... SHE'S ALLOWED ONE LARGE MEAL EVERY ONE HUNDRED YEARS...
...YOUR SACRIFICE IS APPRECIATED AND ISN'T IN VEIN... IT'LL ALLOW ME TO KEEP HER SATIATED AND CONFINED UNTIL THE NEXT CENTENNIAL...
DON'T BE AFRAID...I'LL MAKE SURE YOU DON'T FEEL A THING... HOPEFULLY...

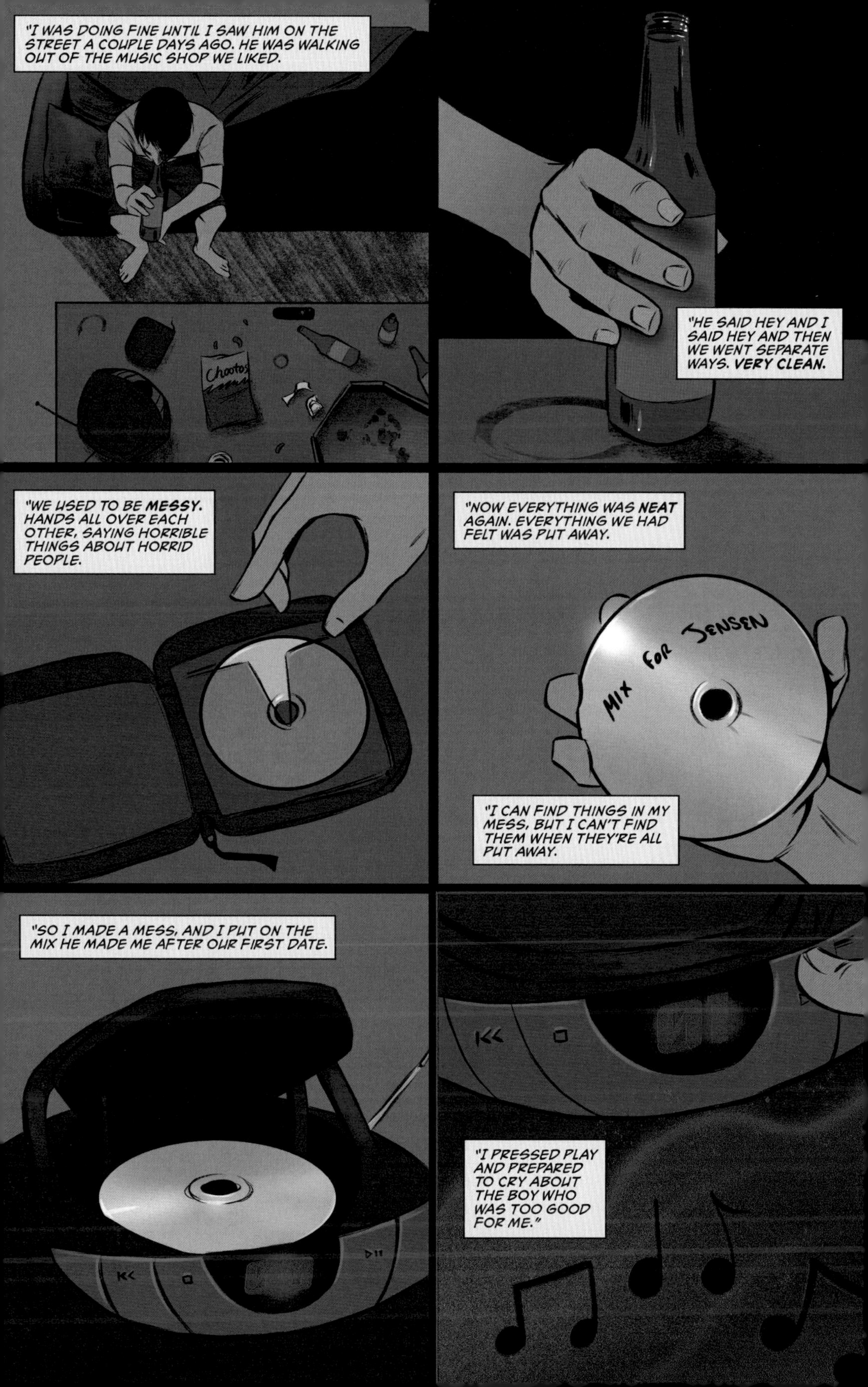
"I WAS DOING FINE UNTIL I SAW HIM ON THE STREET A COUPLE DAYS AGO. HE WAS WALKING OUT OF THE MUSIC SHOP WE LIKED.
Chootos
"HE SAID HEY AND I SAID HEY AND THEN WE WENT SEPARATE WAYS. **VERY CLEAN.**
"WE USED TO BE **MESSY**. HANDS ALL OVER EACH OTHER, SAYING HORRIBLE THINGS ABOUT HORRID PEOPLE.
"NOW EVERYTHING WAS **NEAT** AGAIN. EVERYTHING WE HAD FELT WAS PUT AWAY.
MIX FOR JENSEN
"I CAN FIND THINGS IN MY MESS, BUT I CAN'T FIND THEM WHEN THEY'RE ALL PUT AWAY.
"SO I MADE A MESS, AND I PUT ON THE MIX HE MADE ME AFTER OUR FIRST DATE.
"I PRESSED PLAY AND PREPARED TO CRY ABOUT THE BOY WHO WAS TOO GOOD FOR ME."

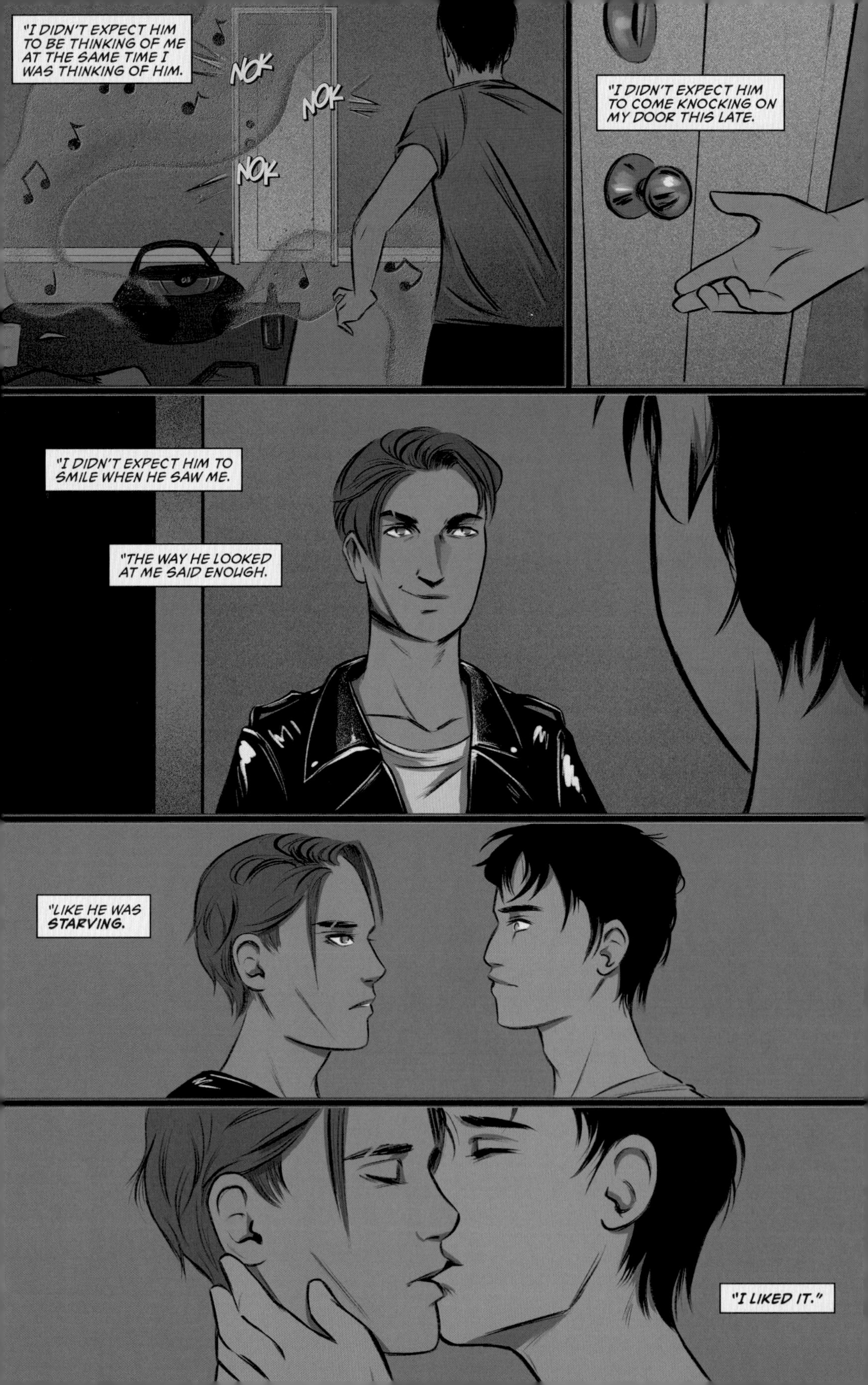
"I DIDN'T EXPECT HIM TO BE THINKING OF ME AT THE SAME TIME I WAS THINKING OF HIM.
NOK
NOK
NOK
"I DIDN'T EXPECT HIM TO COME KNOCKING ON MY DOOR THIS LATE.
"I DIDN'T EXPECT HIM TO SMILE WHEN HE SAW ME.
"THE WAY HE LOOKED AT ME SAID ENOUGH.
"LIKE HE WAS STARVING.
"I LIKED IT."

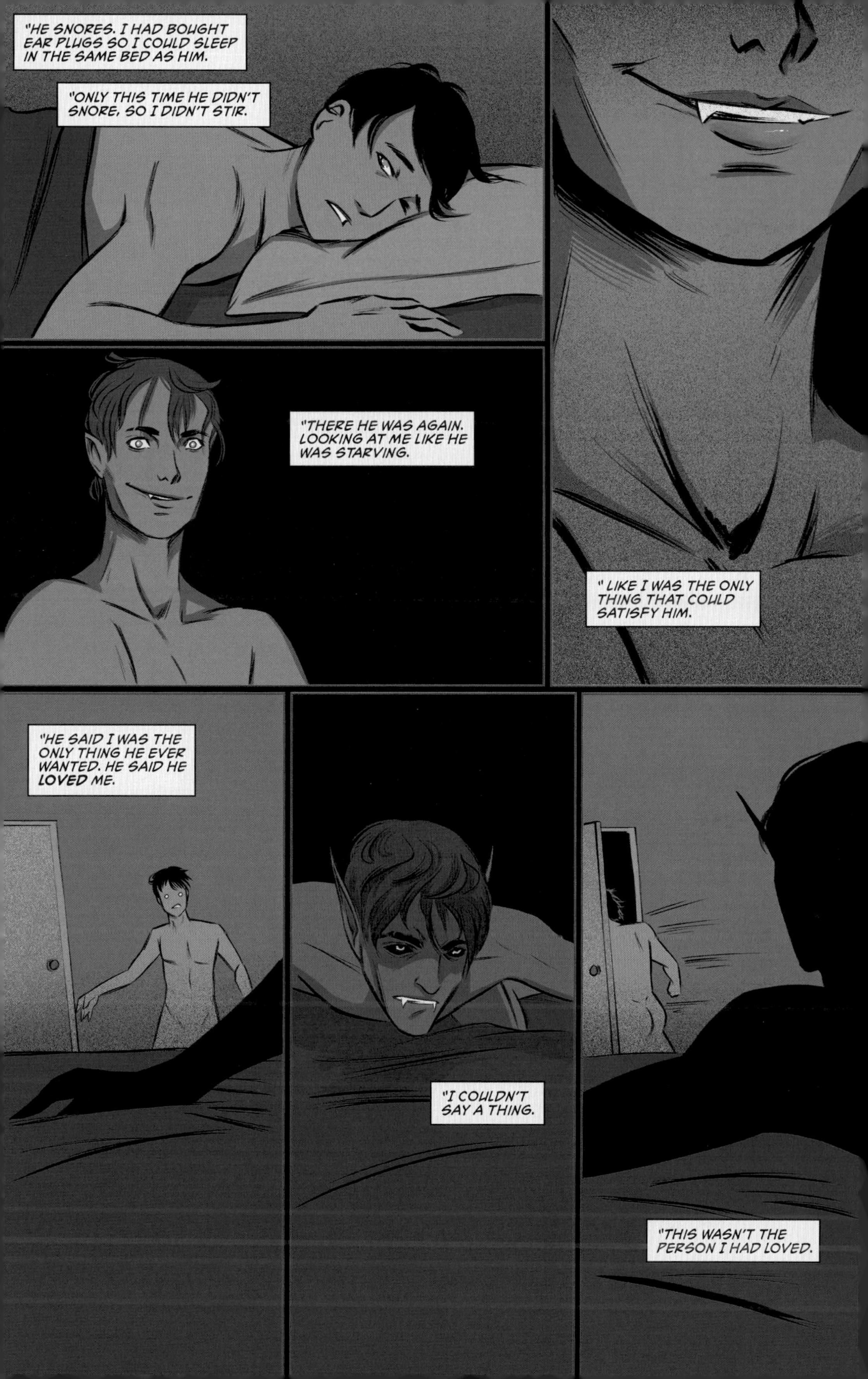
"HE SNORES. I HAD BOUGHT EAR PLUGS SO I COULD SLEEP IN THE SAME BED AS HIM.
"ONLY THIS TIME HE DIDN'T SNORE, SO I DIDN'T STIR.
"THERE HE WAS AGAIN. LOOKING AT ME LIKE HE WAS STARVING.
" LIKE I WAS THE ONLY THING THAT COULD SATISFY HIM.
"HE SAID I WAS THE ONLY THING HE EVER WANTED. HE SAID HE LOVED ME.
"I COULDN'T SAY A THING.
"THIS WASN'T THE PERSON I HAD LOVED.

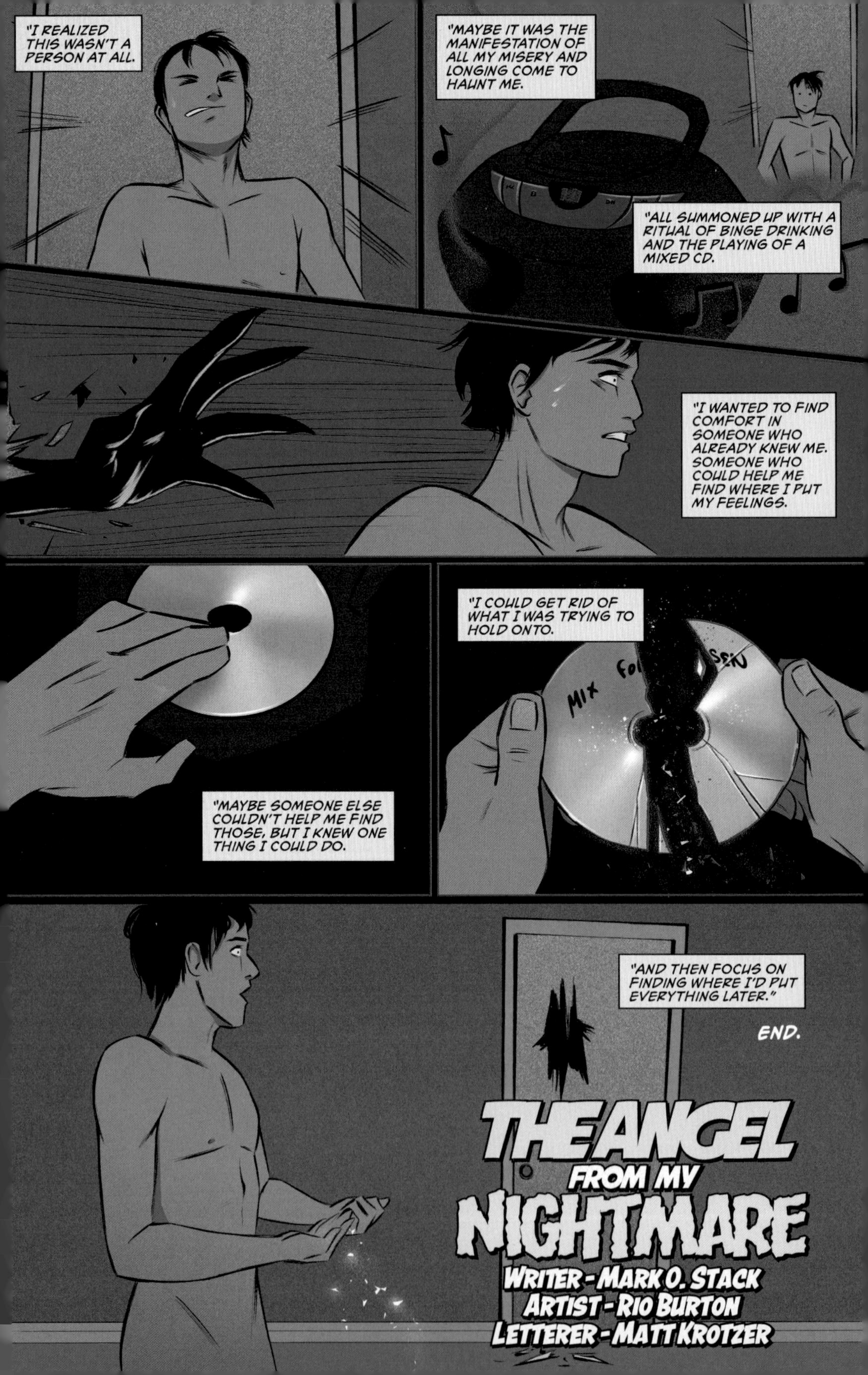
"I REALIZED THIS WASN'T A PERSON AT ALL.
"MAYBE IT WAS THE MANIFESTATION OF ALL MY MISERY AND LONGING COME TO HAUNT ME.
"ALL SUMMONED UP WITH A RITUAL OF BINGE DRINKING AND THE PLAYING OF A MIXED CD.
"I WANTED TO FIND COMFORT IN SOMEONE WHO ALREADY KNEW ME. SOMEONE WHO COULD HELP ME FIND WHERE I PUT MY FEELINGS.
"MAYBE SOMEONE ELSE COULDN'T HELP ME FIND THOSE, BUT I KNEW ONE THING I COULD DO.
"I COULD GET RID OF WHAT I WAS TRYING TO HOLD ONTO.
"AND THEN FOCUS ON FINDING WHERE I'D PUT EVERYTHING LATER."
END.
THE ANGEL FROM MY NIGHTMARE
WRITER - MARK O. STACK
ARTIST - RIO BURTON
LETTERER - MATT KROTZER

APOCALYPSE DEMO

WRITTEN BY DANNY LORE & ART BY MARIE ENGER
COLORS BY DJ CHAVIS & LETTERS BY MICAH MYERS

AND THAT WAS **'THE JAM,'** FEATURING LIL BEATZ.

THE LIVE VERSION IS BETTER.

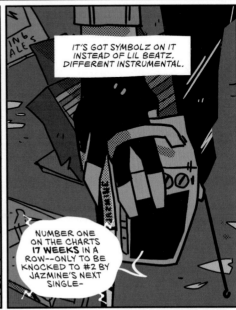

IT'S GOT SYMBOLZ ON IT INSTEAD OF LIL BEATZ. DIFFERENT INSTRUMENTAL.

NUMBER ONE ON THE CHARTS **17 WEEKS** IN A ROW--ONLY TO BE KNOCKED TO #2 BY JAZMINE'S NEXT SINGLE--

JAZMINE IS ALWAYS BETTER IN CONCERT.

...LAST MONTH'S SURPRISE TRACK 'LOVE ME AFTER.'

NOT LIKE THERE'LL EVER BE ANOTHER CONCERT.

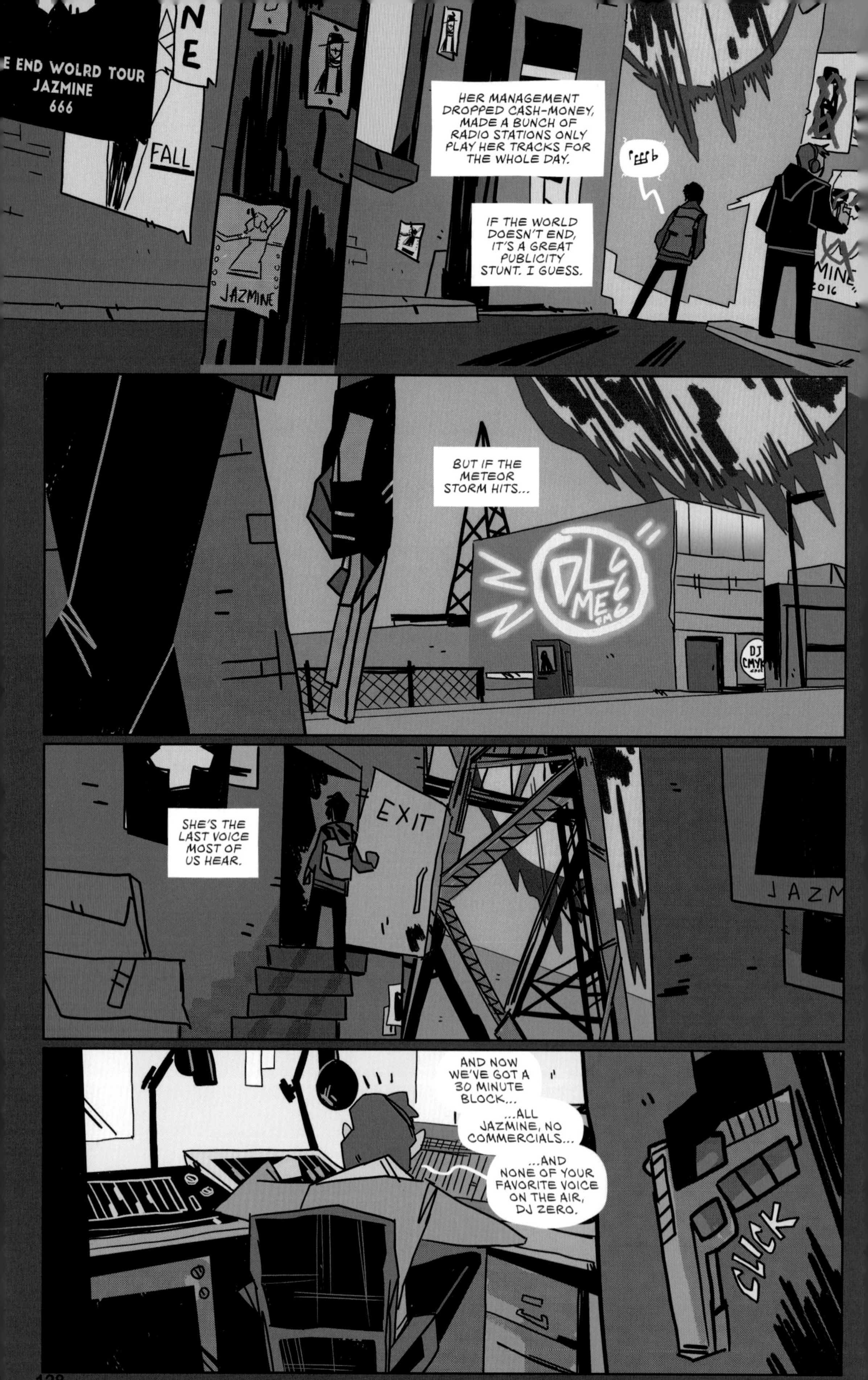

E END WOLRD TOUR
JAZMINE
666
NE
FALL
JAZMINE
HER MANAGEMENT DROPPED CASH-MONEY, MADE A BUNCH OF RADIO STATIONS ONLY PLAY HER TRACKS FOR THE WHOLE DAY.
IF THE WORLD DOESN'T END, IT'S A GREAT PUBLICITY STUNT. I GUESS.
MINE 2016
BUT IF THE METEOR STORM HITS...
DJ CMYK
SHE'S THE LAST VOICE MOST OF US HEAR.
EXIT
JAZM
AND NOW WE'VE GOT A 30 MINUTE BLOCK...
...ALL JAZMINE, NO COMMERCIALS...
...AND NONE OF YOUR FAVORITE VOICE ON THE AIR, DJ ZERO.
CLICK

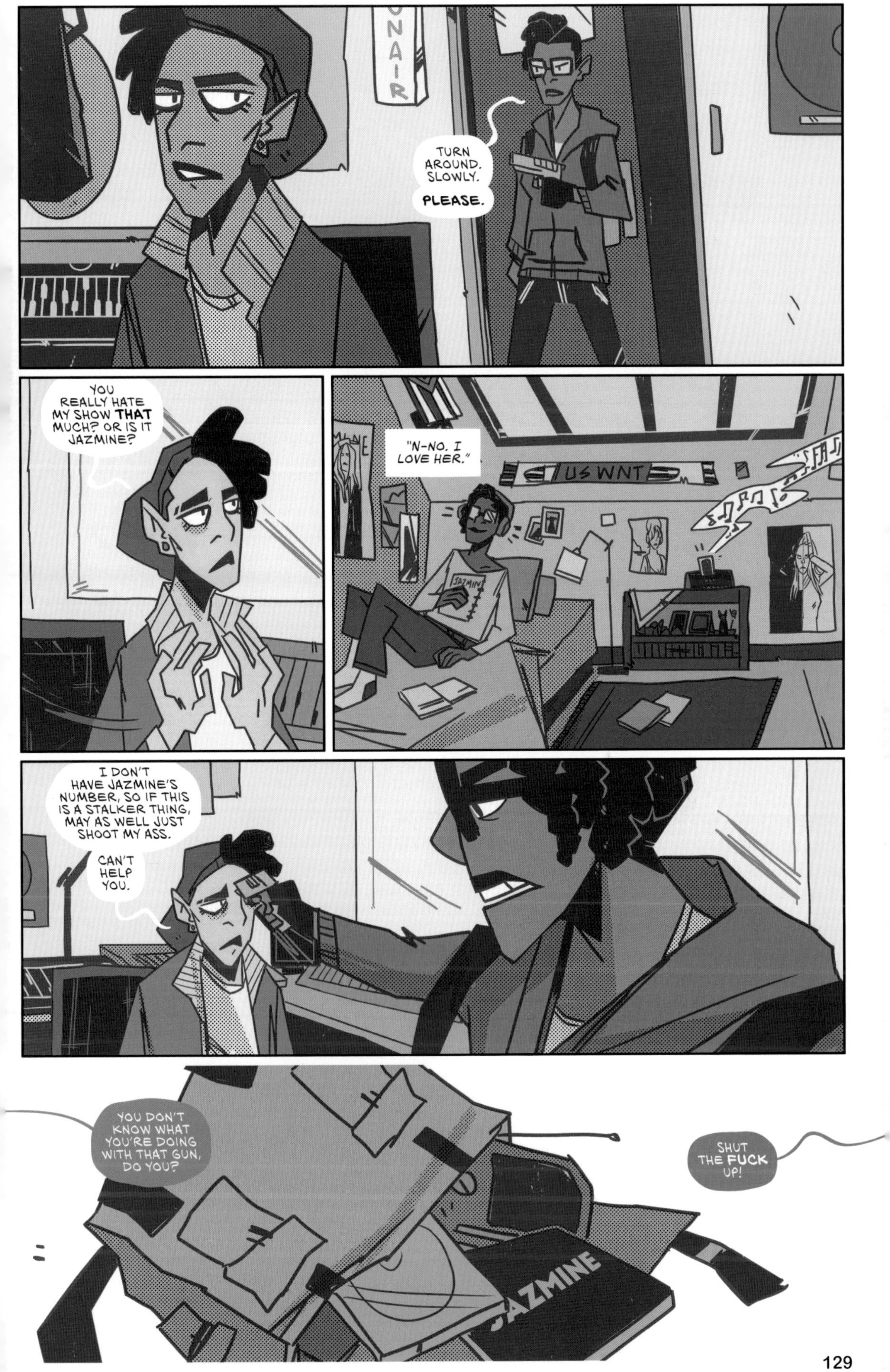
TURN AROUND. SLOWLY.
PLEASE.
YOU REALLY HATE MY SHOW THAT MUCH? OR IS IT JAZMINE?
"N-NO. I LOVE HER."
US WNT
JAZMIN
I DON'T HAVE JAZMINE'S NUMBER, SO IF THIS IS A STALKER THING, MAY AS WELL JUST SHOOT MY ASS.
CAN'T HELP YOU.
YOU DON'T KNOW WHAT YOU'RE DOING WITH THAT GUN, DO YOU?
SHUT THE FUCK UP!
JAZMINE

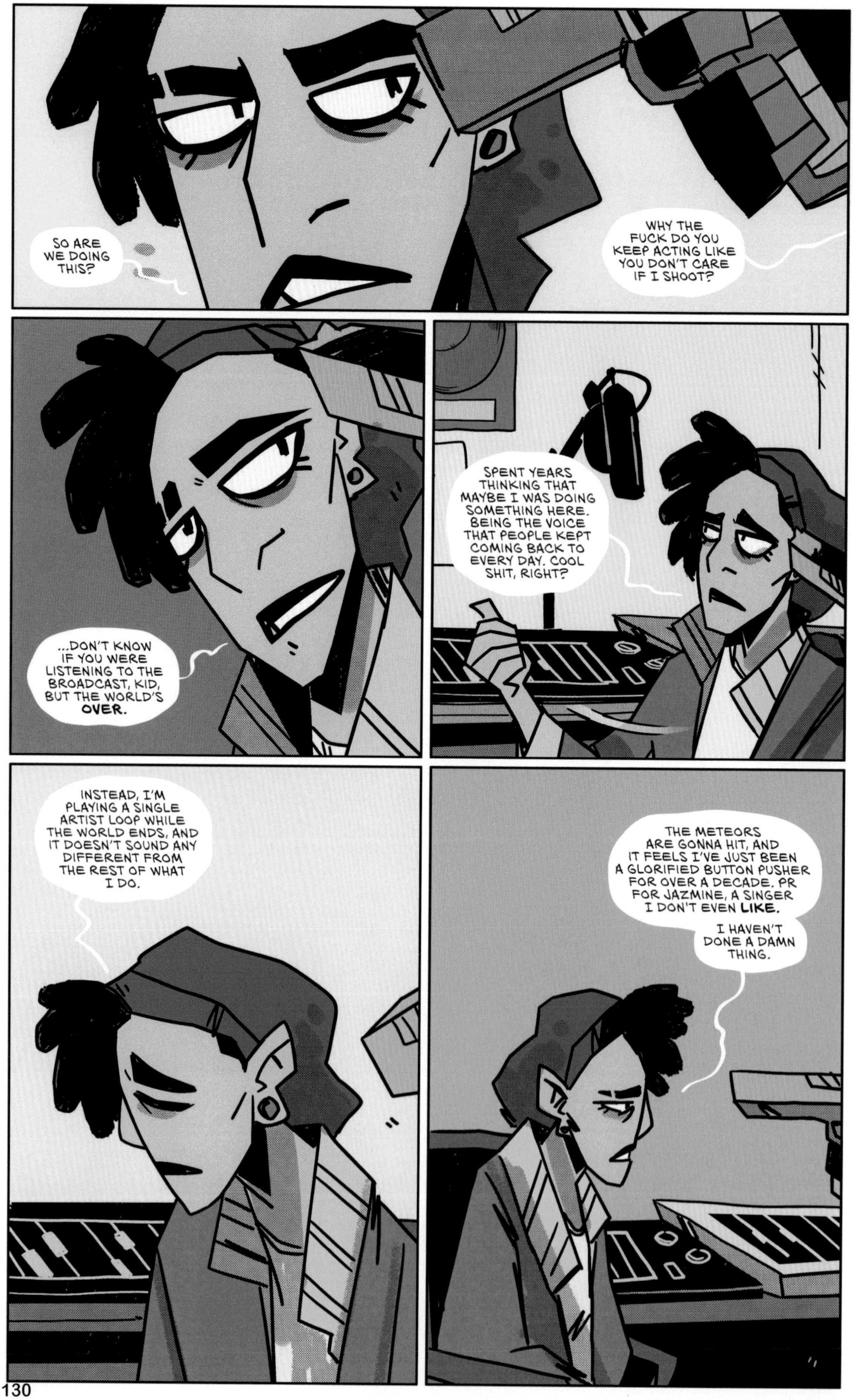
SO ARE WE DOING THIS?
WHY THE FUCK DO YOU KEEP ACTING LIKE YOU DON'T CARE IF I SHOOT?
...DON'T KNOW IF YOU WERE LISTENING TO THE BROADCAST, KID, BUT THE WORLD'S **OVER.**
SPENT YEARS THINKING THAT MAYBE I WAS DOING SOMETHING HERE. BEING THE VOICE THAT PEOPLE KEPT COMING BACK TO EVERY DAY. COOL SHIT, RIGHT?
INSTEAD, I'M PLAYING A SINGLE ARTIST LOOP WHILE THE WORLD ENDS, AND IT DOESN'T SOUND ANY DIFFERENT FROM THE REST OF WHAT I DO.
THE METEORS ARE GONNA HIT, AND IT FEELS I'VE JUST BEEN A GLORIFIED BUTTON PUSHER FOR OVER A DECADE. PR FOR JAZMINE, A SINGER I DON'T EVEN **LIKE.**
I HAVEN'T DONE A DAMN THING.

BUT THEY **HEARD** YOU.

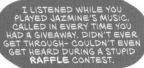

I LISTENED WHILE YOU PLAYED JAZMINE'S MUSIC, CALLED IN EVERY TIME YOU HAD A GIVEAWAY. DIDN'T EVER GET THROUGH— COULDN'T EVEN GET HEARD DURING A STUPID **RAFFLE** CONTEST.

EVERYONE WHO TUNED IN EVERY NIGHT **HEARD** YOU.

I HEARD YOU.

"YOU HAD A CONTEST ONCE. TO MEET HER—ALL I HAD TO DO WAS PUT MYSELF OUT THERE AND **SING.**

"I CHOKED. PANICKED. COULDN'T DO IT.

"NO ONE WILL **EVER** HEAR ME."

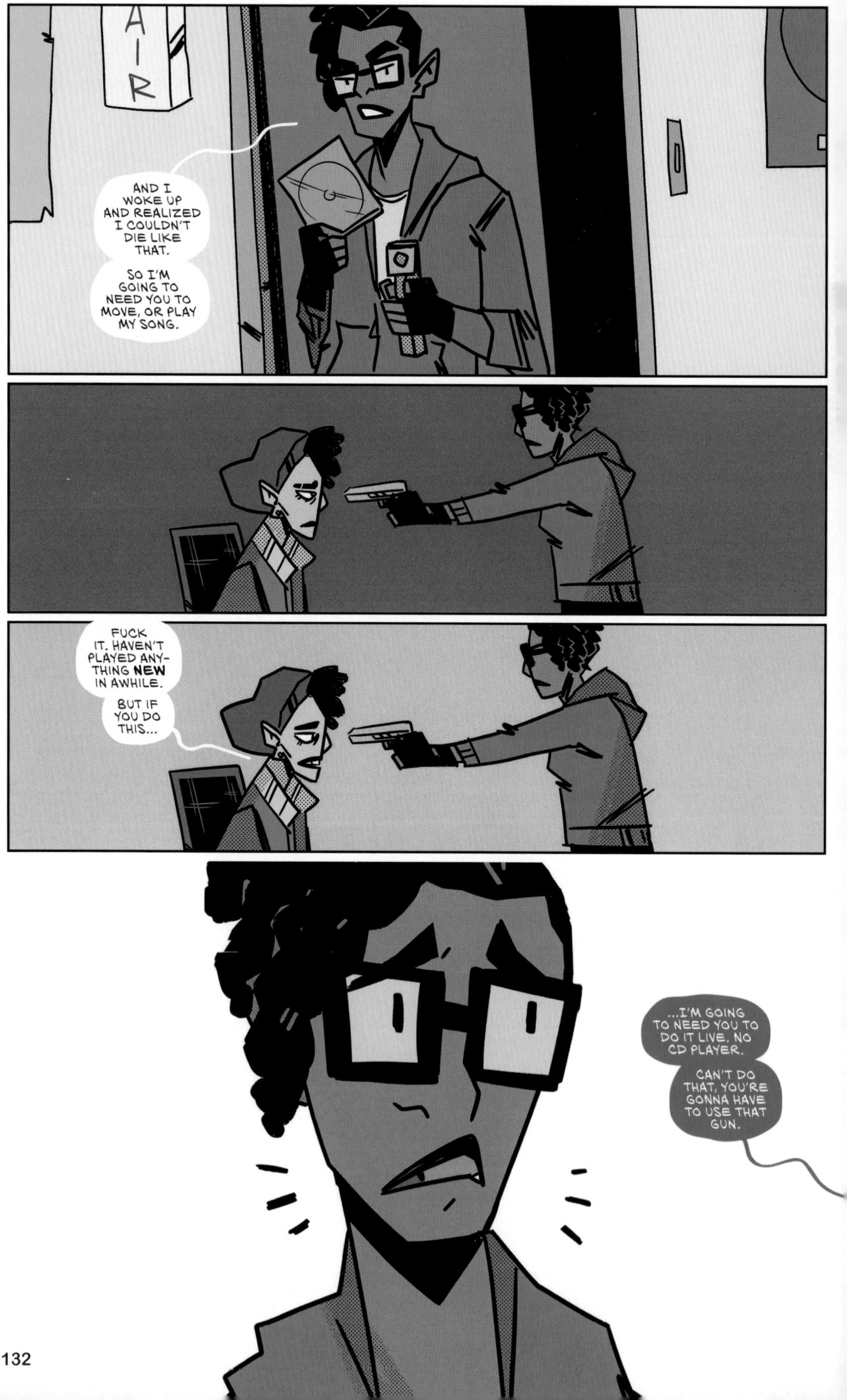
AND I WOKE UP AND REALIZED I COULDN'T DIE LIKE THAT.
SO I'M GOING TO NEED YOU TO MOVE, OR PLAY MY SONG.
AIR
FUCK IT. HAVEN'T PLAYED ANY-THING **NEW** IN AWHILE.
BUT IF YOU DO THIS...
...I'M GOING TO NEED YOU TO DO IT LIVE. NO CD PLAYER.
CAN'T DO THAT, YOU'RE GONNA HAVE TO USE THAT GUN.

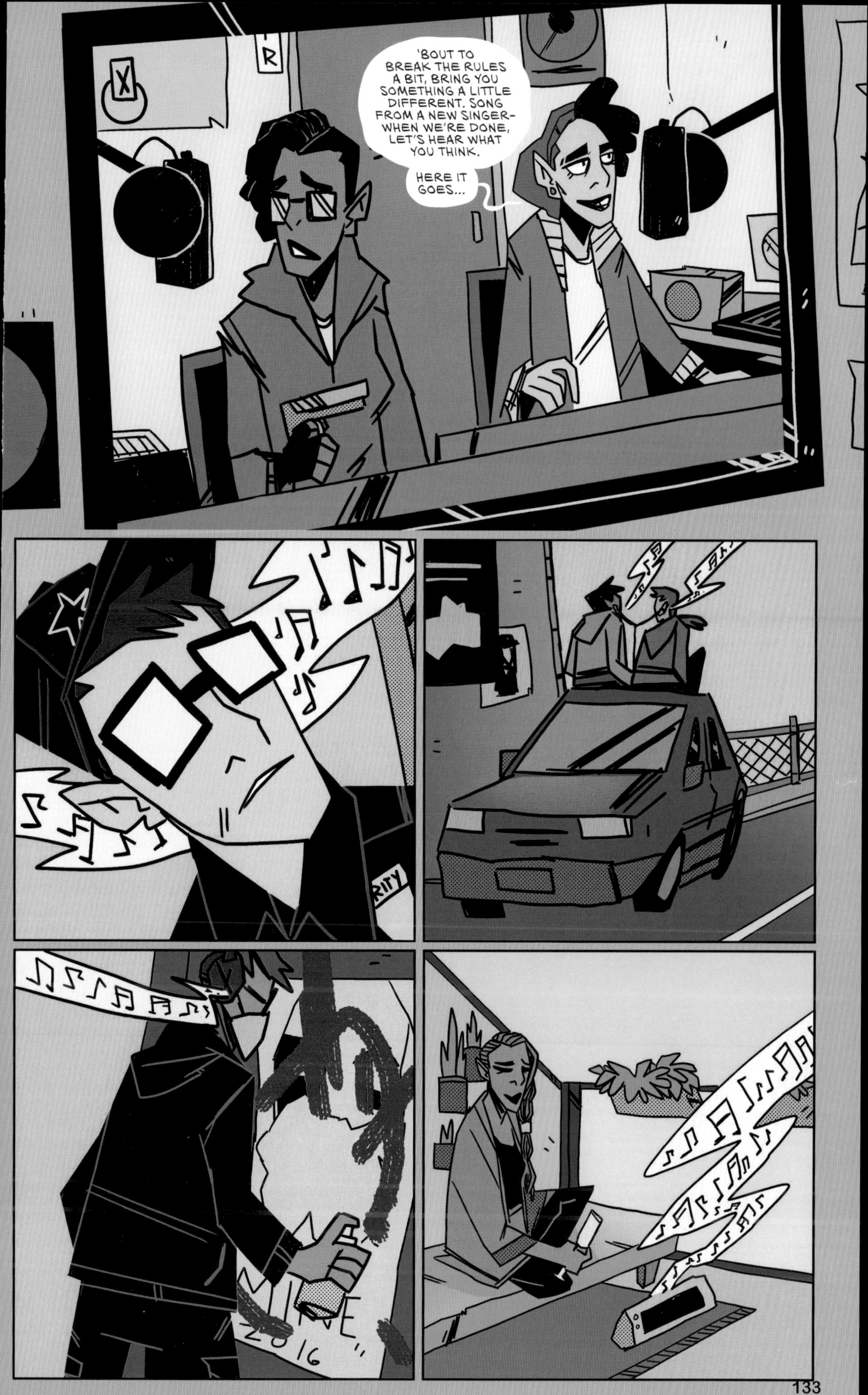
'BOUT TO BREAK THE RULES A BIT, BRING YOU SOMETHING A LITTLE DIFFERENT. SONG FROM A NEW SINGER-WHEN WE'RE DONE, LET'S HEAR WHAT YOU THINK.
HERE IT GOES...
R
RITY
MINE 2016

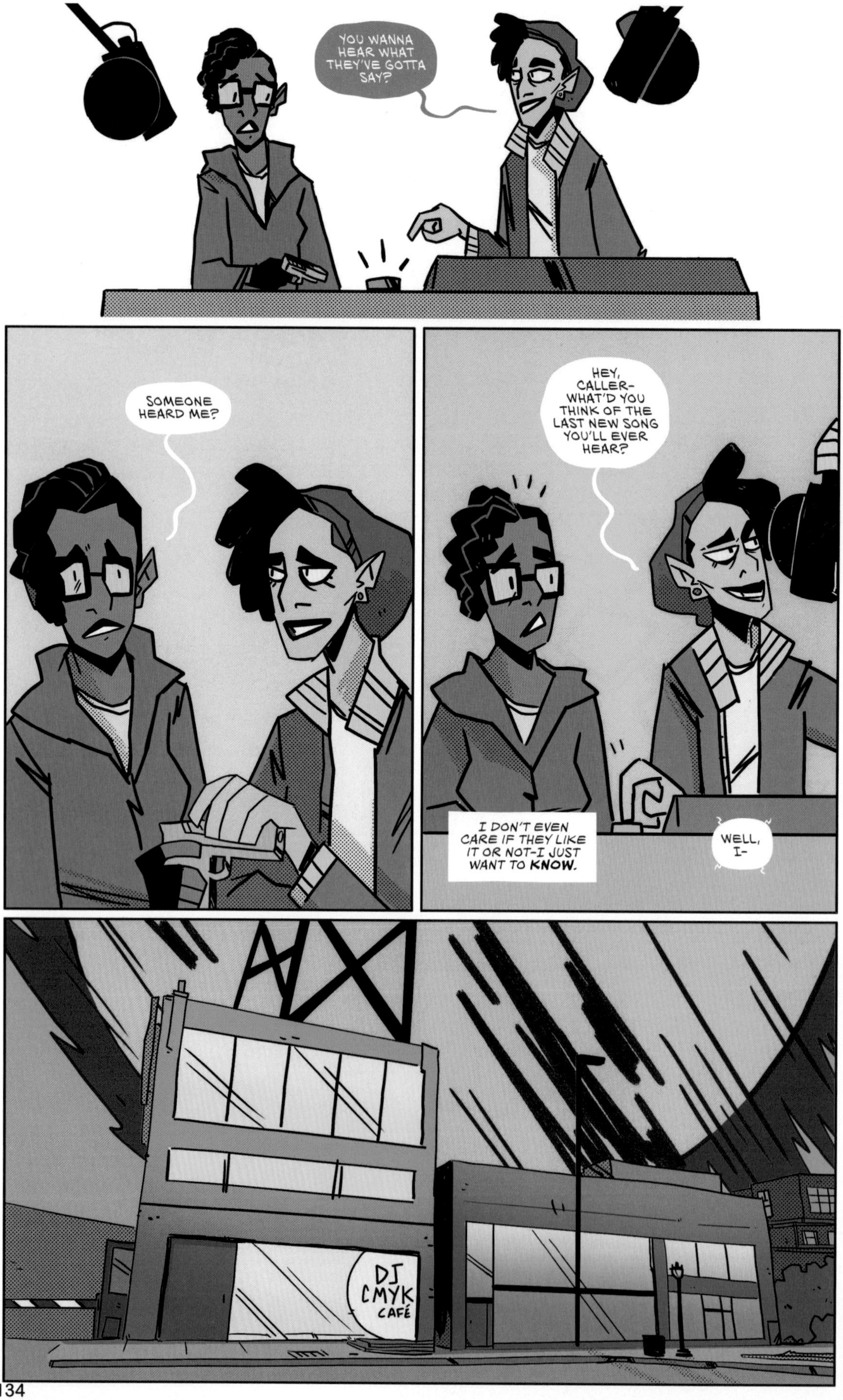
YOU WANNA HEAR WHAT THEY'VE GOTTA SAY?
SOMEONE HEARD ME?
HEY, CALLER- WHAT'D YOU THINK OF THE LAST NEW SONG YOU'LL EVER HEAR?
I DON'T EVEN CARE IF THEY LIKE IT OR NOT-I JUST WANT TO **KNOW**.
WELL, I-
DJ CMYK CAFÉ

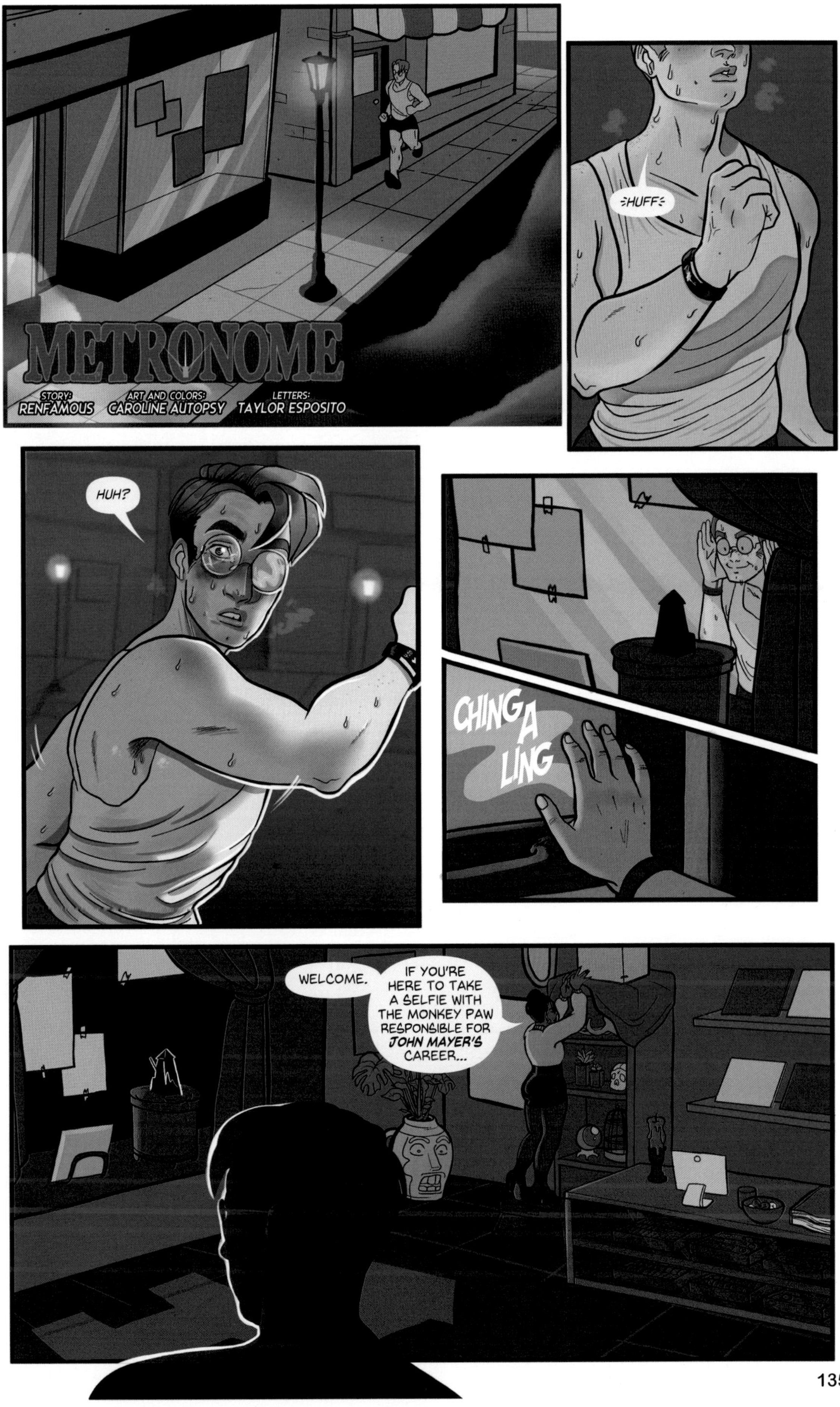
METRONOME
STORY: RENFAMOUS
ART AND COLORS: CAROLINE AUTOPSY
LETTERS: TAYLOR ESPOSITO
HUFF
HUH?
CHING A LING
WELCOME.
IF YOU'RE HERE TO TAKE A SELFIE WITH THE MONKEY PAW RESPONSIBLE FOR JOHN MAYER'S CAREER...

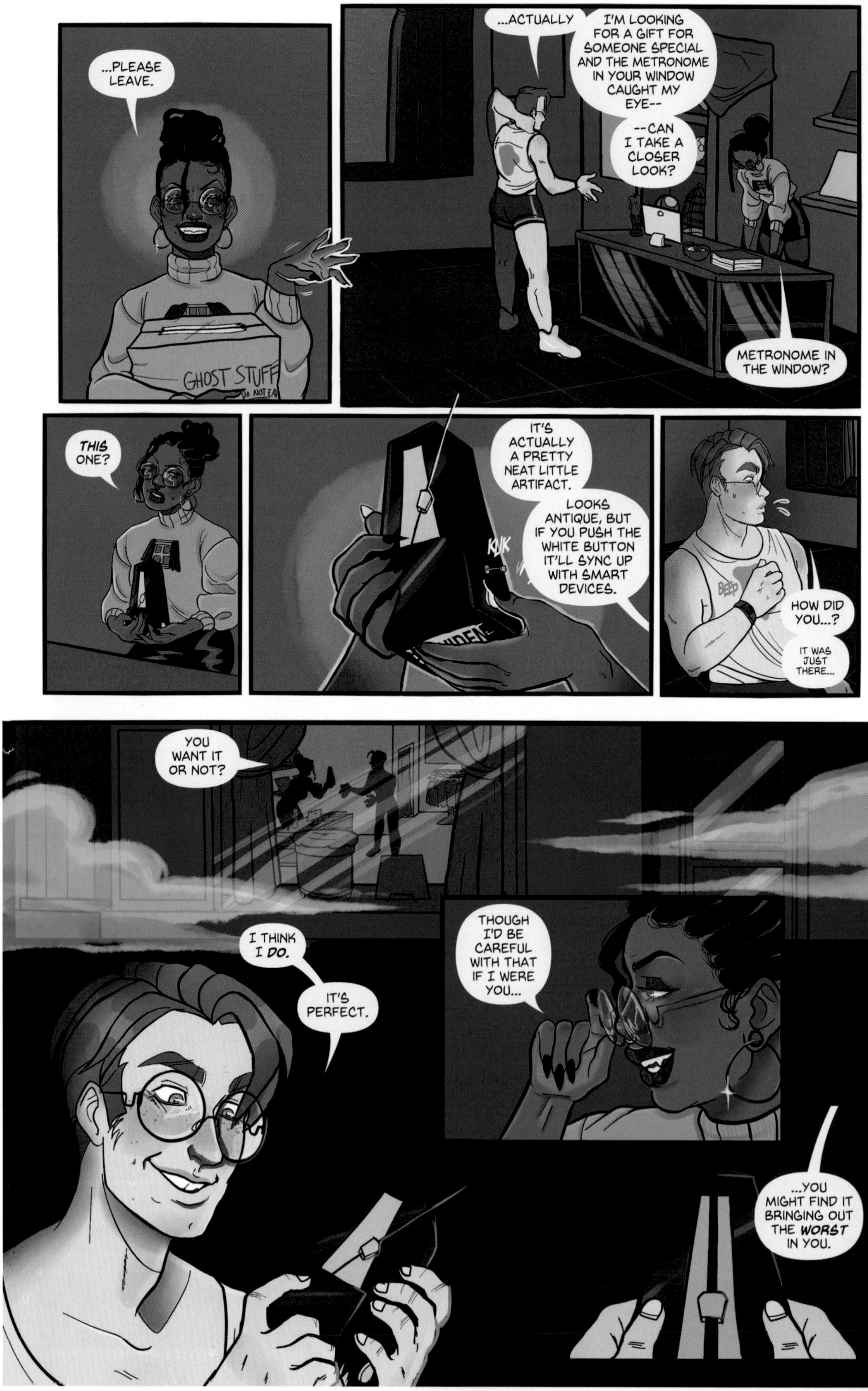
...PLEASE LEAVE.
GHOST STUFF
DO NOT EAT
...ACTUALLY
I'M LOOKING FOR A GIFT FOR SOMEONE SPECIAL AND THE METRONOME IN YOUR WINDOW CAUGHT MY EYE--
--CAN I TAKE A CLOSER LOOK?
METRONOME IN THE WINDOW?
THIS ONE?
IT'S ACTUALLY A PRETTY NEAT LITTLE ARTIFACT.
LOOKS ANTIQUE, BUT IF YOU PUSH THE WHITE BUTTON IT'LL SYNC UP WITH SMART DEVICES.
KLIK
BEEP
HOW DID YOU...?
IT WAS JUST THERE...
YOU WANT IT OR NOT?
I THINK I *DO.*
IT'S PERFECT.
THOUGH I'D BE CAREFUL WITH THAT IF I WERE YOU...
...YOU MIGHT FIND IT BRINGING OUT THE ***WORST*** IN YOU.

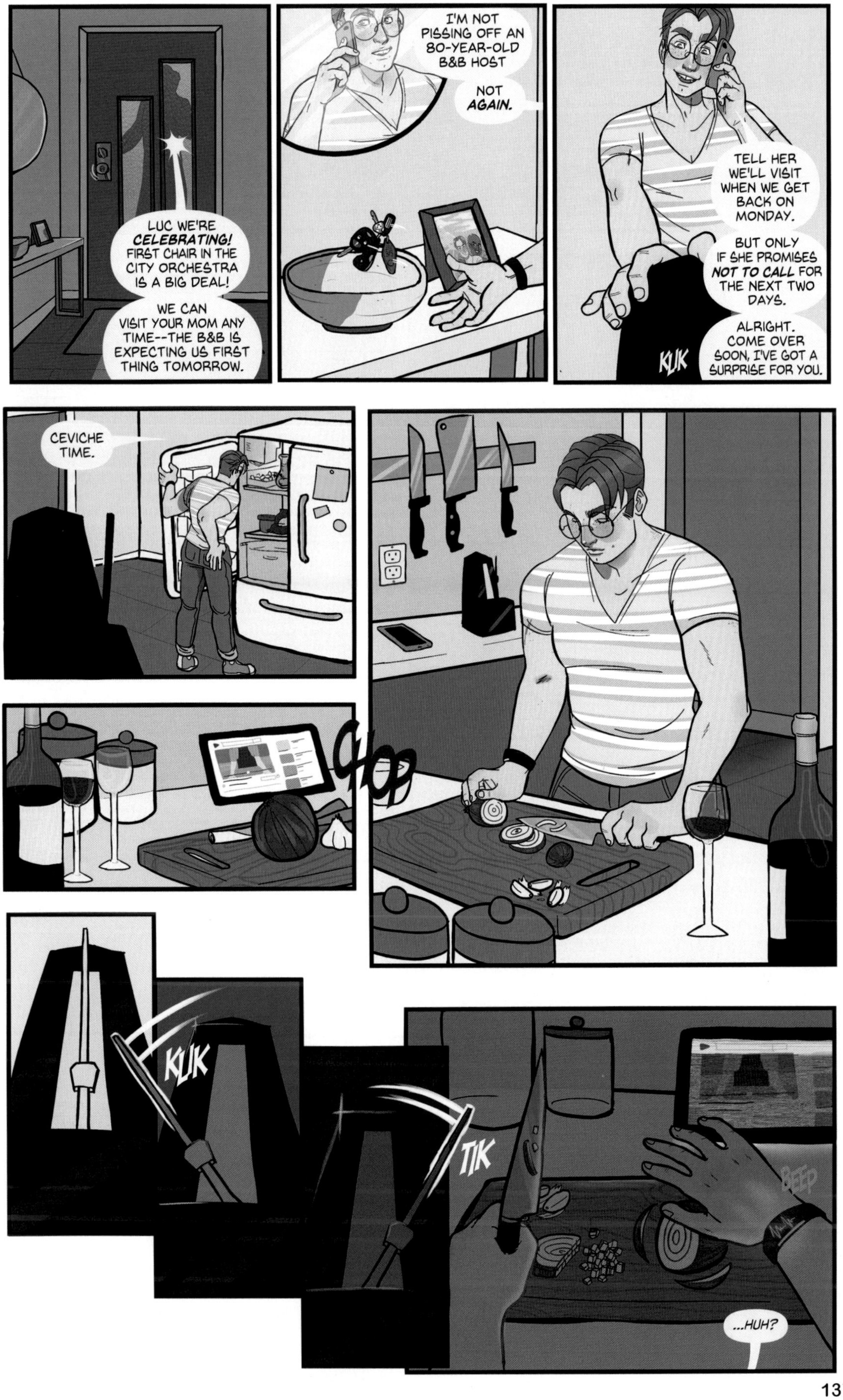
LUC WE'RE CELEBRATING! FIRST CHAIR IN THE CITY ORCHESTRA IS A BIG DEAL!
WE CAN VISIT YOUR MOM ANY TIME--THE B&B IS EXPECTING US FIRST THING TOMORROW.
I'M NOT PISSING OFF AN 80-YEAR-OLD B&B HOST
NOT AGAIN.
TELL HER WE'LL VISIT WHEN WE GET BACK ON MONDAY.
BUT ONLY IF SHE PROMISES NOT TO CALL FOR THE NEXT TWO DAYS.
ALRIGHT. COME OVER SOON, I'VE GOT A SURPRISE FOR YOU.
KLIK
CEVICHE TIME.
CHOP
KLIK
TIK
BEEP
...HUH?

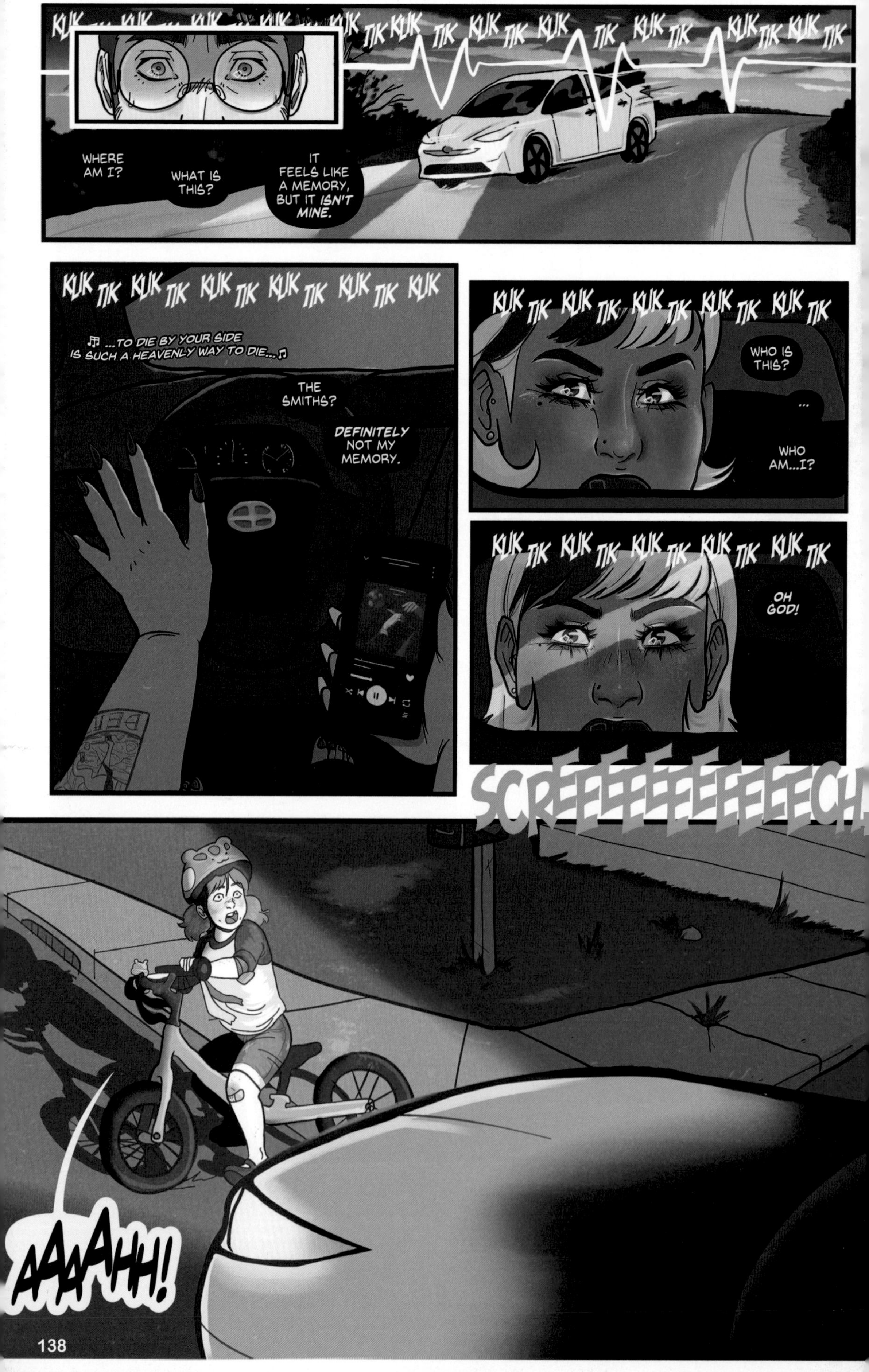
KLIK TIK KLIK TIK KLIK TIK KLIK TIK KLIK TIK KLIK TIK KLIK TIK KLIK TIK KLIK TIK KLIK TIK KLIK TIK
WHERE AM I?
WHAT IS THIS?
IT FEELS LIKE A MEMORY, BUT IT ISN'T MINE.
KLIK TIK KLIK TIK KLIK TIK KLIK TIK KLIK TIK KLIK
♫ ...TO DIE BY YOUR SIDE IS SUCH A HEAVENLY WAY TO DIE...♫
THE SMITHS?
DEFINITELY NOT MY MEMORY.
KLIK TIK KLIK TIK KLIK TIK KLIK TIK KLIK TIK
WHO IS THIS?
...
WHO AM...I?
KLIK TIK KLIK TIK KLIK TIK KLIK TIK KLIK TIK
OH GOD!
SCREEEEEEEEEEECH
AAAAHH!

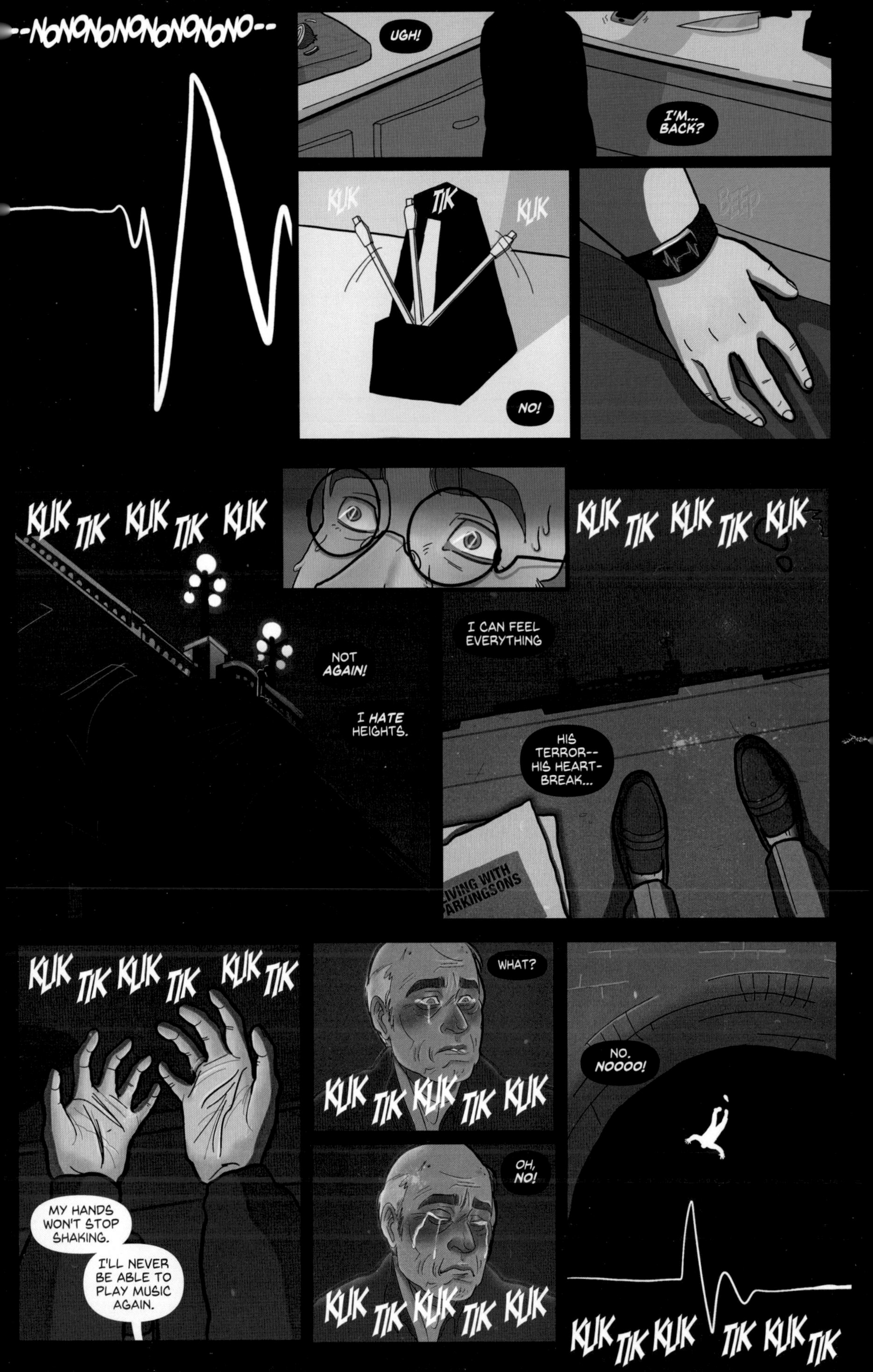
--NONONONONONONONONO--
UGH!
I'M... BACK?
TIK
KLIK
KLIK
NO!
BEEP
KLIK TIK KLIK TIK KLIK
KLIK TIK KLIK TIK KLIK
NOT AGAIN!
I HATE HEIGHTS.
I CAN FEEL EVERYTHING
HIS TERROR-- HIS HEART-BREAK...
IVING WITH ARKINGSONS
KLIK TIK KLIK TIK KLIK TIK
MY HANDS WON'T STOP SHAKING.
I'LL NEVER BE ABLE TO PLAY MUSIC AGAIN.
WHAT?
KLIK TIK KLIK TIK KLIK
OH, NO!
KLIK TIK KLIK TIK KLIK
NO. NOOOO!
KLIK TIK KLIK TIK KLIK TIK

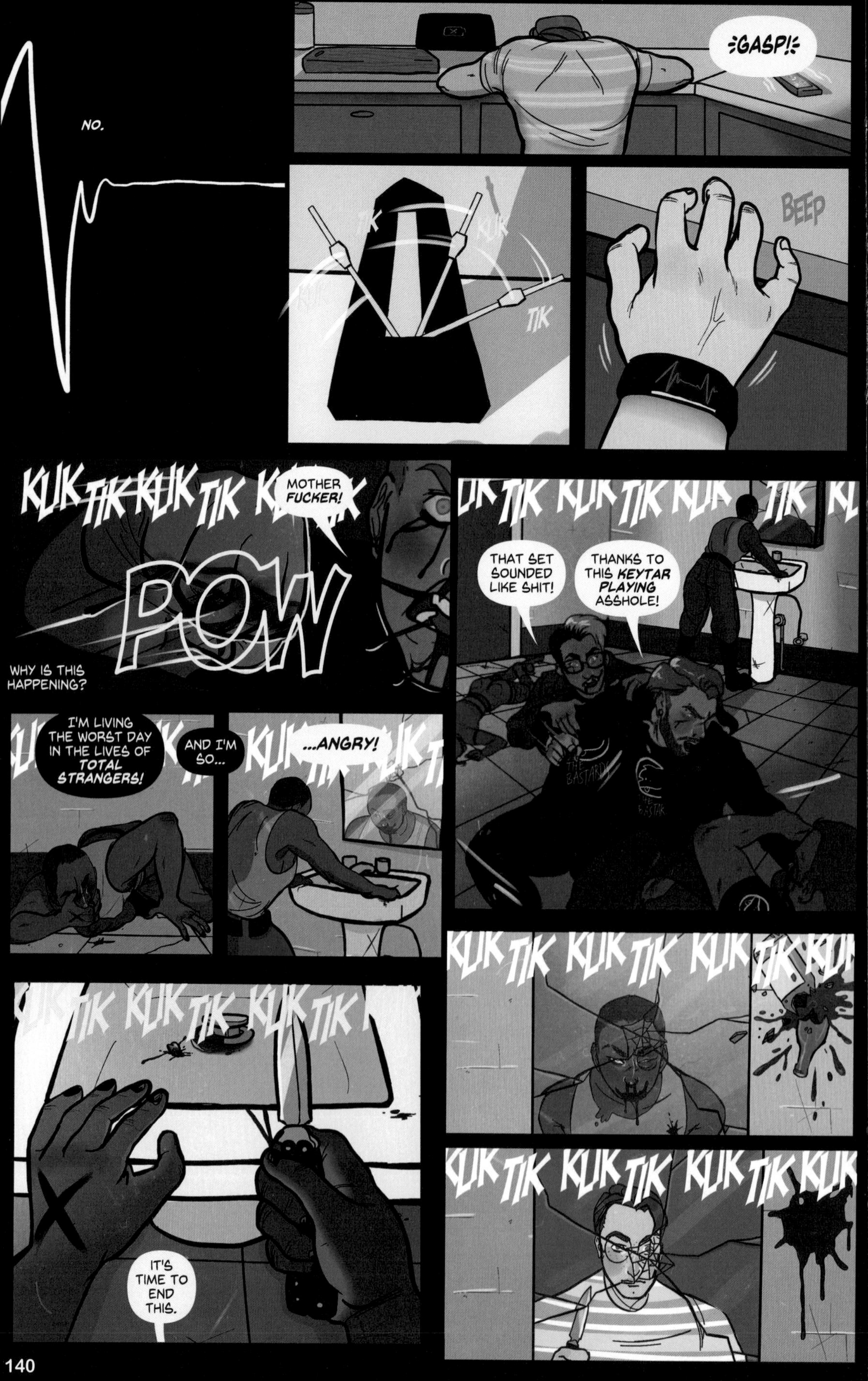

NO.
:GASP!:
TIK
KUK
KUK
TIK
BEEP
KUK TIK KUK TIK
MOTHER FUCKER!
POW
WHY IS THIS HAPPENING?
TIK KUK TIK KUK TIK
THAT SET SOUNDED LIKE SHIT!
THANKS TO THIS KEYTAR PLAYING ASSHOLE!
I'M LIVING THE WORST DAY IN THE LIVES OF TOTAL STRANGERS!
AND I'M SO...
...ANGRY!
TIK KUK TIK KUK TIK
KUK TIK KUK TIK KUK TIK
IT'S TIME TO END THIS.
KUK TIK KUK TIK KUK TIK KUK

KLIK
BEEP
TAP
TAP
I UNDERSTAND.

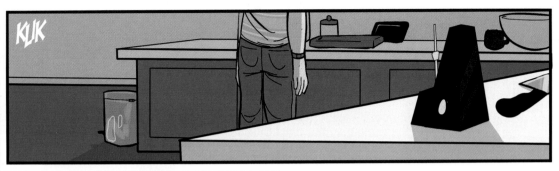

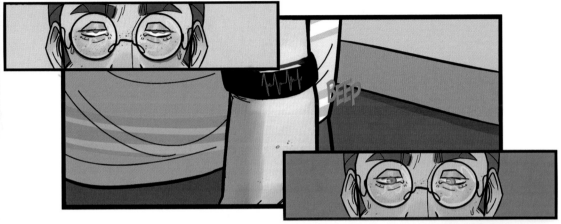

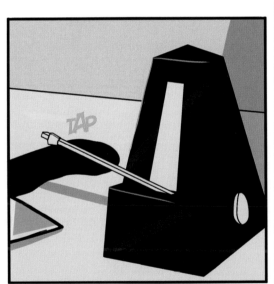

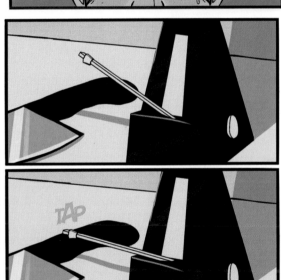

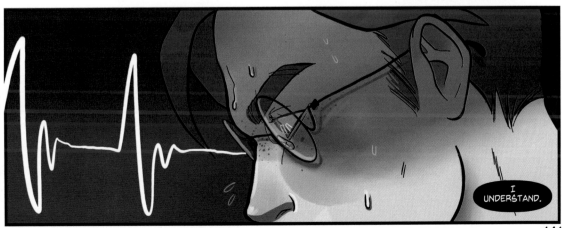

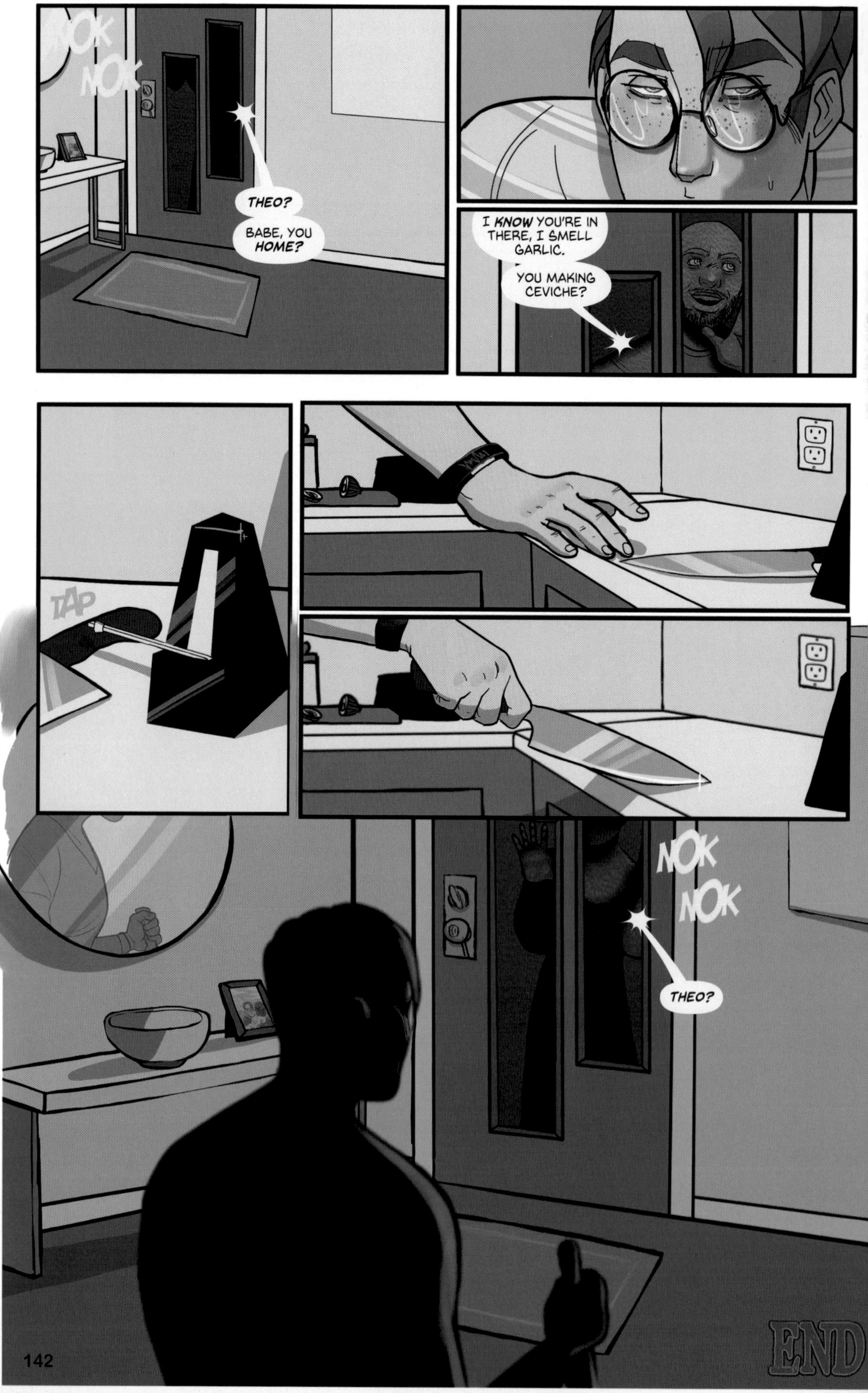
NOK
NOK
THEO?
BABE, YOU HOME?
I KNOW YOU'RE IN THERE, I SMELL GARLIC.
YOU MAKING CEVICHE?
TAP
NOK
NOK
THEO?
END

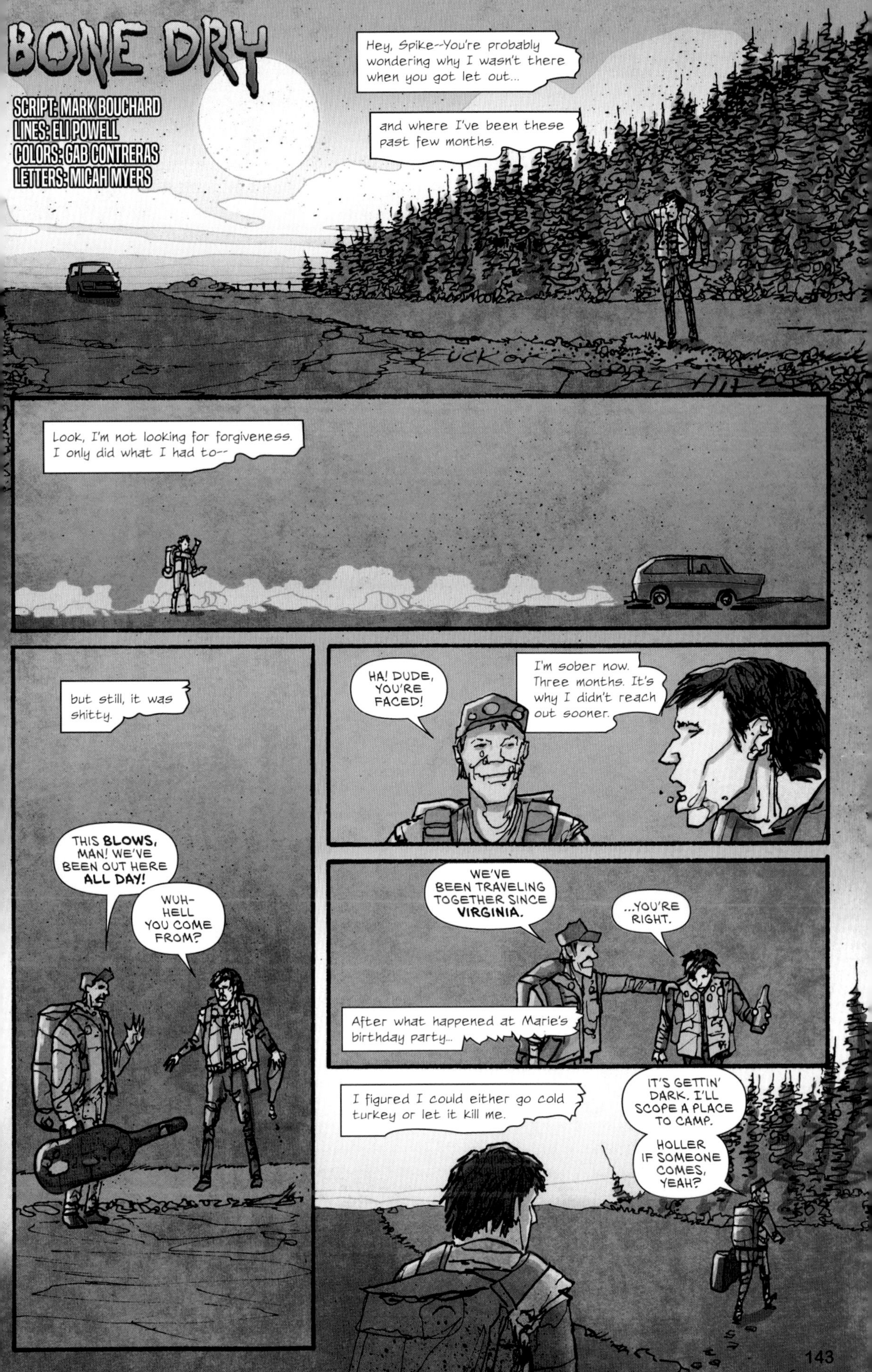
BONE DRY
SCRIPT: MARK BOUCHARD
LINES: ELI POWELL
COLORS: GAB CONTRERAS
LETTERS: MICAH MYERS
Hey, Spike--You're probably wondering why I wasn't there when you got let out...
and where I've been these past few months.
Look, I'm not looking for forgiveness. I only did what I had to--
but still, it was shitty.
THIS **BLOWS,** MAN! WE'VE BEEN OUT HERE **ALL DAY!**
WUH-HELL YOU COME FROM?
HA! DUDE, YOU'RE FACED!
I'm sober now. Three months. It's why I didn't reach out sooner.
WE'VE BEEN TRAVELING TOGETHER SINCE **VIRGINIA.**
...YOU'RE RIGHT.
After what happened at Marie's birthday party...
I figured I could either go cold turkey or let it kill me.
IT'S GETTIN' DARK. I'LL SCOPE A PLACE TO CAMP.
HOLLER IF SOMEONE COMES, YEAH?

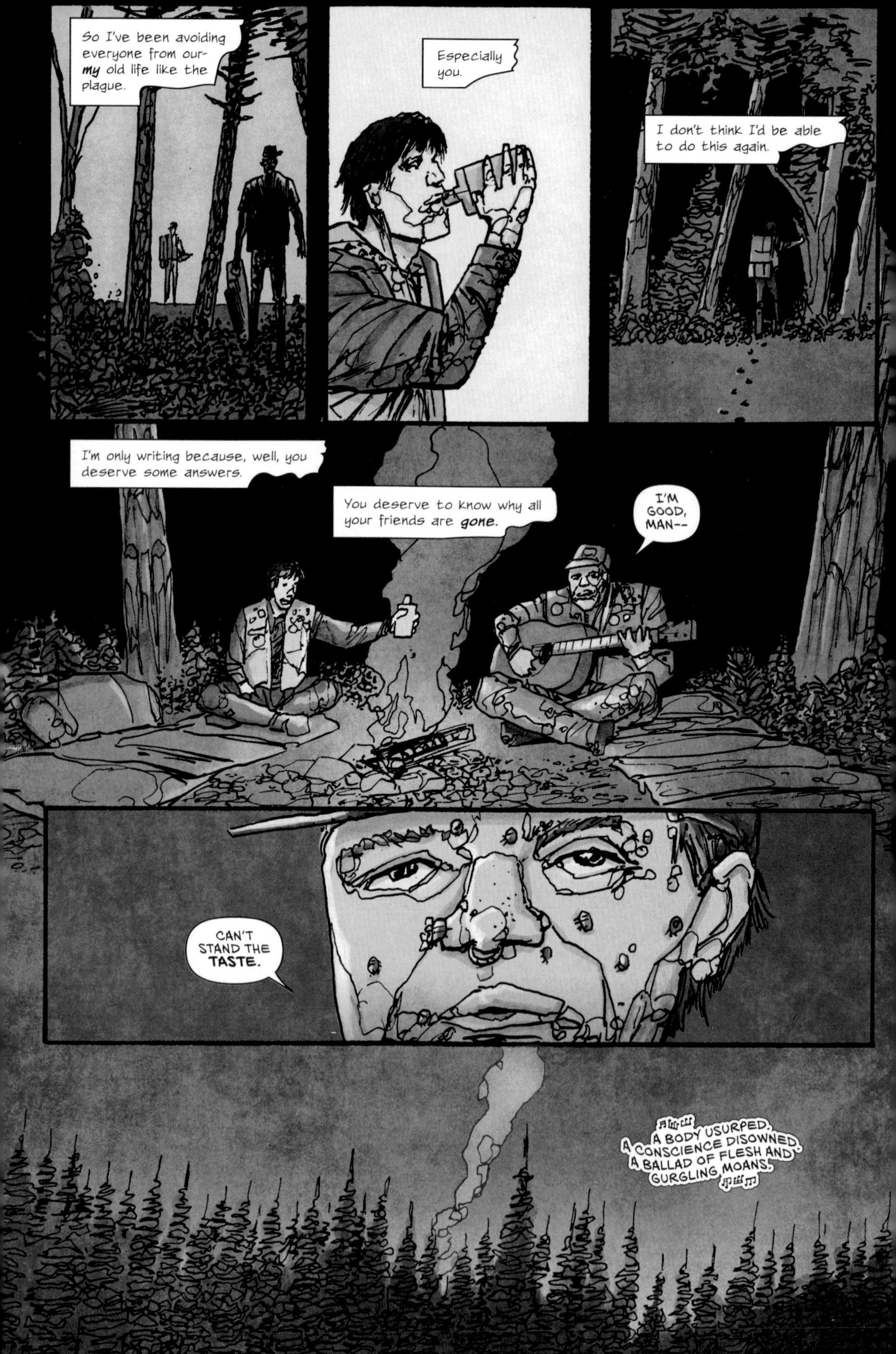

So I've been avoiding everyone from our-**my** old life like the plague.
Especially you.
I don't think I'd be able to do this again.
I'm only writing because, well, you deserve some answers.
You deserve to know why all your friends are **gone**.
I'M GOOD, MAN--
CAN'T STAND THE **TASTE.**
A BODY USURPED. A CONSCIENCE DISOWNED. A BALLAD OF FLESH AND GURGLING MOANS.

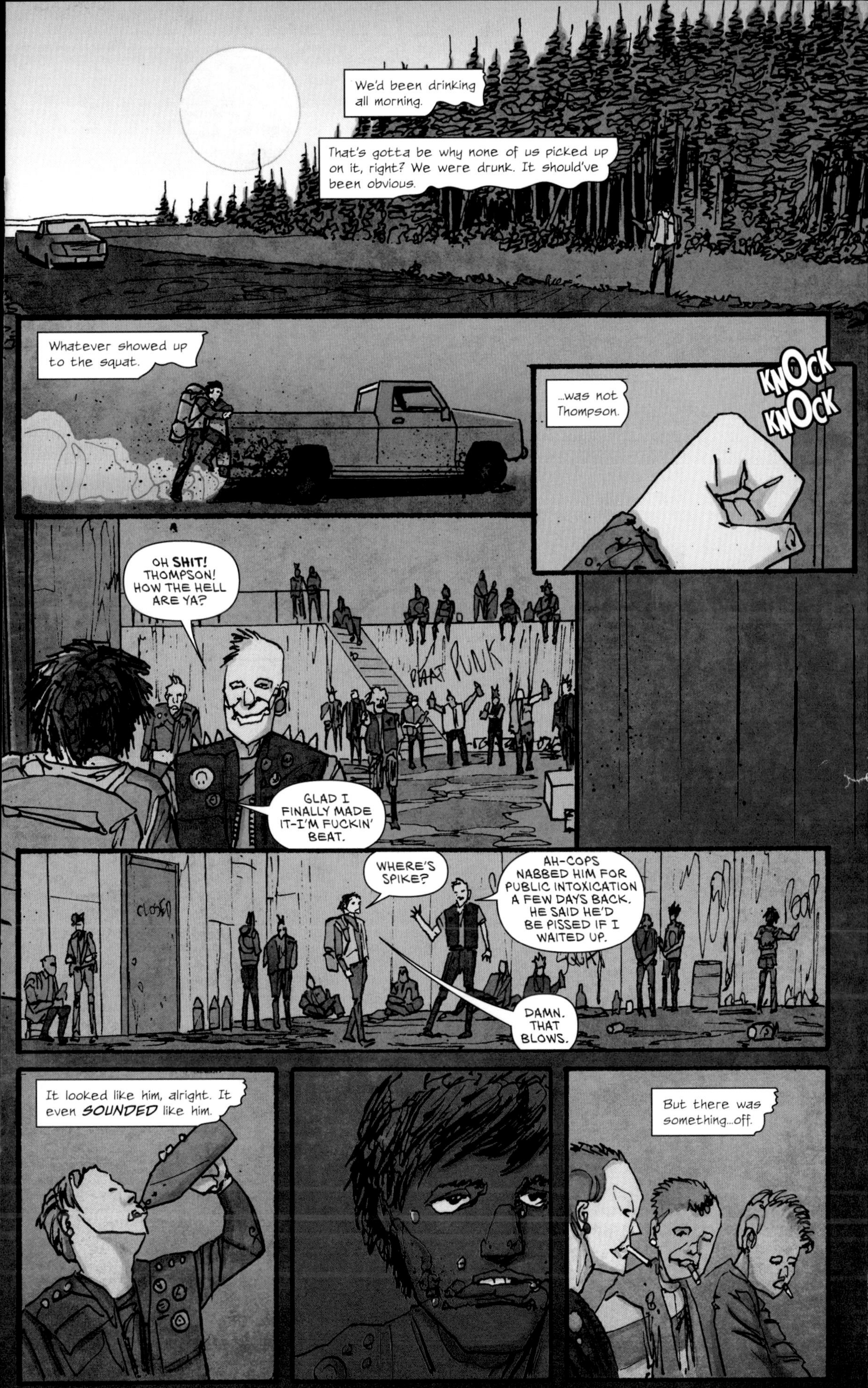
We'd been drinking all morning.
That's gotta be why none of us picked up on it, right? We were drunk. It should've been obvious.
Whatever showed up to the squat.
...was not Thompson.
KNOCK KNOCK
OH SHIT! THOMPSON! HOW THE HELL ARE YA?
PUNK
GLAD I FINALLY MADE IT-I'M FUCKIN' BEAT.
WHERE'S SPIKE?
AH-COPS NABBED HIM FOR PUBLIC INTOXICATION A FEW DAYS BACK. HE SAID HE'D BE PISSED IF I WAITED UP.
CLOSED
DAMN. THAT BLOWS.
It looked like him, alright. It even SOUNDED like him.
But there was something...off.

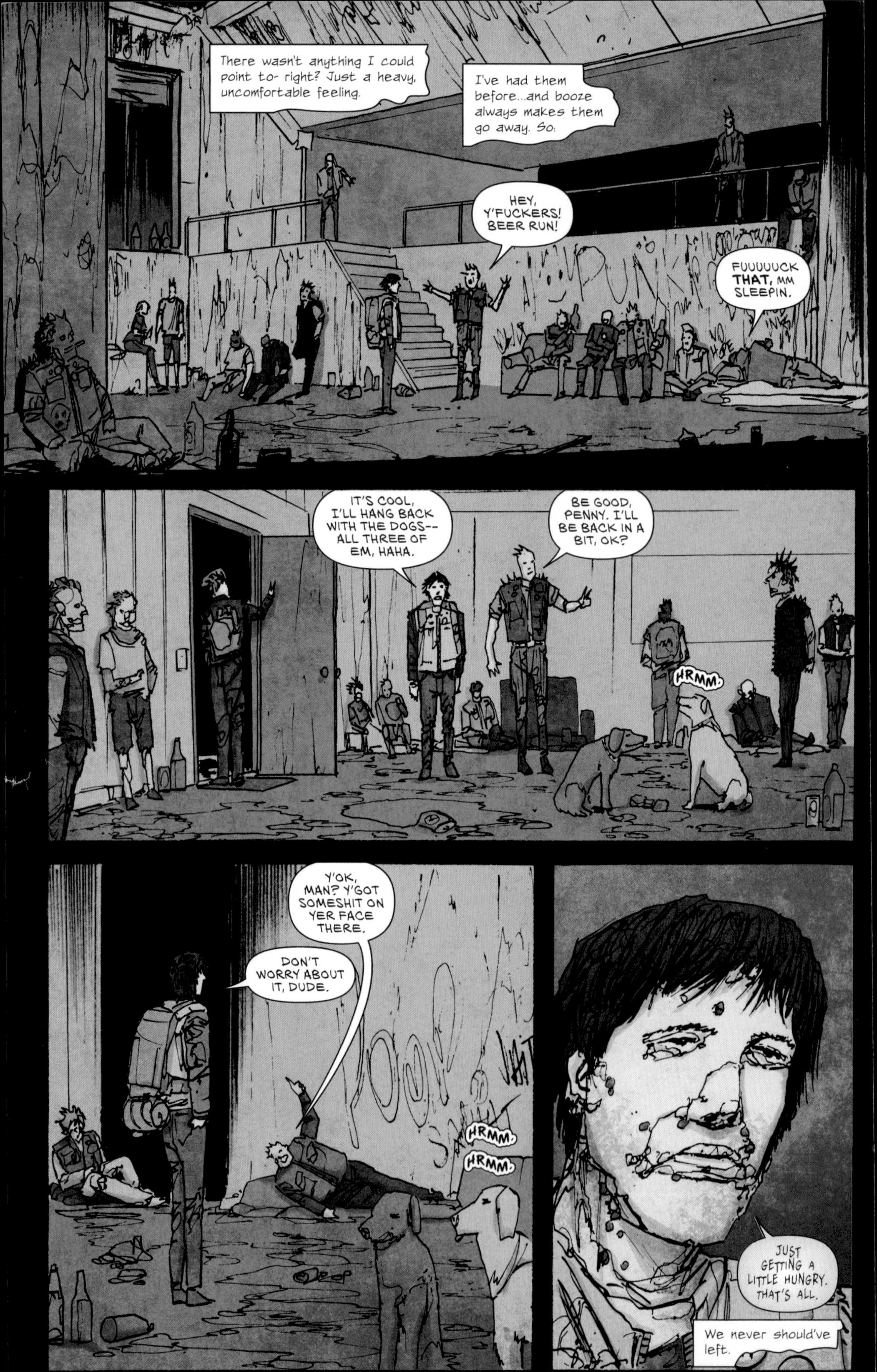
There wasn't anything I could point to- right? Just a heavy, uncomfortable feeling.
I've had them before...and booze always makes them go away. So:
HEY, Y'FUCKERS! BEER RUN!
FUUUUUCK THAT, MM SLEEPIN.
IT'S COOL, I'LL HANG BACK WITH THE DOGS-- ALL THREE OF EM, HAHA.
BE GOOD, PENNY. I'LL BE BACK IN A BIT, OK?
HRMM.
Y'OK, MAN? Y'GOT SOMESHIT ON YER FACE THERE.
DON'T WORRY ABOUT IT, DUDE.
HRMM.
HRMM.
JUST GETTING A LITTLE HUNGRY. THAT'S ALL.
We never should've left.

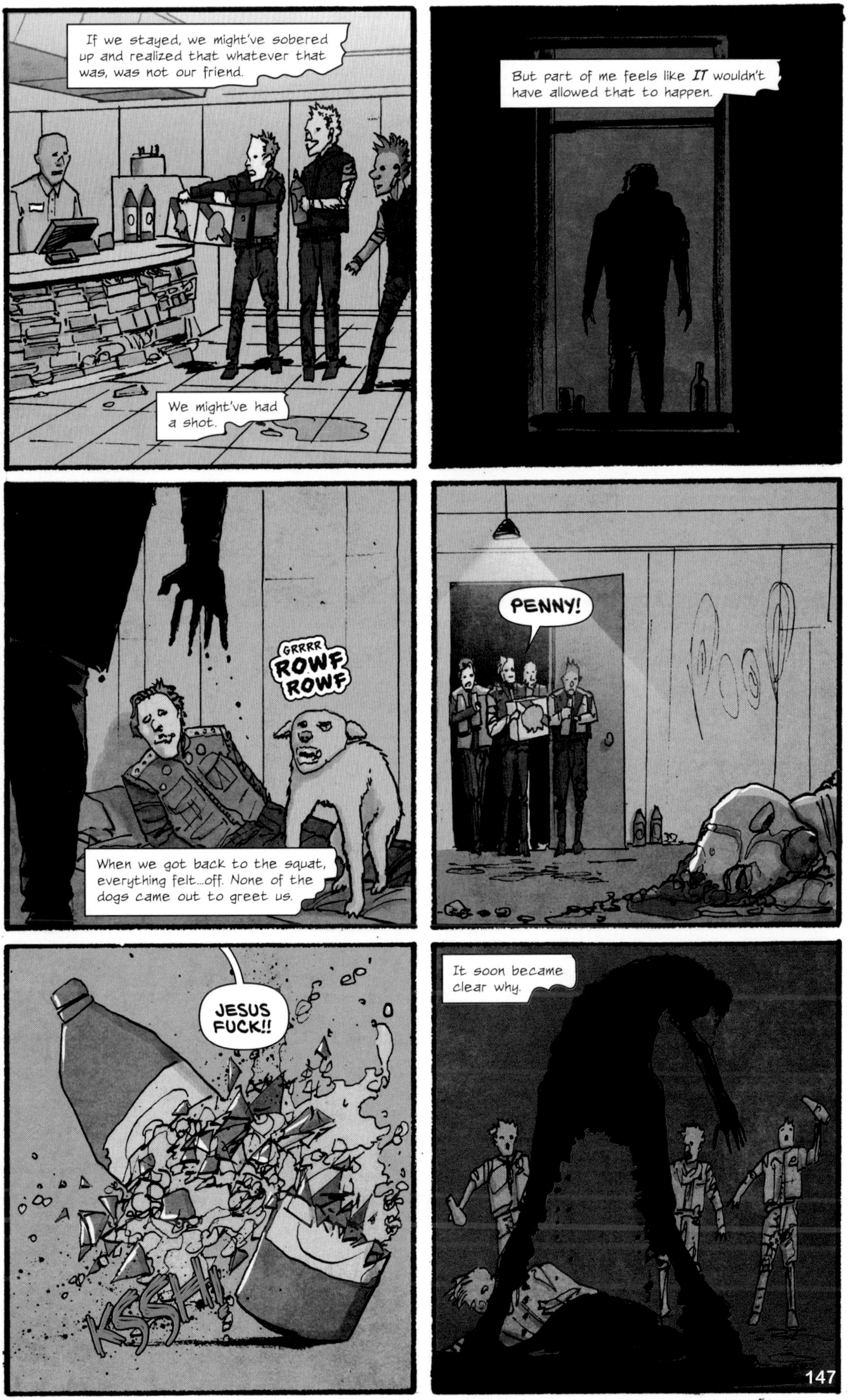

If we stayed, we might've sobered up and realized that whatever that was, was not our friend.
We might've had a shot.
But part of me feels like *IT* wouldn't have allowed that to happen.
GRRRR
ROWF ROWF
When we got back to the squat, everything felt...off. None of the dogs came out to greet us.
PENNY!
JESUS FUCK!!
KSSSH!
It soon became clear why.

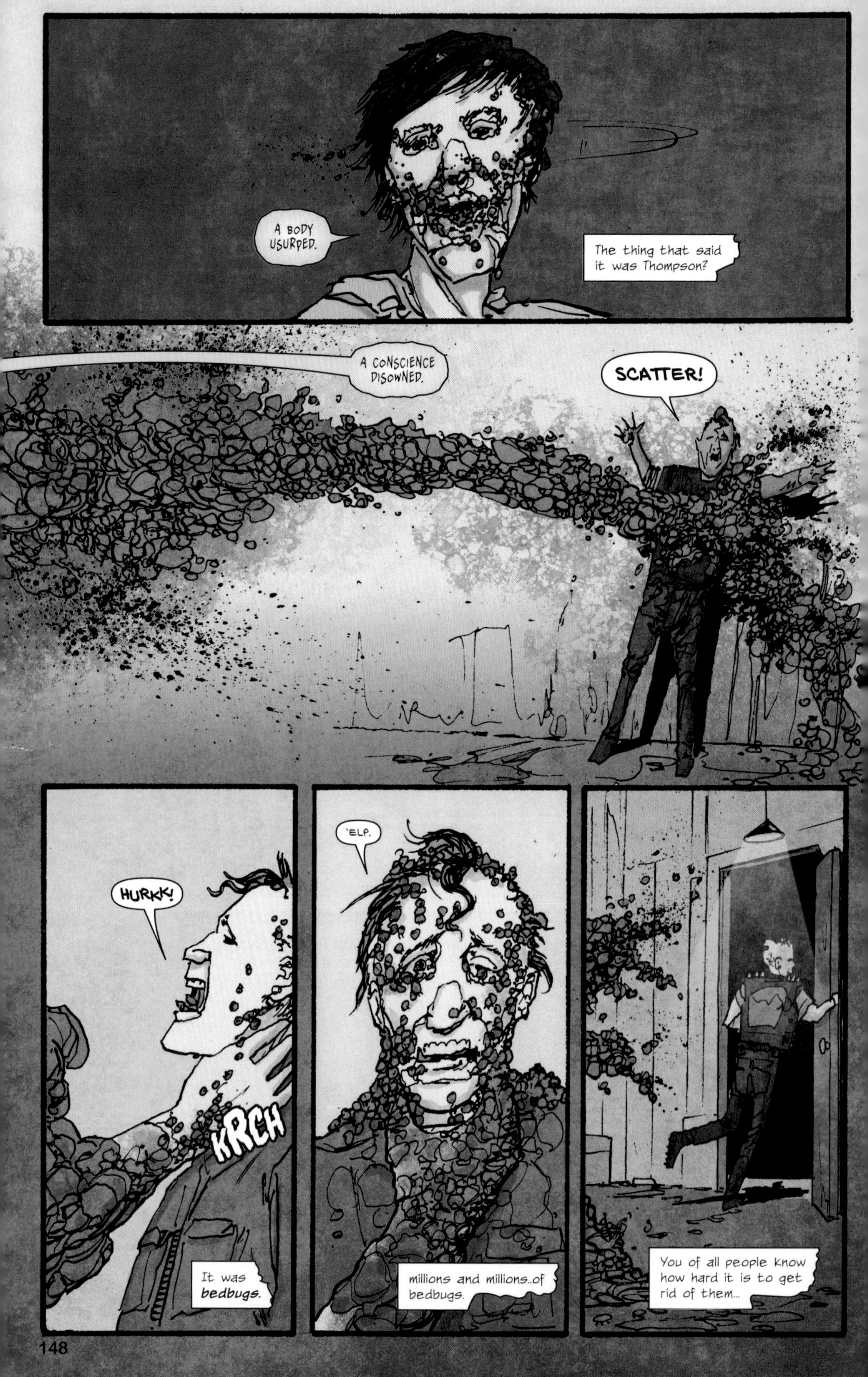
A BODY USURPED.
The thing that said it was Thompson?
A CONSCIENCE DISOWNED.
SCATTER!
HURKK!
KRCH
It was bedbugs.
'ELP.
millions and millions..of bedbugs.
You of all people know how hard it is to get rid of them...

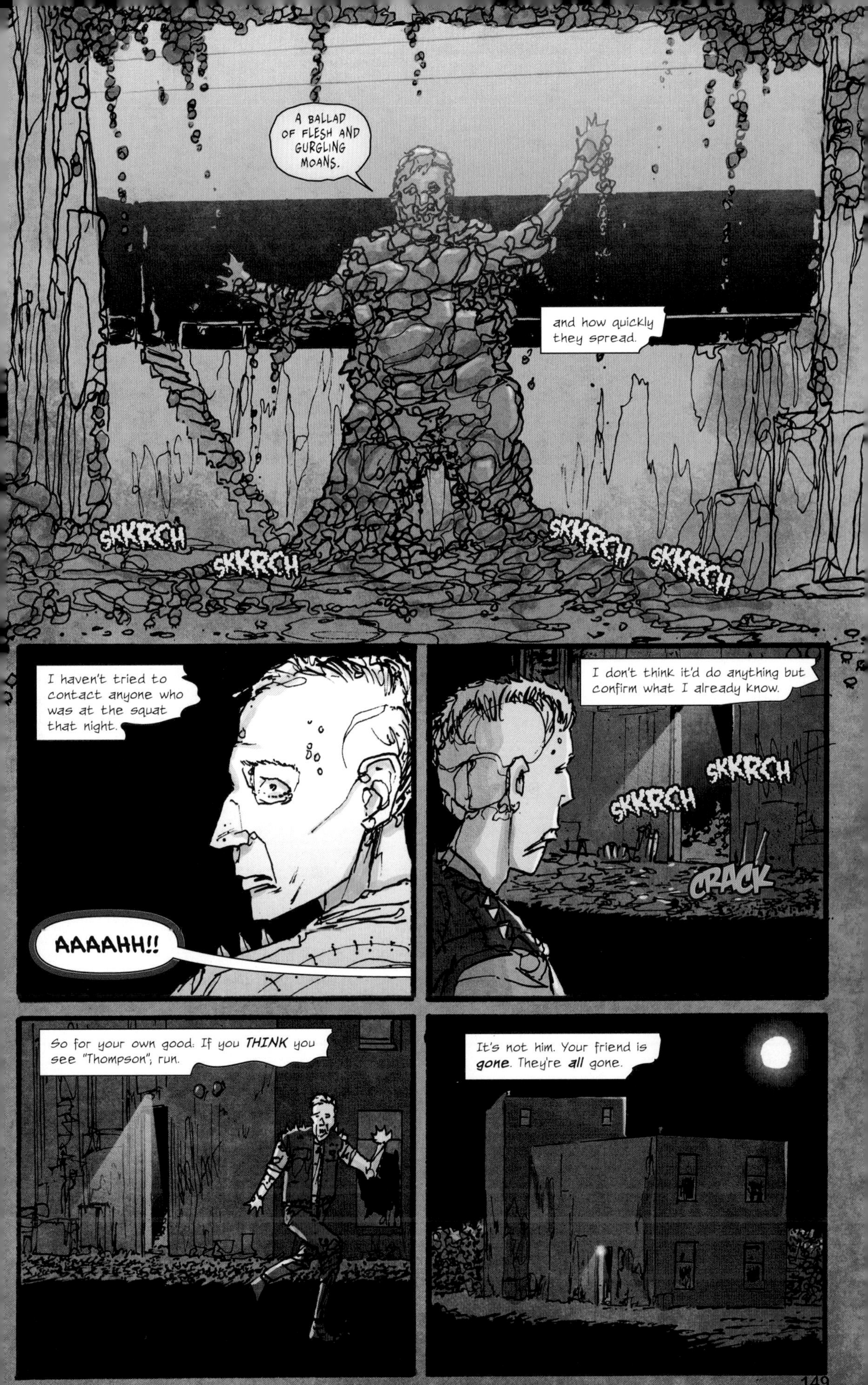
A BALLAD OF FLESH AND GURGLING MOANS.
and how quickly they spread.
SKKRCH
SKKRCH
SKKRCH
SKKRCH
I haven't tried to contact anyone who was at the squat that night.
AAAAHH!!
I don't think it'd do anything but confirm what I already know.
SKKRCH
SKKRCH
CRACK
So for your own good: If you THINK you see "Thompson", run.
It's not him. Your friend is gone. They're all gone.

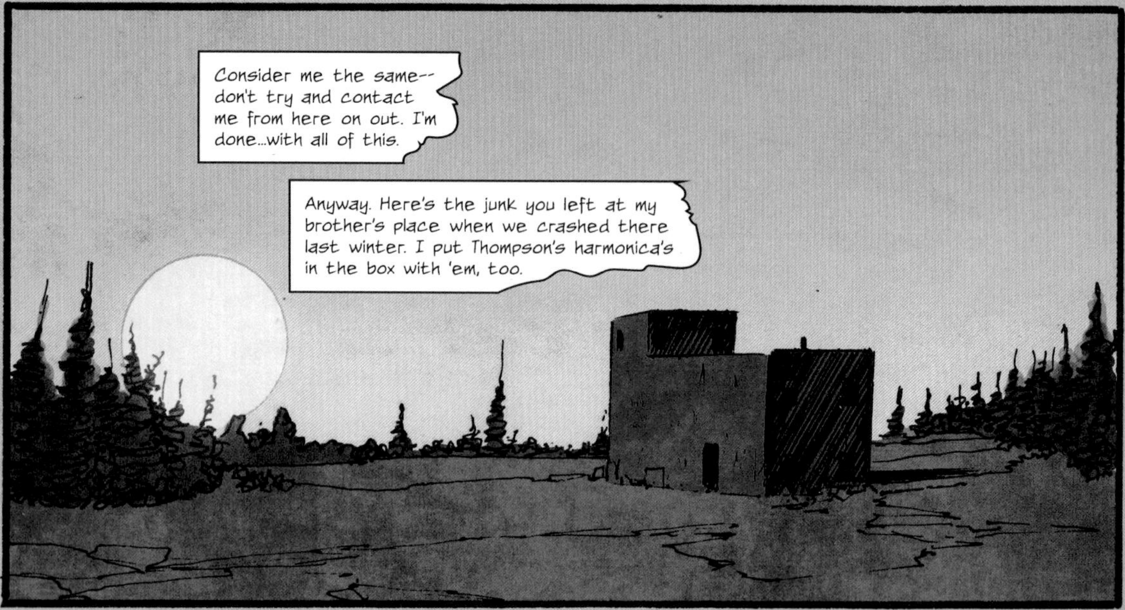
Consider me the same--don't try and contact me from here on out. I'm done...with all of this.
Anyway. Here's the junk you left at my brother's place when we crashed there last winter. I put Thompson's harmonica's in the box with 'em, too.

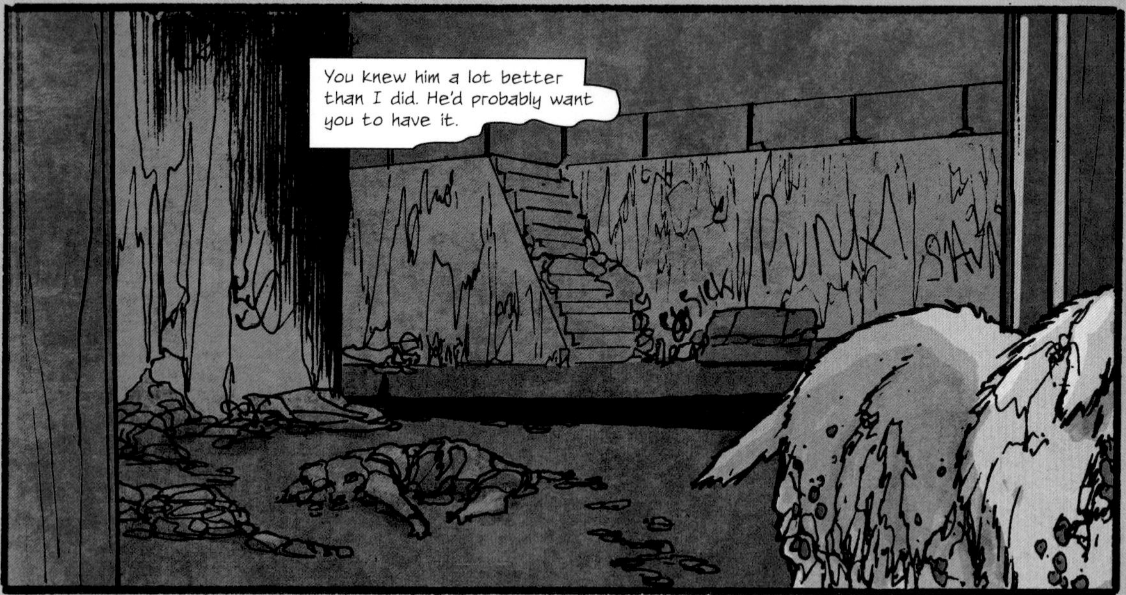
You knew him a lot better than I did. He'd probably want you to have it.
PUNK
SICK

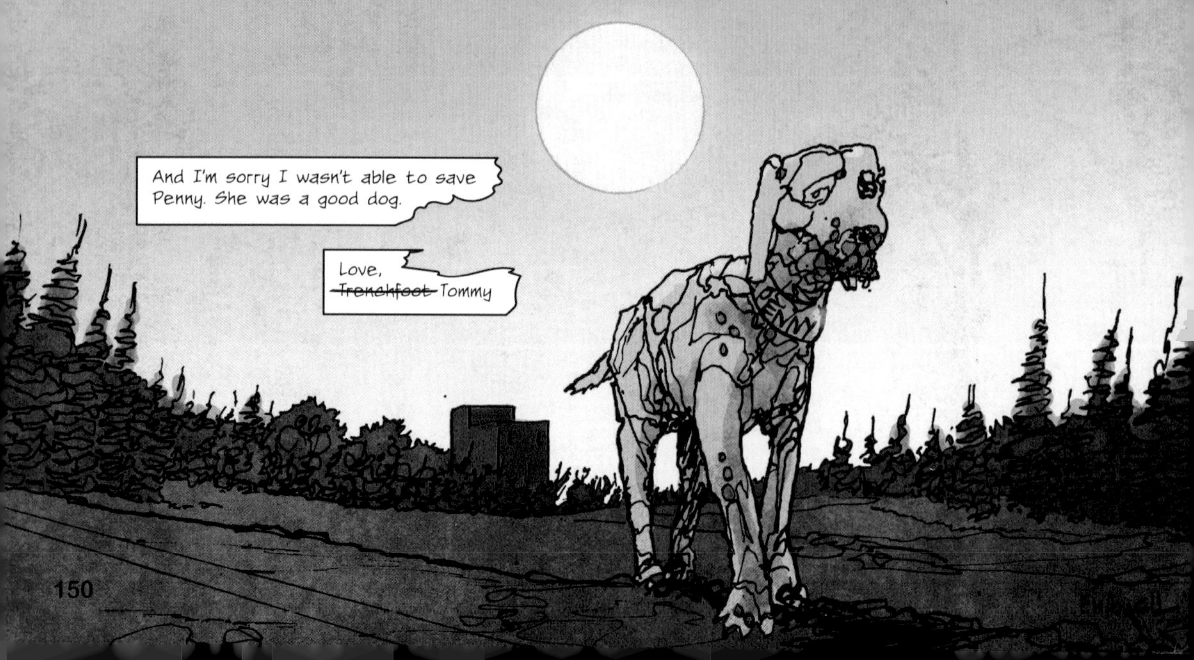
And I'm sorry I wasn't able to save Penny. She was a good dog.
Love, ~~Trenchfoot~~ Tommy

WE GET THESE *PARTICULAR* KIDS IN HERE SOMETIMES.

YOU CAN SPOT THEM A MILE AWAY.

THEY KNOW MUSIC IS *COOL*, BUT THEY DON'T KNOW HOW THEY FIT INTO IT YET. IT'S *DANGEROUS*, AND *SEXY*, AND *INTIMIDATING* AS FUCK.

IN OTHER WORDS, EVERYTHING THEY'RE *NOT*.

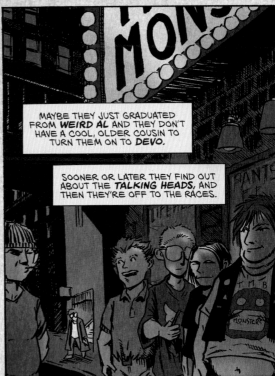

MAYBE THEY JUST GRADUATED FROM *WEIRD AL* AND THEY DON'T HAVE A COOL, OLDER COUSIN TO TURN THEM ON TO *DEVO*.

SOONER OR LATER THEY FIND OUT ABOUT THE *TALKING HEADS*, AND THEN THEY'RE OFF TO THE RACES.

BUT BETWEEN *DR. DEMENTO* AND *ELVIS COSTELLO*, THERE'S A MANDATORY STOP ALONG THE WAY.

AND A WARNING TO THOSE WHO LINGER THERE A LITTLE TOO LONG, FOR IN THAT CONFUSING, PUBESCENT LIMINAL NERD-SPACE...

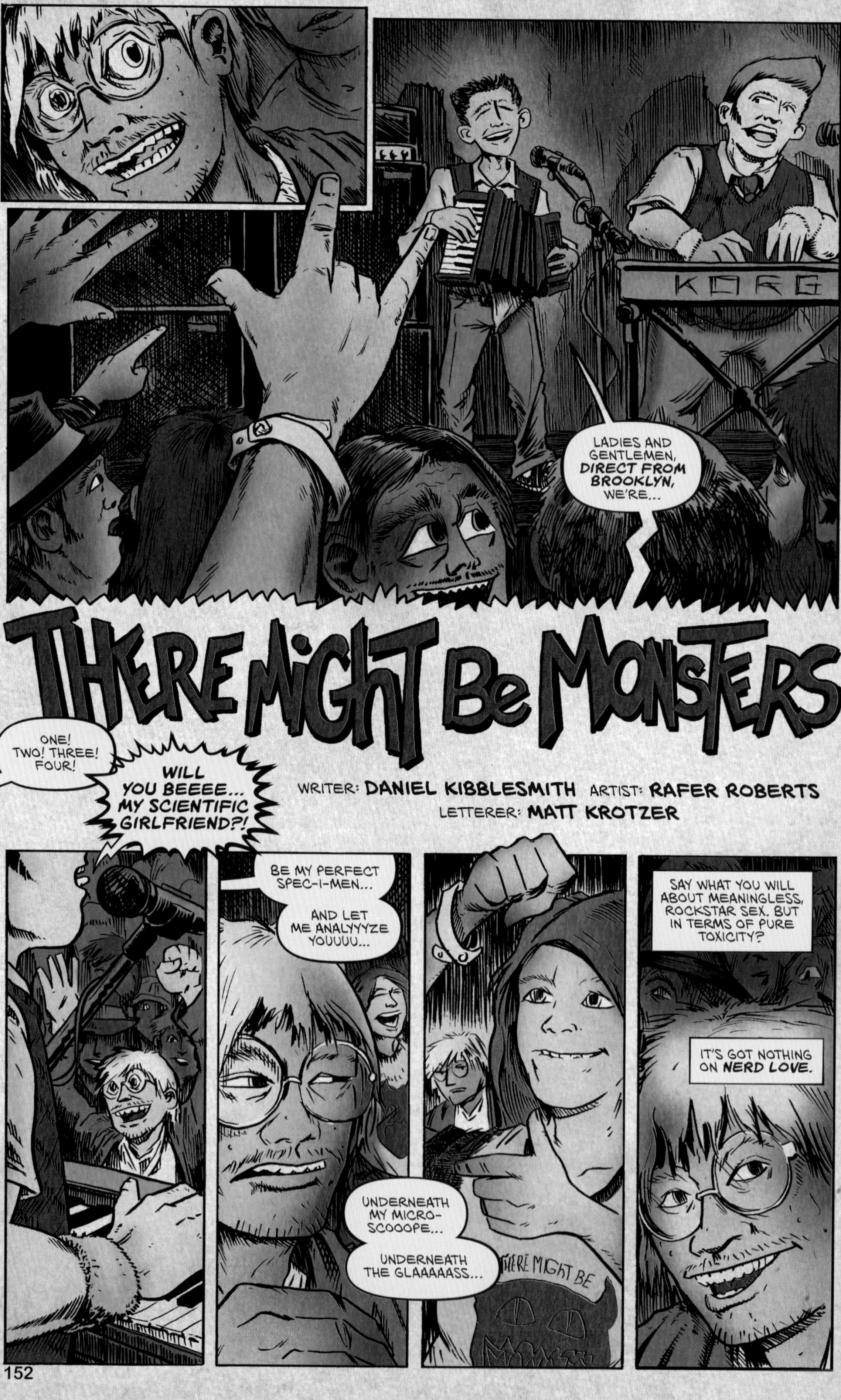
KORG
LADIES AND GENTLEMEN, DIRECT FROM BROOKLYN, WE'RE...
THERE MIGHT BE MONSTERS
ONE! TWO! THREE! FOUR!
WILL YOU BEEEE... MY SCIENTIFIC GIRLFRIEND?!
WRITER: DANIEL KIBBLESMITH ARTIST: RAFER ROBERTS
LETTERER: MATT KROTZER
BE MY PERFECT SPEC-I-MEN...
AND LET ME ANALYYYZE YOUUUU...
UNDERNEATH MY MICRO-SCOOOPE...
UNDERNEATH THE GLAAAAASS...
THERE MIGHT BE
SAY WHAT YOU WILL ABOUT MEANINGLESS, ROCKSTAR SEX. BUT IN TERMS OF PURE TOXICITY?
IT'S GOT NOTHING ON NERD LOVE.

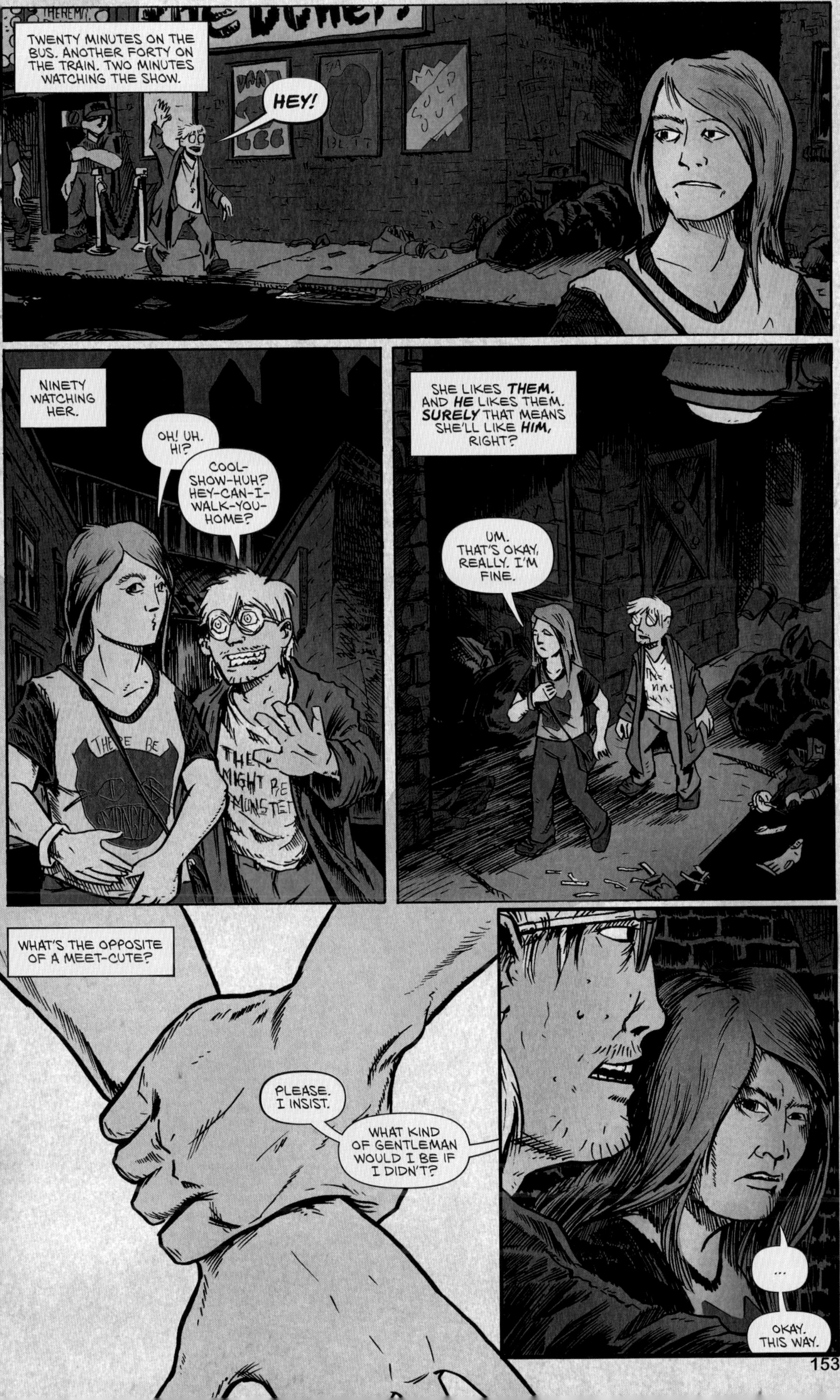
TWENTY MINUTES ON THE BUS. ANOTHER FORTY ON THE TRAIN. TWO MINUTES WATCHING THE SHOW.
HEY!
SOLD OUT
NINETY WATCHING HER.
OH! UH. HI?
COOL-SHOW-HUH? HEY-CAN-I-WALK-YOU-HOME?
SHE LIKES THEM. AND HE LIKES THEM. SURELY THAT MEANS SHE'LL LIKE HIM, RIGHT?
UM. THAT'S OKAY, REALLY. I'M FINE.
WHAT'S THE OPPOSITE OF A MEET-CUTE?
PLEASE. I INSIST.
WHAT KIND OF GENTLEMAN WOULD I BE IF I DIDN'T?
...
OKAY. THIS WAY.

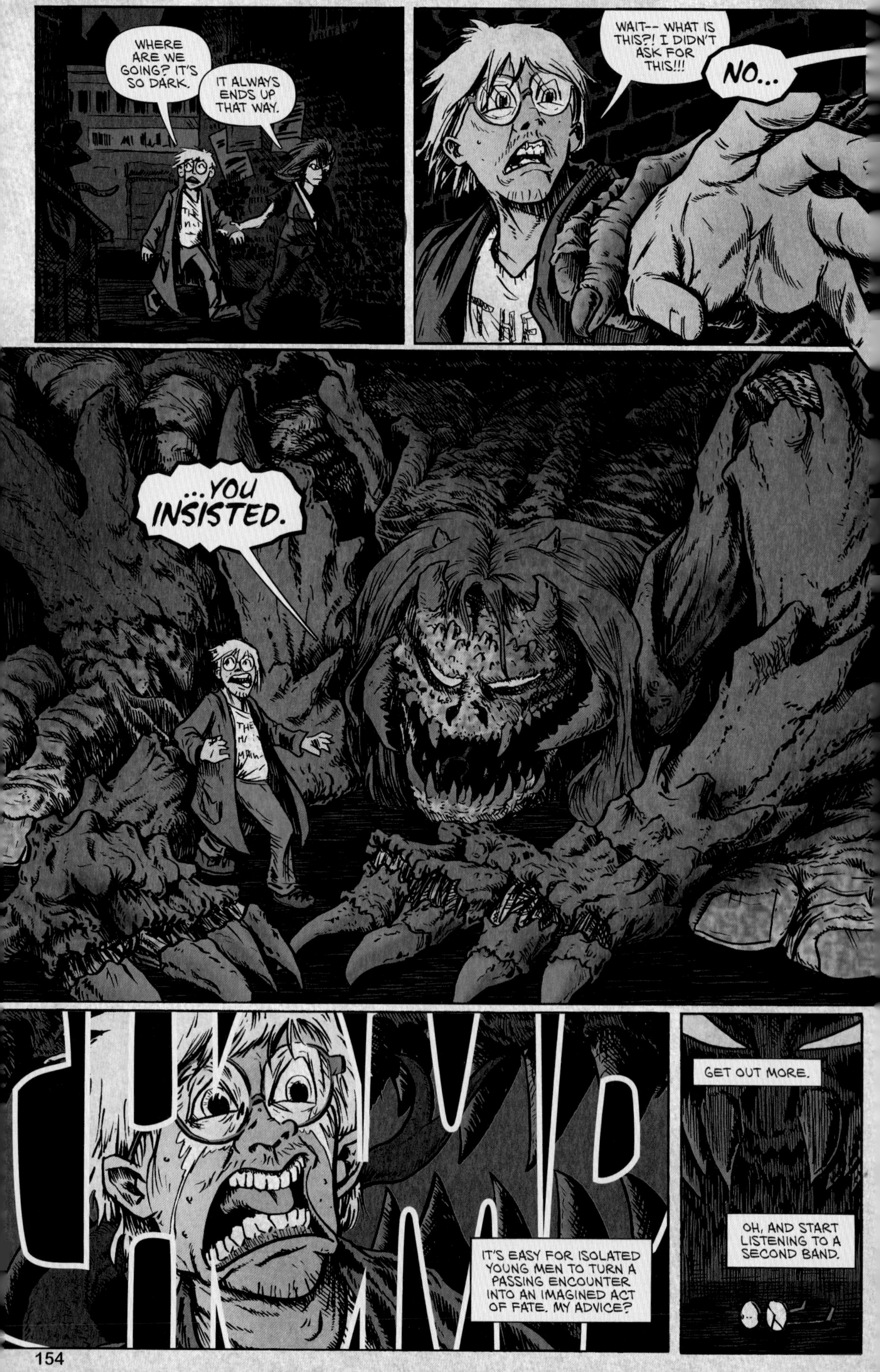
WHERE ARE WE GOING? IT'S SO DARK.
IT ALWAYS ENDS UP THAT WAY.
WAIT-- WHAT IS THIS?! I DIDN'T ASK FOR THIS!!!
NO...
...YOU INSISTED.
IT'S EASY FOR ISOLATED YOUNG MEN TO TURN A PASSING ENCOUNTER INTO AN IMAGINED ACT OF FATE. MY ADVICE?
GET OUT MORE.
OH, AND START LISTENING TO A SECOND BAND.

debaser

story: Joe Corallo
art: Jen Hickman

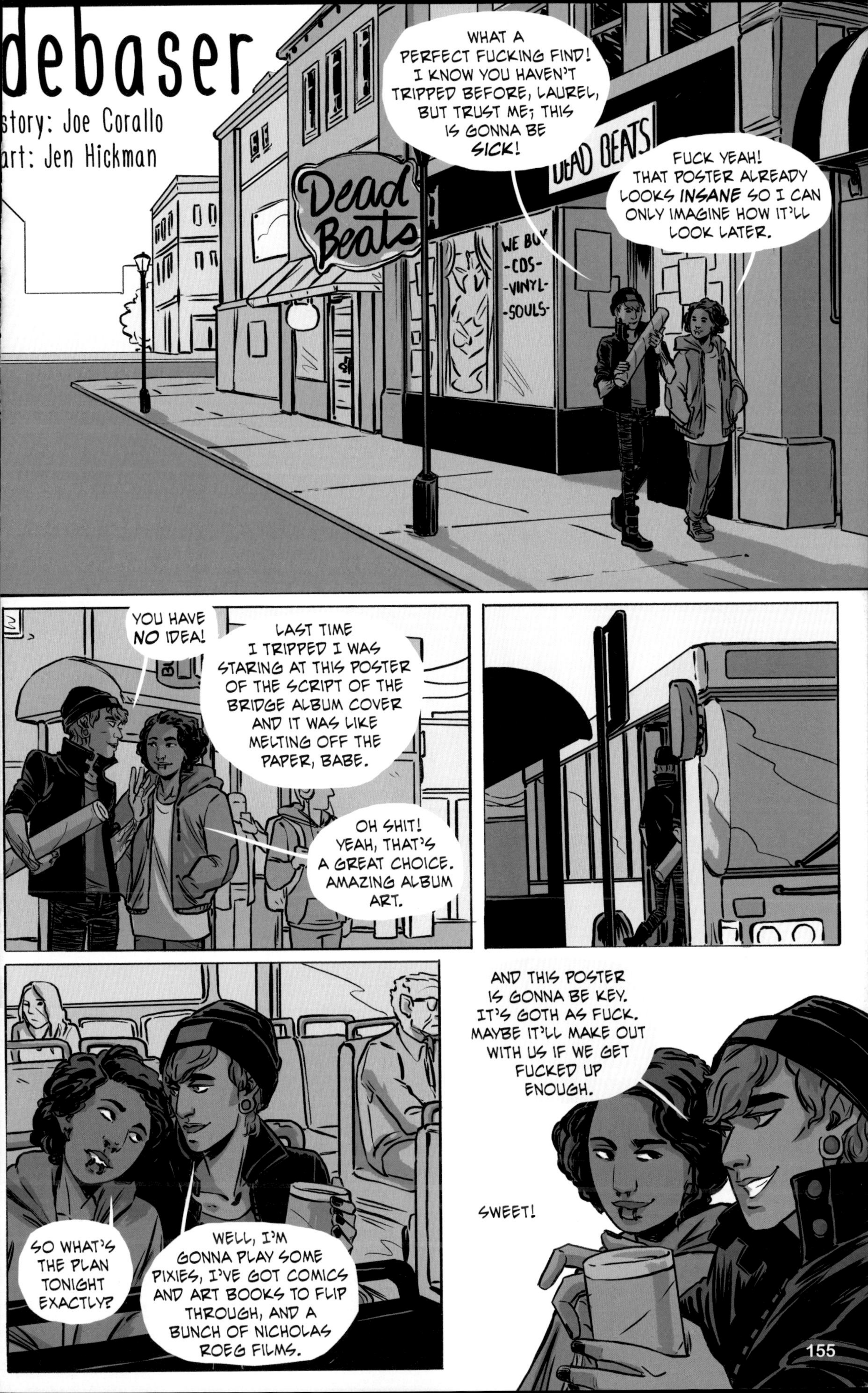

WHAT A PERFECT FUCKING FIND! I KNOW YOU HAVEN'T TRIPPED BEFORE, LAUREL, BUT TRUST ME; THIS IS GONNA BE SICK!
FUCK YEAH! THAT POSTER ALREADY LOOKS INSANE SO I CAN ONLY IMAGINE HOW IT'LL LOOK LATER.
Dead Beats
DEAD BEATS
WE BUY -CDS- -VINYL- -SOULS-
YOU HAVE NO IDEA!
LAST TIME I TRIPPED I WAS STARING AT THIS POSTER OF THE SCRIPT OF THE BRIDGE ALBUM COVER AND IT WAS LIKE MELTING OFF THE PAPER, BABE.
OH SHIT! YEAH, THAT'S A GREAT CHOICE. AMAZING ALBUM ART.
SO WHAT'S THE PLAN TONIGHT EXACTLY?
WELL, I'M GONNA PLAY SOME PIXIES, I'VE GOT COMICS AND ART BOOKS TO FLIP THROUGH, AND A BUNCH OF NICHOLAS ROEG FILMS.
AND THIS POSTER IS GONNA BE KEY. IT'S GOTH AS FUCK. MAYBE IT'LL MAKE OUT WITH US IF WE GET FUCKED UP ENOUGH.
SWEET!

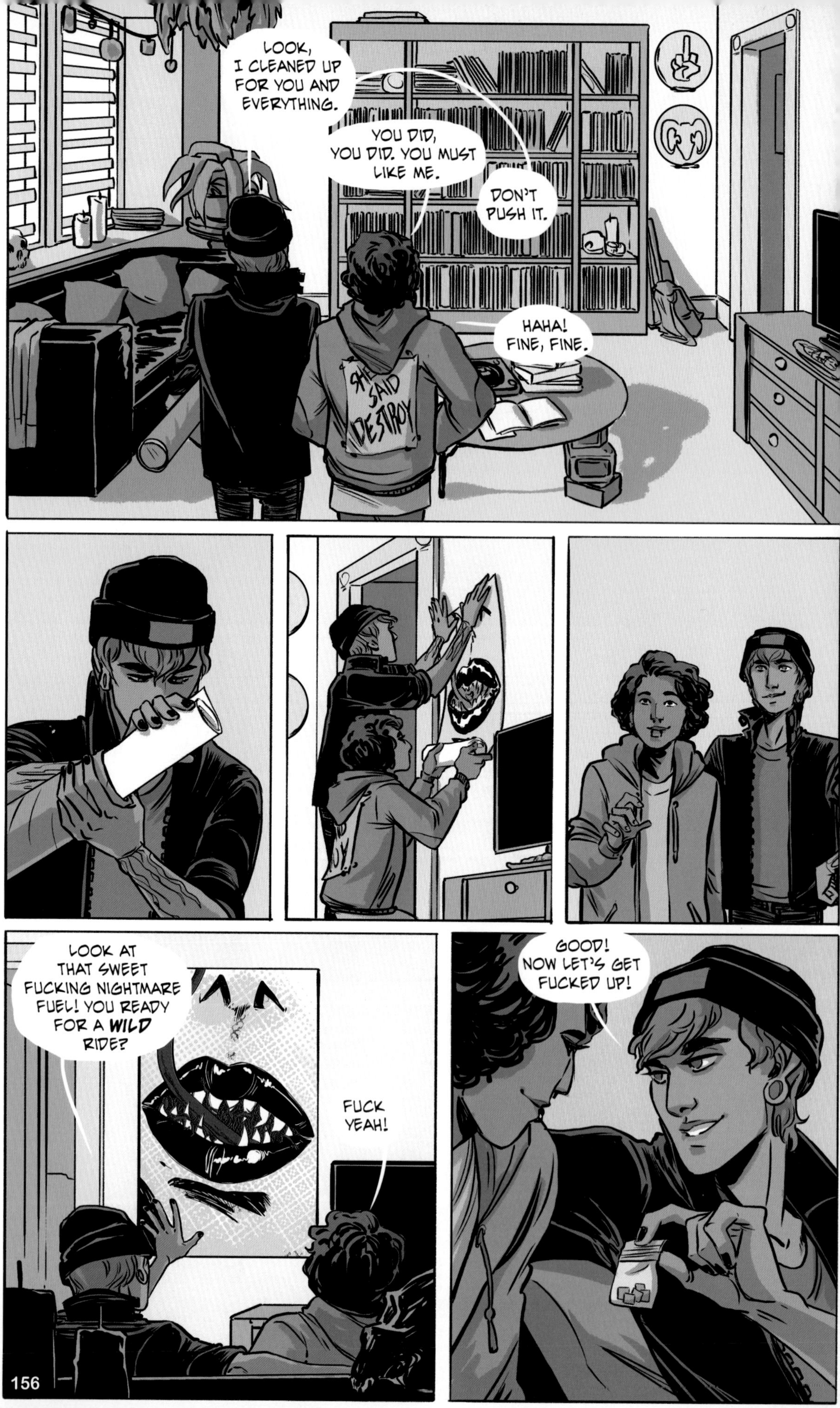
LOOK, I CLEANED UP FOR YOU AND EVERYTHING.
YOU DID, YOU DID. YOU MUST LIKE ME.
DON'T PUSH IT.
HAHA! FINE, FINE.
SHE SAID DESTROY
LOOK AT THAT SWEET FUCKING NIGHTMARE FUEL! YOU READY FOR A ***WILD*** RIDE?
FUCK YEAH!
GOOD! NOW LET'S GET FUCKED UP!

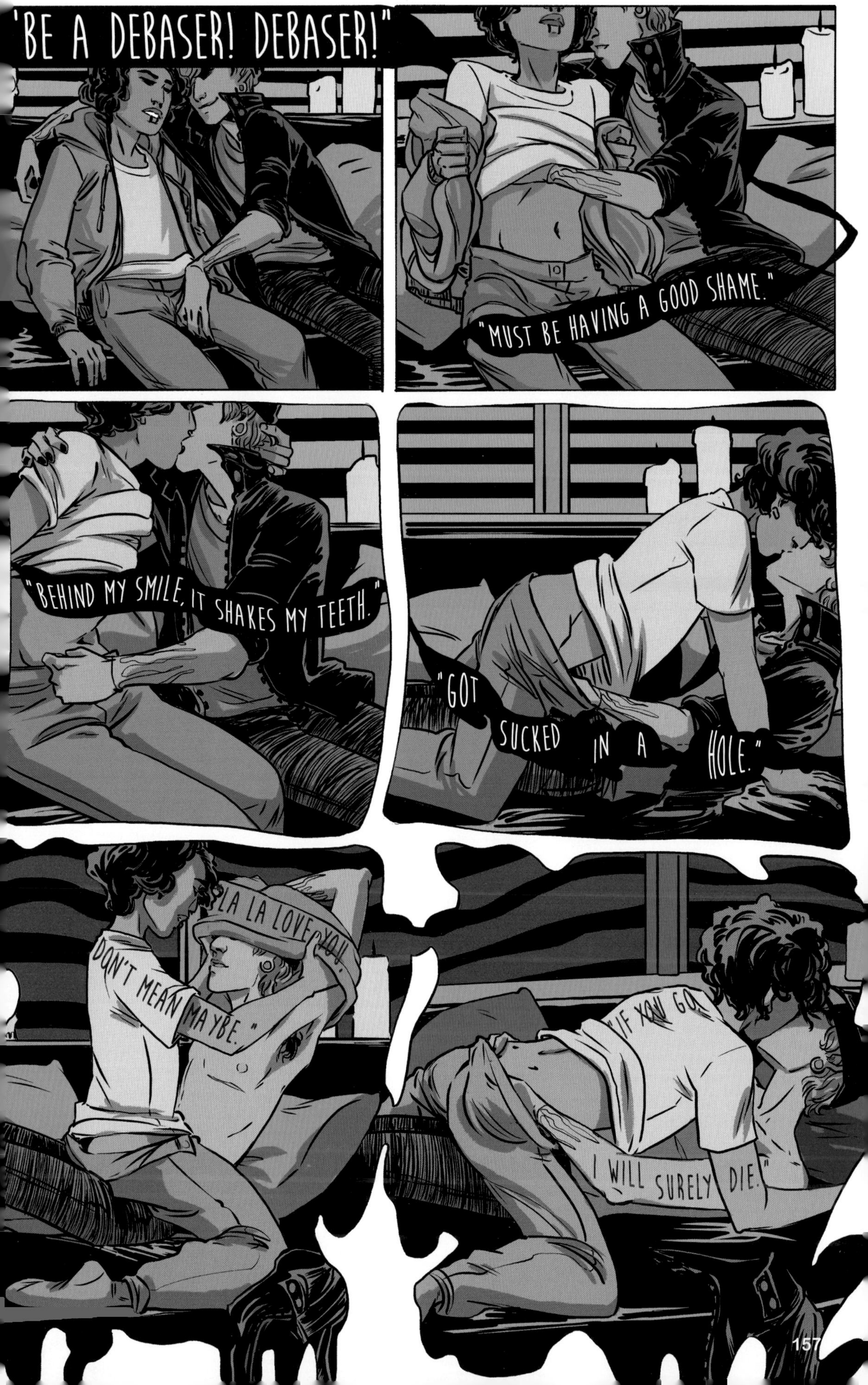
'BE A DEBASER! DEBASER!"
"MUST BE HAVING A GOOD SHAME."
"BEHIND MY SMILE, IT SHAKES MY TEETH."
"GOT SUCKED IN A HOLE."
LA LA LOVE YOU.
DON'T MEAN MAYBE."
IF YOU GO
I WILL SURELY DIE."

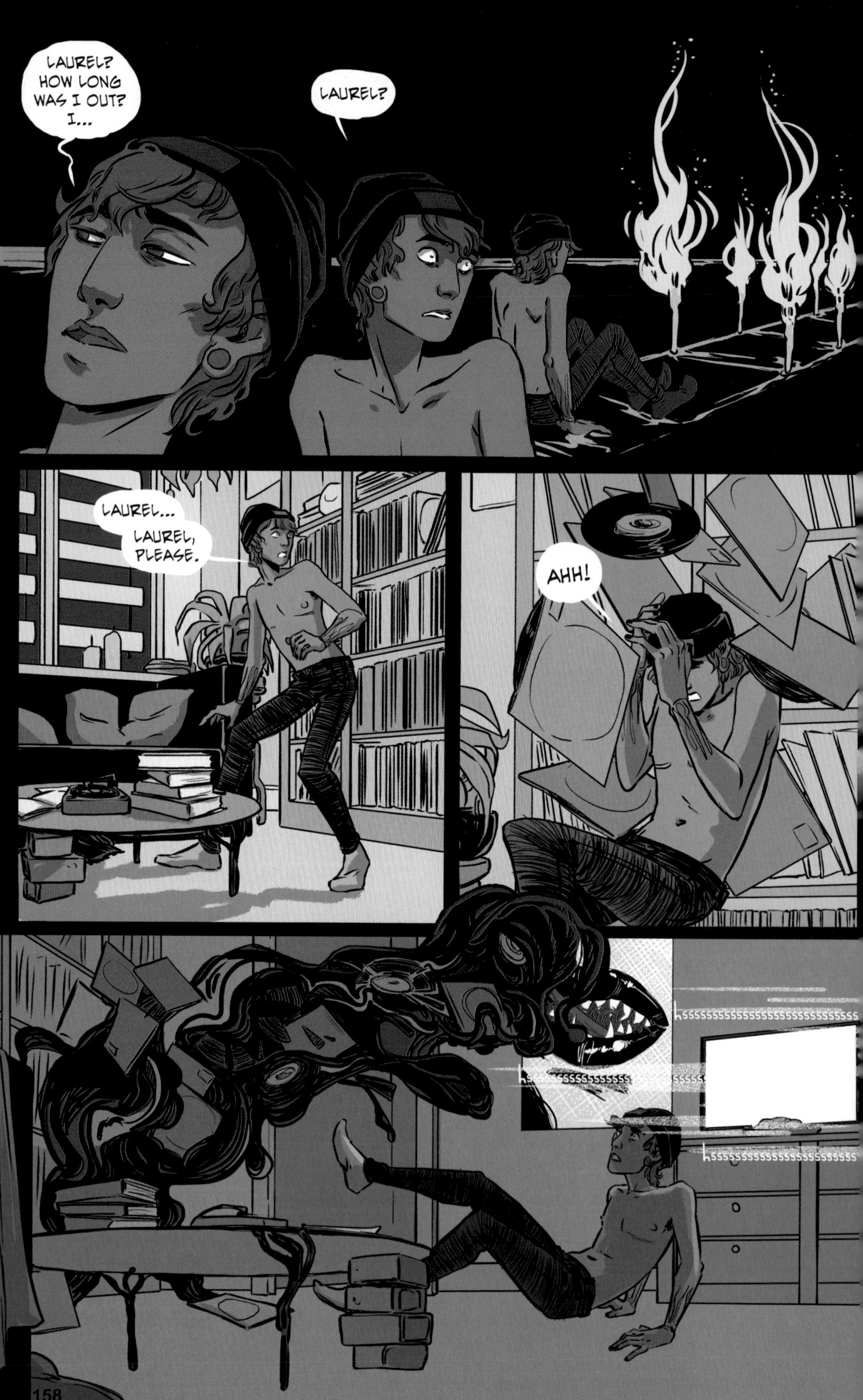
LAUREL? HOW LONG WAS I OUT? I...
LAUREL?
LAUREL... LAUREL, PLEASE.
AHH!
hssssssssssssssssssssssssssssssss
hsssssssssssssssssssssssssssssss
hssssssssssssssssssssssssss

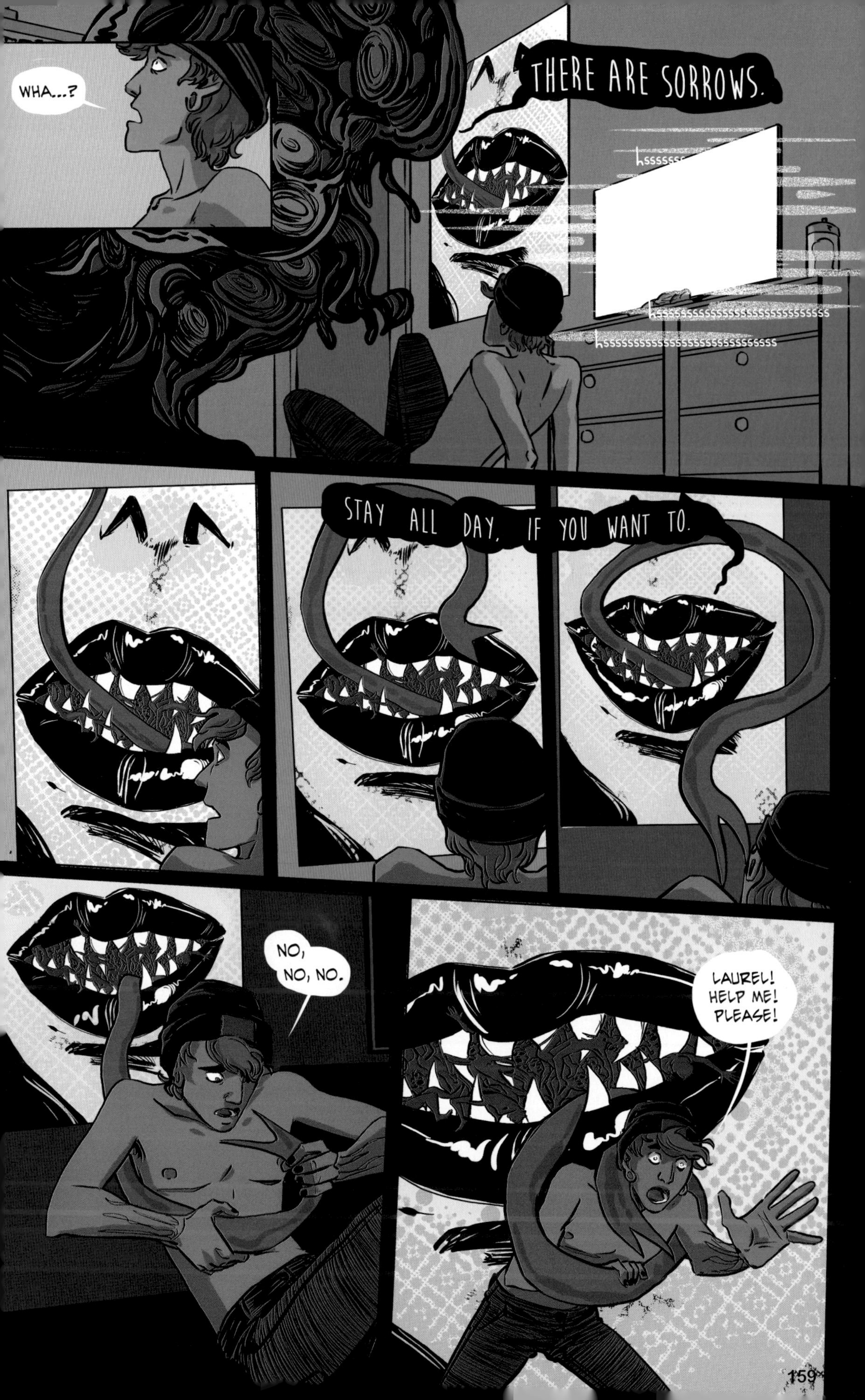
WHA...?
THERE ARE SORROWS.
hsssssss
hsssssssssssssssssssssssssssssss
hssssssssssssssssssssssssssssss
STAY ALL DAY, IF YOU WANT TO.
NO, NO, NO.
LAUREL! HELP ME! PLEASE!

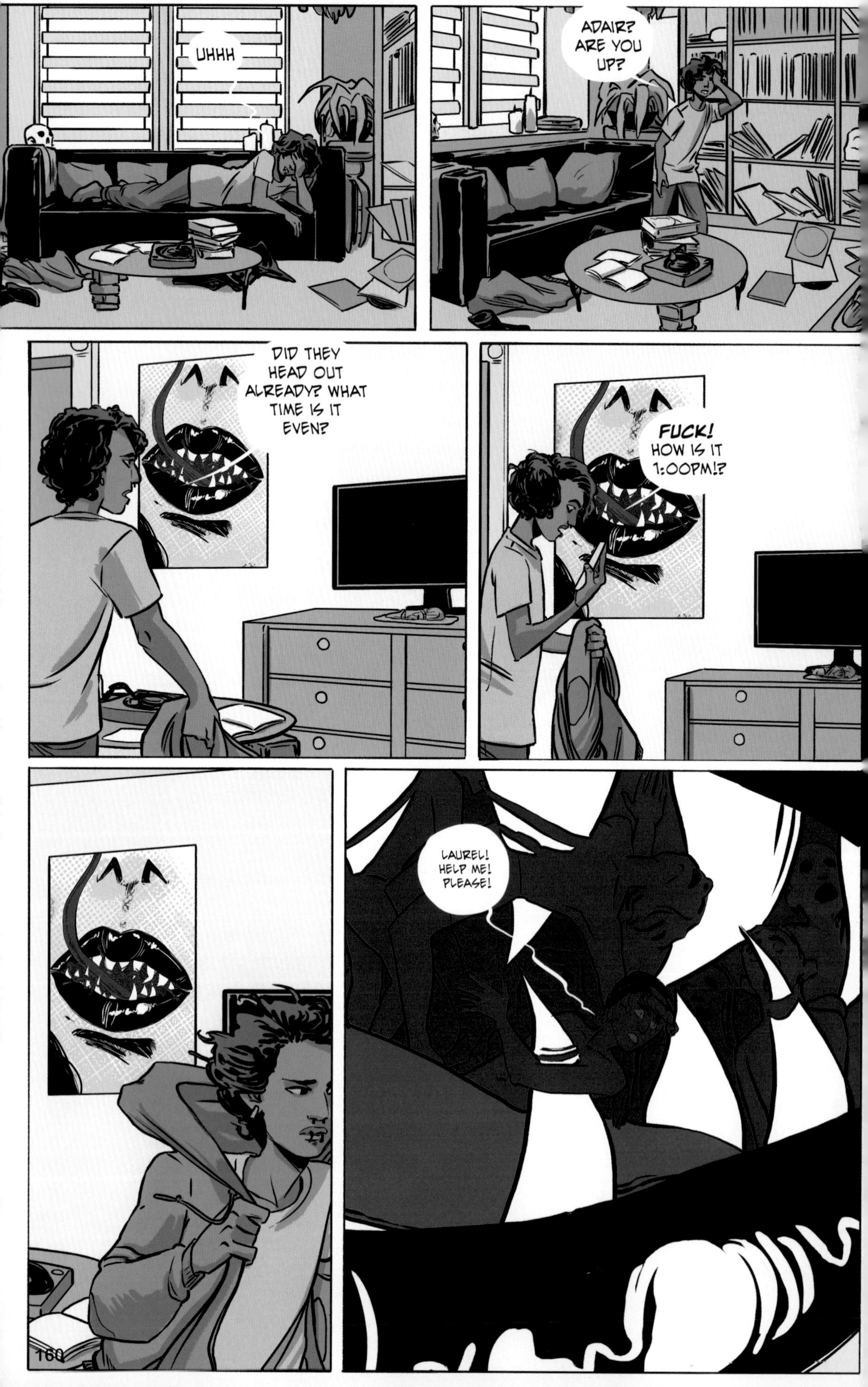
UHHH
ADAIR? ARE YOU UP?
DID THEY HEAD OUT ALREADY? WHAT TIME IS IT EVEN?
FUCK! HOW IS IT 1:00PM!?
LAUREL! HELP ME! PLEASE!

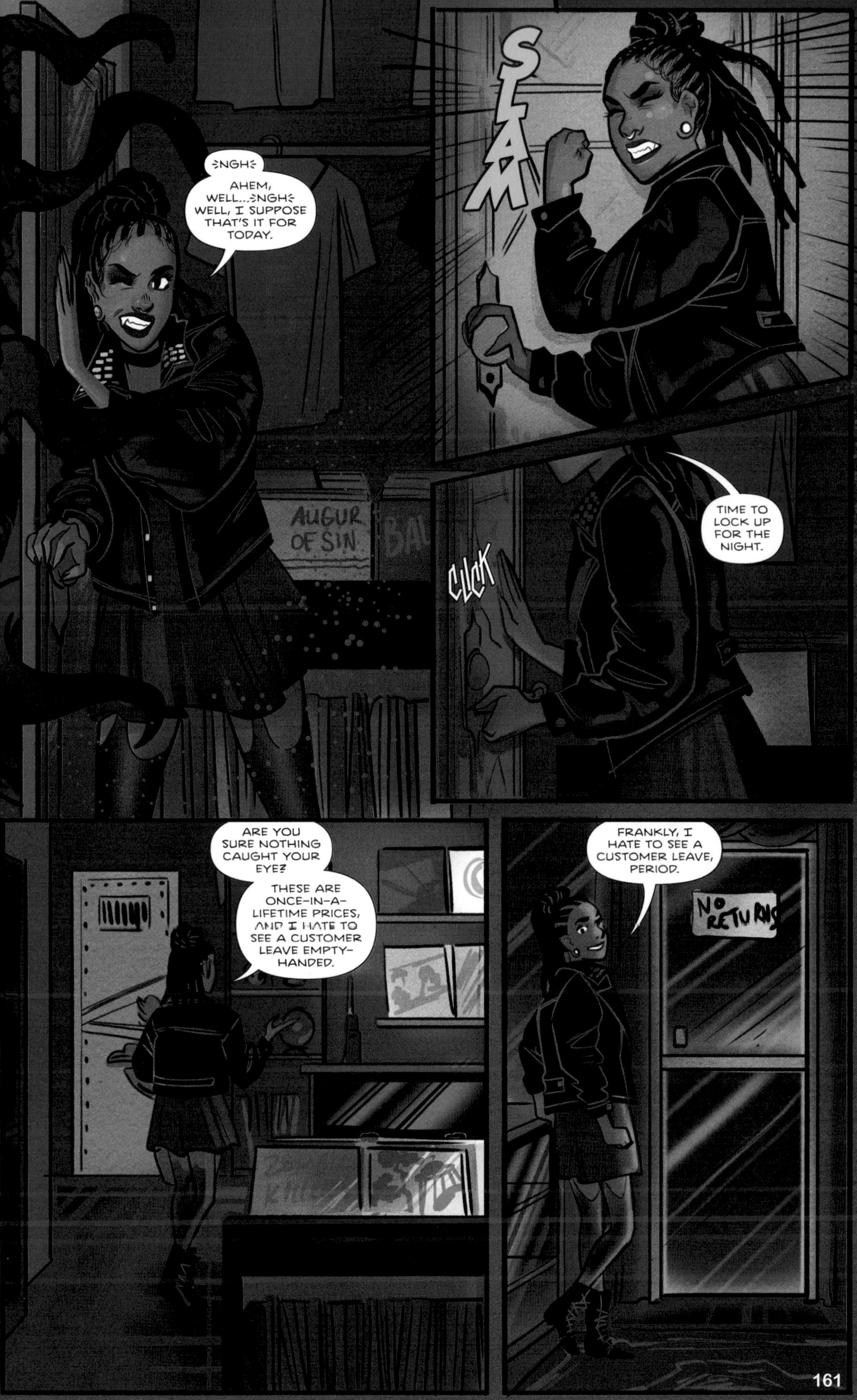
NGH
AHEM, WELL... NGH WELL, I SUPPOSE THAT'S IT FOR TODAY.
AUGUR OF SIN
SLAM
CLICK
TIME TO LOCK UP FOR THE NIGHT.
ARE YOU SURE NOTHING CAUGHT YOUR EYE?
THESE ARE ONCE-IN-A-LIFETIME PRICES, AND I HATE TO SEE A CUSTOMER LEAVE EMPTY-HANDED.
FRANKLY, I HATE TO SEE A CUSTOMER LEAVE, PERIOD.
NO RETURNS

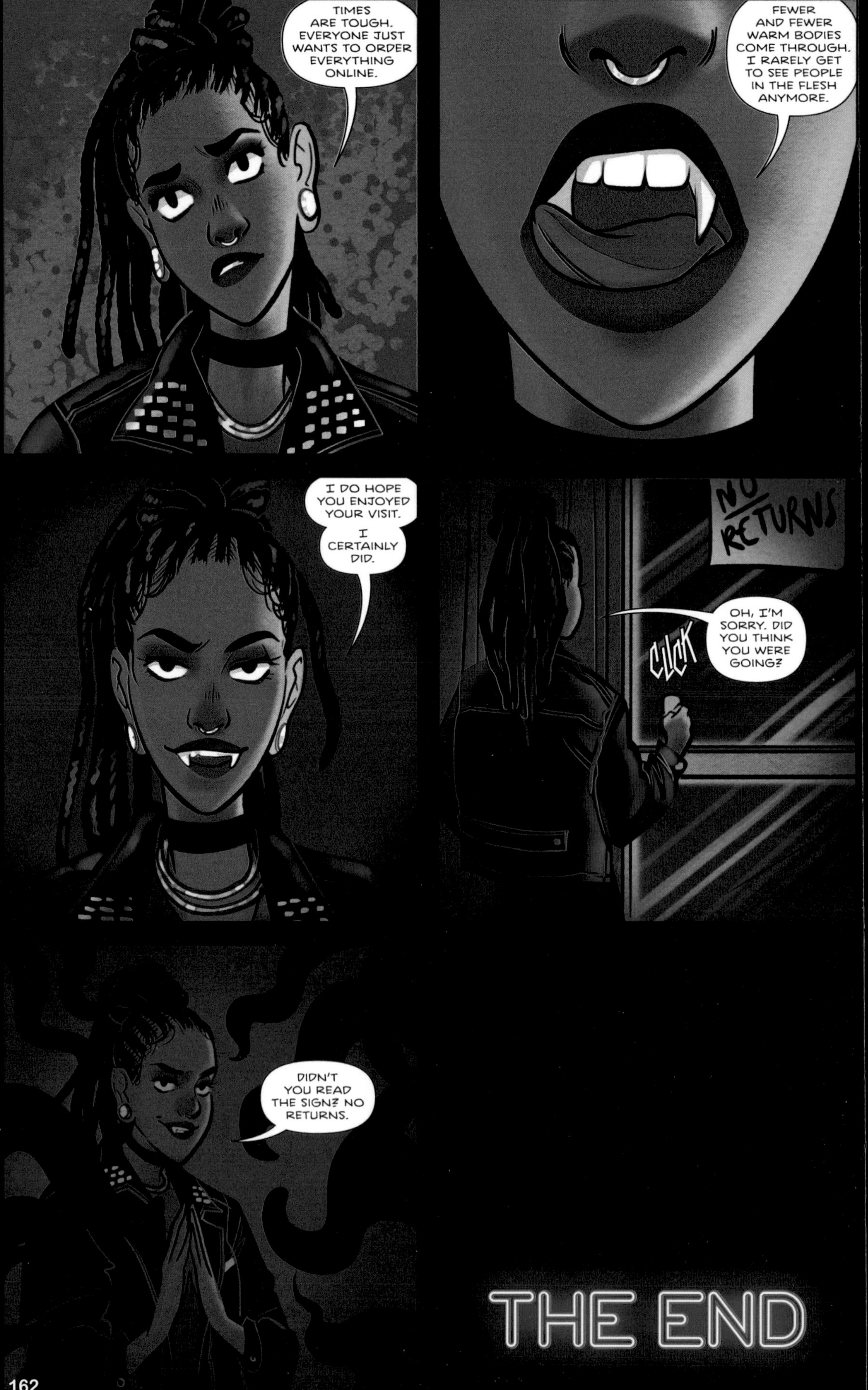
TIMES ARE TOUGH. EVERYONE JUST WANTS TO ORDER EVERYTHING ONLINE.
FEWER AND FEWER WARM BODIES COME THROUGH. I RARELY GET TO SEE PEOPLE IN THE FLESH ANYMORE.
I DO HOPE YOU ENJOYED YOUR VISIT.
I CERTAINLY DID.
NO RETURNS
CLICK
OH, I'M SORRY. DID YOU THINK YOU WERE GOING?
DIDN'T YOU READ THE SIGN? NO RETURNS.
THE END

Letters from the Editors

I've always tied music and horror close together. The first two horror movies I watched as a kid (when my parents deemed me old enough to watch horror) were Halloween and Psycho; two films very well known for their scores. And I always loved anthology style horror, first on TV with Are You Afraid Of The Dark, Tales From The Crypt, Monsters, and The Twilight Zone before finding horror anthology comics like the aforementioned crypt tales.

Over the years I gravitated further to horror that was tied closely to music. Suspiria with its Goblin soundtrack (and Thom Yorke on the remake, which I liked as well), Phantom of the Paradise, or even Wish Upon with its cursed music box that I admittedly enjoy because I think it's hilarious. As goofy as that movie is, the idea of a haunted musical item is a great concept. Finding a way to wed that with a love for anthology horror and the hosts that would serve as your guide helped shape the book you hold in your hands. We hope you love it as much as we loved putting it all together for you.

Joe Corallo
Long Island, New York
27 August 2019

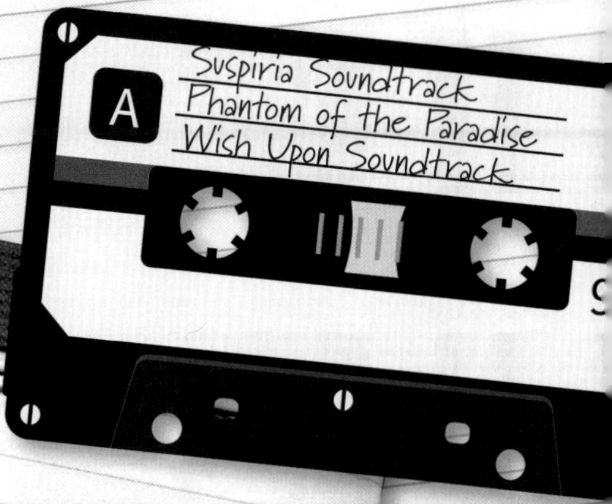
A
Suspiria Soundtrack
Phantom of the Paradise
Wish Upon Soundtrack

I miss mixtapes.

Sure, I've learned to make a halfway decent Spotify playlist, but nothing compares to making a mixtape for someone you care about. It's a gift at once cheap and priceless. In place of mixtapes, I've found a similar joy in making comics anthologies: curating talent I love, arranging it just so, and then passing it along to people--or to a person--I adore. Of course, unlike a mixtape, a comics anthology is anything but cheap, and we couldn't have made this anthology of musically inspired horror stories without a little help. Thank you to the friends and colleagues who agreed to work at a page rate below their station, to the hundreds of Kickstarter backers, to Tyler Chin-Tanner of A Wave Blue World for believing in this book, and to Joe Corallo for inviting me along on the journey to build this crazy project. This book you hold in your hands, it's not quite a mixtape, but it's beautiful.

Eric Palicki
Toledo, Ohio
27 August 2019

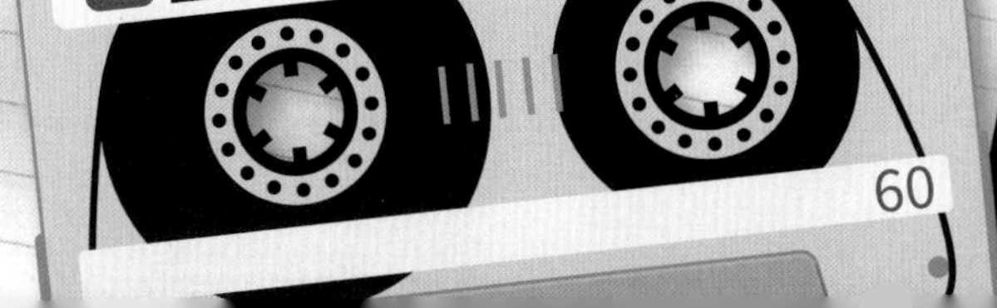
B
'98 Kickass Mix
60

THANK YOU TO OUR KICKSTARTER BACKERS:

Nick A

Matthew Abbott

Michele Abounader

The Accidental Aliens

Ben Acosta

Clay Adams

Ted Adams

Sekinat Adekanbi

AEIOU and Sometimes Why

AgentKaz

Holly Aitchison

akimika

Folarin Akinmade

Cordelia Albertson

Alicat

Ali-Oops

Jon K.G. Allanson

Will Allred

Jordan Alsaqa

Mike Altschwager

Aaron A. Alvarez

Ben Alvarez-Hiscox

Anabel Amis

Ampyluxe

Anaxphone

Suzanna Anderson

David Andry

Tony Anjo

Chris Antzoulis

Kristy Arter

Ash

John-Paul Atley

Jane Aubourg

Azerrvan

B

Allison Babka

Ryan Balkam
(The Comic Lounge)

James Ballard

Krysta Banco

Willyn "Jay" Bandoy

Travis Bannister

Henry Barajas

Adam Bargmeyer

Bryan Barnes

Myra Barnett

Andrew Barton

Elizabeth Bastyr

Terry J Bates

Aly Beard

Brian "Slash" Beardsley

Matt "InterestingMix" Bearup

Kira Beaudoin

Enrique Bedlam

John Behling

Jon Belf

Aaron S Bell

Daryll Benjamin

Scott A. Bennett

Jason Bennett

Scott C. Berg

Shaylyn Berlew

James E. Best III

Glen (Bigneg) Bignell

Aaron Bishop

Ashlee E. Blackwell

ed. blair

Matt Blairstone and
Mad Doctors Comics

Davery Bland

Annie Blitzen

Casey and Lyn Bloss

Bobadilla

Sean Bodnar

Kacy Boggs

Richard Bond

Patrick A Boner

Michael Bones

Bones

Jasmin Bonilla

Eric Bonin

Jason Boone

Gregory Booth

Haley & Jessy Boros

Jeff Rider & Carla Borsoi

JD Boucher

Joel Boutiere

Keith Bowden

Atwood MacMullin Boyd

James Boyle

Madison Bragiel

Rowan Brandou

S. Brandou

Josh Brandt

Alex Breen

Brian J Brennan

John Broglia

Erika Brooks

Jeff T. Brooks

Jeremy Brown

Clint Brown

Ash Brown

Jillian Marie Browning

Julia Din Brunenberg

Whitney Buccicone

Chris Buchner

Wyn PJ Buckley

Elizabeth Buckwalter

Stephan Buksa, Jr

Steve Buksa

Bully the Little Stuffed Bull

Ernie Burnett

Burning Spear Comix

Allie Bustion

Leanna C

Cassie Caccavallo

Lizz & Anthony Caggiano

H.F Calder

Devon Camel

Steph Cannon

Fred Cardona

Ryan Carey

Stephanie Carey

CarlistMaximus

Elsa Carmona

Christian Carnouche

J Carter

Doug "DJ Eternal Darkness" Carter

Frances Joesph Castle-Dredd

Erin Cavanaugh

David Lars Chamerlain

Tucker Chandler

Isaac Chappell

Dylan Charles

Greg Childs

Rick Chillot

Chimera's Comics

Nathan Chio

Ian Chung

Kevin Churcb

Christina Ciminera

Zachary Circo

Perry Clark

Richard P Clark

Jamila Clarke

CMRZ

Shaun Jacob Cobble

Linda H. Codega

Jessica Leigh Codling

Chris Cole

Clifton V. Coleman

Gabriel Coleman

Lyle Coleman

Samuel Coleridge

Andy Conduit-Turner

Chandra Connor

William Conway

Aaron & Becky Cook

Shatayja cooper

Natalie Cooper

Link Copp-Millward

Ray Cornwall

Rebecca Crawford

Josh Crews

Justin Cristelli

Dan Crotty

Daniel Crowley

Alberto G. de la Cruz

Salvatore Cucinotta

Hoang Viet Cuong

Kitty Curran

Alex Currie

Janora Curtis

cyberpilate

Craig Czyz

Eric D.

Danielle

Dan-o

Danny's Mom!

Darren Dare

Joan Dark

Dauchon

Chris Davidson

Joe Davis

William Tyler Davis

Lauren Davis

Maya Davis

Grant DeArmitt

Rhel ná DecVandé

Katie Dee

David DeGeer

Jude Deluca

Tim Dennie

Alexis Dent

The DeOrdio family

Cameron James
Wolfgang DeOrdio

Tom Depoorter

Andy Detloff

Eastin DeVerna

Ava Dickerson

Alex Dionisio

Ian Doherty

Sean Padraic Dolan

Mike Donohue

Eryk Donovan

Colleen Doran

Jason Doring

Rich Douek

Cam Dow

Tara Drake

Jon Duckworth

Duell

Craig Duguay

James H. Duke IV

Sydney Dunstan

Brandon Eaker

Michael S. Edwards

The Effective Nerd Team

EJF

Pierce Elliott

Emma

Cpt Emoji

Kenny Endlich

Jessica Enfante

EngelDreizehn

Bri Engels

Jeff Eppenbach

Rae Epstein

Erstwhile

Roberto Sales Faria Junior

Claire Farmer

Dwayne Farver

Jamie Faulconer

Ben Feldman

Adam Ferris

Kelly Finn

Stephen (Supernovame) Fitch

Alex Fitch

Kelly Fitzpatrick

Jason A Fleece

Christopher Fleming

Joe Flood

Robbie Foggo

Curt Fortenbery

Cait "Mostly Coffee" Fortier

Tom Foss

Minerva Fox

Jim Francesca

Jenevieve Frank

John Frasene

Kelly "K-Fresh" Frazier

Tyler Freshcorn

Hillary (Bee) Froemel

Sean Frost

Will Funderburke

Cameron Funk

Jeremiah Gaboury

Bryan Gaffin

Rae Gaines

Edwin Arsenio Ramirez Garcia

Michael Garcia

Andrew Garda

Nick Gardner

Mike Garley

Jaime M Garmendia III

Darren Garoutte

Mike Garvey

The Gauntlet Podcast

Prachi Gauriar

Sam Gawith

Geek Brunch Podcast

Ghaele

Carlos Giffoni

Geoff Gill

Kieron Gillen

Gilles

Martin Gillin

Jason Giovannettone

Thom Gladhill

Leon Glaser

Jesse Glaspey

Joe Glass

Stephanie Grey Glass

Too Many Goblins

Abi Godsell

Frank Gogol

Adam Goldstein

Samantha Gomez

William Goodwill

Cory Goonan

Michael Gordon

Shawna Gore

Joshua Gorfain

Anthony J. Gramuglia

Che Grayson

Karen Green

Mick Green

GreenChoc

Gerry Green @professorfrenzy

Diana Greenhalgh

Lua Gregory

David Greshel

Dustin Doyke Gret

Mat Groom

The Groundwater Press

Brian Groth

Zabet Groznaya

Grumpy Old Manchild

Kristen Gudsnuk

Erica Guezadilla

Erik Gustafson

Alice H.

Nikolai H.

R.J.H.

Gene Ha

Richard L. Haas III

Lara Haddadin

Barry Hall

Wayne Hall
(Wayne's Comics Podcast)

Chloe Handler

Travis Haney

Russ Harbison

Matt Harding

Bob and Shari Harrison

Kit Harrison

Brentt Harshman

Elizabeth Hasara

Kenn Haspel

Salah Hassanpour

Monica Hastedt

Isabel Hatherell

Thonas Hawksworth

Jay Hazardpay

F. Hazelip

Josh Heake

Crys Helix

Amanda & Sophia
Helstrom-White

Christopher Helton

Jaimel Hemphill

Matty Hemsworth

Alex Henning

Iz hermo

Rick Hernandez

Sven "DrMcCoy" Hesse

Sarah Hickey

Erica D. Hickman

Drew Hicks

Kristel Hill

Russell Hillman/
Freaktown Comics

Tracy Holt

Emma Holt

Travis M. Holyfield

Fermin Serena Hortas

Matt Houck

Robert "Bobby" Howard

Stephanie Howes

Kim Hu

Nick Hughes

Xavier Hugonet

Madeline Hunter

Heather Hurt

Edmond Hyland

HyperToast

I Am Hexed

iamjacquelin

Ian

Aaron Iara

Matthew Isaac

Farah Ismail

Spiral Ivy

Emma J.

Molly Jackson

Amy Lynn Jackson

Seth Jacob

Morgan Jacobs-Leahy

JAKirby

@JamesFerguson

Enrica "Cool Whip" Jang

Captain Jaq

Paul y cod asyn Jarman

Steve Jasiczek

Jamie Jeans

Patricia Jeres

Renie Jesanis

Chandra Jessee

Brian Jimenez

Drewski Johnson

Rose Johnson

Steve Johnson, Hex Games

Zoran Joka

Rodney B Jones

Rhea Jones

M. J. Jones

Jacob Jones-Goldstein

Jonrob5000

Alex Jordan

JP Jordan

S. Jordan

Jessi Jordan

Kristiana Josifi

Jowen

Jvgray

Ben Kahn

Nic Kaitaloipa

Daniel Kalban

Liana Kangas

Mitchell Kaplan

Mrs. KBpool

Levi Keim

Katherine Keller

Allyson Kelley

CHUNK Kelly

Steve Kendall

Viktor Kerney

Kev Ketner

K & M Comics

KG

Joe R. Khachadourian

Anand Khatri

Doug Kieselbach

Rachel Kiley

Mackenzie Kimmel

@Kimota1977

D. Kleymeyer

Krysta A Kluge

Gendou and René Knepper

Justin Knight

Jason Knol

Zach Knowlton

Konner Knudsen

Jim Kosmicki

Jamie Kosmin

Andrew Kossek

KPM

CJ Kral

Hank Kuhfeldt

Tanya Kumar

Shawn Kunstal

Jeremy S. Kuris

KylaTea

Erin L

Daniel Laében-Rosén

Chelsea "DemonRin" LaLicata

Alysha Lancaster

Graham Lanini

Sean D Laughlin

Jason Lavochkin

Mark J Lawson

Matt Lazorwitz

Seedy Leaf
Sam Learmonth
Brendan Leber
Michael A.S. Lee
K. Lee
Adrian Lee
Miranda Leiggi
Andy Leipold
Len @theprophetlen
Whit Leopard
Andy Levy
A. David Lewis
Daniel Lin
S. Lindbloom
Richard Lindsay
Josh Link
Kelly Little
Mark Locy
Jay Lofstead
Marc Lombardi
Michael Long
Cam Lopez
Matt Mair Lowery
Cat X. Lu
Laura Lu
James Lucas
Jarred Luján
Jen Luna
Sara Lunsford
Ginny Lurcock
Ashley Lynch
Evan Lyons
David Lyons
Rachael M
Terry M
M
M&C Limited
Scott Mabe
Lisa Machado
Fester LD MacKrell
Colin Maclaughlin
John MacLeod
Alex MacLeod
James Maddox
Phil Maddox
Andrew Magazzu
Mx. John E Mahoney
Malchus
John Paul Maler
Joshua Malkin
Aaron Malone
Jim Manchester
Zefram Mann
Dirk Manning
Shaun Manning
Sean Mannion
Shawn Marier
Brian Marino

AJ Mark
Christopolis Tiberius Markus
Kevin J. "Womzilla" Maroney
Megan Cosman Marsden
C Marshell
Derek Martino
Michael Martínez
Todd Matthy
Mason Matzker
mb
Ellen McCammon
Kit William McClory
Clay McCormack
Stacey McDonald
Karat McFall
Michael McGrath
Taylor McGruder
Liam McGuire
Colby McHugh
Edward McKee
Grant McLaughlin
Paul McPartlin
Mike McPhillips
Evan Meadow
Mec
Ro Mediavilla
Meesimo
Mel!
Melissa
Kelly Mellings
Maus Merryjest
Oliver Mertz
Kate Meyers
MH
Staci Michaelz and
the Electric Congregation
Evie Michelle
michi
Tim Midura
Mike Seibert Radio Podcast
Ben Miller
Neal Miller
Jefferson Mills
Mindi
shades Misa
mjdidonato
Michael J. Moehring
Chris Mole
Gary Moloney
Ian Mondrick
Heather Mong
Caleb Monroe
Josh Monroe
Jennifer Montgomery
Michelle Montroy
Robyn Moore
William will2bill Moore
Ben Moore
The More You Nerd Podcast

Michelle Moreno
Stacy Morgan
Ilusha Moroz
Chris Morris
Matt "Starman" Morrison
Bonnie Morse
Bee Moser
Cai Murphy
Brian Murray
Rebecca Mutton
Steve Myers
Lukas Myhan
Aaron Nagy
A Napoleon
Roland Nault
Hal Neat
James Nettum
Mike Newhouse-Bailey
Brian Newman
Rob Newstead
Randall Nichols
Joy A. Nickens (@JOYNFINITY)
Steve Nicoll
Niki
Philip Noguchi
Nathan Nolan
Jeremy Noonan
Rick Norman
NOTRock
Meredith Nudo
Kati Nyman
Ciarán "Sarky" O'Brien
Oerglwoergl
Nick OG
Patricia Ogura
Nestine Olidan
Tyler Olson from
The Longbox Podcast
OmniDog
Miguel Angel Torres Ontiveros
Faye O'Reilly
Niki Ortega-Diaz
Meghan O'Sullivan
Ally P
@p3rf3kt
Greg Pak
Rabid Pandaren
Genevieve Paquin-Saikali
Mark A. Parchman
Natalie Parker
Elizabeth Parmeter
Bradley "Kakyoin" Patrick
Skylar Patridge
Andy Patton
Ahren "Plognark" Paulson
Pax
Paul Payabyab-Cruz
Robert Peacock
Matt Penn

Wilee Penner
Peony
David Pepose
Rachel Perciphone
Marcela Peres
Nicholas Petcosky
Doug Peterson
Eraklis Petmezas
Ben Petrila
Erika Petrimoulx
Kae Petrin
Lindsey Petrucci
Nola Pfau
Foxglove Pharm
David Phelps
Charlie Phillips
Stephanie Phillips
Nick Piers
Pirate Sky
Brian K, Pittman
Joshua W. Pittman
Sarah Plissner
Nathan R Plunkett
Kevin Pointer
Tony Santa Cruz Polanco
Nicholas Poonamallee
Marie & George Popichak
Alison Poppy
John Porter
Peyton C. Presgrove
Damen Marie Price
Elliot Price
Pat Prince
Grace Pushman
Amanda Quashie
Noodles Queen
Jason Song Quinn
Jana Quintin
Ahmed Raafat
Alex Rae
Polly Rag
Dan E Raga
Mark Roslan
Michael Rawdon
Ashley Rayner
Chip Reece
Renata
Rentfn
Berry Rhapsody
Rhiannon
John Rice
Justin Richards
Boo Rider
Nate Rider
Kaycie Riead
Carl Rigney
Mark D. Ritchie
George Rivera

Jonathan Robert
Ken Robinson
Lemuel Robinson
Tania Ochoa Robotania
Krista Rockandel
Sebastian Rodriguez-Delgado
Matthew J. Rogers
M C Rolston
Caitlin Rosberg
Zachary Rosenberg
Marwa Roshan
Frances Rowat
Derek Ruiz
Alin Răuțoiu
Keith Rupp
Owen John Ryan
Paul Ryan
Haley Rymel
Anna S
Katherine S
Joshua S.
E.S
Ray Sablack
Mary Safro
Christian Sager
St. Sean of the Knife
Guillermo Sanchez
Darío E. Sanchez
Matt Santori
Tracie Santos
Benjamin Sawyer
Michael Scally
Scott Schaper
Evan Schmalz
Brett A. Schmidt
Greg "schmegs" Schwartz
Robert Secundus
Samantha Sesenton
Pat Shand
Brandon Shanks
James B. Sharkey, Jr.
Dhruv Sharma
Morgan Shaunette
Tracey Sheehy
Lambert Sheng
Christopher Shepard
Blacky Shepherd
Jeremy K. Shober
Gregory Paul Silber
Hoyt Silva
Luis Silva
Sze-Ying Sim
Kofi Jamal Simmons
Gary Simmons
Austin Simmons
sirshannon
Matt Smith
Jeannie Smith

Ryan J Smith
Travis Smith
Peter Smyk
Tim Smyth
Ben Snow
Jesse Snow
Softnum
Michael Solko
Susan Sordo
Allyssa Sosebee
Andrew Sparling
Rob Staeger
Jason Stallman
Daniel Stalter
Thomas and Sarah Stanton
DeAnne Stefanic
Ashley Stephens
Mathew Stevens
Charlie Stickney
Big Tim Stiles
Randy Stone
Maddie Stowe
Thaddeus Strange
Erin Subramanian
Elizabeth Sullivan
summervillain
Emily Swan
Jamie Swedler
Craig A. Taillefer
Emma Tarver
TEXASRAVER
Chace Thibodeaux
Rob Thomas
Cecelia & Thor Thomas
Martha Thomases
Loch Thompson
Jorren Thornton
Brendan Tihane
Trevor Tocco
Mike Toole
Richard Topp
Nicholas Toscani
A. K. Tosh
Rachel "Nausicaa" Tougas
TRACY
Trek Treksson
Paul & Laura Trinies
Gina Trujillo
Noel Tuazon
Aaron Turko
Andrew Turman
William O. Tyler
Chatè Ukwandu
Nick Ulanowski
Alexis Ulrich
Vince Underwood
Lina V
Koomi V

Michael Vallachi
Adam VanderYacht
Jen Vaughn
Matthew Vealey
Lilith Velkor
Amanda Vernon
J Vigants
Jack Lope Vollman
Christopher Wade
Justin Wait
David F. Walker
Gary E. Walker
Lizzy Walker, WiHM Librarian
Sheafe B Walker
Jared Walske
Justin Ward, DVM
Donnalyn Washington
Trey Washington
Watchtower Coffee & Comics
Anthony R Watkins
Claude Weaver III
Mila Webb
Christoph-A. Weber
Thomas Webster
Drew Wendorf
Jason Wentworth
Thomas Werner
Katie Wertz
Colin Westerfield
Michael James Wheeler
Ronell Whitaker
Frankee White
Jon R. White, Jr.
Malissa White
Ashley Why
Jeremy Wiggins
WilatHeroicStudios
Evan Wilber,
he who shall not be tamed
Amie Wilensky
Noel Willett
Kelly Williams
Kate Williams
Stephanie Williams
Akil Wilson
Betty Wilson
Tristan Wilson
Elaine Wilson
Kim Wincen
Ten Van Winkle
Kass Winters
Rus Wooton
Tim Powell Wright
James F. Wright
Sam Wright
Ross Wright
Wuppy
Ian Yarington
Bryan Young

Joel Young
Sheila Z
Paula Z
Vincey Zalkind
Orion and Katie Zangara
Kurt Zauer
James Zeffiro
Andy Zeiner

RETAILERS

Avalon Comics & Games-
Santa Barbara
Big Easy Comics
Black Cat Comics
Books With Pictures
Bulletproof Comics and Games
Doc's Comics & Games
Escape Pod Comics
Excalibur Comics
Fantasy Books Inc Star Clipper
Friendly Neighborhood Comics
Haven Comics: Etc.
Kirwan's Game Store
Pegasus Books of Bend
Royal Collectibles
Sanctum Sanctorum
Comics & Oddities
Soundwave Comics
Space Cadets
Collection Collection
Summit Comics & Games
Urban Legends Comics

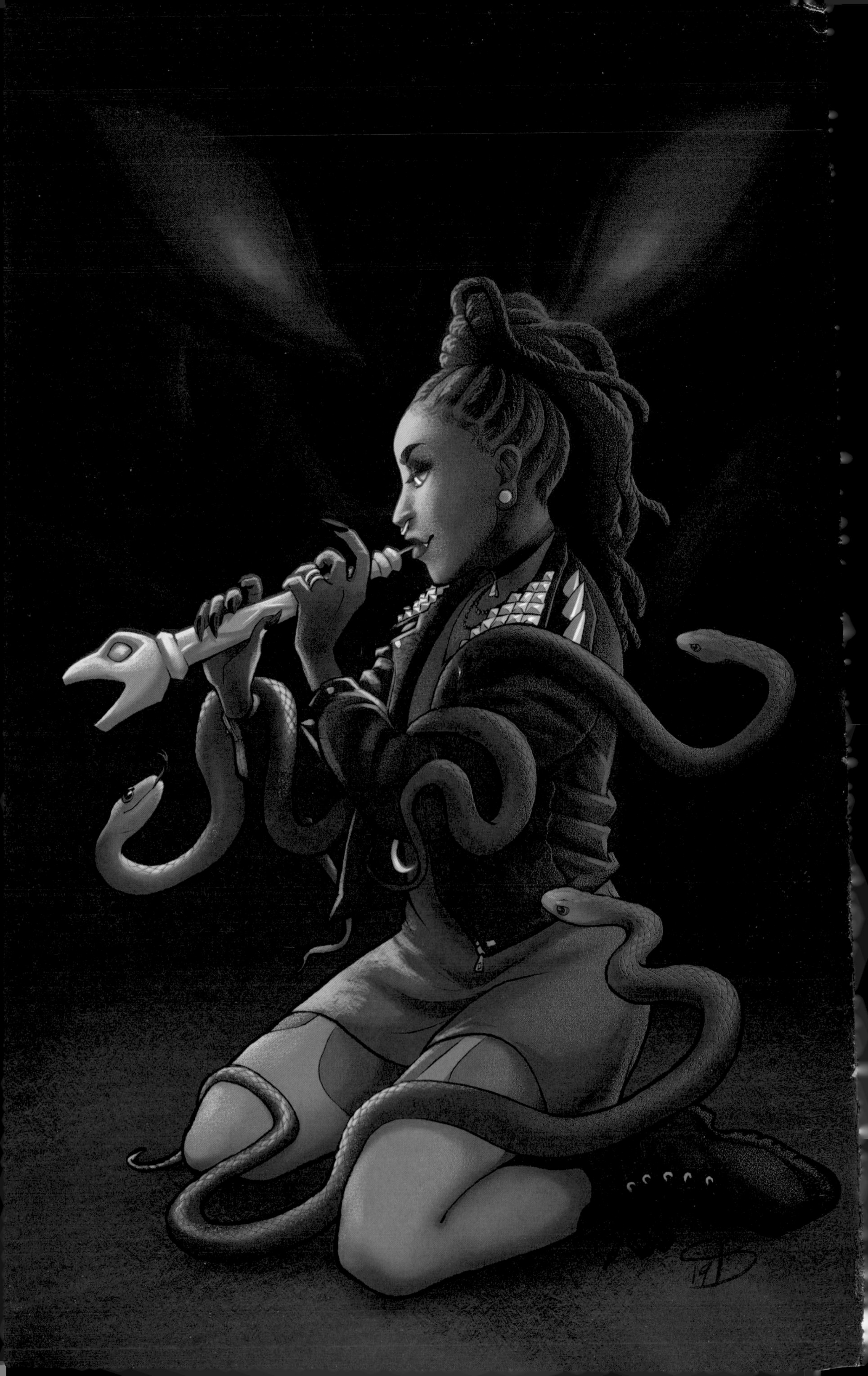